enVisionmath 2.0
SCOTT FORESMAN · ADDISON WESLEY

Volume 2 Topics 9-16

Authors

Randall I. Charles
Professor Emeritus
Department of Mathematics
San Jose State University
San Jose, California

Jennifer Bay-Williams
Professor of Mathematics
Education
College of Education and Human
Development
University of Louisville
Louisville, Kentucky

Robert Q. Berry, III
Associate Professor of
Mathematics Education
Department of Curriculum,
Instruction and Special Education
University of Virginia
Charlottesville, Virginia

Janet H. Caldwell
Professor of Mathematics
Rowan University
Glassboro, New Jersey

Zachary Champagne
Assistant in Research
Florida Center for Research in
Science, Technology, Engineering,
and Mathematics (FCR-STEM)
Jacksonville, Florida

Juanita Copley
Professor Emerita, College of
Education
University of Houston
Houston, Texas

Warren Crown
Professor Emeritus of Mathematics
Education
Graduate School of Education
Rutgers University
New Brunswick, New Jersey

Francis (Skip) Fennell
L. Stanley Bowlsbey Professor
of Education and Graduate and
Professional Studies
McDaniel College
Westminster, Maryland

Karen Karp
Professor of Mathematics
Education
Department of Early Childhood
and Elementary Education
University of Louisville
Louisville, Kentucky

Stuart J. Murphy
Visual Learning Specialist
Boston, Massachusetts

Jane F. Schielack
Professor of Mathematics
Associate Dean for Assessment
and Pre K-12 Education,
College of Science
Texas A&M University
College Station, Texas

Jennifer M. Suh
Associate Professor for
Mathematics Education
George Mason University
Fairfax, Virginia

Jonathan A. Wray
Mathematics Instructional
Facilitator
Howard County Public Schools
Ellicott City, Maryland

Glenview, Illinois   Boston, Massachusetts   Chandler, Arizona   Hoboken, New Jersey

Mathematicians

Roger Howe
Professor of Mathematics
Yale University
New Haven, Connecticut

Gary Lippman
Professor of Mathematics and
Computer Science
California State University,
East Bay
Hayward, California

ELL Consultants

Janice R. Corona
Independent Education
Consultant
Dallas, Texas

Jim Cummins
Professor
The University of Toronto
Toronto, Canada

Common Core State Standards Reviewers

Debbie Crisco
Math Coach
Beebe Public Schools
Beebe, Arkansas

Kathleen A. Cuff
Teacher
Kings Park Central School District
Kings Park, New York

Erika Doyle
Math and Science Coordinator
Richland School District
Richland, Washington

Susan Jarvis
Math and Science Curriculum
Coordinator
Ocean Springs Schools
Ocean Springs, Mississippi

Velvet M. Simington
K-12 Mathematics Director
Winston-Salem/Forsyth County
Schools
Winston-Salem, North Carolina

ISBN-13: 978-0-328-82747-3
ISBN-10: 0-328-82747-9

Digital Resources

You'll be using these digital resources throughout the year!

Go to PearsonRealize.com

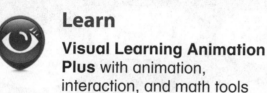

MP

Math Practices Animations to play anytime

Learn

Visual Learning Animation Plus with animation, interaction, and math tools

Practice Buddy

Online Personalized Practice for each lesson

Assessment

Quick Check for each lesson

Games

Math Games to help you learn

ACTIVe-book

Student Edition online for showing your work

Solve

Solve & Share problems plus math tools

Glossary

Animated Glossary in English and Spanish

Tools

Math Tools to help you understand

Help

Another Look Homework Video for extra help

eText

Student Edition online

PEARSON realize™ Everything you need for math anytime, anywhere

KEY

● Major Cluster

● Supporting Cluster

● Additional Cluster

The content is organized to focus on Common Core clusters.

For a list of clusters, see Volume 1 pages F15–F18.

Digital Resources at PearsonRealize.com

And remember your eText is available at PearsonRealize.com!

Contents

TOPICS

PearsonRealize.com

You can use ratio models to help you find equivalent ratios and solve problems.

Footballs
5
3
Soccer balls

TOPIC 9 Ratio Concepts and Reasoning

Rates compare quantity that have different units, like Kilometers per minute.

Distance (km)	Time (min)
5	$1\frac{1}{2}$
10	3
15	$4\frac{1}{2}$
20	6
25	$7\frac{1}{2}$

TOPIC 10 Ratio Concepts: Rates

You can draw diagrams to relate percents, fractions, and decimals.

Number
0   200   600

0      $33\frac{1}{3}\%$ 100%
Percent

TOPIC 11 Ratio Concepts: Percent

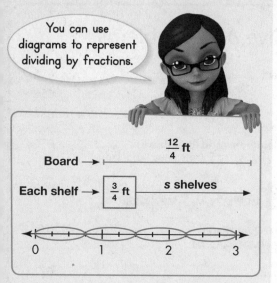

You can use diagrams to represent dividing by fractions.

Board → $\frac{12}{4}$ ft

Each shelf → $\frac{3}{4}$ ft   s shelves

0   1   2   3

TOPIC 12 Divide Fractions by Fractions

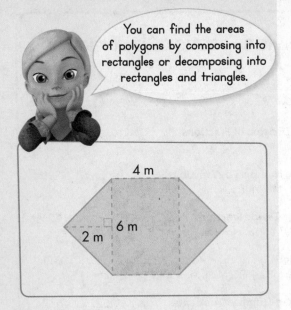

You can find the areas of polygons by composing into rectangles or decomposing into rectangles and triangles.

4 m

6 m

2 m

TOPIC 13 Solve Area Problems

You can use a net to represent a three-dimensional figure, and use the net to find the surface area of the figure.

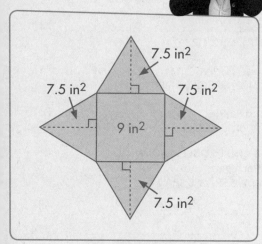

TOPIC 14 Solve Surface Area and Volume Problems

> You can use measures of center, like mean, median, and mode to summarize a set of data.

	9	10	FINAL SCORE
2 95	86 [7] [2]	95 [6] [3] −	95
87	80 [4] [2]	87 [7] [0] −	87
84	77 [5] [1]	84 [4] [3] −	84
81	74 [2] [4]	81 [5] [2] −	81
+ 83	75 [3] [3]	83 [6] [2] −	83
430			

Mean → 430 ÷ 5 = 86

TOPIC 15 Measures of Center and Variability

You can display numerical data, like on the box plot below. The shape of the distribution shows how the data values are centered and how variable they are.

TOPIC 16 Display and Summarize Data

STEP UP to Grade 7

These lessons help prepare you for Grade 7.

© Math Practices and Problem Solving Handbook

Math practices are ways we think about and do math.

Math practices will help you solve problems.

Math Practices

MP.1 Make sense of problems and persevere in solving them.

MP.2 Reason abstractly and quantitatively.

MP.3 Construct viable arguments and critique the reasoning of others.

MP.4 Model with mathematics.

MP.5 Use appropriate tools strategically.

MP.6 Attend to precision.

MP.7 Look for and make use of structure.

MP.8 Look for and express regularity in repeated reasoning.

There are good Thinking Habits for each of these math practices.

MP.1 Make sense of problems and persevere in solving them.

Good math thinkers make sense of problems and think of ways to solve them.

If they get stuck, they don't give up.

Here I listed what I know and what I am trying to find.

Jon earns $15.50 per week for helping his dad deliver newspapers. He has helped his dad for 3 weeks. Jon uses part of his earnings to buy a new video game that costs $42.39, including tax. How much of his earnings does he have left?

What I know:

• Jon earns $15.50 per week.
• Jon has worked 3 weeks.
• Jon buys a game that costs $42.39.

What I need to find:

• The amount of earnings Jon has left.

Thinking Habits

Be a good thinker! These questions can help you.

• What do I need to find?

• What do I know?

• What's my plan for solving the problem?

• What else can I try if I get stuck?

• How can I check that my solution makes sense?

Good math thinkers know how to think about words and numbers to solve problems.

I drew a bar diagram that shows how the quantities in the problem are related.

Jacie bought a 6-pack of juice drinks for $4.50. How much does each drink in the pack of juice cost?

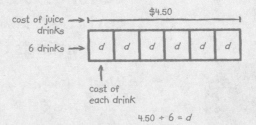

cost of juice drinks → | $4.50

6 drinks → | d | d | d | d | d | d |

↑ cost of each drink

$4.50 ÷ 6 = d$

Thinking Habits

Be a good thinker! These questions can help you.

- What do the numbers and symbols in the problem mean?

- How are the numbers or quantities related?

- How can I represent a word problem using pictures, numbers, or equations?

Construct viable arguments and critique the reasoning of others.

Good math thinkers use math to explain why they are right. They can talk about the math that others do, too.

I wrote a clear argument with words, numbers, and symbols.

Jo said that when you multiply a nonzero whole number by a fraction less than 1, the product is always less than the whole number. Do you agree? Explain.

You can think of multiplying by a fraction less than one as finding a part of a whole group. So, the product of a nonzero whole number and a fraction less than one is always less than the whole number. For example:

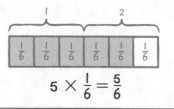

$$5 \times \frac{1}{6} = \frac{5}{6}$$

Thinking Habits

Be a good thinker! These questions can help you.

- How can I use numbers, objects, drawings, or actions to justify my argument?

- Am I using numbers and symbols correctly?

- Is my explanation clear and complete?

- What questions can I ask to understand other people's thinking?

- Are there mistakes in other people's thinking?

- Can I improve other people's thinking?

- Can I use a counterexample in my argument?

MP.4 | Model with mathematics.

Good math thinkers choose and apply math they know to show and solve problems from everyday life.

Sally's dad is building shelving in his garage. He fills a 32.5-foot long wall with 6 identical shelves. How wide is each shelf?

I can use what I know about division to solve this problem. I drew a diagram to help.

| w | w | w | w | w | w |

32.5 ft

$32.5 \div 6 = w$

Thinking Habits

Be a good thinker! These questions can help you.

- How can I use math I know to help solve the problem?

- How can I use pictures, objects, or an equation to represent the problem?

- How can I use numbers, words, and symbols to solve the problem?

Math Practices and Problem Solving Handbook

MP.5 Use appropriate tools strategically.

Good math thinkers know how to pick the right tools to solve math problems.

I decided to use unit cubes to show how I could fill the box.

Alex has a pencil box that is 9 inches long, 6 inches wide, and 3 inches high. What is the volume of his pencil box?

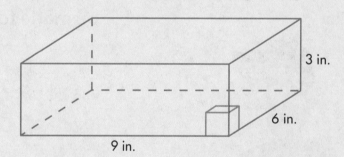

3 in.

6 in.

9 in.

Thinking Habits

Be a good thinker! These questions can help you.

- Which tools can I use?
- Why should I use this tool to help me solve the problem?
- Is there a different tool I could use?
- Am I using the tool appropriately?

MP.6 Attend to precision.

Good math thinkers are careful about what they write and say, so their ideas about math are clear.

I was precise with my work and the way that I wrote my solution.

A party planner says that $\frac{2}{3}$ pound of chicken should be made for each person at a party. There will be 8 people at a dinner party. How much chicken should be made for the party?

$$8 \times \frac{2}{3}$$
$$= 8 \times 2 \times \frac{1}{3}$$
$$= 16 \times \frac{1}{3}$$
$$= \frac{16}{3}$$
$$= 5\frac{1}{3}$$

$5\frac{1}{3}$ pounds of chicken should be made for the party.

Thinking Habits

Be a good thinker! These questions can help you.

- Am I using numbers, units, and symbols appropriately?

- Am I using the correct definitions?

- Am I calculating accurately?

- Is my answer clear?

Math Practices and Problem Solving Handbook

MP.7 Look for and make use of structure.

Good math thinkers look for patterns in math to help solve problems.

I used place-value structure to multiply a decimal and solve this problem.

A gardener is planting a row of spinach with seeds every 0.25 meter. How many centimeters apart is each seed?

1 m = 100 cm

0.25×10^2
$= 0.25 \times 100$
$= 25$

Each *seed* is 25 centimeters apart.

Thinking Habits

Be a good thinker! These questions can help you.

- What patterns can I see and describe?

- How can I use the patterns to solve the problem?

- Can I see expressions and objects in different ways?

- What equivalent expressions can I use?

MP.8 Look for and express regularity in repeated reasoning.

> Good math thinkers look for things that repeat, and they make generalizations.

> I used reasoning to generalize about the operations.

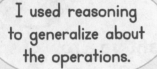

Use <, >, or = to compare the expressions without calculating.

$534 \div 10 \bigcirc 534 \times 10$

534 ÷ 10 < 534 × 10
because the result of dividing a number by 10 is less than the result of multiplying the same number by 10.

Thinking Habits

Be a good thinker! These questions can help you.

- Are any calculations repeated?
- Can I generalize from examples?
- What shortcuts do I notice?

Math Practices Land Problem Solving Handbook

Problem Solving Guide

Math practices can help you solve problems.

Make Sense of the Problem

Reason Abstractly and Quantitatively

- What do I need to find?
- What given information can I use?
- How are the quantities related?

Think About Similar Problems

- Have I solved problems like this before?

Persevere in Solving the Problem

Model with Math

- How can I use the math I know?
- How can I represent the problem?
- Is there a pattern or structure I can use?

Use Appropriate Tools Strategically

- What math tools could I use?
- How can I use those tools strategically?

Check the Answer

Make Sense of the Answer

- Is my answer reasonable?

Check for Precision

- Did I check my work?
- Is my answer clear?
- Did I construct a viable argument?
- Did I generalize correctly?

Some Ways to Represent Problems

- Draw a Picture
- Make a Bar Diagram
- Make a Table or Graph
- Write an Equation

Some Math Tools

- Objects
- Grid Paper
- Rulers
- Technology
- Paper and Pencil

Problem Solving Recording Sheet

This sheet helps you organize your work.

Name **Carlos**

Teaching Tool
1

Problem Solving Recording Sheet

Problem:
One of the Thorny Devil lizard's favorite foods is ants. It can eat up to 45 ants per minute. How long would it take it to eat 1,080 ants? Express your answer in seconds.

MAKE SENSE OF THE PROBLEM

Need to Find	**Given**
How many seconds it takes the Thorny Devil to eat 1,080 ants	The Thorny Devil lizard can eat 45 ants per minute.

PERSEVERE IN SOLVING THE PROBLEM

Some Ways to Represent Problems

☐ Draw a Picture
☑ Make a Bar Diagram
☐ Make a Table or Graph
☑ Write an Equation

Some Math Tools

☐ Objects
☐ Grid Paper
☐ Rulers
☐ Technology
☑ Paper and Pencil

Solution and Answer

1,080 ÷ 45

1,080 ants ⟶ | 1,080
m minutes ⟶ [45] | m ⟶
↑
ants each minute

It takes 24 minutes for the lizard to eat 1,080 ants. There are 60 seconds in each minute.
24 × 60 = 1,440

Answer:
The Thorny Devil lizard would take 1,440 seconds to eat 1,080 ants.

CHECK THE ANSWER

Check
1,440 ÷ 60 = 24 minutes   My answer is correct.
24 × 45 = 1,080

T1

Bar Diagrams

You can draw a **bar diagram** to show how the quantities in a problem are related. Then you can write an equation to solve the problem.

Add To

Draw this **bar diagram** for situations that involve *adding* to a quantity.

Result →

432	
102	330

↑ Start   ↑ Change

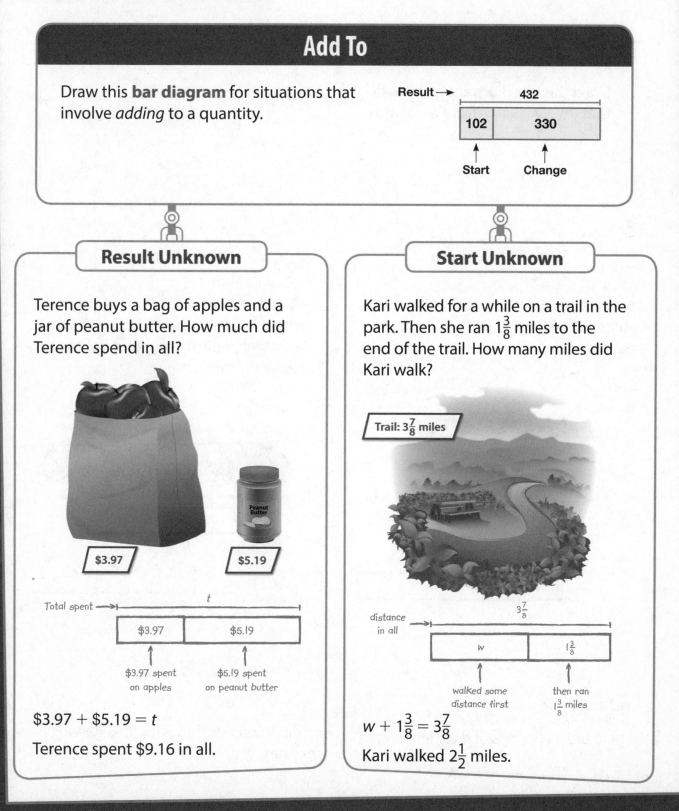

Result Unknown

Terence buys a bag of apples and a jar of peanut butter. How much did Terence spend in all?

$3.97

$5.19

Total spent →

$3.97	$5.19

↑ $3.97 spent on apples   ↑ $5.19 spent on peanut butter

$3.97 + $5.19 = t

Terence spent $9.16 in all.

Start Unknown

Kari walked for a while on a trail in the park. Then she ran $1\frac{3}{8}$ miles to the end of the trail. How many miles did Kari walk?

Trail: $3\frac{7}{8}$ miles

distance in all →

$3\frac{7}{8}$	
w	$1\frac{3}{8}$

↑ walked some distance first   ↑ then ran $1\frac{3}{8}$ miles

$w + 1\frac{3}{8} = 3\frac{7}{8}$

Kari walked $2\frac{1}{2}$ miles.

Bar Diagrams

You can use bar diagrams to make sense of addition and subtraction problems.

Take From

Draw this **bar diagram** for situations that involve *taking* from a quantity.

Start → 18,600

12,000	6,600

↑ Change   ↑ Result

Result Unknown

Bristol had $15\frac{1}{4}$ cups of flour. She used some of the flour to make a pie. How many cups of flour are left?

$3\frac{1}{3}$ cups of flour used

cups of flour to start → $15\frac{1}{4}$

$3\frac{1}{3}$	f

↑ flour used   ↑ flour left

$15\frac{1}{4} - 3\frac{1}{3} = f$

There are $11\frac{11}{12}$ cups of flour left.

Start Unknown

Mr. Adkins used 2.4 gallons of gas doing errands on Saturday. Including the gas he has left, how many gallons of gas did he start with?

6.73 gallons of gas left

gallons of gas to start → g

2.4	6.73

↑ gallons of gas used   ↑ gallons of gas left

$g - 2.4 = 6.73$

Mr. Adkins started with 9.13 gallons of gas.

The **bar diagrams** on this page can help you make sense of more addition and subtraction situations.

Put Together/Take Apart

Draw this **bar diagram** for situations that involve *putting together* or *taking apart* quantities.

Total → 21,400

7,250	14,150

One Quantity ↑   Another Quantity ↑

Whole Unknown

Joseph planted soybeans and corn in separate sections of his farm. How many acres did Joseph plant?

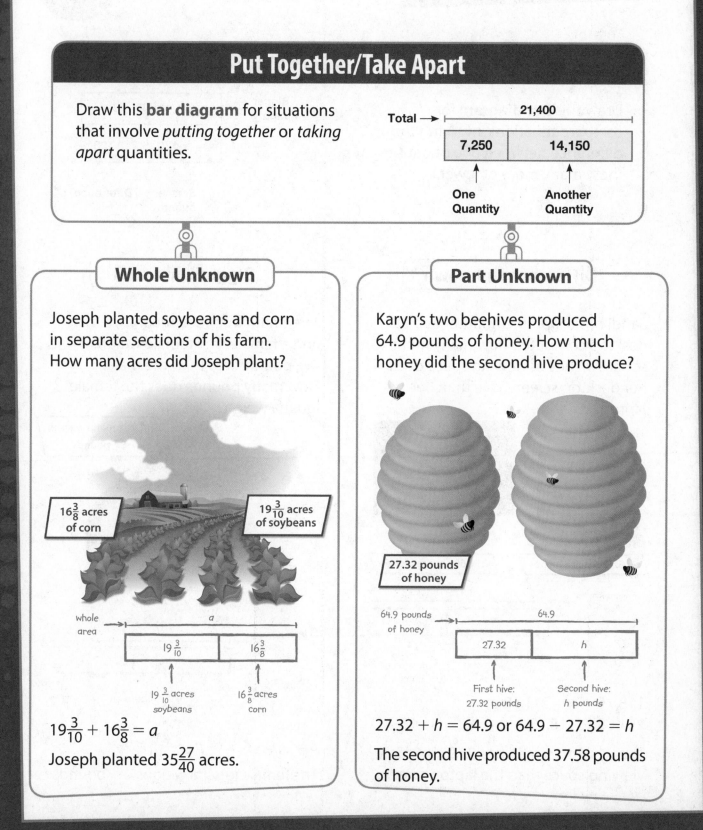

$16\frac{3}{8}$ acres of corn

$19\frac{3}{10}$ acres of soybeans

whole area →

a

$19\frac{3}{10}$	$16\frac{3}{8}$

↑ $19\frac{3}{10}$ acres soybeans   ↑ $16\frac{3}{8}$ acres corn

$19\frac{3}{10} + 16\frac{3}{8} = a$

Joseph planted $35\frac{27}{40}$ acres.

Part Unknown

Karyn's two beehives produced 64.9 pounds of honey. How much honey did the second hive produce?

27.32 pounds of honey

64.9 pounds of honey →

64.9	

27.32	h

↑ First hive: 27.32 pounds   ↑ Second hive: h pounds

$27.32 + h = 64.9$ or $64.9 - 27.32 = h$

The second hive produced 37.58 pounds of honey.

Bar Diagrams

Pictures help you understand. Don't trust key words in a problem.

Compare: Addition and Subtraction

Draw this **bar diagram** for *compare* situations involving the difference between two quantities (how many more or fewer.)

Bigger quantity →
| 1,890 |

| 1,170 | 720 |

↑ Smaller quantity ↑ Difference

Difference Unknown

Sandi has a laptop computer and a desktop computer. How many more square inches of viewing space does her desktop screen have than her laptop screen?

118.75 square inches

211.68 square inches

Desktop screen: 211.68 in²

| 118.75 | s |

Laptop screen: 118.75 in²   ? more screen area

$118.75 + s = 211.68$ or
$211.68 - 118.75 = s$

The desktop screen has 92.93 in² more viewing space than the laptop screen.

Bigger Unknown

Jared has two green iguanas, a male and a female. The female weighs $4\frac{1}{10}$ pounds less than the male. How many pounds does the female iguana weigh?

Male iguana weighs $8\frac{4}{5}$ pounds

male iguana: $8\frac{4}{5}$ pounds $8\frac{4}{5}$

| p | $4\frac{1}{10}$ |

female iguana: p pounds $4\frac{1}{10}$ fewer pounds

$8\frac{4}{5} - p = 4\frac{1}{10}$ or $p + 4\frac{1}{10} = 8\frac{4}{5}$

The female iguana weighs $4\frac{7}{10}$ pounds.

The **bar diagrams** on this page can help you solve problems involving multiplication and division.

Equal Groups: Multiplication and Division

Draw this **bar diagram** for situations that involve *equal groups*.

Total → 2,184

Number of → equal groups 728 | 728 | 728

↑ Group Size

Number of Groups Unknown

Sierra's parents spent $390 on passes to the amusement park. How many passes did Sierra's parents purchase?

$65 for each pass

$390 →| 390

p passes → 65 | P →

↑ $65 for each pass

$p \times 65 = 390$ or $390 \div 65 = p$

Sierra's parents purchased 6 passes to the amusement park.

Group Size Unknown

With the money he has saved, Ben plans to go to 3 major league baseball games this summer. If he spends the same amount, how much can he spend at each game?

$133.47

$133.47 →| 133.47

3 games → m | m | m

↑ m for each game

$3 \times m = 133.47$ or $133.47 \div 3 = m$

Ben can spend $44.49 at each game.

Bar Diagrams

Bar diagrams can be used to show how quantities that are being compared are related.

Compare: Multiplication and Division

Draw this **bar diagram** for *compare* situations involving how many times one quantity is of another quantity.

| 1,650 | | | Multiplier: 3 times as many |

Bigger quantity → | 550 | 550 | 550 |

Smaller quantity → | 550 |

Bigger Unknown

Marci's horse eats $2\frac{1}{4}$ bales of hay in a week. How many bales of hay do Craig's horses below eat in a week?

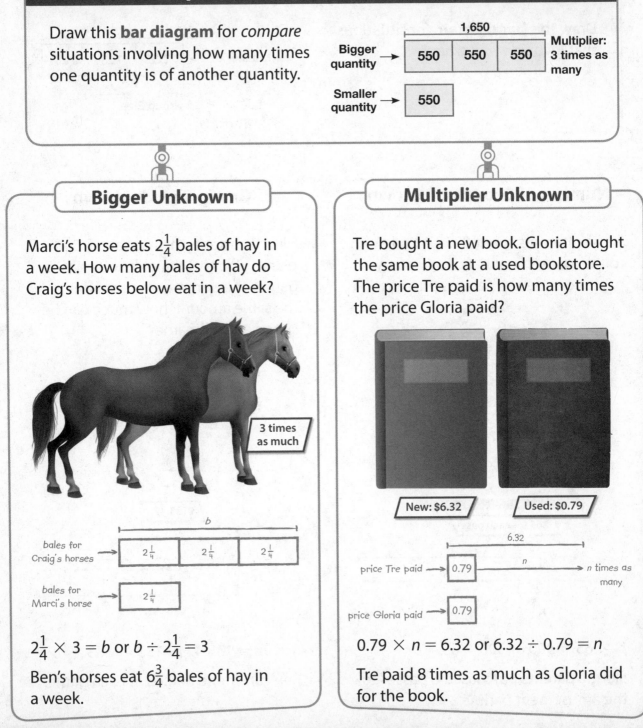

3 times as much

| b | | |
bales for Craig's horses → | $2\frac{1}{4}$ | $2\frac{1}{4}$ | $2\frac{1}{4}$ |

bales for Marci's horse → | $2\frac{1}{4}$ |

$2\frac{1}{4} \times 3 = b$ or $b \div 2\frac{1}{4} = 3$

Ben's horses eat $6\frac{3}{4}$ bales of hay in a week.

Multiplier Unknown

Tre bought a new book. Gloria bought the same book at a used bookstore. The price Tre paid is how many times the price Gloria paid?

New: $6.32   Used: $0.79

| 6.32 | |
price Tre paid → | 0.79 | n | → n times as many

price Gloria paid → | 0.79 |

$0.79 \times n = 6.32$ or $6.32 \div 0.79 = n$

Tre paid 8 times as much as Gloria did for the book.

Ratio Concepts and Reasoning

Essential Questions: What is a ratio? How can you use ratios to describe quantities?

Digital Resources

Solve   Learn   Glossary   Practice Buddy

Tools   Assessment   Help   Games

Scientists use ratios in determining scale properties of objects in the solar system, including Earth.

The temperature at the center of Earth is about 6,000°C.

Ratio relationships run deep! Here's a project on the layers of Earth and ratios.

Math and Science Project: Earth's Ratios

Do Research Use the Internet or other sources to learn about the thickness of each layer within Earth.

Journal: Write a Report Include what you found. Also in your report:

- Calculate the ratio of the thickness of each layer to the average thickness of Earth's crust.

- Use the ratios to draw a scale model of Earth's layers. Describe how the thicknesses of the layers compare.

Review What You Know

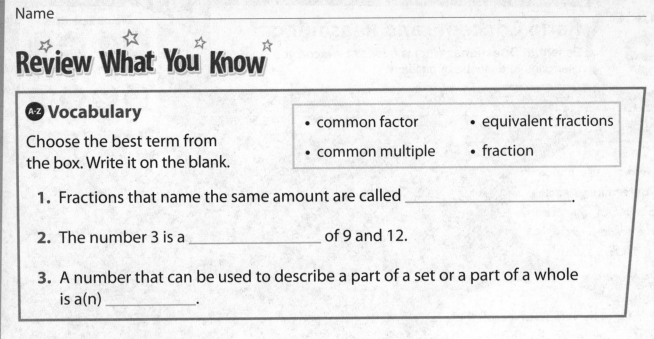

Vocabulary

Choose the best term from the box. Write it on the blank.

• common factor	• equivalent fractions
• common multiple	• fraction

1. Fractions that name the same amount are called _____.

2. The number 3 is a _____ of 9 and 12.

3. A number that can be used to describe a part of a set or a part of a whole is a(n) _____.

Equivalent Fractions

Write two fractions equivalent to the given fraction.

4. $\frac{3}{4}$ 5. $\frac{7}{8}$ 6. $\frac{12}{5}$

7. $\frac{1}{2}$ 8. $\frac{8}{9}$ 9. $\frac{2}{3}$

Equation

Write an equation that represents the pattern in each table.

10.

x	2	3	4	5	6
y	16	24	32	40	48

11.

x	2	4	6	8	10
y	5	7	9	11	13

The Coordinate Plane

12. Describe how to locate and plot the point (4, 6) on the coordinate plane.

My Word Cards

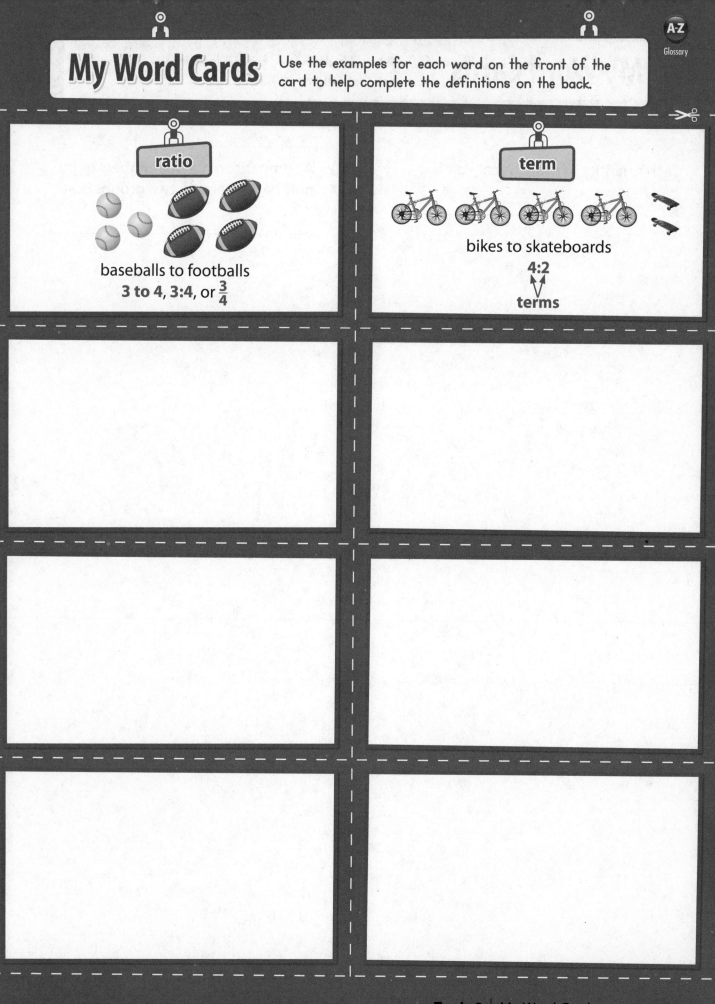

Use the examples for each word on the front of the card to help complete the definitions on the back.

A-Z Glossary

ratio

baseballs to footballs
3 to 4, 3:4, or $\frac{3}{4}$

term

bikes to skateboards
4:2
terms

My Word Cards

Complete each definition. Extend learning by writing your own definitions.

Each quantity in a ratio is called a

_____.

A comparison of two numbers or the number of items in two groups is a

_____.

Name _____

☆ ☆
Solve & Share

In a newspaper article, for every 58 words there are 6 sentences. Show the relationship between the number of words and the number of sentences in different ways.

I can ...
use a ratio to describe the relationship between two quantities.

ⓒ Content Standard 6.RP.A.1
Mathematical Practices MP.2, MP.6, MP.7

You can reason about the quantities to compare the number of words and the number of sentences.

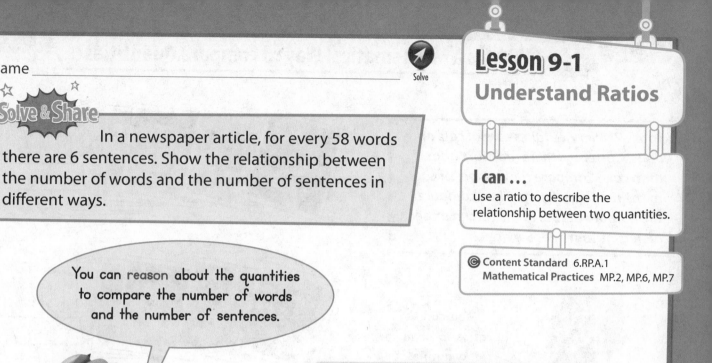

In a newspaper article I saw:	
Number of words	
Number of sentences	
Number of words to sentences	
Number of sentences to words	

Look Back! ⓒ **MP.6 Be Precise** If another sentence with 10 words were added to the article, how could you write the comparison of words to sentences?

Essential Question # What is a Mathematical Way to Compare Quantities?

A

Tom's Pet Service takes care of cats and dogs. Currently, there are more dogs than cats. Compare the number of cats to the number of dogs. Then compare the number of cats to the total number of pets at Tom's Pet Service.

17 dogs

14 cats

You can use ratios to compare quantities.

B A ratio is a relationship where for every x units of one quantity there are y units of another quantity.

A ratio can be written three ways.

x to y

$x:y$

$\frac{x}{y}$

The quantities x and y in a ratio are called terms.

C Use a ratio to compare the number of cats to the number of dogs.

14 to 17

14:17

$\frac{14}{17}$

This ratio compares one part to another part.

D Use a ratio to compare the number of cats to the total number of pets.

14 to 31

14:31

$\frac{14}{31}$

This ratio compares one part to the whole.

Convince Me! ⓒ **MP.6 Be Precise** What are three ways to write the ratio of the number of dogs to the total number of pets?

Name_____

☆ Guided Practice *

Do You Understand?

1. **© MP.2 Reasoning** What are two different types of comparisons a ratio can be used to make? How is this different from a fraction?

2. A science classroom has 5 turtles and 7 frogs. What is the ratio of frogs to total animals?

Do You Know How?

In **3–5**, use three different ways to write a ratio for each comparison below.

A sixth-grade basketball team has 3 centers, 5 forwards, and 6 guards.

3. Forwards to guards

4. Centers to total players

5. Guards to centers

☆ Independent Practice ☆

In **6–15**, use the data to write a ratio for each comparison in three different ways.

A person's blood type is denoted with the letters A, B, and O, and the symbols + and −. The blood type A+ is read as *A positive*. The blood type B− is read as *B negative*.

Blood Donors	
Type	**Donors**
A+	45
B+	20
AB+	6
O+	90
A−	21
B−	0
AB−	4
O−	9
Total	195

DATA

6. O+ donors to A+ donors

7. AB− donors to AB+ donors

8. B+ donors to total donors

9. O− donors to A− donors

10. B− donors to B+ donors

11. O− donors to total donors

12. A+ and B+ donors to AB+ donors

13. A− and B− donors to AB− donors

14. Which comparison does the ratio $\frac{90}{9}$ represent?

15. Which comparison does the ratio 20:21 represent?

*For another example, see Set A on page 465.

Math Practices and Problem Solving

16. **MP.7 Look for Relationships** Complete the pattern in the table.

Number of students with pets	1	3	9		81
Total number of students	3	9		81	

17. **Number Sense** What is the sum of $2\frac{3}{10} + 6\frac{1}{6}$?

18. Martin's quilt is made of 6 purple squares and 18 teal squares. Write a ratio that compares the number of teal squares to the total number of squares in the quilt.

19. A math class surveyed students about their musical preferences and recorded the results in the table. Use the data to write a ratio for each comparison in three different ways.

   a. Students who prefer classical to students who prefer techno

   b. Students who prefer hip-hop to total number of students surveyed

DATA

Favorite Music	
Music Type	**Number of Students**
Rock	10
Classical	4
Techno	12
Hip-Hop	15
Country	8
Alternative	4

20. **Higher Order Thinking** A recipe calls for 2 cups of flour for every $\frac{1}{4}$ cup of raisins. If $1\frac{1}{2}$ cups of raisins were used, how many cups of flour would be added?

21. **MP.2 Reasoning** Rita's class has 14 girls and 16 boys. How does the ratio 14:30 describe Rita's class?

Common Core Assessment

22. There are 12 strawberries, 18 pineapple slices, and 48 other pieces of fruit in a fruit basket. Which ratio compares the number of pineapple slices to the total number of pieces of fruit?

   Ⓐ 12 to 30

   Ⓑ 18 to 48

   Ⓒ 18 to 78

   Ⓓ 30 to 78

Help   Practice   Tools   Games
       Buddy

Another Look!

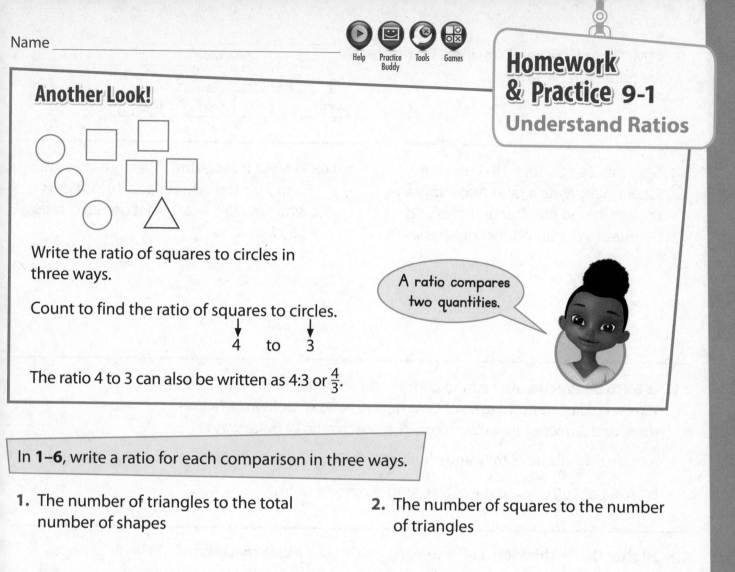

Write the ratio of squares to circles in three ways.

Count to find the ratio of squares to circles.

4   to   3

The ratio 4 to 3 can also be written as 4:3 or $\frac{4}{3}$.

A ratio compares two quantities.

In **1–6**, write a ratio for each comparison in three ways.

1. The number of triangles to the total number of shapes

2. The number of squares to the number of triangles

3. The number of triangles to the number of squares

4. The number of triangles to the number of circles

5. The number of circles to the total number of shapes

6. The total number of shapes to the number of squares

7. There are 14 boys and 16 girls in Mr. Allen's class. What is the ratio of girls to the total number of students in the class? Write the ratio 3 ways.

8. © **MP.7 Look for Relationships** Complete the pattern in the table.

Animals					
Squirrels	2	4	5		15
Birds	8		20	40	

9. Gary has 24 quarters, 16 dimes, and 32 pennies. Write a ratio that compares the combined number of dimes and pennies to the number of quarters.

10. © **MP.2 Reasoning** There are 12 students who play the clarinet and 16 students who play the viola. What does the ratio 16:12 describe?

11. © **MP.6 Be Precise** An orchard contains 12 rows of Granny Smith trees, 10 rows of Fuji trees, 15 rows of Gala trees, 2 rows of Golden Delicious trees, and 2 rows of Jonathan trees. Write each ratio in three ways.

a. rows of Gala trees to Granny Smith trees

b. rows of Fuji trees to the total number of rows of trees

12. **Higher Order Thinking** Lori is 6 years old. In three years, her cousin Philip will be twice as old as Lori will be. Write the ratio of Philip's age now to Lori's age now.

13. **Algebra** Gil has $128 in his savings account. He saves n dollars each week. Write an expression for the amount of money in his account in 10 weeks. Use the expression to find how much he will have saved if $n = 25$.

© Common Core Assessment

14. There are 4 sports stores, 9 clothing stores, and 6 jewelry stores in a shopping center. Which ratio compares the number of sports stores to the total number of stores?

Ⓐ 9:10

Ⓑ 4:19

Ⓒ 4:15

Ⓓ 15:4

Name _____

☆ ★ ☆
Solve & Share

A band just released a new album. For every 3 pop songs, the album has 2 R&B songs. If the album has 12 pop songs, how many R&B songs does it have? Explain how you know.

I can ...
draw diagrams to help solve ratio problems.

© Content Standard 6.RP.A.3
Mathematical Practices MP.1, MP.2, MP.3, MP.4, MP.7

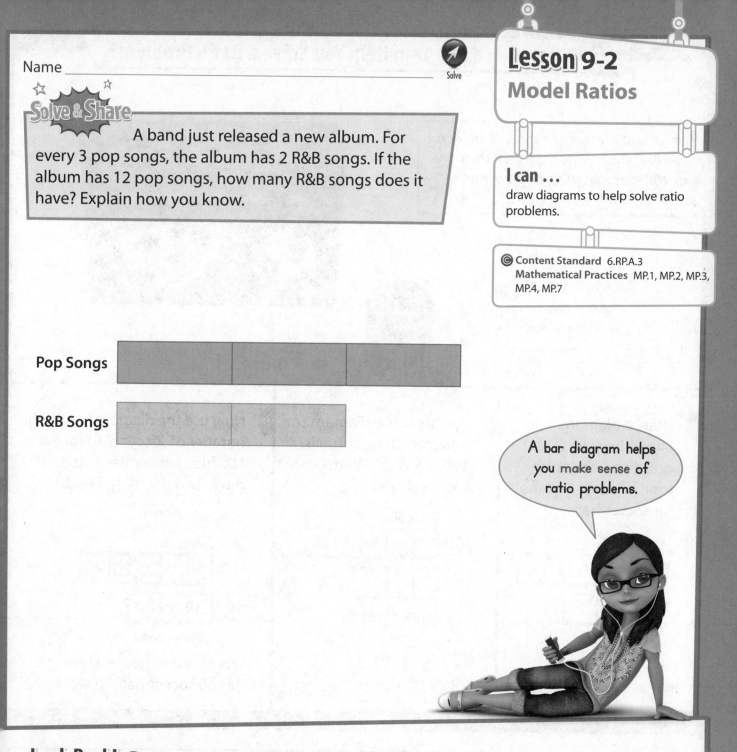

Pop Songs

R&B Songs

A bar diagram helps you make sense of ratio problems.

Look Back! © **MP.2 Reasoning** On another album the ratio of pop songs to R&B songs is 5 to 2. How would a bar diagram for this album compare to the one shown above?

How Can a Diagram Help You Solve a Ratio Problem?

A

The ratio of footballs to soccer balls at a sporting goods store is 5 to 3. If the store has 100 footballs in stock, how many soccer balls does it have ?

In a bar diagram, every box represents the same number.

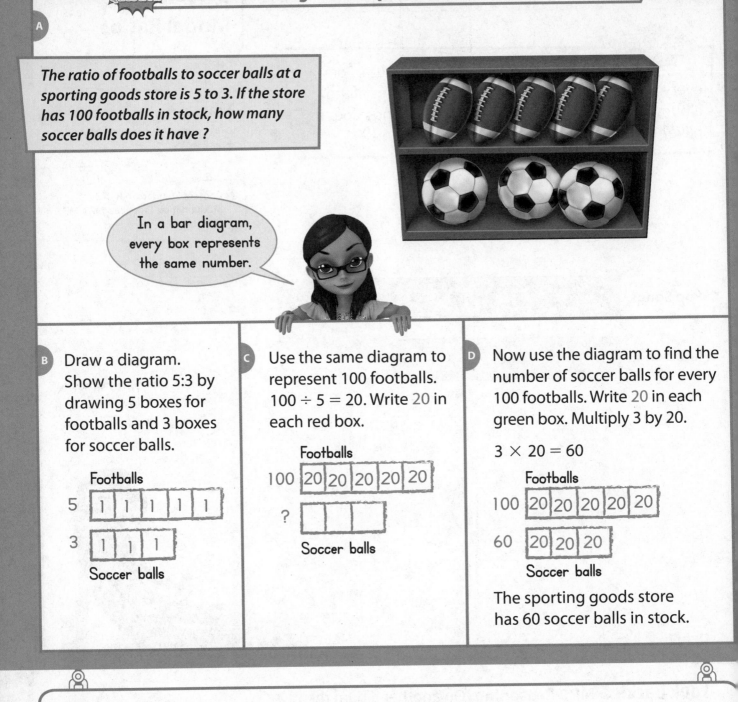

B Draw a diagram. Show the ratio 5:3 by drawing 5 boxes for footballs and 3 boxes for soccer balls.

Footballs
5 | 1 | 1 | 1 | 1 | 1 |
3 | 1 | 1 | 1 |
Soccer balls

C Use the same diagram to represent 100 footballs. 100 ÷ 5 = 20. Write 20 in each red box.

Footballs
100 | 20 | 20 | 20 | 20 | 20 |
? | | | |
Soccer balls

D Now use the diagram to find the number of soccer balls for every 100 footballs. Write 20 in each green box. Multiply 3 by 20.

3 × 20 = 60

Footballs
100 | 20 | 20 | 20 | 20 | 20 |
60 | 20 | 20 | 20 |
Soccer balls

The sporting goods store has 60 soccer balls in stock.

Convince Me! © **MP.7 Use Structure** Suppose the store has 30 footballs in stock and the ratio of footballs to soccer balls is still 5 to 3. How would the diagram for this situation be the same? How would the diagram be different? Draw a diagram for this new situation.

Another Example

You can use a double number line diagram to solve problems involving ratios.

A crew can mow 2 miles of grass along a highway in 45 minutes. At this rate, how long will it take to mow 10 miles of grass?

Draw a double number line diagram. Use equal spaces. Count by 2s until you get to 10 miles. Count by 45s the same number of spaces.

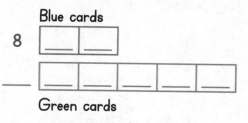

It will take 225 minutes to mow 10 miles.

☆ Guided Practice

Do You Understand?

In **1** and **2**, draw a diagram to solve each problem.

1. Tye is making trail mix with 3 cups of nuts for every 4 cups of granola. If Tye has 6 cups of nuts, how many cups of granola should he use?

2. Angela can paint 3 sections in 25 minutes. How many minutes will it take Angela to paint 12 sections?

Do You Know How?

3. ⓒ **MP.4 Model with Math** The ratio of blue cards to green cards is 2 to 5. There are 8 blue cards. Complete the diagram and explain how you can find the number of green cards.

    Blue cards
    8 ☐☐

    _ ☐☐☐☐☐
    Green cards

☆ Independent Practice ☆

In **4** and **5**, draw a diagram to solve the problem.

4. Jeremy made 4 out of every 5 free throws. If Jeremy attempted 35 free throws, how many free throws did he make?

5. Anne's family drove 165 miles in 3 hours. At that rate, how long would it take them to drive 825 miles?

For another example, see Set A on page 465.

Math Practices and Problem Solving

6. © **MP.3 Construct Arguments** Justin used blocks to model the following situation: A car dealer sells 7 cars for every 4 minivans it sells.

   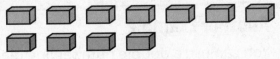

   How can Justin use his model to find the number of minivans the dealer sells if it sells 35 cars?

---

7. © **MP.1 Make Sense and Persevere** The ratio of adult dogs to puppies at a park on Monday was 3:2. There were 12 puppies there that day. Tuesday, 15 adult dogs were at the park. What is the difference between the number of adult dogs at the park on Monday and Tuesday?

8. Fourteen cousins bought their grandmother a patio table for $374 and a patio umbrella for $118. Sales tax was $40. If they shared the cost equally, how much did each cousin pay?

---

9. **Algebra** If $c = 8$, which expression has the greater value, $5c^3 + 982$ or $2c^4 - 7c$?

10. **Higher Order Thinking** At 9:30 A.M., Sean started filling a 4,500-gallon swimming pool. At 11:30 A.M., he had filled 1,800 gallons. At what time will the pool be full?

© **Common Core Assessment**

11. Of the students taking a foreign language class, 8 students take Spanish for every 5 students who take French. This is represented in the diagram below.

    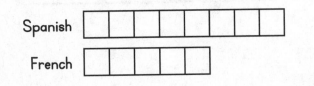

    Explain how you can use the diagram to find the number of students who are taking French if there are 72 students taking Spanish

    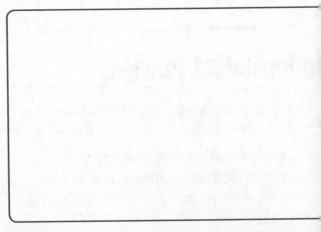

Help   Practice   Tools   Games
        Buddy

Another Look!

Chen can ride his bike 3 miles in 15 minutes. At this rate, how long will it take him to ride 18 miles?

You can solve this problem in more than one way.

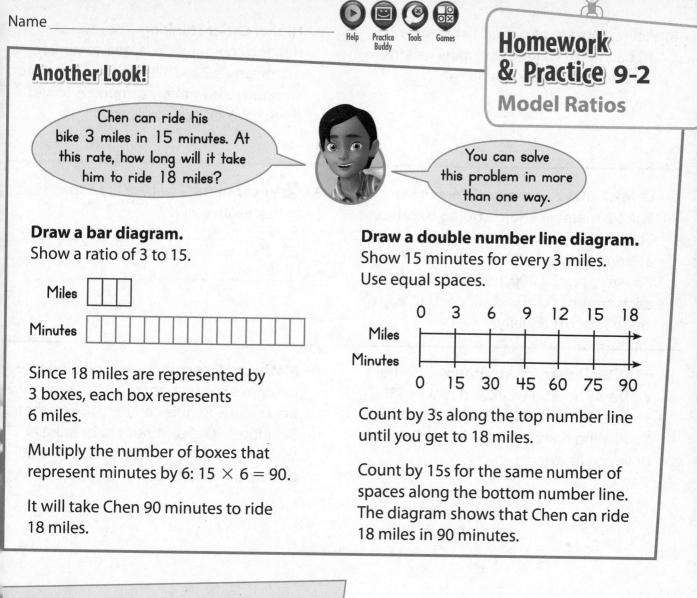

Draw a bar diagram.
Show a ratio of 3 to 15.

Miles

Minutes

Since 18 miles are represented by 3 boxes, each box represents 6 miles.

Multiply the number of boxes that represent minutes by 6: $15 \times 6 = 90$.

It will take Chen 90 minutes to ride 18 miles.

Draw a double number line diagram.
Show 15 minutes for every 3 miles.
Use equal spaces.

Miles   0   3   6   9   12   15   18
Minutes   0   15 30 45 60   75   90

Count by 3s along the top number line until you get to 18 miles.

Count by 15s for the same number of spaces along the bottom number line. The diagram shows that Chen can ride 18 miles in 90 minutes.

In **1–4**, draw a diagram to solve the problem.

1. A cleaning crew can clean 5 offices in 6 hours. How many offices can they clean in 12 hours?

2. Joseph is planting a vegetable garden. He plants 2 tomato plants for every 5 pepper plants. If Joseph plants 14 tomato plants, how many pepper plants does he plant?

3. There are 4 adult chaperones for every 15 students who attend a school field trip. If there were 135 students, how many adults would there be on the field trip?

4. Ms. Dawson spent $28 for 8 notebooks. If each notebook sells for the same price, how much would she have to spend for 48 notebooks?

5. A pet store keeps 4 small fish in every 10 gallons of water. How many gallons of water are needed for 36 fish?

6. Higher Order Thinking The ratio of desktop computers to laptop computers at a company is 2 to 9. If there were 108 laptop computers, how many computers would there be in all at the company?

7. 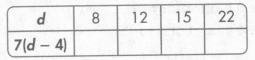 **MP.1 Make Sense and Persevere** The 52-member choir is going to camp. The total cost for the entire choir to attend camp is $12,736. If the Music Boosters pay $4,000, how much would each member of the choir need to pay to share the cost equally?

8. 🅰🆉 **Vocabulary** *Evaluate* the expression for each value of *d*.

d	8	12	15	22
$7(d - 4)$				

9. Ⓒ **MP.3 Construct Arguments** Harriet works 35 hours a week and makes $560. Jenny works 40 hours a week and makes $600. Who makes more per hour? Explain how you know.

10. Math and Science Your respiration rate measures the number of breaths you take per minute. Reggie counted 48 breaths in 3 minutes. If he continues to breathe at the same rate, how many breaths would he take in 10 minutes?

Ⓒ **Common Core Assessment**

11. A company makes uniforms for a fast-food restaurant. For every 8 yards of blue fabric, they use 13 yards of white fabric. This is represented in the diagram below.

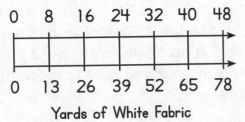

Yards of Blue Fabric

0   8   16   24   32   40   48

0   13   26   39   52   65   78

Yards of White Fabric

Explain how you would use the diagram to find the number of yards of white fabric used when 64 yards of blue fabric are used.

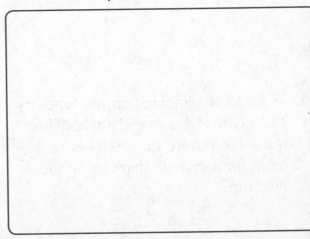

Name _____

Solve & Share

Sally used all of the paint shown below to make a certain tint of orange paint. How many pints of red paint should be mixed with 24 pints of yellow paint to make the same tint of orange? *Solve this problem any way you choose.*

I can ...
find equal ratios.

© Content Standard 6.RP.A.3a
Mathematical Practices MP.2, MP.3, MP.5, MP.6, MP.7

You can look for relationships and use them to write equal ratios.

Look Back! © MP.2 Reasoning Using the same ratio of yellow paint to red paint, how many pints of yellow paint should be mixed with 16 pints of red paint?

Essential Question: How Can You Find Equivalent Ratios?

A

For every 16 basketball players in Crystal County schools, there are 48 baseball players. If there are 64 basketball players, how many baseball players are there?

You can use the structure in a ratio table to find equivalent ratios.

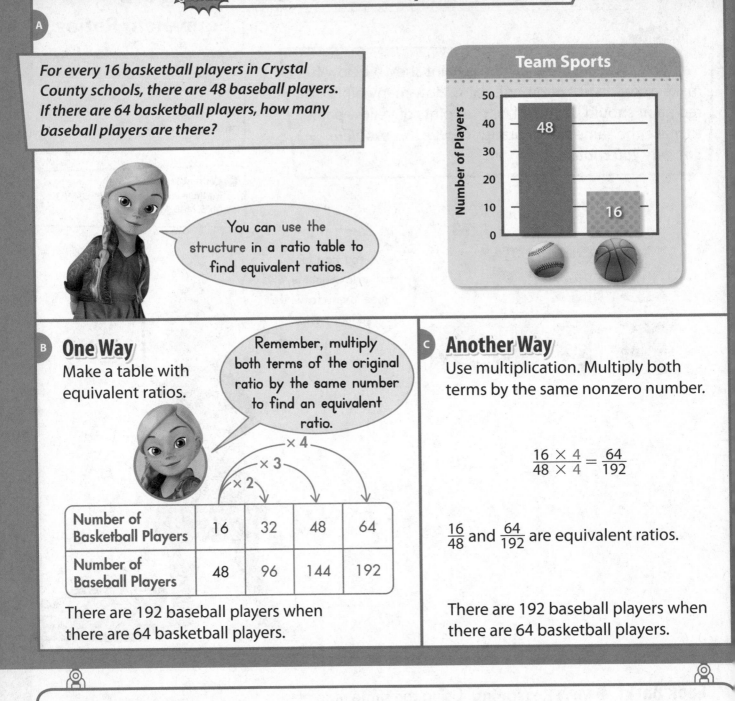

Team Sports

Number of Players

48

16

B ## One Way
Make a table with equivalent ratios.

Remember, multiply both terms of the original ratio by the same number to find an equivalent ratio.

× 4
× 3
× 2

Number of Basketball Players	16	32	48	64
Number of Baseball Players	48	96	144	192

There are 192 baseball players when there are 64 basketball players.

C ## Another Way
Use multiplication. Multiply both terms by the same nonzero number.

$$\frac{16 \times 4}{48 \times 4} = \frac{64}{192}$$

$\frac{16}{48}$ and $\frac{64}{192}$ are equivalent ratios.

There are 192 baseball players when there are 64 basketball players.

Convince Me! © **MP.7 Look for Relationships** If you extend the table above, how would you find the next ratio of basketball players to baseball players?

Another Example

Sarah took 18 shots in a basketball game and made 12 baskets.
How many baskets will she likely make in her next 6 shots?

One Way

Make a table with equivalent ratios.

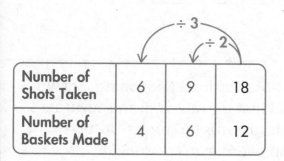

Number of Shots Taken	6	9	18
Number of Baskets Made	4	6	12

Sarah will likely make 4 baskets in her next 6 shots.

Another Way

Use division. Divide both terms by the same nonzero number.

$$\frac{18 \div 3}{12 \div 3} = \frac{6}{4}$$

$\frac{18}{12}$ and $\frac{6}{4}$ are equivalent ratios.

Sarah will likely make 4 baskets in her next 6 shots.

☆ Guided Practice *

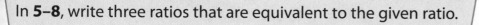

Do You Understand?

1. What are two ways you can find an equivalent ratio for $\frac{12}{16}$?

Do You Know How?

In **2–4**, write an equivalent ratio for each given ratio.

2. $\frac{12}{21}$

3. 1:3

4. 6 to 8

☆ Independent Practice ☆

In **5–8**, write three ratios that are equivalent to the given ratio.

5. $\frac{6}{7}$

6. $\frac{9}{5}$

7. 8:14

8. 7:9

Math Practices and Problem Solving

9. **MP.5 Use Appropriate Tools** Equivalent ratios can be found by extending pairs of rows or columns in a multiplication table. Write three ratios equivalent to $\frac{2}{5}$ using the multiplication table.

X	0	1	2	3	4	5	6
0	0	0	0	0	0	0	0
1	0	1	2	3	4	5	6
2	0	2	4	6	8	10	12
3	0	3	6	9	12	15	18
4	0	4	8	12	16	20	24
5	0	5	10	15	20	25	30
6	0	6	12	18	24	30	36

10. **MP.2 Reasoning** The ratio of the maximum speed of Car A to the maximum speed of Car B is 2:3. Explain whether Car A or Car B is faster.

11. **MP.3 Critique Reasoning** Shawn said that the ratios 5:6 and 40:48 are equivalent. Is he correct? Justify or improve Shawn's reasoning.

12. **Vocabulary** How is the word *term* defined when used to describe a ratio relationship? How is the word *term* defined in the context of an expression?

13. **Higher Order Thinking** If 5 miles ≈ 8 km, about how many miles would be equal to 50 km? Show how you decided.

Common Core Assessment

14. Select all of the ratios that are equivalent to 18:8.

   ☐ 9:4
   ☐ 6:3
   ☐ $\frac{48}{24}$
   ☐ $\frac{90}{40}$

15. Select all of the ratios that are equivalent to 3:5.

   ☐ 5 to 7
   ☐ 2:4
   ☐ 9:15
   ☐ $\frac{18}{30}$

Help Practice Tools Games
      Buddy

Another Look!

You can find equivalent ratios just like you find equivalent fractions.

Multiply or divide by common factors of the ratio terms to find equivalent ratios.

Find ratios equivalent to $\frac{30}{40}$ by multiplying.

Multiply both terms by the same number.

$\frac{30 \times 2}{40 \times 2} = \frac{60}{80}$ $\frac{30 \times 3}{40 \times 3} = \frac{90}{120}$

$\frac{30 \times 4}{40 \times 4} = \frac{120}{160}$ $\frac{30 \times 10}{40 \times 10} = \frac{300}{400}$

Find ratios equivalent to $\frac{30}{40}$ by dividing.

Divide both terms by the same number.

$\frac{30 \div 2}{40 \div 2} = \frac{15}{20}$ $\frac{30 \div 5}{40 \div 5} = \frac{6}{8}$ $\frac{30 \div 10}{40 \div 10} = \frac{3}{4}$

In **1–9**, write three ratios equivalent to the given ratio.

1. $\frac{3}{5}$

2. $\frac{4}{8}$

3. $\frac{6}{18}$

4. 8:10

5. 6:8

6. 10:12

7. 12 to 18

8. 16 to 18

9. 5 to 25

In **10–12**, use = or ≠ to show whether the ratios are equivalent.

10. 3:12 ◯ 6:24

11. $\frac{28}{16}$ ◯ $\frac{7}{4}$

12. 4 to 20 ◯ 1 to 4

---

13. **Math and Science** Scientists study ways to increase the population of wild salmon. How many salmon eggs may be needed to produce 18 adult salmon?

For every 8,000 eggs, only 2 adults may survive.

14. **Number Sense** Tell why you cannot multiply or divide by zero to find equivalent ratios.

15. Ⓒ **MP.3 Critique Reasoning** Dale says the ratios 3:5 and 2:10 are equivalent. Is he correct? Explain.

16. Is the ratio of length to width equivalent for these two rectangles? Tell how you know.

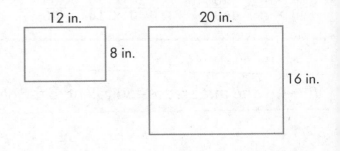

12 in.

8 in.

20 in.

16 in.

17. **Higher Order Thinking** An animal shelter can hold a total of 60 cats and dogs. For every 5 cats the shelter can house, there is room for 7 dogs. How many cats and dogs are at the shelter when it is completely full?

18. Ⓒ **MP.6 Be Precise** For a small music concert, each child in attendance will get a free toy trumpet. Five adults are expected for every 2 children. Find how many children are expected if there are 15 adults, 25 adults, and 40 adults.

Ⓒ **Common Core Assessment**

19. In a section of a lake, there are 8 sailboats for every 6 motorboats. Which could be the number of sailboats and motorboats? Choose all that apply.

- [ ] 14 sailboats, 12 motorboats
- [ ] 24 sailboats, 18 motorboats
- [ ] 32 sailboats, 24 motorboats
- [ ] 4 sailboats, 2 motorboats

20. For every 8 boys in Kaley's class, there are 10 girls. Which could describe the students in Kaley's class? Choose all that apply.

- [ ] 4 boys, 5 girls
- [ ] 10 boys, 12 girls
- [ ] 12 boys, 14 girls
- [ ] 16 boys, 20 girls

Name_____

Solve & Share

Scott is making a snack mix using almonds and raisins. For every 2 cups of almonds in the snack mix, there are 3 cups of raisins. Ariel is making a snack mix that has 3 cups of almonds for every 5 cups of sunflower seeds. If Scott and Ariel each use 6 cups of almonds to make a batch of snack mix, who would make a larger batch?

I can ...
compare ratios to solve problems.

© Content Standard 6.RP.A.3a
Mathematical Practices MP.1, MP.2, MP.4, MP.6, MP.7

You can use ratio tables to model with math.

Scott's Snack Mix in Cups					
Almonds					
Raisins					

Ariel's Snack Mix in Cups					
Almonds					
Sunflower Seeds					

Look Back! © **MP.7 Look for Relationships** Scott and Ariel want to make as much snack mix as possible, but no more than 25 cups of mix. If they can only use full cups of ingredients, who can make more mix without going over?

Essential Question **How Can You Compare Ratios to Solve a Problem?**

A

Dustin had 3 hits for every 8 at bats. Adrian had 4 hits for every 10 at bats. Who has the better hits to at bats ratio?

You can make a ratio table to compare ratios.

DATA

Dustin	
Hits	**At Bats**
3	8

DATA

Adrian	
Hits	**At Bats**
4	10

B Extend and complete the ratio tables for Dustin and Adrian until the number of hits or the number of at bats is the same in each table.

DATA

Dustin	
Hits	**At Bats**
3	8
6	16
9	24
12	32
15	40

DATA

Adrian	
Hits	**At Bats**
4	10
8	20
12	30
16	40

C Now you can compare the number of hits that Dustin and Adrian each get with 40 at bats.

Dustin gets 15 hits for every 40 at bats. Adrian gets 16 hits for every 40 at bats.

Since Adrian gets more hits, he has the better hits to at bats ratio.

Convince Me! **©** **MP.7 Look for Relationships** Marlon had 6 hits in 15 at bats. How does Marlon's hits to at bats ratio compare to Adrian's?

☆ Guided Practice *

Do You Understand?

1. In the example on the previous page, how many hits would Adrian have in 50 at bats?

2. Ⓒ **MP.2 Reasoning** In the first week, 2 out of 3 campers were boys. In the second week, 3 out of 5 campers were boys. There were 15 total campers each week. In which week were there more boy campers? Explain how you know.

Do You Know How?

3. To make plaster, Kevin mixes 3 cups of water with 4 pounds of plaster powder. Complete the ratio table. How much water will he mix with 20 pounds of powder?

Cups of water	3			
Pounds of powder	4	8	12	

4. Jenny makes plaster using a ratio of 4 cups of water to 5 pounds of plaster powder. Whose plaster recipe uses more water? Use the ratio tables to compare.

Water (cups)	4	8		
Powder (lb)	5			

Independent Practice ☆

In **5–7**, use the ratio table at the right.

5. Local radio station *WMTH* schedules 2 minutes of news for every 20 minutes of music. Complete the ratio table.

6. What is the ratio of minutes of music to minutes of news?

7. Radio station *WILM* broadcasts 4 minutes of news for every 25 minutes of music. Which radio station broadcasts more news each hour?

> You can make a ratio table like this one to compare the music to news ratios.

Minutes of Music	20	30	40	50	60
Minutes of News	2	3			

Math Practices and Problem Solving

8. **© MP.2 Reasoning** The ratio tables to the right show the comparison of HD discs to DVDs for sale at Bert's Store and at Gloria's Store. Complete the ratio tables. Which store has the greater ratio of HD discs to DVDs? Explain how you know.

Bert's Store					
HD Discs	4				
DVDs	6				

Gloria's Store					
HD Discs	5				
DVDs	8				

9. Anya rode 4 miles on her bicycle in 20 minutes. If she continues at the same rate of speed, how long will it take her to ride 24 miles?

10. **© MP.1 Make Sense and Persevere** Carol uses $\frac{1}{3}$ yard of ribbon for each bow she makes. If she has $5\frac{1}{2}$ yards of ribbon, how many complete bows can she make?

11. **Higher Order Thinking** Lauren can drive her car 320 miles on 10 gallons of gasoline. Melissa can drive her car 280 miles on 8 gallons of gasoline. Who can drive farther on 40 gallons of gasoline? Complete the ratio tables to justify your solution.

Lauren's Car					
Miles Driven					
Gallons					

Melissa's Car					
Miles Driven					
Gallons					

© Common Core Assessment

12. Fran buys socks in packages with 9 pairs of white socks for every 3 pairs of blue socks. Mia buys socks in packages with a ratio of 2 blue pairs to 4 white pairs. If the girls each bought 6 pairs of blue socks, how many pairs of white socks would each have bought?

Part A

Complete the ratio tables.

Fran's Sock Packages			
White socks			
Blue socks			

Mia's Sock Packages			
White socks			
Blue socks			

Part B

Explain how you can solve this problem.

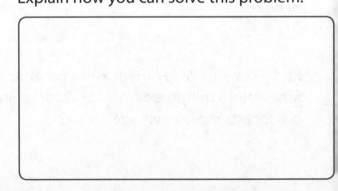

Another Look!

Due to compatibility and size restrictions, only certain types of fish can live together in an aquarium. There is a ratio of 4 guppies for every 5 mollies in one aquarium. In another aquarium, there are 2 angelfish for every 3 mollies. If there are 15 mollies in each aquarium, which aquarium has more fish?

Use tables to compare the numbers of fish in each aquarium.

Make a table that shows the ratio of guppies to mollies in an aquarium.

DATA					
Guppies	4	8	12	16	20
Mollies	5	10	15	20	25

Make a table to show the ratio of angelfish to mollies.

DATA					
Angelfish	2	4	6	8	10
Mollies	3	6	9	12	15

Compare the number of guppies and angelfish when there are 15 mollies in each aquarium.

There are 12 guppies for every 15 mollies. There are 10 angelfish for every 15 mollies.

The aquarium with 12 guppies and 15 mollies has more fish than the aquarium with 10 angelfish and 15 mollies.

In **1** and **2**, complete the ratio tables to solve.

1. There are 3 boys for every 5 girls in Mrs. Smith's class. In Mr. Addy's class there are 5 boys for every 6 girls. If each class has 15 boys, which class has fewer girls?

Mrs. Smith's Class					
Number of Boys					
Number of Girls					

Mr. Addy's Class					
Number of Boys					
Number of Girls					

2. Explain how you used the data in the ratio tables to solve Exercise 1.

3. **MP.4 Model with Math** Every 5 days during the week, Morgan sleeps 40 hours. How many days would it take him to sleep 200 hours? Complete and use the ratio table to show how you found the answer.

Morgan's Sleep Ratio Table					
Days					
Hours of Sleep					

4. **MP.2 Reasoning** Alice sleeps 50 hours every 6 days. Does Alice or Morgan have greater days to hours of sleep ratio? Explain how you know.

Alice's Sleep Ratio Table					
Days					
Hours of Sleep					

5. **MP.6 Be Precise** Susie claims that every ratio can be written as a fraction and a decimal. Do you agree? Use the ratio 32:80 in your answer.

6. **Higher Order Thinking** Mrs. Henderson has 16 boys in her class of 24 students. Mr. Gregory has 18 boys in his class of 30 students. Which class has the greater ratio of boys to students? Explain how you know.

Common Core Assessment

7. Jan makes a party punch that requires 2 gallons of orange juice for every $\frac{1}{2}$ gallon of lemonade. Matt's favorite punch recipe calls for 3 gallons of orange juice for every 2 gallons of pineapple juice. What would the ratio of orange juice to lemonade or pineapple juice be for 4 batches of each punch recipe?

Part A

Complete the ratio tables.

Jan's Party Punch				
Orange Juice				
Lemonade				

Matt's Party Punch				
Orange Juice				
Pineapple				

Part B

If Matt and Jan each make 10 gallons of punch, how many more gallons of orange juice would Jan use than Matt?

Name _____

Solve & Share

For every 4 adults at the beach one afternoon, there were 3 children. How many children were at the beach if there were 8, 12, 16, or 20 adults at the beach?

I can ...
solve problems by using tables and graphs to show equal ratios.

Content Standard 6.RP.A.3a
Mathematical Practices MP.1, MP.2, MP.3, MP.4, MP.7

Number of Adults					
Number of Children					

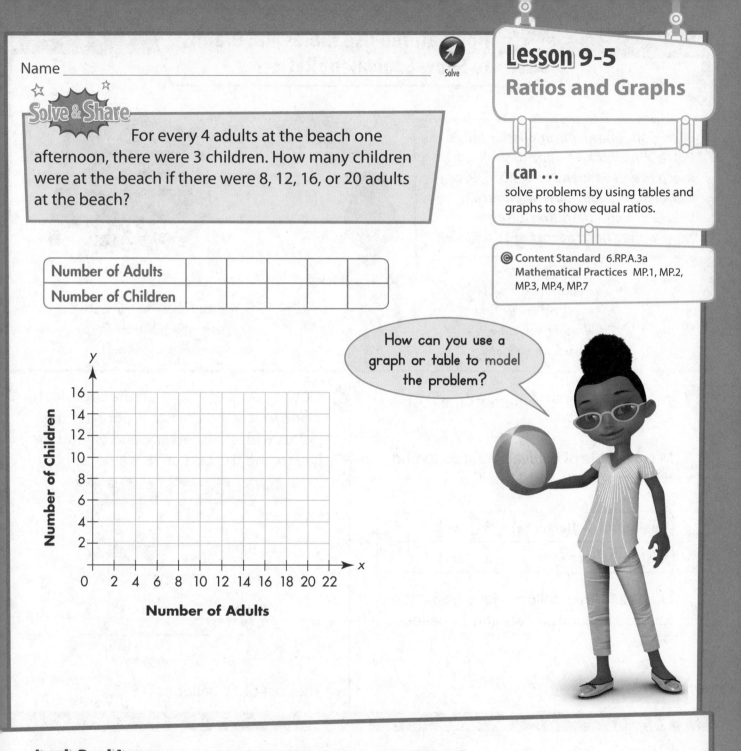

How can you use a graph or table to model the problem?

Look Back! MP.3 Critique Reasoning Emery said that if there were 5 children for every 3 adults at the beach and there were 25 children, then there were 15 adults at the beach. Is he correct?

Essential Question **How Can You Use Tables and Graphs to Show Equivalent Ratios?**

A

Ellen is shopping for supplies at Jake's Party Store. Make a table to show how much Ellen will spend to buy 3, 6, 9, or 12 balloons. Then plot the pairs of values in a coordinate graph and use the graph to find the cost of 18 balloons.

Jake's Party Store
Balloons 3 for $2
Hats 5 for $3
Streamers 4 for $1

You can make a table of equal ratios to find the costs for other numbers of balloons.

You can plot the ratios from the table on a coordinate plane.

B

The ratio $\frac{3\text{ balloons}}{\$2}$ represents the cost of the balloons.

Make a table of equivalent ratios to find the costs of 6, 9, and 12 balloons.

Number of Balloons (x)	3	6	9	12
Cost in Dollars (y)	2	4	6	8

Ellen can buy 3 balloons for $2, 6 balloons for $4, 9 balloons for $6, and 12 balloons for $8.

C

Plot the pairs of values on the coordinate plane for each ratio, x to y. Connect the points with a dashed line and extend the line to find the cost of 18 balloons.

Cost of Balloons

The cost of 18 balloons is $12.

Convince Me! © MP.2 Reasoning How can you use the graph to find the cost of 15 balloons?

Another Example

A healthy juice recipe calls for 5 celery sticks for every 2 apples. Jack has 25 celery sticks. How many apples does he need to make the juice?

Find equivalent ratios to complete the table.

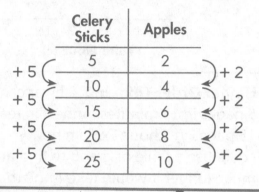

Plot the pairs of values on a coordinate plane.

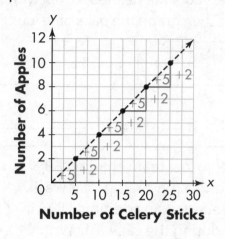

☆ Guided Practice ☆

Do You Understand?

1. © **MP.7 Look for Relationships** In Another Example, how could you use the graph to find the ratio of apples to 30 celery sticks?

Do You Know How?

2. Complete the table to show equivalent ratios for $\frac{3}{8}$. Then write the pairs of values as points to be plotted on the coordinate plane.

3	8

☆ Independent Practice ☆

In **3** and **4**, complete the table and graph the pairs of values.

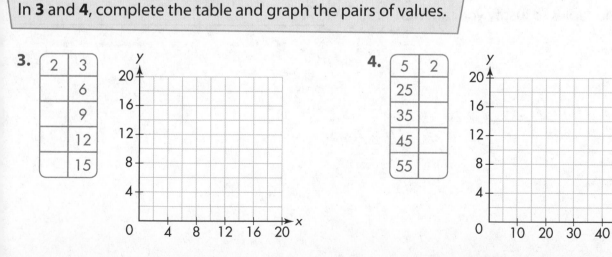

3.

2	3
	6
	9
	12
	15

4.

5	2
25	
35	
45	
55	

Math Practices and Problem Solving

5. © **MP.4 Model with Math** A bread recipe calls for 4 cups of white flour for every 3 cups of whole-wheat flour. Complete the table to show how many cups of whole-wheat flour are needed to mix with 20 cups of white flour. Then graph the pairs of values.

Cups of White Flour	4	8	12	16	20
Cups of Whole-Wheat Flour					

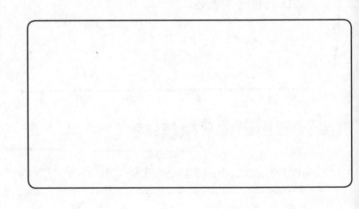

6. **Algebra** A soccer team charged $8 per car during a fund-raising car wash. The team received an additional $45 in donations during the car wash. Write an expression that represents the total amount of money the team raised if it washed *c* cars.

7. **Higher Order Thinking** Ishwar can read 5 pages in 15 minutes. Anne can read 15 pages in 1 hour. Explain how you could use a table or graph to find how much longer it would take Anne to read a 300-page book than Ishwar.

© **Common Core Assessment**

8. At Manny's store, for every 4 cartons of brown eggs, there are 6 cartons of white eggs. At Calvin's store, for every 6 cartons of brown eggs, there are 10 cartons of white eggs. If each store has the same number of brown eggs, which store would have the greater number of white eggs? Use ratio tables to justify your answer.

Name _____

Another Look!

> You can make a table of equivalent ratios and graph the values on a coordinate plane.

For every 3 tennis rackets sold at a sports store, 4 cans of tennis balls are sold. At this rate, how many cans of tennis balls were sold if 12 tennis rackets were sold?

Make a table to show equivalent ratios for $\frac{3}{4}$.

Plot the points for each ratio, x to y, of rackets to tennis balls sold. Draw a dashed line from (0, 0) and extending through the points representing 6, 9, and 12 rackets sold.

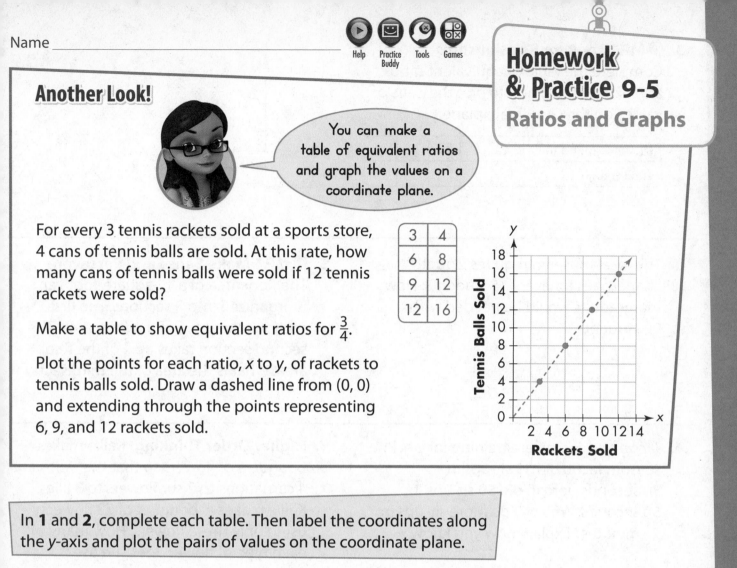

3	4
6	8
9	12
12	16

In **1** and **2**, complete each table. Then label the coordinates along the y-axis and plot the pairs of values on the coordinate plane.

1.

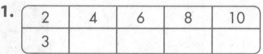

2	4	6	8	10
3				

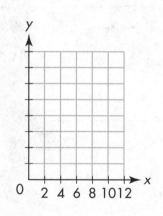

2.

1	2	3	4	5
2				

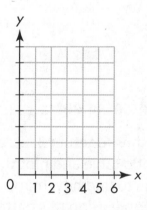

3. © **MP.7 Look for Relationships**
   Complete the table of equivalent ratios and extend the graph to plot the pairs of values on the coordinate plane.

Distance Biked (mi)	4	8	12	16	20
Time (min)	15				

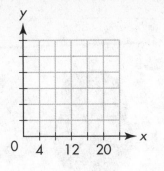

4. The local museum requires 2 adult chaperones for every 15 students. How many adults would be needed with 90 students?

5. © **MP.1 Make Sense and Persevere**
   The floor area of a 12-square-foot van is organized into 3 sections. The first section takes up $\frac{1}{2}$ of the floor area. The second section takes up $\frac{3}{8}$ of the floor area. What is the area of the third section?

6. Jacob and Jordan are training for track season. Jacob did 39 sit-ups in 30 seconds. Jordan did 59 sit-ups in 50 seconds. Who will do more sit-ups in $2\frac{1}{2}$ minutes? Explain how you know.

7. **Higher Order Thinking** Kallie makes bouquets of flowers so that the ratios are 4 carnations to 2 sunflowers to 3 lilies. Kallie makes a bouquet of 72 flowers using only these flowers. How many of each type of flower does she use?

> You can make a table to compare the ratios to the total flowers in each bouquet.

© **Common Core Assessment**

8. A restaurant pushes together 3 tables to seat 13 people. Complete the ratio table and plot the pairs of values on the coordinate plane to find how many tables are needed to seat up to 65 people using this pattern.

Tables	3				
People					65

Name _____

Solve & Share

Sam is packing gift boxes with apples, oranges, and plums. For every apple, he packs 3 plums and 5 oranges. If a gift box contains 4 apples, how many oranges and plums are there?

I can ...
make sense of problems and keep working if I get stuck.

© **Mathematical Practices** MP.1 Also MP.4, MP.6, MP.8
Content Standards 6.RP.A.1, 6.RP.A.3a

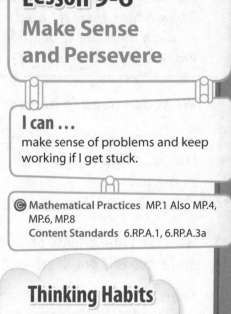

Thinking Habits

Be a good thinker!
These questions can help you.

- What do I need to find?

- What do I know?

- What's my plan for solving the problem?

- What else can I try if I get stuck?

- How can I check that my solution makes sense?

Look Back! © **MP.1 Make Sense and Persevere** How did the number of apples help you find the number of oranges and plums in the gift box? Explain your reasoning.

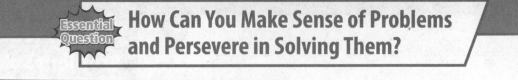

Essential Question

How Can You Make Sense of Problems and Persevere in Solving Them?

A

Lucinda is making a necklace of beads. For every 3 blue beads, there is 1 gold bead and 2 purple beads. If there are 48 beads in the necklace, how many of each color are there?

What do I need to do to solve this problem?

I need to make sense of the problem before I can solve it. I need to find the correct number of beads for each color in the necklace.

B **How can I make sense of and solve this problem?**

I can

- identify what I know and what I need to find.

- think about how the quantities are related.

- choose and implement a strategy.

- check that my solution makes sense.

C

Here's my thinking...

I can draw a diagram to show how the beads are related.

Blue beads
Gold beads
Purple beads

Then I can use the same diagram to show 48 beads.

$48 \div 6 = 8$

Blue beads   8 8 8
Gold beads   8
Purple beads 8 8

The necklace has 24 blue beads, 8 gold beads, and 16 purple beads.

Convince Me! © **MP.1 Make Sense and Persevere** Explain how to check your solution.

Practice Buddy   Tools   Assessment

☆ Guided Practice *

© MP.1 Make Sense and Persevere

A factory produces 5 green jellybeans and 2 orange jellybeans for every 8 pink jellybeans. There are 75 jellybeans in a bag. How many green jellybeans are in the bag?

> Think about ways to show ratio relationships.

1. How can you make sense of the problem?

2. How can you solve this problem? Explain your thinking.

Independent Practice ☆

© MP.1 Make Sense and Persevere

Three sisters are saving for a special vacation. The ratio of Ada's savings to Ellie's savings is 7:3 and the ratio of Ellie's savings to Jasmine's savings is 3:4. Together all three girls have saved $56. How much has each girl saved?

3. How can you use a diagram to make sense of the problem?

4. Complete the table. Describe how the table can be used to solve the problem.

Ada's savings	$7		$21	
Ellie's savings		$6		
Jasmine's savings	$4			$16

*For another example, see Set E on page 466.

Math Practices and Problem Solving

© Common Core Performance Assessment

Gas Guzzlers?

A car magazine reports the number of miles driven for different amounts of gas. Which car travels the farthest on 1 gallon of gas?

Miles Driven		200	300		500	
Gallons of Gas	4	8		16		40

Car B can travel 140 miles for every 5 gallons of gas.

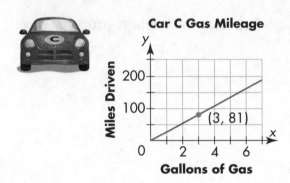

Car C Gas Mileage

(3, 81)

5. **MP.4 Model with Math** Complete the ratio table for Car A.

6. **MP.1 Make Sense and Persevere** What do you know? What are you asked to find?

7. **MP.1 Make Sense and Persevere** Describe your plan or strategy to solve the problem.

8. **MP.6 Be Precise** Solve the problem. Explain why your answer makes sense.

Another Look!

For every 2 SUVs in a parking lot, there are 5 minivans and 8 cars. If there are 45 minivans, how many SUVs and cars are in the parking lot?

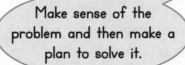

Make sense of the problem and then make a plan to solve it.

Tell how you can make sense of the problem.

- I can identify what I know and what I need to find out.

- I can make a plan to find the number of SUVs and cars in the parking lot when there are 45 minivans.

- I can try a different strategy if I get stuck.

Make a plan. Use it to solve the problem.

SUVs	2	4	6	8	10	12	14	16	18
Minivans	5	10	15	20	25	30	35	40	45
Cars	8	16	24	32	40	48	56	64	72

I made a ratio table to show the relationship of 2 SUVs for every 5 minivans and 8 cars.

It lists equivalent ratios and shows that when there are 45 minivans in the parking lot, there will be 18 SUVs and 72 cars.

When I divide each of these terms by 9, I get the original ratio. So, my answer checks.

© MP.1 Make Sense and Persevere

Tyler, Kristin, and Nadine ran for student council president. The ratio of votes for Tyler to votes for Kristin was 6:5, and the ratio of votes for Tyler to votes for Nadine was 6:10. Kristin got 50 votes. How many votes did Tyler and Nadine get?

Remember, diagrams and tables can help you make sense of the problem.

1. How can you make sense of the problem?

2. Solve the problem. If you get stuck, try another method. Explain how you solved the problem.

Mixing Paints

Dana mixes yellow, blue, and white paint to make her favorite shade of light green. For every 7 ounces of yellow paint, she uses 6 ounces of blue and 3 ounces of white paint. How much yellow, blue, and white paint should she mix to make 128 ounces of light green paint?

3. **MP.4 Model with Math** Use a bar diagram to represent the ratio relationship in the problem. Explain how the diagram represents the given quantities.

4. **MP.6 Be Precise** Dana says she should mix 56 ounces, 48 ounces, and 24 ounces of paint. What did she forget to include in her answer?

> To be precise in solving ratio problems, you need to use appropriate labels and units to describe amounts.

5. **MP.8 Generalize** Explain how you can use a bar diagram to find the number of ounces of each paint Dana needs to mix.

6. **MP.1 Make Sense and Persevere** Check Dana's solution by using another method to solve the problem. Explain what you did.

Name _____

Find a Match

Work with a partner. Point to a clue.

Read the clue.

Look below the clues to find a match. Write the clue letter in the box next to the match.

Find a match for every clue.

I can ...
add and subtract multi-digit decimals.

© **Content Standard** 6.NS.B.3

Clues

A The difference is between 0.1 and 0.5.

I The ones digit in the sum is 10 times the value of the tenths digit.

T The difference is greater than 0.5 and less than 1.

N The sum is greater than 12.5 and less than 14.5.

Q The sum has a 2 in the tenths place.

U The tenths digit in the difference is $\frac{1}{10}$ the value of the ones digit.

Y The hundredths digit in the sum is less than the tenths digit.

T The difference has a 9 in the tenths place.

□	□	□	□
6.3 + 4.9	18 − 9.103	2.06 − 1.87	4.23 + 9.905

□	□	□	□
12.4 − 6.45	0.68 + 3.8	4.012 − 3.3	8 + 6.73

Vocabulary Review

Glossary

Word List

- common factor
- equivalent ratios
- ordered pair
- ratio
- term

Understand Vocabulary

Choose the best term from the Word List. Write it on the blank.

1. A relationship in which there are *y* units of a quantity for every *x* units of a quantity is a(n) _____.

2. _____ are two fractions that describe the same comparison.

3. A _____ is a factor shared by two or more numbers.

4. Each quantity in a ratio is a _____.

Write T for *true* and F for *false*.

There are 9 snakes, 8 lizards, 12 newts, and 4 scorpions at a nature center. Write T for *true* and F for *false* for each statement.

_____ 5. The ratio of snakes to lizards is 8:9.

_____ 6. The ratio of newts to snakes is $\frac{12}{9}$.

_____ 7. The ratio of lizards to scorpions is 8 to 4.

_____ 8. The ratio of scorpions to all creatures is 4:29.

Use Vocabulary in Writing

9. There are 5 girls and 4 boys on a volleyball team. Explain how to write the ratio of boys to girls in three different ways. Use at least two words from the Word List.

Name _____

TOPIC
9

Set A pages 427–438 _____

The ratio of men to women at a small wedding is 6:4. This ratio can also be written as 6 to 4 and $\frac{6}{4}$.

If there are 16 women at the wedding, how many men are at the wedding?

Draw a diagram to represent the ratio. Since 4 boxes represent 16 women, each box represents 4 women.

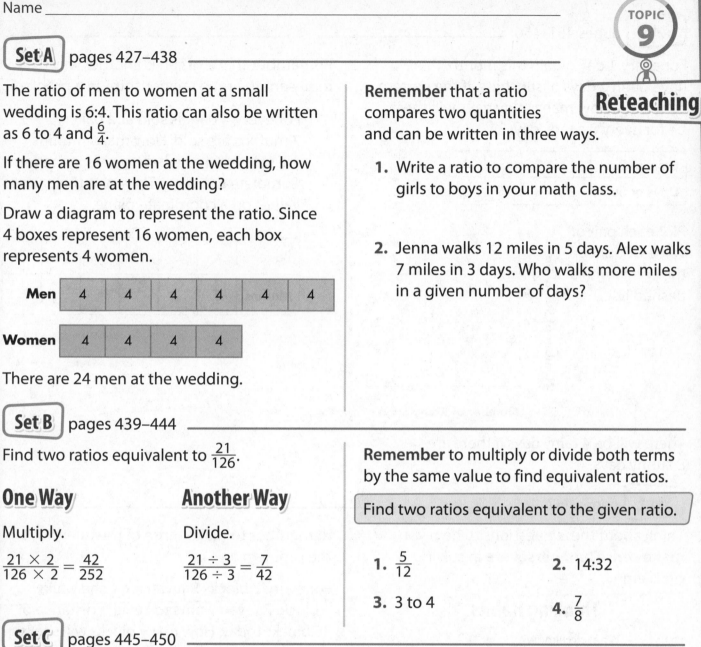

| Men | 4 | 4 | 4 | 4 | 4 | 4 |

| Women | 4 | 4 | 4 | 4 |

There are 24 men at the wedding.

Remember that a ratio compares two quantities and can be written in three ways.

Reteaching

1. Write a ratio to compare the number of girls to boys in your math class.

2. Jenna walks 12 miles in 5 days. Alex walks 7 miles in 3 days. Who walks more miles in a given number of days?

Set B pages 439–444 _____

Find two ratios equivalent to $\frac{21}{126}$.

One Way

Multiply.

$$\frac{21 \times 2}{126 \times 2} = \frac{42}{252}$$

Another Way

Divide.

$$\frac{21 \div 3}{126 \div 3} = \frac{7}{42}$$

Remember to multiply or divide both terms by the same value to find equivalent ratios.

Find two ratios equivalent to the given ratio.

1. $\frac{5}{12}$ 2. 14:32

3. 3 to 4   4. $\frac{7}{8}$

Set C pages 445–450 _____

Erica can complete 25 math facts every 30 seconds. Klayton can complete 38 math facts every 50 seconds. Who can complete more facts in the same amount of time? Use ratio tables to solve.

Erica	
Math Facts	Seconds
25	30
50	60
75	90
100	120
125	**150**
150	180

Klayton	
Math Facts	Seconds
38	50
76	100
114	**150**
152	200
190	250
228	300

Erica can complete more facts than Klayton.

Remember that to compare ratios, one quantity must be the same.

1. Sally saves $10 every 6 days. Mike saves $12 every 7 days. How long will it take for Sally and Mike to have saved the same amount? How much have they each saved?

For every 1 day of rain this month, there have been 2 days of sunshine. If the pattern continues, how many rainy days will there be for every 8 sunny days?

Days of Rain	1	2	3	4
Days of Sun	2	4	6	8

Plot each pair of values. Connect the points with a dashed line.

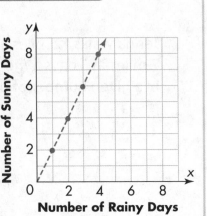

There will be 4 rainy days if there are 8 sunny days.

Remember that a graph is another way to represent the ratio relationships in a problem.

1. For every 4 bagels sold at a bakery, 7 muffins are sold. How many muffins are sold when the bakery sells 24 bagels? Complete the table. Then plot the pairs of values on a coordinate plane.

Bagels	4	8	12	16	20	24
Muffins	7					

Think about these questions to help you **make sense and persevere** in solving problems.

Thinking Habits

- What do I know?

- What do I need to find?

- What is my plan for solving the problem?

- What else can I try if I get stuck?

- How can I check that my solution makes sense?

Remember to make sense of the quantities in the problem.

For every 2 blocks Raevan jogs, she walks 1 block. Raevan wants to cover a distance of 36 blocks today. How many blocks will she jog?

1. What ratio will help you solve the problem?

2. What is your plan to find how far Raevan will jog?

3. How many blocks will Raevan jog? How do you know your answer is correct?

Name _____

1. A preschool has a student to teacher ratio of 5:2. Which of the following ratios is equivalent to this ratio?

   Ⓐ 45 teachers to 18 students

   Ⓑ 45 students to 18 teachers

   Ⓒ 35 students to 10 teachers

   Ⓓ 10 students to 7 teachers

2. The table shows the relationship of the number of yellow flowers to the number of purple flowers in Chloe's garden. Use the numbers from the box below to complete the table.

40	24	20	10	8

Yellow	2	4	6		
Purple	8	16		32	

3. The table shows the number of units that are rented and owned in a building. Which ratios compare the number of the rented units to the total number of units in the building? Choose *Yes* or *No*.

DATA	Type of Occupancy	Number of Units
	Rented	24
	Owned	52

   3a. 6 to 19   ○ Yes ○ No

   3b. 6 to 13   ○ Yes ○ No

   3c. 19 to 6   ○ Yes ○ No

   3d. 13 to 6   ○ Yes ○ No

   3e. 12 to 13   ○ Yes ○ No

4. There are 7 campers for every 2 counselors at summer camp. How many counselors are there if there are 84 campers?

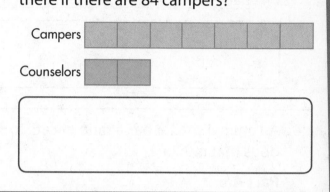

5. José is using 12 brown tiles and 8 white tiles to design a section of an outdoor patio. Which ratio compares the number of brown tiles to the total number of tiles in one section?

   Ⓐ 12:8

   Ⓑ 8:12

   Ⓒ 12:20

   Ⓓ 8:20

6. The table shows the party affiliations of the 100 Senate members of the 109th Congress. The ratio of Republicans to Democrats is 5:4. How many senators are Democrats? Independents?

DATA	Party Affiliation	Number of Senators
	Republican	55
	Democrat	
	Independent	

7. The ratio of width to height of a picture frame is 4 to 3. What is the perimeter of the picture frame if the height is 18 inches?

Width inches	4	8	12	16		
Height inches	3	6	9	12	15	18

8. An animal shelter has a ratio of cats to dogs that is 9:7.

Part A

If the shelter only houses dogs and cats, what is the ratio of dogs to total animals?

Part B

A second shelter has a ratio of cats to dogs of 6 to 5. If both shelters have 18 cats, which shelter has more dogs?

9. Max has 4 baseball cards for every 3 football cards in his collection. Circle all of the ratios that are equivalent to the ratio of baseball cards to football cards in Max's collection.

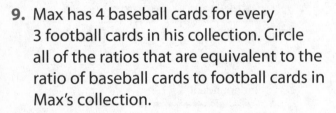

$\frac{16}{9}$ $\frac{8}{6}$ $\frac{32}{24}$ $\frac{48}{36}$

$\frac{36}{30}$ $\frac{24}{18}$ $\frac{6}{5}$ $\frac{14}{13}$

10. Complete the ratio table. Then plot the pairs of values on the coordinate plane.

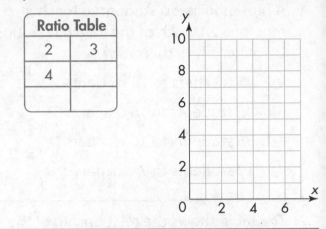

Ratio Table

2	3
4	

11. A lemonade stand sold 48 drinks in 1 hour. The ratio of small to large drinks sold was 6:1. The ratio of small to medium drinks sold was 6:5.

Part A

Draw a diagram or make a table to make sense of the problem.

Part B

How many of each size drink were sold?

Name _____

© **Performance Assessment**

Bradley is planning to publish a cookbook. He consults with the author and they decide to include 150 recipes, one on each page. They also decide to divide the book into three sections: vegetarian dishes, meat dishes, and desserts.

1. After looking at other cookbooks, Bradley decides that 25 recipes should be desserts.

   Part A

   What is the ratio of the number of dessert recipes to the total number of recipes in the book?

   Part B

   What do you think the ratio of vegetarian recipes to all recipes and the ratio of meat recipes to all recipes should be? Complete the table below. Write ratios with 1 as the first term.

Recipe Type	Vegetarian	Meat	Dessert
Ratio to Total Recipes			
Number of Recipes			

2. Explain how you decided what the ratio of vegetarian and meat recipes should be to all recipes.

3. Bradley decides to include 5 pages of photographs for every 15 pages. Use equivalent ratios to find how many pages of photographs will be in the cookbook. Explain how you know the ratios are equivalent.

4. The printer gives Bradley three options for printing the books. The table shows the number of books to be printed and the cost for each option. In addition to the printing costs, Bradley estimates it will cost $47,000 in other fees to market the books and to pay the author and photographer.

	Option A	Option B	Option C
Number of Books	5,000	8,000	12,000
Printing Cost	$27,000	$32,040	$37,480

Part A

Explain how to find the cost per book for each option.

Part B

Which plan do you think Bradley should choose? Explain.

TOPIC 10

Ratio Concepts: Rates

Essential Questions: What are ratios and rates and how are they used in solving problems? How can customary and metric measurements be converted to other units?

Digital Resources

Solve   Learn   Glossary   Practice Buddy

Tools   Assessment   Help   Games

Did you know that the Atlantic Ocean was once a much narrower body of water?

New ocean floor is continually generated at the Mid-Atlantic Ridge, an underwater mountain range.

Mid-Atlantic Ridge

Hey, I catch your drift! Everything is on the go, but at what speed? Here's a project about plate motion and rates.

Math and Science Project: Underwater Mountain Ranges

Do Research Use the Internet or other sources to learn about the Mid-Atlantic Ridge and other seafloor structures, such as trenches and volcanoes. How far does a particular plate or structure move in a given time period?

Journal: Write a Report Include what you found. Also in your report:

• Convert measurements from metric to customary.

• Calculate and compare rates of plate motion.

• Write a general conclusion about the movement of plate motion using the rates you found.

Review What You Know

A-Z Vocabulary

Choose the best term from the box.
Write it on the blank.

- capacity
- ratio
- length
- term
- mass
- weight

1. The _____ of an object can be measured in inches and centimeters.

2. A _____ compares two amounts and can be written as a fraction.

3. The _____ of an object can be measured in pints and liters.

4. The _____ of an object can be measured in pounds.

5. A quantity being compared in a ratio is called a _____.

Units of Measure

Choose the best unit of measurement by writing *inch, foot, yard, ounce, pound, ton, cup, quart,* or *gallon.*

6. serving of trail mix

7. height of a person

8. weight of a newborn kitten

9. gasoline

10. weight of a truck

11. length of a soccer field

Ratios

12. A chef is preparing a vegetable tray. She wants to keep a ratio of 5 carrots for every 3 cherry tomatoes. Circle the ratios that are equivalent to the ratio of carrots to tomatoes the chef wants.

$\frac{6}{10}$ $\frac{25}{15}$ $\frac{50}{30}$ $\frac{10}{8}$

Measurement Conversions

13. Michael is 4 feet tall. Explain how Michael could find his height in inches. Then explain how he could find his height in yards.

My Word Cards

Use the examples for each word on the front of the card to help complete the definitions on the back.

A-Z
Glossary

rate

ratio
$\dfrac{20 \text{ blue balloons}}{7 \text{ red balloons}}$

rate
$\dfrac{20 \text{ blue balloons}}{5 \text{ tables}}$

unit rate

rate
$\dfrac{15 \text{ miles biked}}{5 \text{ days}}$

unit rate
$\dfrac{5 \text{ miles biked}}{1 \text{ day}}$

unit price

rate
$\dfrac{\$12.50}{2 \text{ movie tickets}}$

unit price
$\dfrac{\$6.25}{\text{movie ticket}}$

constant speed

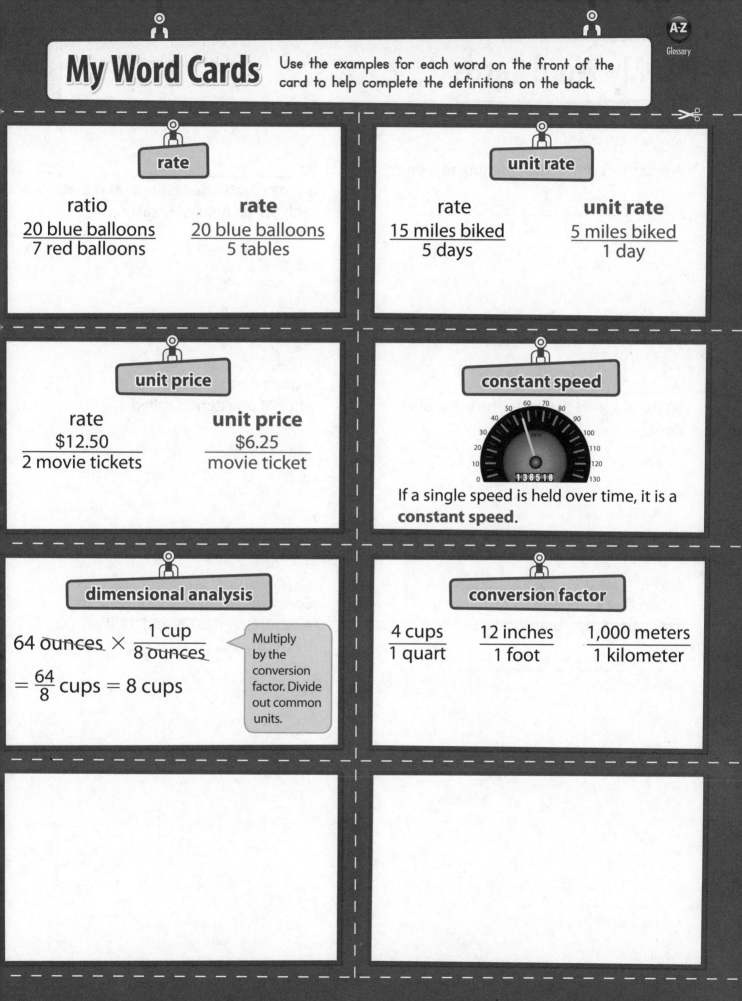

If a single speed is held over time, it is a **constant speed**.

dimensional analysis

$64 \text{ ounces} \times \dfrac{1 \text{ cup}}{8 \text{ ounces}}$

$= \dfrac{64}{8} \text{ cups} = 8 \text{ cups}$

Multiply by the conversion factor. Divide out common units.

conversion factor

$\dfrac{4 \text{ cups}}{1 \text{ quart}}$ $\dfrac{12 \text{ inches}}{1 \text{ foot}}$ $\dfrac{1,000 \text{ meters}}{1 \text{ kilometer}}$

Topic 10 | My Word Cards   **473**

My Word Cards

A rate that compares a quantity to 1 unit is a _____.

A _____ is a type of ratio that compares quantities with unlike units of measure.

A _____ is a rate of speed that stays the same over time.

A unit rate that gives the price of one item is called a

_____.

A rate that compares equivalent measures is called a

_____.

Converting measures by including measurement units and multiplying by a conversion factor is called

_____.

Name _____

Solve & Share

What is the cost of 10 bottles of fruit juice? **Solve this problem any way you choose.**

I can ...
solve problems involving rates.

© Content Standards 6.RP.A.2, 6.RP.A.3a
Mathematical Practices MP.1, MP.2, MP.3, MP.4, MP.6

You can use a ratio table to make sense of the quantities in the problem.

FRUIT JUICE
4 for $10

Cost	$10.00			
Bottles of Fruit Juice	4			

Look Back! © MP.3 Critique Reasoning Monica says that you can use number sense to find the cost of 10 bottles of fruit juice. If 4 bottles cost $10, then 2 bottles cost $5, and 8 bottles cost $20. So 10 bottles cost $5 + $20. Is Monica correct? Explain.

Essential Question **What Is a Rate?**

A

A rate is a special type of ratio that compares quantities with unlike units of measure.

If the race car continues to travel at the same rate, how long will it take it to travel 25 kilometers?

10 km in 3 min

You can find equivalent rates the same ways that you find equivalent ratios.

B **One Way**

Use a ratio table to find rates equivalent to $\frac{10 \text{ km}}{3 \text{ min}}$.

Distance (km)	Time (min)
5	$1\frac{1}{2}$
10	3
15	$4\frac{1}{2}$
20	6
25	$7\frac{1}{2}$

It will take the race car $7\frac{1}{2}$ minutes to travel 25 kilometers.

C **Another Way**

Write the rate as a fraction. Multiply both terms of the rate by the same number to find an equivalent rate.

$$\frac{10 \text{ km}}{3 \text{ min}} = \frac{25 \text{ km}}{x \text{ min}}$$

Think $10 \times ? = 25$

Multiply both terms by 2.5.

$$\frac{10 \text{ km} \times 2.5}{3 \text{ min} \times 2.5} = \frac{25 \text{ km}}{7.5 \text{ min}}$$

It will take the race car 7.5 minutes to travel 25 kilometers.

Convince Me! © **MP.3 Critique Reasoning** Sal draws the double number line diagram at the right. He says that it shows that at this rate, the race car will travel 35 kilometers in 10.5 minutes. Critique Sal's reasoning. Is he correct? Explain.

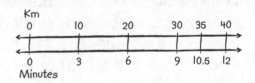

Km
0   10   20   30 35 40
0   3   6   9 10.5 12
Minutes

Name _____

☆ Guided Practice *

Do You Understand?

1. © **MP.6 Be Precise** Use what you know about ratios to explain how a rate is different from a fraction.

2. © **MP.3 Critique Reasoning** A semi truck uses 40 gallons of diesel fuel to travel 320 miles. Steve says this ratio can be written as two different rates: $\frac{40\ gal}{320\ mi}$ or $\frac{320\ mi}{40\ gal}$. Do you agree? Explain.

Do You Know How?

3. Jenny packaged 108 eggs in 9 cartons. Write this statement as a rate.

In **4** and **5**, find the value of *n*.

4.

DATA			
Miles	45	135
Hours	4	n

5. Pounds

```
  0           1              n
  |-----------|--------------|-->
<-|-----------|--------------|-->
  0           2              5
cost ($)
```

☆ Independent Practice ☆

In **6** and **7**, write each statement as a rate.

6. It took Hannah 38 minutes to run 8 laps.

7. Jan saw 9 full moons in 252 days.

In **8** and **9**, find the value of *x*.

8.

DATA		
Fish	16	48
Bowls	2	x

9. Miles

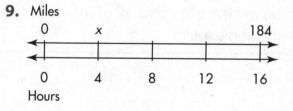

```
  0       x                184
<-|---|---|---|---|---|---|-->
  0   4   8   12   16
Hours
```

Math Practices and Problem Solving

In **10** and **11**, use the table.

10. © **MP.2 Reasoning** Elena completed the hiking trail in 30 minutes. How many calories did Elena burn? Explain how you know.

Calories Burned in 20 Minutes	
Type of Activity	**Calories**
Hiking	118
Bird watching	49
Rock climbing	218

11. **Higher Order Thinking** Tom says he would burn more calories rock climbing for half an hour than he would bird watching for two hours. Is Tom correct? Explain.

12. Roberto solved 6 math problems in 15 minutes. At that rate, how long will it take him to solve 15 math problems?

Quantities that are located at the same distance from 0 on their respective lines represent equivalent ratios.

13. © **MP.4 Model with Math** Over the summer Alexis read 15 books in 12 weeks. The diagram below can be used to track her progress. If Alexis read at the same rate each week, how many books had she read in 4 weeks? In 8 weeks? Complete the diagram.

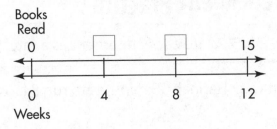

© **Common Core Assessment**

14. The quality inspector at a canning factory inspects 12 packages in 45 minutes. The inspector is expected to inspect 20 packages every hour. At this rate, will the inspector meet the goal? Complete the table and explain.

Packages Inspected	12			
Minutes	45	15	60	75

Name _____

Another Look!

Shauna can keyboard 30 words in 24 seconds on her tablet. This can be written as the rate $\frac{30 \text{ words}}{24 \text{ s}}$. At this rate, how long would it take Shauna to keyboard in 75 words?

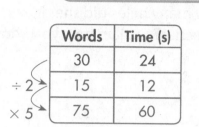

Words	Time (s)
30	24
15	12
75	60

$\div 2$
$\times 5$

To find equivalent rates you can multiply or divide both terms of a rate by the same number.

Shauna can keyboard 75 words in 60 seconds.

In **1** and **2**, write each statement as a rate.

1. Jon buys 3 shirts for $20.

2. Brenda records 76 songs on 4 CDs.

In **3–6**, find the value of *m*.

3.

Apples	*m*		220
Bags	4	8	10

4.

Players	108		*m*
Teams	9	18	21

5.

Markers	24	*m*	
Packages	2	4	12

6.

Miles Ran	60	180	240
Weeks	5		*m*

7. Megabytes

8. Pints

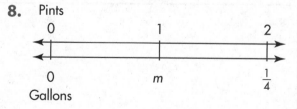

In **9–11**, use the table.

9. © **MP.2 Reasoning** Ms. Ellis used 25 gallons of gas delivering flowers in her delivery van. How many miles did she drive making the deliveries? Explain how you know.

Distance Driven Using 10 Gallons of Gasoline	
Vehicle	**Miles**
Car	285
Van	140
Motorcycle	640

10. **Higher Order Thinking** Mr. Tobias says that he can travel farther on 5 gallons of gasoline using his motorcycle than he can on 15 gallons of gasoline using his car. Is Mr. Tobias correct? Explain.

11. © **MP.3 Construct Arguments** A car has a gasoline tank that holds 18 gallons of gasoline. Can someone use this car to make a 500-mile trip on one tank of gasoline? Explain.

12. **Number Sense** Which is less, 3^4 or 4^3?

13. It took Perla 8 games to score 30 points. At that rate, how many games will it take her to score 45 points?

Games
0   8   ?

0   30   45
Points

© **Common Core Assessment**

14. A circus clown can inflate and tie 18 balloons in 4 minutes. The clown needs 45 balloons for a party. At this rate, will the clown be ready for a party that starts in 10 minutes? Complete the table and explain.

Balloons	18		
Minutes	4	8	10

Name _____

Solve & Share

Galina's high-speed model train can travel 10 meters in 4 seconds at a constant speed. How far can the train travel in 30 seconds? *Solve this problem any way you choose.*

I can ...
solve problems involving unit rates.

Content Standards 6.RP.A.3b, 6.RP.A.2
Mathematical Practices MP.1, MP.2, MP.3, MP.7

You can use structure to find rates equivalent to the speed of the train.

Meters	10		
Seconds	4	1	30

Look Back! MP.3 Construct Arguments Explain how finding the distance a train can travel in 1 second helps you solve the problem.

How Can You Find and Use a Unit Rate to Solve a Problem?

A

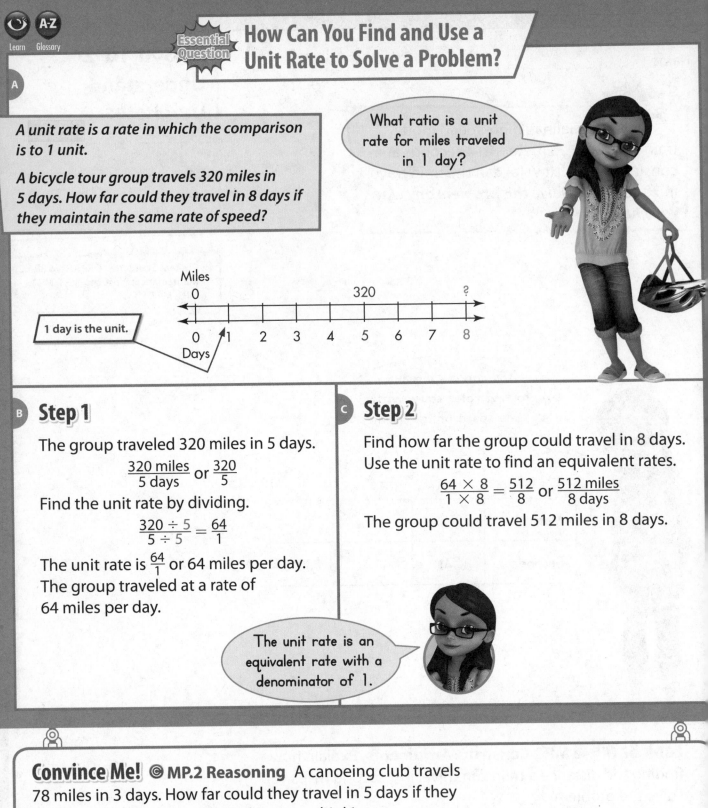

A unit rate is a rate in which the comparison is to 1 unit.

A bicycle tour group travels 320 miles in 5 days. How far could they travel in 8 days if they maintain the same rate of speed?

What ratio is a unit rate for miles traveled in 1 day?

Miles
0   320   ?

1 day is the unit.

0   1   2   3   4   5   6   7   8
Days

B ## Step 1

The group traveled 320 miles in 5 days.

$$\frac{320 \text{ miles}}{5 \text{ days}} \text{ or } \frac{320}{5}$$

Find the unit rate by dividing.

$$\frac{320 \div 5}{5 \div 5} = \frac{64}{1}$$

The unit rate is $\frac{64}{1}$ or 64 miles per day. The group traveled at a rate of 64 miles per day.

C ## Step 2

Find how far the group could travel in 8 days. Use the unit rate to find an equivalent rates.

$$\frac{64 \times 8}{1 \times 8} = \frac{512}{8} \text{ or } \frac{512 \text{ miles}}{8 \text{ days}}$$

The group could travel 512 miles in 8 days.

The unit rate is an equivalent rate with a denominator of 1.

Convince Me! © **MP.2 Reasoning** A canoeing club travels 78 miles in 3 days. How far could they travel in 5 days if they maintain the same speed? Explain your thinking.

☆ Guided Practice*

Do You Understand?

1. **ⓒ MP.2 Reasoning** A bathroom shower streams 5 gallons of water in 2 minutes.

   a. Find the unit rate for gallons per minute and describe it in words.

   b. Find the unit rate for minutes per gallon and describe it in words.

Do You Know How?

In **2** and **3**, use the unit rates you found in Exercise 1.

2. How many gallons of water does the shower stream in 6 minutes?

3. How long can someone shower in order to use only 10 gallons of water?

☆ Independent Practice ☆

Leveled Practice In **4–7**, find the unit rate.

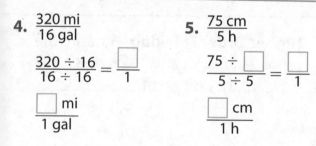

4. $\dfrac{320 \text{ mi}}{16 \text{ gal}}$

$\dfrac{320 \div 16}{16 \div 16} = \dfrac{\square}{1}$

$\dfrac{\square \text{ mi}}{1 \text{ gal}}$

5. $\dfrac{75 \text{ cm}}{5 \text{ h}}$

$\dfrac{75 \div \square}{5 \div 5} = \dfrac{\square}{1}$

$\dfrac{\square \text{ cm}}{1 \text{ h}}$

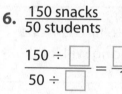

6. $\dfrac{150 \text{ snacks}}{50 \text{ students}}$

$\dfrac{150 \div \square}{50 \div \square} = \dfrac{\square}{1}$

$\dfrac{\square \text{ snacks}}{1 \text{ student}}$

7. $\dfrac{54 \text{ songs}}{3 \text{ h}}$

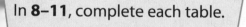

In **8–11**, complete each table.

8.

Pages	9			
Minutes	18	1	10	15

9.

Beans	186			
Bags	3	1	7	11

10.

Ounces		24.6		123
Bag	1	2	5	

11.

Miles	25		125	
Gallon		3	5	12

*For another example, see Set A on page 531.

Topic 10 | Lesson 10-2

Math Practices and Problem Solving

In **12–14**, use the table at the right.

12. © **MP.2 Reasoning** Write two different unit rates that describe Martha's time and number of laps. Then explain how these two rates might be used to find equivalent rates for Martha.

Runner	Laps	Time
Martha	20	32 min
Allison	16	25 min
Rachel	17	27.2 min

13. If Allison continues to run at the same pace, what will her time be for 20 laps?

14. © **MP.1 Make Sense and Persevere** Which runner set the fastest pace? Explain.

15. Math and Science Elephants can charge at speeds of 0.7 kilometer per minute. An elephant charges an object that is 0.35 kilometers away. How long will it take the elephant to reach the object?

16. A machine takes 1 minute to fill 6 cartons of eggs. At this rate, how long will it take to fill 420 cartons?

17. Higher Order Thinking How are the ratios 24 laps:1 h and 192 laps:8 h alike? How are they different?

© **Common Core Assessment**

18. A cook mixes rice into boiling water in the amounts shown at the right. Choose all of the statements that are true.

☐ $\frac{0.8 \text{ lb rice}}{1 \text{ qt water}}$ is a unit rate for the mix.

☐ $\frac{1.25 \text{ qt water}}{1 \text{ lb rice}}$ is a unit rate for the mix.

☐ Using the same rate, the cook should mix 12.5 pounds of rice with 10 quarts of water.

☐ Using the same rate, the cook should mix 10 pounds of rice with 12.5 quarts of water.

Water 5 quarts

Rice 4 pounds

Another Look!

A factory produces 100 laundry baskets in 4 hours. What is the unit rate? At that rate, how many baskets can the factory make in 7 hours?

> A unit rate compares a quantity to 1 unit of another quantity.

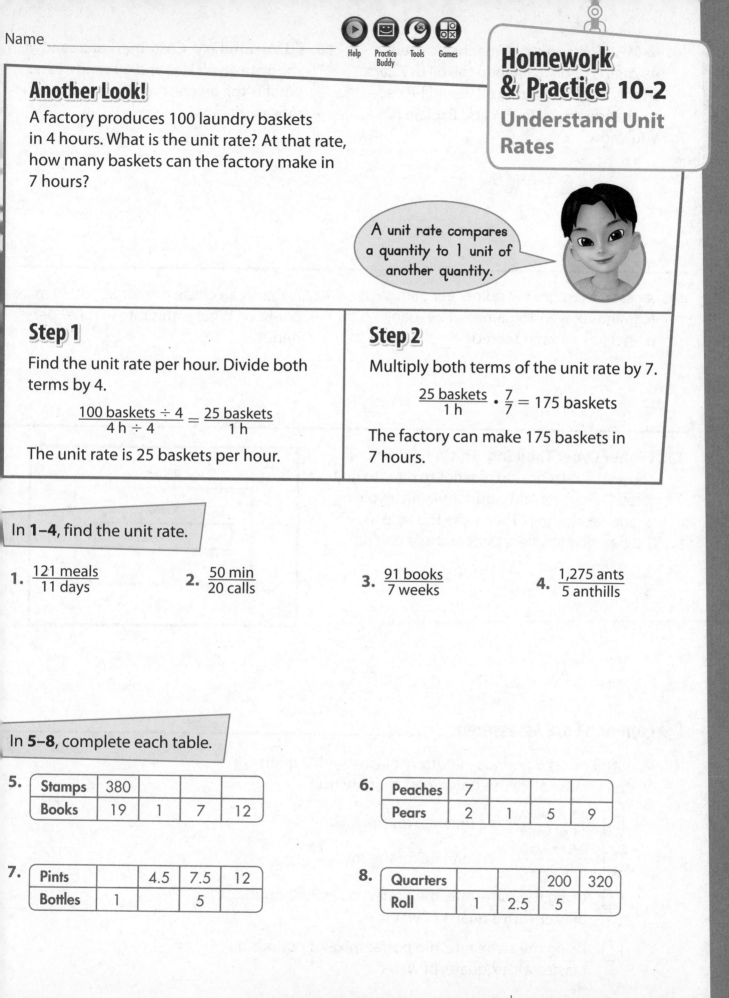

Step 1

Find the unit rate per hour. Divide both terms by 4.

$$\frac{100 \text{ baskets} \div 4}{4 \text{ h} \div 4} = \frac{25 \text{ baskets}}{1 \text{ h}}$$

The unit rate is 25 baskets per hour.

Step 2

Multiply both terms of the unit rate by 7.

$$\frac{25 \text{ baskets}}{1 \text{ h}} \cdot \frac{7}{7} = 175 \text{ baskets}$$

The factory can make 175 baskets in 7 hours.

In **1–4**, find the unit rate.

1. $\dfrac{121 \text{ meals}}{11 \text{ days}}$

2. $\dfrac{50 \text{ min}}{20 \text{ calls}}$

3. $\dfrac{91 \text{ books}}{7 \text{ weeks}}$

4. $\dfrac{1{,}275 \text{ ants}}{5 \text{ anthills}}$

In **5–8**, complete each table.

5.

Stamps	380			
Books	19	1	7	12

6.

Peaches	7			
Pears	2	1	5	9

7.

Pints		4.5	7.5	12
Bottles	1		5	

8.

Quarters			200	320
Roll	1	2.5	5	

9. © **MP.2 Reasoning** A mechanic used 49 quarts of oil to change the oil in 7 cars. At this rate, how much oil would he use to change the oil in 17 cars? Explain how you know.

10. **A-Z Vocabulary** Customers at a sandwich shop ate 48 pickles and 60 sandwiches. What is the *greatest common factor* of these numbers?

11. Jackson averages 6.2 points per game. His team has played 15 games. How many points has Jackson scored?

12. A shark can chase prey at about 30 miles per hour. What is this rate in miles per minute?

13. **Higher Order Thinking** This Venn diagram shows the relationship of ratios to rates to unit rates. Describe a real-world situation involving a ratio relationship. Then write the ratio as 2 different equivalent rates and as a unit rate.

Ratios

Rates

Unit Rates

© **Common Core Assessment**

14. A potter mixes 5 pounds of pottery plaster with 2 quarts of water. Choose all of the statements that are true.

☐ $\frac{2.5 \text{ lb plaster}}{1 \text{ qt water}}$ is a unit rate for the mix.

☐ $\frac{0.5 \text{ qt water}}{1 \text{ lb plaster}}$ is a unit rate for the mix.

☐ Using the same rate, the potter mixes 7.5 pounds of plaster with 3 quarts of water.

☐ Using the same rate, the potter mixes 4 pounds of plaster with 7 quarts of water.

Name _____

Solve & Share

Rick and Nikki own remote-control cars. They use a stopwatch to record the speeds of each car. Rick's car travels 150 feet every 30 seconds. Nikki's car travels 80 feet in 20 seconds. Whose car is faster? **Solve this problem any way you choose.**

I can ...
compare rates to solve problems.

Content Standards 6.RP.A.3b, 6.RP.A.3a
Mathematical Practices MP.1, MP.2, MP.3, MP.4, MP.6

Remember to be precise when using numbers and units to describe and compare rates.

Speed of Rick's Car	
Distance (feet)	Time (seconds)
150	30

Speed of Nikki's Car	
Distance (feet)	Time (seconds)
80	20

Look Back! MP.1 Make Sense and Persevere If each car maintains its rate of speed, how long will it take Rick's car to travel 300 feet? How long will it take Nikki's car to travel the same distance? Explain your reasoning.

Essential Question

How Can You Use Unit Rates to Make Comparisons?

A

Ethan swam 11 laps in the pool in 8 minutes.
Austin swam 7 laps in the same pool in 5 minutes.
Which boy swam at a faster rate?

You can make sense of the problem by finding how fast each swimmer swam per minute.

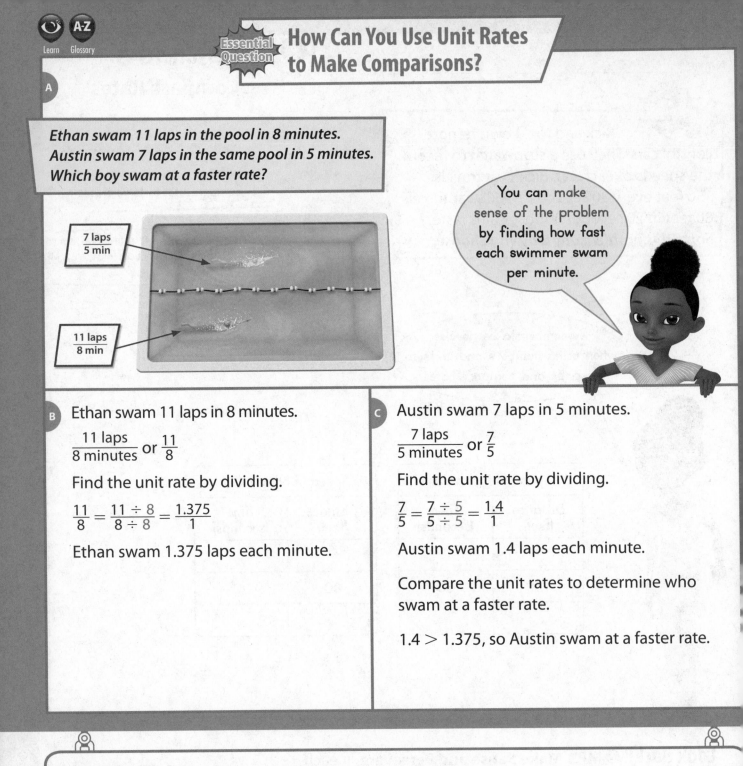

7 laps / 5 min

11 laps / 8 min

B Ethan swam 11 laps in 8 minutes.

$$\frac{11 \text{ laps}}{8 \text{ minutes}} \text{ or } \frac{11}{8}$$

Find the unit rate by dividing.

$$\frac{11}{8} = \frac{11 \div 8}{8 \div 8} = \frac{1.375}{1}$$

Ethan swam 1.375 laps each minute.

C Austin swam 7 laps in 5 minutes.

$$\frac{7 \text{ laps}}{5 \text{ minutes}} \text{ or } \frac{7}{5}$$

Find the unit rate by dividing.

$$\frac{7}{5} = \frac{7 \div 5}{5 \div 5} = \frac{1.4}{1}$$

Austin swam 1.4 laps each minute.

Compare the unit rates to determine who swam at a faster rate.

$1.4 > 1.375$, so Austin swam at a faster rate.

Convince Me! © **MP.2 Reasoning** Ashley is Austin's older sister. She trains in the same pool and can swim 9 laps in 6 minutes. Is she a faster swimmer than Austin? Explain.

Practice Buddy   Tools   Assessment

Guided Practice

Do You Understand?

1. © MP.3 Construct Arguments How does finding unit rates allow you to compare two rates?

2. © MP.2 Reasoning Car A drives 115 miles on 5 gallons of gas. Car B drives 126 miles on 6 gallons of gas. How can you find which car gets better gas mileage?

Do You Know How?

3. Hakim's car travels 600 feet in 20 seconds. Andre's motorcycle travels 300 feet in 12 seconds. Which is faster, the car or the motorcycle? Show how you know.

   a. Find the unit rates.

   b. Compare the unit rates.

Independent Practice

In **4–6**, compare the rates to find which is greater.

4. 35 points in 20 minutes or 49 points in 35 minutes

5. 12 laps in 8 minutes or 16 laps in 10 minutes

6. 45 strikeouts in 36 innings or 96 strikeouts in 80 innings

In **7–9**, compare the rates to find which is the better value.

7. $30 for 100 flyers or $65 for 250 flyers

8. $27 for 4 large pizzas or $32 for 5 large pizzas

9. 36 pictures for $8 or 24 pictures for $5

Math Practices and Problem Solving

10. © MP.4 Model with Math Katrina and Becca exchanged 270 text messages in 45 minutes. An equal number of texts was sent each minute. The girls can send 90 more text messages before they are charged additional fees. Complete the double number line diagram. At this rate, how many more minutes can the girls exchange texts before they are charged extra?

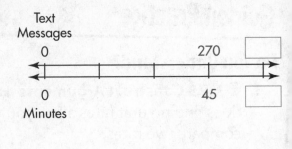

Text Messages

0   270

0   45

Minutes

---

11. Julia is comparing the gas mileage of a red car to that of a black car to decide which car she should buy. The red car can travel 360 miles on 20 gallons of gas. The black car can travel 336 miles on 21 gallons of gas. Find the unit rates and tell which car gets better gas mileage.

12. **Higher Order Thinking** Amil and Abe rode in a bike-a-thon. Amil rode 15 miles in 55 minutes. Abe rode for 77 minutes at a faster rate per mile than Amil. Find Amil's unit rate. Then explain how you could use it to find a possible unit rate for Abe.

© **Common Core Assessment**

13. Darius can run 300 meters in 50 seconds. Patrick can run 200 meters in 32 seconds.

Part A

Who runs faster, Darius or Patrick?

Part B

Use the unit rates to find how much time it would take each boy to run 600 meters if both could maintain the same rates of speed over the longer distance. Explain your reasoning.

Name _____

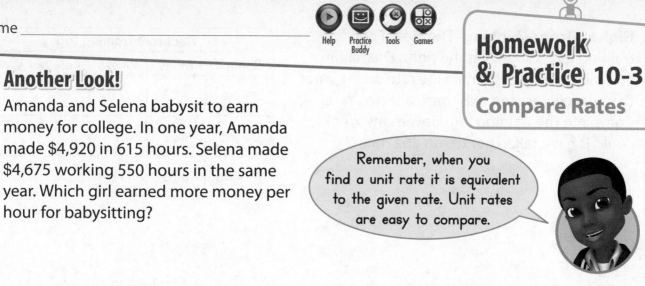
Another Look!

Amanda and Selena babysit to earn money for college. In one year, Amanda made $4,920 in 615 hours. Selena made $4,675 working 550 hours in the same year. Which girl earned more money per hour for babysitting?

> Remember, when you find a unit rate it is equivalent to the given rate. Unit rates are easy to compare.

Amanda earned $4,920 in 615 hours.

$$\frac{4,920}{615}$$

Find the unit rate by dividing.

$$\frac{4,920}{615} = \frac{4,920 \div 615}{615 \div 615} = \frac{8}{1}$$

Amanda earned $8 per hour babysitting.

Selena earned $4,675 in 550 hours.

$$\frac{4,675}{550}$$

Find the unit rate by dividing.

$$\frac{4,675}{550} = \frac{4,675 \div 550}{550 \div 550} = \frac{8.5}{1}$$

Selena earns $8.50 per hour babysitting.

Compare the unit rates to determine who earned more per hour.
$8.50 > $8.00, so Selena earned more money per hour for babysitting.

In **1–3**, compare the rates to find which is greater.

1. 510 visitors in 30 hours or 960 visitors in 60 hours

2. 660 miles on 20 gallons or 850 miles on 25 gallons

3. 1,080 labels on 90 sheets or 2,250 labels on 150 sheets

In **4–6**, compare the rates to find which is the better value.

4. $285 for 150 ft² of carpet or $252 for 120 ft² of carpet

5. $74 for 4 theater tickets or $91 for 5 theater tickets

6. $960 for 30 textbooks or $1,625 for 50 textbooks

7. **Higher Order Thinking** The Fleet Feet training log is shown at the right. Deana ran 462 miles. Her weekly mileage rate was greater than Pavel's rate but less than Alberto's rate. Complete the training log. How many weeks could it have taken her to run 462 miles?

Fleet Feet Training Log			
Runner	Miles	Weeks	Rate per Week
Pavel	672	21	
Deana	462	?	
Alberto	420	12	

8. **A-Z Vocabulary** Chen is using bottle caps and pennies to make coasters for a craft fair. He uses 5 bottle caps for every 2 pennies in each coaster. The _____ of bottle caps to pennies is 5:2.

9. **© MP.6 Be Precise** On Monday, it snowed 30 inches in 16 hours. On Thursday, it snowed 21 inches in 6 hours. On which day did it snow at a greater rate each hour? How much more per hour?

© **Common Core Assessment**

10. The new *Vigo the Vampire Hunter* novel is 520 pages. Skyler has read 145 pages in 5 hours. Ramon has read 124 pages in 4 hours.

Part A

Who reads faster, Skyler or Ramon?

Part B

How long will it take Ramon to read the entire novel if he continues to read at his current rate?

Name _____

Solve

☆ Solve & Share ☆

Daniella is shopping for movies online. She sees the three different offers shown below. Which offer is the best buy? Explain your thinking. *Solve this problem any way you choose.*

I can ...
find, compare, and use unit prices.

© Content Standard 6.RP.A.3b
Mathematical Practices MP.2, MP.3, MP.4, MP.7, MP.8

How can you use reasoning to relate the different prices?

Movies
for
SALE

Offer 1   4 for $33.00
Offer 2   2 for $18.70
Offer 3   5 for $42.50

Look Back! © **MP.4 Model with Math** Jenna found another online sale that offers 3 movies for $27.75. Complete the double number line diagram. What is the cost of each movie for this offer?

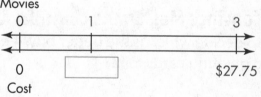

Movies
0   1   3

0   [   ] $27.75
Cost

Essential Question

How Can You Compare the Prices of Different Amounts of the Same Item?

A

A unit price is a unit rate that gives the price of one item.

Is the lunch special or the weekend special a better deal?

Lunch special
3 tacos for $2.40

Weekend special
4 tacos for $3.40

You can compare unit prices of the same item to determine which is a better deal.

B **Step 1**

Find the unit price of the lunch special.

Cost

0   ? $2.40

0   1   3

Tacos

Write the cost of the lunch special as a rate. Then find the unit rate.

$$\frac{\$2.40}{3} \div \frac{3}{3} = \frac{\$0.80}{1}$$

The unit price for the lunch special is $0.80 per taco.

C **Step 2**

Find the unit price of the weekend special.

Cost

0   ? $3.40

0   1   4

Tacos

Write the cost of the weekend special as a rate. Then find the unit rate.

$$\frac{\$3.40}{4} \div \frac{4}{4} = \frac{\$0.85}{1}$$

The unit price for the weekend special is $0.85 per taco.

Now compare.
$0.80 per taco < $0.85 per taco, so the lunch special is a better buy.

Convince Me! © MP.3 Construct Arguments Explain how to decide which is the better buy, 4 greeting cards for $10 or 6 greeting cards for $14.

Name _____

☆ Guided Practice *

Do You Understand?

1. ⓒ **MP.8 Generalize** Why is a unit price a special kind of unit rate?

2. ⓒ **MP.3 Critique Reasoning** Paul says that a lower unit rate is only a better buy if you can use all of the items purchased to get the lower unit rate. Do you agree? Explain.

Do You Know How?

In **3** and **4**, find each unit price.

3. 7 movie tickets for $56

4. 12 ounces of shampoo for $2.76

In **5**, tell which is the better buy.

5. 2 books for $15 or 6 books for $45

☆ Independent Practice ☆

Leveled Practice In **6–9**, find each unit price.

6. 9 pens for $3.60

$$\frac{\$3.60 \div 9}{9 \div 9} = \frac{\boxed{}}{1}$$

7. 15 ounces of canned beans for $2.25

$$\frac{\$2.25 \div \boxed{}}{15 \div \boxed{}} = \frac{\boxed{}}{\boxed{}}$$

8. $\frac{1}{4}$ gallon of paint for $8.99

9. 50 paper clips for 40¢

In **10** and **11**, determine which is the better buy.

10. 3 kilograms of charcoal for $7.95 or
    5 kilograms of charcoal for $12.50

11. 50 envelopes for $2.99 or
    90 envelopes for $5.50

For another example, see Set B on page 531.

Math Practices and Problem Solving

12. © **MP.2 Reasoning** Which container of milk is the better buy? Explain how you know.

$\frac{1}{2}$ gallon for $2.29

1 gallon for $3.99

13. © **MP.7 Use Structure** Company A sells a 500-minute calling card for $30. Company B sells a 1,000-minute calling card for $50. How can you determine the better buy without finding the unit prices?

14. Which is the better buy, a 12-ounce bag of raisins for $2.19 or a 1-pound bag of raisins for $3.40?

15. Mario bought 70 feet of speaker wire for $18.20. He needs 30 more feet. If the unit price is the same, how much will he pay for the extra 30 feet of wire?

16. **Number Sense** The area of a rectangle is 3,600 square inches. The perimeter is 400 inches. What are the length and width of the rectangle?

17. **Higher Order Thinking** There are 5 people in the Fazio family. They are buying matching T-shirts at the Summer Safari Expo. They can buy 1 T-shirt for $12, 2 T-shirts for $22, or 3 T-shirts for $32.40. Which combination of shirts is the best buy? Explain.

© **Common Core Assessment**

18. A food warehouse sells cans of soup in boxes. Bargain shoppers have four options. Find the unit price for each option and complete the table to identify the best buy.

Boxes of Soup	Unit Price
12 cans for $10.56	
16 cans for $13.60	
20 cans for $17.20	
24 cans for $21.36	

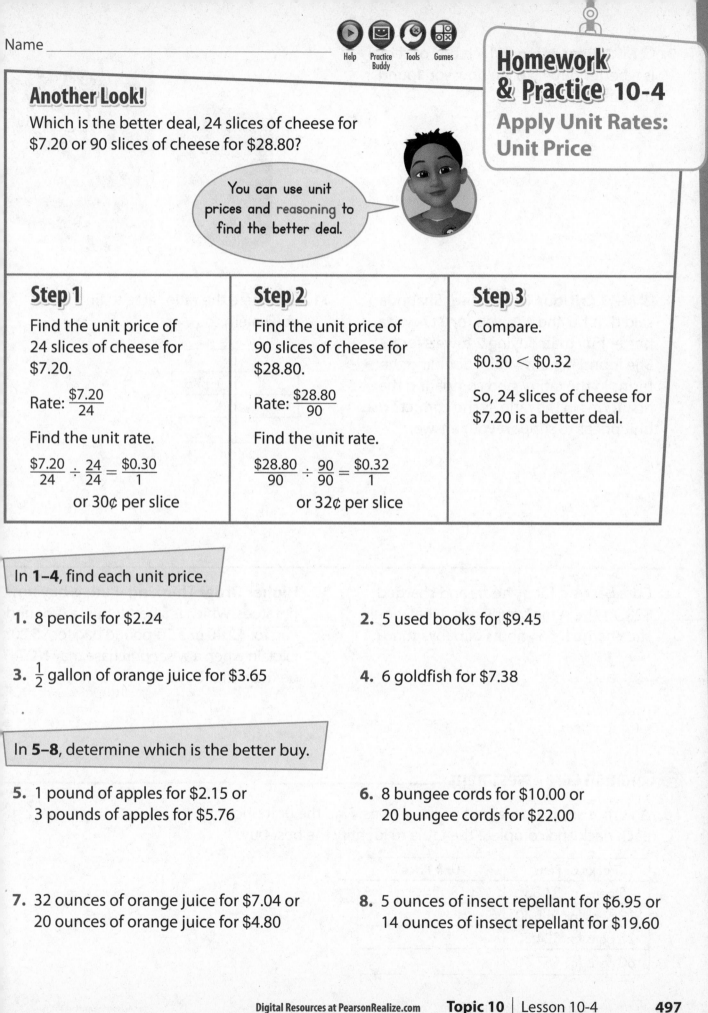

Help   Practice   Tools   Games
        Buddy

Another Look!

Which is the better deal, 24 slices of cheese for $7.20 or 90 slices of cheese for $28.80?

You can use unit prices and reasoning to find the better deal.

Step 1

Find the unit price of 24 slices of cheese for $7.20.

Rate: $\frac{\$7.20}{24}$

Find the unit rate.

$\frac{\$7.20}{24} \div \frac{24}{24} = \frac{\$0.30}{1}$

or 30¢ per slice

Step 2

Find the unit price of 90 slices of cheese for $28.80.

Rate: $\frac{\$28.80}{90}$

Find the unit rate.

$\frac{\$28.80}{90} \div \frac{90}{90} = \frac{\$0.32}{1}$

or 32¢ per slice

Step 3

Compare.

$0.30 < $0.32

So, 24 slices of cheese for $7.20 is a better deal.

In **1–4**, find each unit price.

1. 8 pencils for $2.24

2. 5 used books for $9.45

3. $\frac{1}{2}$ gallon of orange juice for $3.65

4. 6 goldfish for $7.38

In **5–8**, determine which is the better buy.

5. 1 pound of apples for $2.15 or 3 pounds of apples for $5.76

6. 8 bungee cords for $10.00 or 20 bungee cords for $22.00

7. 32 ounces of orange juice for $7.04 or 20 ounces of orange juice for $4.80

8. 5 ounces of insect repellant for $6.95 or 14 ounces of insect repellant for $19.60

9.  **⊚ MP.2 Reasoning** Which box of cereal is a better buy? Explain how you found the answer.

10. **⊚ MP.3 Critique Reasoning** Shaunda said that buying 4 towels for $17 was a better buy than buying 2 towels for $9. She found her answer by doubling the terms in the ratio $\frac{9}{2}$ and comparing the first terms in the ratio. Is she correct? Use unit prices to support your answer.

11. Complete the ratio table to find ratios equivalent to $\frac{3}{12.75}$.

1	
3	12.75
6	
	34

12. Cora babysat for $3\frac{1}{2}$ hours and charged $28. At the same hourly rate, what would she charge for $5\frac{1}{2}$ hours of babysitting?

13. **Higher Order Thinking** Ruth is buying potatoes. Which is a better buy: a 4-pound bag for $2.40 or a 10-pound bag for $5.20? Explain when a wiser purchase may **NOT** be the better buy.

⊚ Common Core Assessment

14. An office supply store sells packs of pens. Find the unit price for each pack and complete the table to identify the best buy.

Packs of Pens	Unit Price
5 pens for $4.85	
12 pens for $11.40	
25 pens for $24.50	
60 pens for $57.60	

Name _____

Solve & Share

Suppose you are traveling by train to visit a friend who lives 275 miles away. If the train travels at a constant speed of 55 miles per hour, how long will the trip take? Moving at the same speed, how long would it take the train to travel 385 miles? *Solve this problem any way you choose.*

I can ...
use unit rates to solve constant speed problems.

Content Standard 6.RP.A.3b
Mathematical Practices MP.2, MP.3, MP.4, MP.7

How can you use what you know about unit rates to model and solve this problem?

Time	Distance

Look Back! MP.2 Reasoning Suppose the train were traveling at a constant speed that is twice as fast as 55 miles per hour. How long would it take the train to go 275 miles? Explain.

A-Z

Essential Question

How Can You Use Unit Rates to Solve Constant Speed Problems?

A

The jet flies at a constant speed. If the jet continues to fly at the same rate, how far could the jet fly in 85 minutes?

The jet flies 175 miles in 7 minutes.

Constant speed means that the speed stays the same over time.

B **One Way**

Use a table to record equivalent rates to find how far the jet could fly in 85 minutes.

Time (min)	Distance (miles)
1	25
7	175
25	625
50	1,250
85	2,125

×85   ×85

At this rate, the jet could fly 2,125 miles in 85 minutes.

C **Another Way**

Use the unit rate to find how far the jet could fly in 85 minutes.

$$\frac{175 \text{ miles} \div 7}{7 \text{ minutes} \div 7} = \frac{25 \text{ miles}}{1 \text{ minute}}$$

Find an equivalent rate.

$$\frac{25 \text{ miles} \times 85}{1 \text{ minute} \times 85} = \frac{2,125 \text{ miles}}{85 \text{ minutes}}$$

The table and the equation represent the same relationships.

The jet could fly 2,125 miles in 85 minutes.

Convince Me! © **MP.7 Use Structure** Would it be easier to use the table or the unit rate to find how far the jet could fly in 75 minutes? Explain.

Name _____

☆ Guided Practice*

Do You Understand?

1. © **MP.3 Construct Arguments** An ostrich runs 6 miles in 12 minutes at a constant speed. Explain how you can use a unit rate to find how far the ostrich could run in 40 minutes.

2. A baseball pitcher throws a fastball 60.5 feet in 2 seconds. If the ball travels at a constant speed per second, how can you write this as a unit rate?

Do You Know How?

In **3** and **4**, use unit rates to solve.

3. A football player runs 80 yards in 25 seconds. If he maintains the same rate of speed, how far could he run in 60 seconds?

4. On a family vacation, Amy's dad drove the car at a constant speed and traveled 585 miles in 13 hours. At this rate, how long would it have taken the family to travel 810 miles? What was the car's rate of speed?

Independent Practice ☆

Leveled Practice In **5** and **6**, use ratio reasoning to solve.

5. A horse named Northern Dancer won the Kentucky Derby by running $1\frac{1}{4}$ miles in exactly 2 minutes. At this constant rate, how long does it take Northern Dancer to run the $1\frac{1}{2}$-mile Belmont Stakes?

Use the unit rate.

$$\frac{1.25 \text{ miles} \div \boxed{}}{2 \text{ minutes} \div 2} = \frac{\boxed{} \text{ miles}}{1 \text{ minute}}$$

Find an equivalent rate.

$$\frac{\boxed{} \text{ mile} \times 2.4}{1 \text{ minute} \times \boxed{}} = \frac{1.5 \text{ miles}}{\boxed{} \text{ minutes}}$$

6. If a cyclist rides at a constant rate of 24 miles per hour, how long would it take the cyclist to ride 156 miles?

For another example, see Set C on page 531.

Math Practices and Problem Solving

7. Algebra Jessica wrote the equation $470 \cdot h = 3{,}008$, where h is the number of hours it took a plane flying at a constant speed of 470 miles per hour to travel 3,008 miles. Solve for h.

8. © MP.2 Reasoning A bird travels at a constant speed of 2 kilometers per hour and an insect travels at a constant speed of 1,000 meters per hour. Which is faster, the bird or the insect? Explain how you can solve without calculating.

9. Marcus took a train to visit his aunt. The train traveled at a constant speed of 60 mph. Complete the table. Then write an equation to find the total distance, d, traveled after t hours.

Time, t (in hours)	1	2	3	4
Distance, d (in miles)	60			

10. Write an inequality to represent that there are only 15 seconds remaining to finish a test.

11. Higher Order Thinking Sasha runs at a constant speed of 3.8 meters per second for $\frac{1}{2}$ hour. Then she walks at a rate of 1.5 meters per second for $\frac{1}{2}$ hour. How far did Sasha run and walk in 60 minutes?

© Common Core Assessment

12. Suppose that a leatherback turtle swam 7.5 kilometers in 3 hours at a constant speed.

Part A

How many kilometers per hour did the turtle swim?

Part B

At this rate, how long will it take the turtle to swim 10 kilometers?

Name _____

Another Look!

If an ant is moving at a constant speed and travels 6 centimeters in 1.5 seconds, how long will it take for the ant to travel 24 centimeters?

One Way

Use a ratio table to solve.

Time (s)	Distance (cm)
1	4
1.5	6
3	12
4.5	18
6	24

×6   ×6

It will take 6 seconds for the ant to travel 24 centimeters.

Another Way

Use the unit rate to solve.

Find the unit rate.

$$\frac{6 \text{ centimeters} \div 1.5}{1.5 \text{ seconds} \div 1.5} = \frac{4 \text{ centimeters}}{1 \text{ second}}$$

Find an equivalent rate.

$$\frac{4 \text{ centimeters} \times 6}{1 \text{ second} \times 6} = \frac{24 \text{ centimeters}}{6 \text{ seconds}}$$

It will take 6 seconds for the ant to travel 24 centimeters.

Leveled Practice In **1** and **2**, use ratio reasoning to solve.

1. Jason and his family travel 160 miles in 3.2 hours. If they continue at this constant speed, how long will it take them to travel 300 miles?

   Make and complete a ratio table.

   It will take Jason and his family _____ hours to travel _____ miles.

Time (hours)	Distance (miles)
1	
3.2	160
	300

2. A space shuttle orbits Earth at a rate of about 4,375 miles in 15 minutes. At this rate, how far does the space shuttle travel around Earth in 1 hour?

You can use a unit rate to find how far the shuttle travels in any number of minutes. Remember, 1 hour = 60 minutes.

3. © **MP.4 Model with Math** Kenny is walking at a constant speed of 3.5 miles per hour. How far can he walk in 6 hours? Complete the table and plot the points on the coordinate plane to solve.

time (t)	1	2	3	4
distance (d)	3.5			

4. If the maglev train travels at a constant speed of 480 kilometers per hour for $\frac{1}{4}$ hour, how far does the train travel?

5. If the maglev train traveled at a constant rate of its top speed for 10 kilometers, what is the approximate amount of time the train would have traveled?

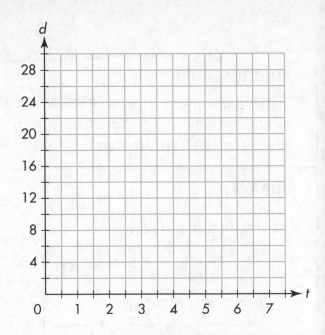

Because maglev trains use magnets to levitate, they can reach rates of up to 500 kilometers per hour.

6. In Jamie's class, there are 17 students with brown hair, 9 with blonde hair, and 2 with red hair. What is the ratio of students with blonde hair to students in Jamie's class?

7. **Higher Order Thinking** A cyclist rode at a constant speed of 21 mph for 3 hours. Then she decreased her rate of speed to 17 mph for 4 hours. How far did the cyclist ride in 7 hours?

© **Common Core Assessment**

8. Jack drove 325 miles in 5 hours.

   Part A

   How many miles per hour did Jack drive?

   Part B

   Jack will drive 520 more miles at the same rate. How long will it take Jack to drive the 520 miles?

Name _____

Solve & Share

During a twenty-four hour period in April of 1921, a record 75.8 inches of snow fell in Silver Lake, Colorado. If 6.5 feet of snow were to fall in a later twenty-four hour period, would the 1921 record be broken? *Solve this problem any way you choose.*

I can ...
use ratio reasoning to convert measurements.

© Content Standard 6.RP.A.3d
Mathematical Practices MP.1, MP.2, MP.3, MP.7

You can use reasoning to evaluate the relationship between inches and feet and solve the problem.

DATA

Customary Units of Length

1 ft = 12 in.

Look Back! © MP.1 Make Sense and Persevere How many feet of snow would need to fall in Silver Lake, Colorado, to break the 1921 twenty-four-hour snowfall record?

Essential Question How Can You Use Ratios to Convert Customary Units of Measure?

A

The sidewalk in front of a store is 4.5 feet wide. The city regulations require the width of a sidewalk to be a maximum of 66 inches. Does the sidewalk meet the city regulations?

The equations in the table can be written as rates that compare equivalent measurements.

Customary Units		
Length	**Capacity**	**Weight**
1 ft = 12 in.	1 tbsp = 3 tsp	1 lb = 16 oz
1 yd = 36 in.	1 fl oz = 2 tbsp	1 T = 2,000 lb
1 yd = 3 ft	1 c = 8 fl oz	
1 mi = 5,280 ft	1 pt = 2 c	
1 mi = 1,760 yd	1 qt = 2 pt	
	1 gal = 4 qt	

B ## One Way

Write the width of the sidewalk in inches.

Identify the conversion rate that relates to the measurement.

$$12 \text{ in.} = 1 \text{ ft}$$

Find an equivalent rate.

$$\frac{12 \text{ in.}}{1 \text{ ft}} = \frac{\square \text{ in.}}{4.5 \text{ ft}}$$

$$\frac{12 \text{ in.} \times 4.5}{1 \text{ ft} \times 4.5} = \frac{54 \text{ in.}}{4.5 \text{ ft}}$$ ← Multiply both terms of the rate by 4.5.

The sidewalk is 54 inches wide.
It meets the city regulations.

C ## Another Way

Use dimensional analysis to convert measures by including measurement units when you multiply by a conversion factor. A conversion factor is a rate that compares equivalent measures.

$$4.5 \text{ ft} \times \frac{12 \text{ in.}}{1 \text{ ft}}$$ ← Multiply by the conversion factor that relates the measures. Divide out the common units.

$$= 4.5 \times 12 \text{ in.}$$
$$= 54 \text{ in.}$$

Use the conversion factor so that you are left with the units needed to solve the problem.

The sidewalk is 54 inches wide.
It meets the city regulations.

Convince Me! © **MP.2 Reasoning** According to city regulations, how many feet wide is the maximum sidewalk width? Write an equation to solve.

Name _____

Practice Buddy   Tools   Assessment

Another Example

The alpine pika is a small mammal in the rabbit family. An alpine pika at a local zoo weighs 10 ounces. How much does the alpine pika weigh in pounds?

One Way

Identify the conversion rate.
$$16 \text{ oz} = 1 \text{ lb}$$

Find an equivalent rate.
$$\frac{16 \text{ oz}}{1 \text{ lb}} = \frac{10 \text{ oz}}{\square \text{ lb}}$$

$$\frac{16 \text{ oz} \div 1.6}{1 \text{ lb} \div 1.6} = \frac{10 \text{ oz}}{0.625 \text{ lb}}$$ ← Divide both terms of the rate by 1.6.

The alpine pika weighs 0.625 pound.

Another Way

Use dimensional analysis.

$$10 \text{ oz} \times \frac{1 \text{ lb}}{16 \text{ oz}}$$

$$= \frac{10}{16} \text{ lb}$$

$$= 0.625 \text{ lb}$$

The alpine pika weighs 0.625 pound.

☆ Guided Practice ☆

Do You Understand?

1. What is a conversion factor that relates miles to yards?

2. Ⓒ MP.3 Construct Arguments Jenna used the conversion factor $\frac{1T}{2,000 \text{ lb}}$ to convert 50 tons to pounds. Did she use the correct conversion factor? Explain.

Do You Know How?

3. Ⓒ MP.3 Critique Reasoning Sam is tripling a recipe for an organic cleaning solution. The new recipe calls for 15 tsp of orange oil. To find how many tbsp this is, Sam converted this way:

conversion factor: $\frac{3 \text{ tsp}}{1 \text{ tbsp}}$

$$15 \text{ tsp} \times \frac{3 \text{ tsp}}{1 \text{ tbsp}} = \frac{45}{1} \text{ tbsp} = 45 \text{ tbsp}$$

What error did Sam make?

☆ Independent Practice ☆

In **4–6**, complete each conversion.

4. $5 \text{ pt} = \square \text{ c}$

5. $2\frac{1}{2} \text{ gal} = \square \text{ qt}$

6. $2,640 \text{ yd} = \square \text{ mi}$

*For another example, see Set D on page 532.

Topic 10 | Lesson 10-6

507

Math Practices and Problem Solving

In **7** and **8**, use the recipe card.

7. 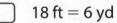 **MP.7 Look for Relationships** Cheryl has 3 cups of water. Is this enough water for Cheryl to make 2 recipes of green slime for a class project? Explain.

Green Slime Recipe
- 1 pint water
- 1/2 cup cornstarch
- Green food coloring

Add hot water to cornstarch and stir constantly. Then add green food coloring, and stir. Allow the slime to cool to room temperature. This makes a messy slime that goes from liquid to solid. Make sure to play with it on a plastic covered surface. Always have adult supervision when using hot water.

8. There are 16 tablespoons in 1 cup. How many tablespoons of cornstarch would Cheryl need to use to make 15 recipes of green slime?

9. Ⓒ **MP.1 Make Sense and Persevere** Len plans to run at least 3 miles each day to get ready for a cross-country race. One lap of the school track is 440 yards. If Len runs 10 laps each day, will he cover at least 3 miles? Explain.

10. **Higher Order Thinking** Hunter is splitting a quart of ice cream with 7 members of his family. If the quart is split evenly, how many cups will each family member get? Explain.

11. **Algebra** Using dimensional analysis, write an expression you could use to convert x ounces to pounds.

12. A fully loaded and fueled space shuttle can weigh close to 4.5 million pounds at liftoff. What is this weight converted to tons?

Ⓒ Common Core Assessment

13. Choose all of the conversions that are true.

- ☐ 18 ft = 6 yd
- ☐ 18 yd = 6 ft
- ☐ 0.5 mi = 10,560 ft
- ☐ 0.5 mi = 2,640 ft
- ☐ $\frac{1}{2}$ mi = 880 yd

Units of Length

DATA

1 ft = 12 in.
1 yd = 3 ft
1 mi = 5,280 ft

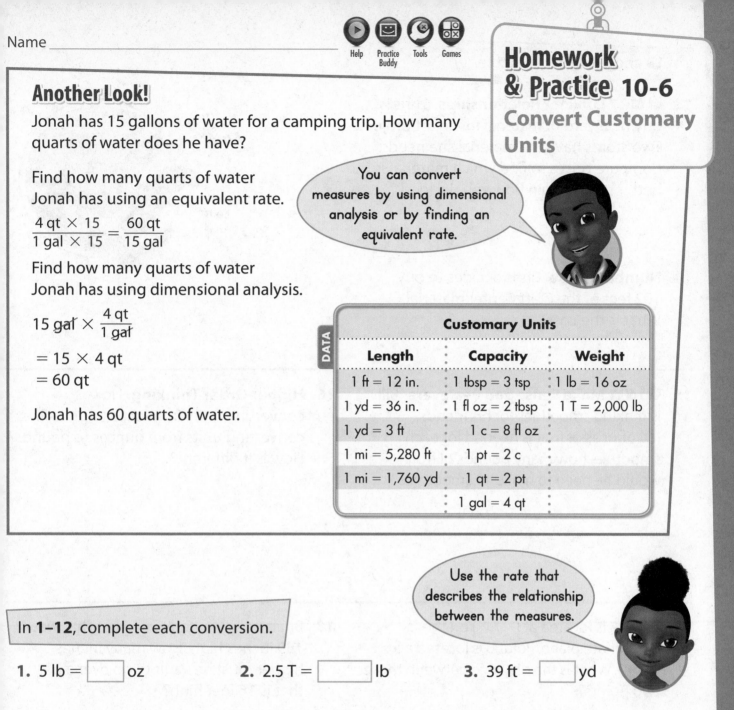
Another Look!

Jonah has 15 gallons of water for a camping trip. How many quarts of water does he have?

Find how many quarts of water Jonah has using an equivalent rate.

$$\frac{4 \text{ qt} \times 15}{1 \text{ gal} \times 15} = \frac{60 \text{ qt}}{15 \text{ gal}}$$

Find how many quarts of water Jonah has using dimensional analysis.

$$15 \text{ gal} \times \frac{4 \text{ qt}}{1 \text{ gal}}$$
$$= 15 \times 4 \text{ qt}$$
$$= 60 \text{ qt}$$

Jonah has 60 quarts of water.

> You can convert measures by using dimensional analysis or by finding an equivalent rate.

DATA

Customary Units		
Length	**Capacity**	**Weight**
1 ft = 12 in.	1 tbsp = 3 tsp	1 lb = 16 oz
1 yd = 36 in.	1 fl oz = 2 tbsp	1 T = 2,000 lb
1 yd = 3 ft	1 c = 8 fl oz	
1 mi = 5,280 ft	1 pt = 2 c	
1 mi = 1,760 yd	1 qt = 2 pt	
	1 gal = 4 qt	

> Use the rate that describes the relationship between the measures.

In **1–12**, complete each conversion.

1. 5 lb = ☐ oz

2. 2.5 T = ☐ lb

3. 39 ft = ☐ yd

4. 22 pt = ☐ qt

5. 4.5 lb = ☐ oz

6. 3 qt = ☐ gal

7. 5 qt = ☐ gal

8. 13 pt = ☐ qt

9. $\frac{1}{2}$ mi = ☐ ft

10. 1.5 mi = ☐ yd

11. 17 yd = ☐ ft

12. 25,000 lb = ☐ T

In **13** and **14**, use the picture.

13. © **MP.7 Look for Relationships** Chris is buying a yard of material for an art project. Two stores have the material she needs. Compare prices to find which material is the better buy. Explain how you decided.

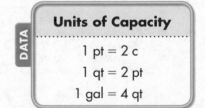

14. **Number Sense** Chris decides to buy 102 feet of the Craft Center material. What is the cost?

15. © **MP.1 Make Sense and Persevere** Bill is making smoothies for his friends. If 4 ounces of fruit is needed for each smoothie, how many pounds of fruit would he need to make 10 smoothies?

16. **Higher Order Thinking** How is converting units from cups to pints like converting units from ounces to pounds? How is it different?

17. Point A is located at $(-7, 4)$ on the coordinate plane. Point B is located at $(10, 4)$. What is the distance between these two points?

18. Brian pole-vaulted over a bar that was 189 inches high. How many inches higher must he vault to go over a bar that is 16 feet high?

© **Common Core Assessment**

19. Choose all of the conversions that are true.

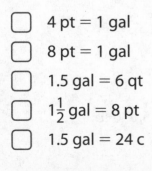

- ☐ 4 pt = 1 gal
- ☐ 8 pt = 1 gal
- ☐ 1.5 gal = 6 qt
- ☐ $1\frac{1}{2}$ gal = 8 pt
- ☐ 1.5 gal = 24 c

Units of Capacity
1 pt = 2 c
1 qt = 2 pt
1 gal = 4 qt

DATA

Name_____

Solve & Share

Sam has a water bottle that holds 250 milliliters of water when full. He needs to fill a 5-liter water jug for his team. If Sam uses the water bottle to fill the jug, how many times does he need to fill the water bottle in order to fill the jug? **Solve this problem any way you choose.**

I can ...
use unit rates to convert metric measurement units.

© Content Standard 6.RP.A.3d
Mathematical Practices MP.2, MP.3, MP.6, MP.7

You can use reasoning to decide how many milliliters are in 5 liters.

Metric Units of Capacity

1,000 milliliters (mL) = 1 liter (L)
100 centiliters (cL) = 1 liter
10 deciliters (dL) = 1 liter
1 dekaliter (daL) = 10 liters
1 hectoliter (hL) = 100 liters
1 kiloliter (kL) = 1,000 liters

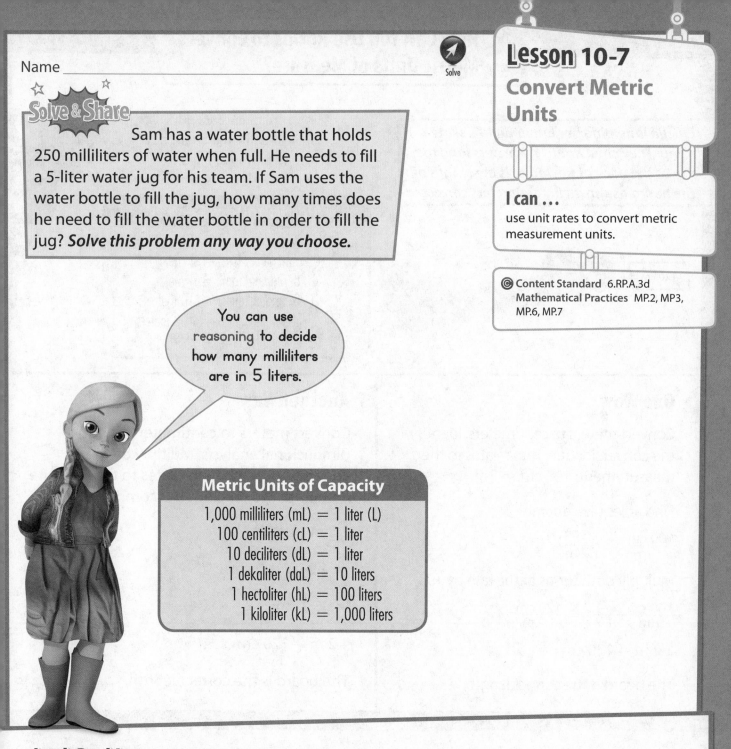

Look Back! © MP.6 Be Precise How many liters of water does Sam's water bottle hold when full?

Essential Question **How Can You Use Ratios to Convert Metric Units of Measure?**

A

Emelia is helping her father build a skate ramp. They cut a board 1.2 meters long to use as the back of the ramp. Is the length of the board as shown in centimeters correct?

You can convert metric units the same way as customary units.

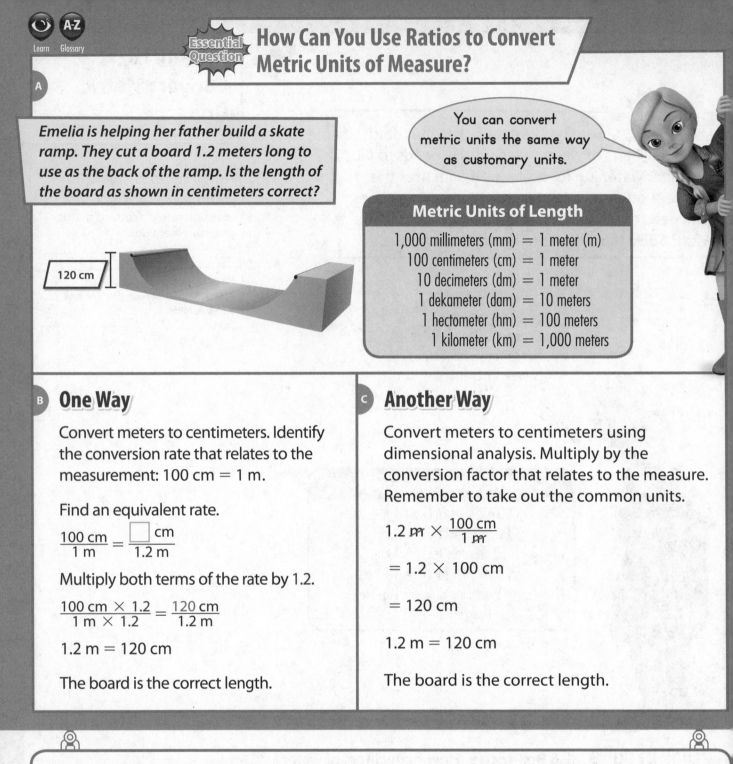

120 cm

Metric Units of Length

1,000 millimeters (mm) = 1 meter (m)
100 centimeters (cm) = 1 meter
10 decimeters (dm) = 1 meter
1 dekameter (dam) = 10 meters
1 hectometer (hm) = 100 meters
1 kilometer (km) = 1,000 meters

B **One Way**

Convert meters to centimeters. Identify the conversion rate that relates to the measurement: 100 cm = 1 m.

Find an equivalent rate.

$$\frac{100 \text{ cm}}{1 \text{ m}} = \frac{\square \text{ cm}}{1.2 \text{ m}}$$

Multiply both terms of the rate by 1.2.

$$\frac{100 \text{ cm} \times 1.2}{1 \text{ m} \times 1.2} = \frac{120 \text{ cm}}{1.2 \text{ m}}$$

1.2 m = 120 cm

The board is the correct length.

C **Another Way**

Convert meters to centimeters using dimensional analysis. Multiply by the conversion factor that relates to the measure. Remember to take out the common units.

$$1.2 \text{ m} \times \frac{100 \text{ cm}}{1 \text{ m}}$$

$$= 1.2 \times 100 \text{ cm}$$

$$= 120 \text{ cm}$$

1.2 m = 120 cm

The board is the correct length.

Convince Me! © **MP.7 Look for Relationships** The middle of the skate ramp is 2.5 meters wide. Emelia and her father want to use a board that is 23.5 decimeters long. Is this board wide enough for them to use? Convert the decimeters to meters to explain.

Practice Buddy   Tools   Assessment

☆ Guided Practice *

Do You Understand?

1. © **MP.6 Be Precise** How are the metric units kilometer and kilogram the same? How are they different?

2. © **MP.2 Reasoning** Which is greater, 250 m or 0.25 km? Justify your reasoning.

Do You Know How?

3. What is the conversion factor when converting from liters to milliliters?

4. © **MP.3 Critique Reasoning** Maddy wants to know how many centigrams are in 0.75 gram. She converted 0.75 gram to its equivalent in centigrams as shown. Is her work correct? Explain.

$$\frac{10 \text{ cg} \times 0.75}{1 \text{ g} \times 0.75} = \frac{7.5 \text{ cg}}{0.75 \text{ g}}$$

☆ Independent Practice ☆

Leveled Practice In **5** and **6**, complete each conversion using an equivalent rate.

5. 4 m = [　] cm

$$\frac{100 \text{ cm} \times \boxed{}}{1 \text{ m} \times \boxed{}} = \frac{\boxed{} \text{ cm}}{4 \text{ m}}$$

6. 800 mL = [　] L

$$\frac{1,000 \text{ mL} \div \boxed{}}{1 \text{ L} \div \boxed{}} = \frac{800 \text{ mL}}{\boxed{} \text{ L}}$$

Leveled Practice In **7** and **8**, complete each conversion using dimensional analysis.

7. 200 cL = [　] L

$$200 \text{ cL} \times \frac{\boxed{} \text{ L}}{\boxed{} \text{ cL}} = \frac{\boxed{}}{\boxed{}} \text{ L} = \boxed{} \text{ L}$$

8. 2.5 kg = [　] g

$$2.5 \text{ kg} \times \frac{\boxed{} \text{ g}}{\boxed{} \text{ kg}} =$$

$$2.5 \times 1,000 \text{ g} = \boxed{} \text{ g}$$

In **9–11**, complete each conversion.

You can use ratio reasoning to convert units of measure.

9. 80 cm = [　] m

10. 2.1 g = [　] mg

11. 0.75 L = [　] mL

Math Practices and Problem Solving

12. Math and Science Since there are 10 millimeters in 1 centimeter, about how many millimeters long is this dinosaur fossil bone? Explain how you calculated your answer.

About 22 cm

13. Jess is competing in a 20 km bike race. He has just passed the 17,000 m marker. How many meters does he have left in the race?

14. Tara is the editor of the school newspaper. She devotes $\frac{1}{2}$ of the paper to news, $\frac{1}{3}$ to pictures, and the rest of the paper to advertising. How much of the paper is devoted to advertising?

15. Higher Order Thinking Louis has a bag of 25 pencils. Each pencil is 18 centimeters long. What is the combined length of the pencils in meters?

16. © MP.4 Model with Math Lucas hiked 14.3 km in the morning. After lunch he continued hiking. When he finished the hike, he had covered 31.5 km in all. Write an equation that can be used to find how far Lucas hiked after lunch.

© **Common Core Assessment**

17. Choose all of the conversions that are true for the capacity of the pitcher of lemonade at the right.

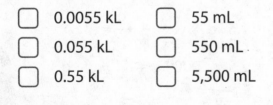

☐ 0.0055 kL   ☐ 55 mL

☐ 0.055 kL   ☐ 550 mL

☐ 0.55 kL   ☐ 5,500 mL

5.5 liters

Help Practice Tools Games
       Buddy

Another Look!

Amelia wants to convert 200 grams to kilograms.
What are two ways she can do this?

Identify the conversion rate.

$$1,000 \text{ g} = 1 \text{ kg}$$

Use an equivalent rate.

$$\frac{1,000 \text{ g}}{1 \text{ kg}} = \frac{200 \text{ g}}{\square \text{ kg}}$$

Divide both terms of the rate by 5.

$$\frac{1,000 \text{ g} \div 5}{1 \text{ kg} \div 5} = \frac{200 \text{ g}}{0.2 \text{ kg}}$$

$$200 \text{ g} = 0.2 \text{ kg}$$

Use dimensional analysis.

$$\frac{200 \text{ g} \times 1 \text{ kg}}{1,000 \text{ g}}$$

$$= \frac{200}{1,000} \text{ kg}$$

$$= 0.2 \text{ kg}$$

200 grams
are equal to
0.2 kilogram.

Metric Units of Mass

1,000 milligrams (mg) = 1 gram (g)
100 centigrams (cg) = 1 gram
10 decigrams (dg) = 1 gram
1 dekagram (dag) = 10 grams
1 hectogram (hg) = 100 grams
1 kilogram (kg) = 1,000 grams

In **1–12**, complete each conversion.

Remember, 10 millimeters
equal 1 centimeter, and
100,000 centimeters equal
1 kilometer.

1. 45 g = ☐ mg

2. 3,450 mL = ☐ L

3. 6.5 m = ☐ mm

4. 1.68 L = ☐ mL

5. 28 cm = ☐ mm

6. 7,658 g = ☐ kg

7. 600 cm = ☐ m

8. 5,000 dg = ☐ g

9. 5.1 km = ☐ m

10. 0.178 L = ☐ mL

11. 4,300 m = ☐ km

12. 2.7 m = ☐ cm

The Persistence of Memory, by Salvador Dali, and Water Lilies, by Claude Monet, are two famous paintings. In **13–15**, use the table.

13. © **MP.6 Be Precise** What is the length and height of The Persistence of Memory in centimeters?

DATA	Painting Title	Length (meters)	Height (meters)
	The Persistence of Memory	0.33	0.241
	Water Lilies	5.99	1.995

14. What is the length and height of Water Lilies in millimeters?

15. **Number Sense** The height of Water Lilies is about how many times the height of The Persistence of Memory?

16. © **MP.3 Construct Arguments** A banana has a mass of 122 g. Explain how to find the mass of the banana in milligrams.

17. **Higher Order Thinking** A kilometer is about $\frac{5}{8}$ of a mile. If a car is traveling at 40 kilometers per hour, about how many miles per hour is the car traveling?

18. A computer disk has a mass of 20 g. How many of these disks would you need to equal a total mass of 1 kg?

19. A chemist needs 2,220 mL of potassium chloride to complete an experiment. She has 2 L. How many more liters does she need?

© **Common Core Assessment**

20. Choose all of the conversions that are true for the distance between the towers of the suspension bridge at the right.

← 725 meters →

☐ 725,000 mm   ☐ 7.25 km

☐ 72,500 cm   ☐ 0.725 km

☐ 7,250 cm   ☐ 0.0725 km

Name _____

Solve & Share

Sasha bought a 1-gallon jug of lemonade at the store. She wants to pour the lemonade into two empty 2-liter bottles. Is the capacity of the 2-liter bottles enough to contain 1 gallon of lemonade? Explain. **Solve this problem any way you choose.**

I can ...
convert between customary and metric units.

© **Content Standard** 6.RP.A.3d
Mathematical Practices MP.1, MP.2, MP.3, MP.6, MP.7, MP.8

How can you use reasoning to compare the liquid volumes of containers measured in customary and metric units?

Units of Capacity Conversion Chart	
1 gal ≈ 3.79 L	1 L ≈ 0.26 gal
1 gal = 4 qt	1 L ≈ 1.06 qt
1 qt ≈ 0.95 L	

The ≈ symbol means "about" or "approximately".

Look Back! © **MP.8 Generalize** Can 4 quarts of lemonade be poured into two empty 2-liter bottles? Use what you know about converting units of capacity to write an equation and to justify your answer.

How Can You Use Ratios to Convert Customary and Metric Units of Measure?

A

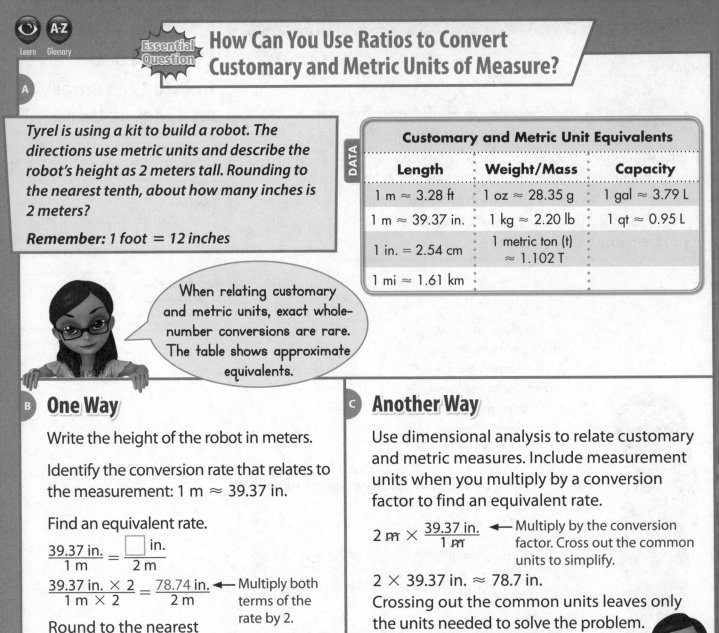

Tyrel is using a kit to build a robot. The directions use metric units and describe the robot's height as 2 meters tall. Rounding to the nearest tenth, about how many inches is 2 meters?

Remember: 1 foot = 12 inches

DATA

Customary and Metric Unit Equivalents

Length	Weight/Mass	Capacity
1 m ≈ 3.28 ft	1 oz ≈ 28.35 g	1 gal ≈ 3.79 L
1 m ≈ 39.37 in.	1 kg ≈ 2.20 lb	1 qt ≈ 0.95 L
1 in. = 2.54 cm	1 metric ton (t) ≈ 1.102 T	
1 mi ≈ 1.61 km		

When relating customary and metric units, exact whole-number conversions are rare. The table shows approximate equivalents.

B ## One Way

Write the height of the robot in meters.

Identify the conversion rate that relates to the measurement: 1 m ≈ 39.37 in.

Find an equivalent rate.

$$\frac{39.37 \text{ in.}}{1 \text{ m}} = \frac{\boxed{} \text{ in.}}{2 \text{ m}}$$

$$\frac{39.37 \text{ in.} \times 2}{1 \text{ m} \times 2} = \frac{78.74 \text{ in.}}{2 \text{ m}}$$ ← Multiply both terms of the rate by 2.

Round to the nearest tenth of an inch.

So, 2 m ≈ 78.7 in.

C ## Another Way

Use dimensional analysis to relate customary and metric measures. Include measurement units when you multiply by a conversion factor to find an equivalent rate.

$$2 \text{ m} \times \frac{39.37 \text{ in.}}{1 \text{ m}}$$ ← Multiply by the conversion factor. Cross out the common units to simplify.

2 × 39.37 in. ≈ 78.7 in.

Crossing out the common units leaves only the units needed to solve the problem.

78.7 inches is about 6 feet 7 inches tall.

Convince Me! © **MP.6 Be Precise** Jacob is building a robot named T3-X that is 75 inches tall. Rounding to the nearest tenth, how many centimeters tall is T3-X? Show your work.

Practice Buddy   Tools   Assessment

☆ Guided Practice ☆

Do You Understand?

1. © **MP.2 Reasoning** When converting centimeters to inches, do you multiply or divide by 2.54? Explain your reasoning.

2. © **MP.7 Use Structure** How can you find the approximate amount of liters in 1 pint?
Remember: 1 quart = 2 pints.

Do You Know How?

In **3–6**, find the equivalent measure. Round to the nearest tenth.

3. 5 in. = ☐ cm

4. 2 mi ≈ ☐ km

5. 113 g ≈ ☐ oz

6. 14 kg ≈ ☐ lb

Independent Practice ☆

In **7–18**, find the equivalent measure. Round to the nearest tenth. Show your work.

7. 9 qt ≈ ☐ L

8. 2 gal ≈ ☐ L

9. 2 in. ≈ ☐ cm

10. 5 km ≈ ☐ mi

11. 196 in. ≈ ☐ m

12. 10 L ≈ ☐ qt

13. 5.5 t ≈ ☐ T

14. 25 in. = ☐ cm

15. 50 lb ≈ ☐ kg

16. 51.6 gal ≈ ☐ L

17. 10 oz ≈ ☐ g

18. 3.5 m ≈ ☐ in.

Math Practices and Problem Solving

19. ©**MP.3 Construct Arguments** Francesca wants to convert 1 foot to centimeters. Use what you know about customary units to explain how she can do this.

20. ©**MP.2 Reasoning** To convert pounds to their approximate measure in kilograms on Earth, which operation should you use? Use reasoning to explain your answer.

21. ©**MP.6 Be Precise** Mount McKinley is the highest mountain in the United States. What is its height in meters? Round to the nearest whole number.

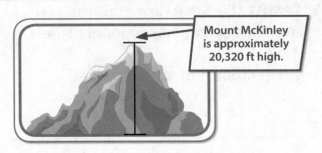

Mount McKinley is approximately 20,320 ft high.

22. Number Sense Explain how you can find the equivalent of 28.3 grams in kilograms without doing any calculation.

23. Higher Order Thinking At the State Fair, a person must be at least 138 centimeters tall to ride the roller coaster. Billy wants to ride the coaster. He is 4 feet 7 inches tall. Is Billy tall enough to ride the coaster? Explain.

© Common Core Assessment

24. The posted speed limit is 65 miles per hour. Choose all the metric measures that are faster than 65 miles per hour.

☐ 65 km per hour

☐ 97.5 km per hour

☐ 104 km per hour

☐ 105.7 km per hour

☐ 120.3 km per hour

25. Boys competing in the long jump event must jump at least 15 feet to qualify for the state track and field meet. Choose all metric measures that are less than 15 feet.

☐ 6.5 m

☐ 5.0 m

☐ 4.5 m

☐ 3.92 m

☐ 3.5 m

Help Practice   Tools   Games
      Buddy

Another Look!

Jenna's Alaskan husky has a mass of 21 kilograms. On Earth, about how many pounds are equal to a mass of 21 kilograms? Round your answer to the nearest tenth.

> You can use what you know about converting within one measurement system to generalize when relating customary and metric units.

Customary and Metric Unit Equivalents

Length	Weight/Mass	Capacity
1 in. = 2.54 cm	1 oz ≈ 28.35 g	1 qt ≈ 0.95 L
1 m ≈ 39.37 in.	1 kg ≈ 2.20 lb	1 gal ≈ 3.79 L
1 mi ≈ 1.61 km	1 metric ton (t) ≈ 1.102 T	

One Way

Identify the conversion rate that applies.
$$1 \text{ kg} \approx 2.20 \text{ lb}$$

Find the equivalent rate.

$$\frac{2.20 \text{ lb} \times 21}{1 \text{ kg} \times 21} = \frac{46.2 \text{ lb}}{21 \text{ kg}}$$ ← Multiply both terms of the rate by 21.

Round to the nearest tenth, if needed.

On Earth, Jenna's dog weighs about 46.2 lb.

Another Way

Use dimensional analysis to find an equivalent rate.

$$21 \text{ kg} \times \frac{2.20 \text{ lb}}{1 \text{ kg}}$$ ← Multiply by the conversion factor. Cross out the common units to simplify.

Crossing out leaves only the units needed to solve the problem: 21 × 2.20 lb = 46.2 lb.

On Earth, Jenna's dog weighs about 46.2 lb.

In **1–9**, find the equivalent measure. Round to the nearest tenth. Show your work.

1. 4 in. ≈ ☐ cm

2. 12 gal ≈ ☐ L

3. 35 lb ≈ ☐ kg

4. 20 km ≈ ☐ mi

5. 125 in. ≈ ☐ m

6. 18 L ≈ ☐ qt

7. 55 oz ≈ ☐ g

8. 34 in. ≈ ☐ cm

9. 70 mi ≈ ☐ km

10. © **MP.3 Critique Reasoning** A recipe Carmen is making calls for 4 cups of milk. She has 1 liter of milk. Her sister says she has enough milk. Is her sister correct? Explain.

Units of Capacity Conversion Chart	
1 pt = 2 c	1 gal ≈ 3.79 L
1 qt = 2 pt	1 qt ≈ 0.95 L
1 gal = 4 qt	

11. **A-Z** **Vocabulary** Eamon purchased 8 packs of sports cards for $26. Each pack is the same price. Find the *unit price* of each pack.

12. © **MP.6 Be Precise** Keiko is using metric units of capacity to find an equivalent measure for 3 gallons. She records the liquid volume using milliliters and deciliters. Which unit will give a more precise measure? Explain.

13. © **MP.1 Make Sense and Persevere** A 1-mile race is 5,280 feet long. To the nearest tenth, about how many meters are there in 1 mile? Explain how you solved the problem.

14. **Higher Order Thinking** Six juice boxes have a total liquid volume of 48 fluid ounces. There are 8 fluid ounces in 1 cup. There are about 4.23 cups in 1 liter. About how many liters are there in 48 fluid ounces? Round your answer to the nearest tenth.

© **Common Core Assessment**

15. A gorilla has a mass of 156 kilograms. Choose all of the customary measures that are less than 156 kilograms.

☐ 400 lb
☐ 350 lb
☐ 300 lb
☐ 250 lb
☐ 200 lb

16. The public library has a mural that measures 15 meters wide. Choose all customary measures that are greater than 15 meters.

☐ 500 in.
☐ 550 in.
☐ 600 in.
☐ 45 ft
☐ 50 ft

Name _____

Solve & Share

Alanna, Jordan and Xavier work in a frozen yogurt store and are paid an hourly rate. In their state, the minimum hourly wage is $7.50. Is each employee earning at least the state minimum wage? How much less or more than minimum wage does each employee earn? **Solve this problem any way you choose.**

Employee	Hours Worked	Earnings
Alanna	8	$63.60
Jordan	4	$29.00
Xavier	6	$45.90

I can ...
be precise when solving math problems.

© Mathematical Practices MP.6, MP.1, MP.2, MP.3, MP.4
Content Standards 6.RP.A.3b, 6.RP.A.3d

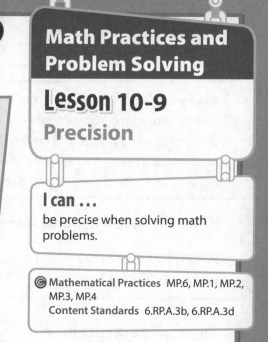

Thinking Habits

Be a good thinker!
These questions can help you.

- Am I using numbers, units, and symbols appropriately?

- Am I using the correct definitions?

- Am I calculating accurately?

- Is my answer clear and appropriate?

Look Back! © **MP.6 Be Precise** How did you use words, numbers, and symbols to make sure your answer is clear and correct?

How Can You Be Precise When Solving Math Problems?

A

To prepare for a battle of the books competition, Gabby is reading a book that is 273 pages long. She can read 84 pages in 3 hours. If she continues reading at the same rate, will she finish the book before the competition begins in 8 hours?

Hours	Pages
1	?
2	?
3	84
4	?
5	?

What do I need to do to solve the problem?

I need to be precise when finding how long it will take Gabby to read her book.

Here's my thinking...

B How can I be precise in solving this problem?

I can

- correctly use the information given.

- calculate accurately.

- decide if my answer is clear and appropriate.

- use the correct units.

C

I can use a unit rate to solve the problem. Gabby has read 84 pages of a book in 3 hours.

$$\frac{84 \text{ pages} \div 3}{3 \text{ hours} \div 3} = \frac{28 \text{ pages}}{1 \text{ hour}}$$

Find an equivalent rate.

$$\frac{28 \text{ pages} \times 8}{1 \text{ hour} \times 8} = \frac{224 \text{ pages}}{8 \text{ hours}}$$

Gabby will only read 224 pages of the book in 8 hours, so she will not finish the book in time for the competition.

Convince Me! © **MP.6 Be Precise** How long it will take Gabby to read her entire book to the nearest hour? Explain.

Name _____

☆ Guided Practice ☆

© MP.6 Be Precise

Township workers painted lines on 96 miles of roadway in 4 hours. The town manager says it will take more than 8 hours to paint 210 miles of road. Is this statement accurate? Explain.

> To be precise, you need to check that the words, numbers, symbols, and units you use are correct and that your calculations are accurate.

1. How can you use rate reasoning to solve this problem? Explain.

2. Show how to use numbers, units, and symbols to justify or disprove the manager's statement.

Independent Practice ☆

© MP.6 Be Precise

The Garcia family is driving from San Diego, California, to Bar Harbor, Maine. In 5 days, they have traveled 2,045 miles. At this rate, how long will it take them to travel from San Diego to Bar Harbor?

3. How can you use rate reasoning to solve this problem? Explain.

Bar Harbor, Maine

3,272 miles

San Diego, California

4. Show how to use numbers, units, and symbols precisely to solve the problem.

For another example, see Set F on page 532.   **Topic 10** | Lesson 10-9   **525**

Math Practices and Problem Solving

© Common Core Performance Assessment

Keyboard Challenge

Kevin and Valeria have just completed a keyboarding class. Their test results are shown in the table. They each have a 9,000-word report to type. Who will finish first? Explain your answer.

Student	Minutes	Words Typed	Errors/ 100 words
Kevin	7	441	2
Valeria	5	360	3

5. **MP.1 Make Sense and Persevere** How can you use the information given in the problem?

6. **MP.3 Construct Arguments** Explain how rate reasoning can be used to find who will finish the report first.

Be precise. Use the correct numbers, terms, and operations, calculate accurately, and clearly explain how to solve problems.

7. **MP.6 Be Precise** Could the number of errors each student makes affect who finishes first? Explain.

8. **MP.4 Model with Math** Use rate reasoning to write and solve equations to solve the problem.

Name _____

Another Look!

Noah does odd jobs for his neighbors. The table shows the number of jobs and the amount earned during his first 3 weeks. His friend, Jim, says that Noah's earnings per job increased each week. Do you agree? Explain.

Week	Number of Jobs	Total Earnings
Week 1	3	$411
Week 2	4	$450
Week 3	6	$696

> You can be precise by carefully considering and using the information you are given to solve problems.

How can you be precise when solving this problem?

- I can make sure I am using numbers, units, and symbols correctly.

- I can make sure my calculations are accurate.

Use numbers, units, and symbols precisely to solve the problem.

Find the unit rate for each week.

Week 1	Week 2	Week 3
$\dfrac{\$411 \div 3}{3 \text{ jobs} \div 3} = \dfrac{\$137}{1 \text{ job}}$	$\dfrac{\$450 \div 4}{4 \text{ jobs} \div 4} = \dfrac{\$112.50}{1 \text{ job}}$	$\dfrac{\$696 \div 6}{6 \text{ jobs} \div 6} = \dfrac{\$116}{1 \text{ job}}$

Noah earned the most per job in Week 1. Jim is not correct.

© MP.6 Be Precise

Hanna and Dien are both getting a raise.
Who will earn more per hour after the raise?

1. How can you use rate reasoning to find Hanna's and Dien's new earnings per hour? Explain.

	Hours Worked	Earnings	Raise (per hour)
Hanna	8	$78.00	$1.00
Dien	6	$60.60	$0.50

2. Use numbers, units, and symbols to solve the problem.

Portrait Painting

Diego is an artist. Every weekend he paints portraits in the park for a fee. He can paint 3 small portraits in 36 minutes, a medium portrait in 30 minutes, and 2 large portraits in 84 minutes. Last weekend, he spent 294 minutes painting large portraits and 60 minutes painting small portraits. How much money did he earn?

Portrait Size	Price
Small	$9.00
Medium	$16.50
Large	$36.50

3. **MP.1 Make Sense and Persevere** What given information do you need to solve the problem?

4. **MP.6 Be Precise** Do you need to find the total number of minutes Diego spent painting in order to find the total amount Diego earned? Explain.

5. **MP.2 Reasoning** Describe a strategy you can use to find how much money Diego earned painting small portraits.

6. **MP.4 Model with Math** Write and solve equations to find how much Diego earned painting portraits. Explain your reasoning.

Follow the Path

Shade a path from **START** to **FINISH**. Follow quotients that are between 4 and 40. You can only move up, down, right, or left.

Start				
$12\overline{)384}$	$100\overline{)14,500}$	$8\overline{)496}$	$10\overline{)3,300}$	$3\overline{)255}$
$1,000\overline{)4,800}$	$16\overline{)896}$	$12\overline{)816}$	$4\overline{)232}$	$12\overline{)636}$
$16\overline{)128}$	$36\overline{)828}$	$2\overline{)176}$	$16\overline{)912}$	$64\overline{)192}$
$3\overline{)5,280}$	$10\overline{)309}$	$64\overline{)1,536}$	$10\overline{)3,700}$	$100\overline{)82,300}$
$8\overline{)328}$	$36\overline{)1,620}$	$100\overline{)1,785}$	$16\overline{)592}$	$4\overline{)92}$

Finish

Vocabulary Review

Word List

- constant speed
- conversion factor
- dimensional analysis
- rate
- unit price
- unit rate

Understand Vocabulary

Choose the best term from the Word List. Write it on the blank.

1. Use _____ to convert measures by including measurement units and multiplying by a conversion factor.

2. The price of a single item is called its _____.

3. A _____ that compares equivalent measures is a _____.

4. A rate of speed that stays the same over time is a _____.

5. Circle the *conversion factor* needed to convert 13,200 feet to miles.

$$\frac{5,280\ ft}{1\ mi} \qquad \frac{1\ mi}{5,280\ ft} \qquad \frac{3\ ft}{1\ mi} \qquad \frac{1\ mi}{3\ ft}$$

Write T for *true* and F for *false*.

_____ 6. A *unit rate* always compares two different units of measure.

_____ 7. A *unit price* is a ratio that compares money amounts.

_____ 8. When you ride your bicycle, you always travel at a *constant speed*.

Use Vocabulary in Writing

9. Explain how you can convert 52 ounces to pounds. Use at least 2 words from the Word List in your explanation.

Name _____

Set A pages 475–480, 481–486 _____

Write 20 meters in 4 minutes as a rate and as a unit rate.

Write "20 meters in 4 minutes" as a rate, a special type of ratio that compares quantities with unlike units of measure.

$$\frac{20\text{ meters}}{4\text{ minutes}}$$

The unit rate is an equivalent rate with a denomintor of 1 unit.

$$\frac{20\text{ meters} \div 4}{4\text{ minutes} \div 4} = \frac{5\text{ meters}}{1\text{ minute}}$$

Remember that a unit rate is a comparison to 1 unit.

Write each phrase as a unit rate.

1. 78 miles on 3 gallons

2. 18 laps in 6 minutes

3. 48 sandwiches for 16 people

4. 49 houses in 7 blocks

Set B pages 487–492, 493–498 _____

On Pet Day, Meg's turtle crawled 30 feet in 6 minutes, and Pat's turtle crawled 25 feet in 5 minutes. Whose turtle crawled at a faster rate?

Find each unit rate and determine which rate is greater.

Write each rate: $\quad \frac{30\text{ ft}}{6\text{ min}}, \frac{25\text{ ft}}{5\text{ min}}$

Find each unit rate: $\quad \frac{5\text{ ft}}{1\text{ min}}, \frac{5\text{ ft}}{1\text{ min}}$

Both turtles crawled at the same rate.

Remember that converting rates to unit rates or unit prices makes them easy to compare.

1. Which is the better buy? Circle it.
$5.00 for 4 mangoes
$6.00 for 5 mangoes

2. Who earned more each month?
Atif: $84 over 3 months
Jafar: $100 over 4 months

Set C pages 499–504 _____

A plane travels at a rate of 780 miles in 2 hours. At this rate, how far will it travel in 3.5 hours?

Find the unit rate.

$$\frac{780\text{ miles} \div 2}{2\text{ hours} \div 2} = \frac{390\text{ miles}}{1\text{ hour}}$$

Find an equivalent rate.

$$\frac{390\text{ miles} \times 3.5}{1\text{ hour} \times 3.5} = \frac{1{,}365\text{ miles}}{3.5\text{ hours}}$$

The plane will travel 1,365 miles in 3.5 hours.

Remember that you can use a unit rate to find any constant speed or distance.

1. Doug has 5 hours to make an on-time delivery 273 miles away. Doug drives at a constant speed of 55 miles per hour. Will he make the delivery by the deadline? Explain.

Set D pages 505–510, 511–516

How many feet is 5 miles?

$$5 \text{ mi} \times \frac{5{,}280 \text{ ft}}{1 \text{ mi}} = 26{,}400 \text{ ft}$$

$$5 \text{ mi} = 26{,}400 \text{ ft}$$

How many kilometers is 15,100 meters?

$$15{,}100 \text{ m} \times \frac{1 \text{ km}}{1{,}000 \text{ m}} = \frac{15{,}100}{1{,}000} \text{ km} = 15.1 \text{ km}$$

Remember to use dimensional analysis to convert units of measure.

Find the equivalent measure.

1. 1 mi = _____ ft
2. 36 in = _____ yd
3. 3 m = _____ mm
4. 3,520 mm = _____ c

Set E pages 517–522

Gwen has a cooler that holds 3 quarts. How many liters does the cooler hold?

$$1 \text{ qt} \approx 0.95 \text{ L}$$

$$3 \text{ qt} \times \frac{0.95 \text{ L}}{1 \text{ qt}} = (3 \times 0.95) \text{ L} = 2.85 \text{ L}$$

Gwen's cooler holds approximately 2.85 liters.

Remember to use a conversion factor to approximate equivalent metric and customary measures.

Find the equivalent measure. Round to the nearest tenth.

1. 100 g ≈ _____ oz
2. 6 ft ≈ _____ m
3. 57 gal ≈ _____ L
4. 27 km ≈ _____ mi

Set F pages 523–528

Think about these questions to help you **be precise** in solving problems.

Thinking Habits

- Am I using numbers, units, and symbols appropriately?
- Am I using the correct definitions?
- Am I calculating accurately?
- Is my answer clear and appropriate?

Remember to be precise when solving problems.

Carla is making a craft project with marbles. Store 1 sells 100 marbles for $3.38. Store 2 sells 1,000 marbles for $35. She needs at least 750 marbles. Which store offers the better price?

1. How can you use rate reasoning to solve this problem? Explain.

2. Use numbers, units, and symbols correctly to solve the problem.

Name _____

1. If Mrs. Banks made 44 quarts of jelly, how many gallons did she make?

   Ⓐ 11 gallons

   Ⓑ 22 gallons

   Ⓒ 88 gallons

   Ⓓ 176 gallons

2. In one hour, 32 cars pass through a particular intersection. At the same rate, how long would it take for 96 cars to pass through the intersection?

   Ⓐ 2 hours

   Ⓑ 3 hours

   Ⓒ 8 hours

   Ⓓ 16 hours

3. Nick flew 1,560 miles in 3 hours on his airline flight. The plane flew at a constant speed. How far did Nick fly in 1 hour?

4. A shower uses 5 gallons of water each minute. Which of the following can be used to find the number of gallons of water used during an 8-minute shower?

   Ⓐ $\frac{5 \text{ gal}}{1 \text{ min}} = \frac{n \text{ gal}}{8 \text{ min}}$

   Ⓑ $\frac{5 \text{ gal}}{1 \text{ min}} = \frac{8 \text{ min}}{n \text{ gal}}$

   Ⓒ $\frac{5 \text{ gal}}{n \text{ min}} = \frac{1 \text{ gal}}{8 \text{ min}}$

   Ⓓ $\frac{5 \text{ gal}}{8 \text{ min}} = \frac{n \text{ gal}}{1 \text{ min}}$

5. How many milliliters of liquid are in the container shown?

   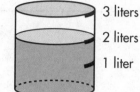

   3 liters
   2 liters
   1 liter

6. The table shows the results of typing tests given to four job applicants. Each applicant typed at the same rate. Choose the correct numbers from the box to complete the table.

21	24	63	96
120	126	164	168
210	252	336	420

DATA	Applicant	Words Typed	Time (in minutes)
	Smith	84	2
	Johnson		3
	Ramirez		4
	Yates		5

7. April can buy a package of 10 folders for $1.20 or a package of 8 folders for $1.12.

Part A

How much does each folder cost in each package?

Part B

Which is the better buy?

Part C

April needs 1 folder for each of her six classes. Which package of folders should she buy? Explain your reasoning.

8. Jessica is buying several bunches of bananas to make desserts for a fundraiser. She can buy 10 pounds of bananas for $14.90 or 8 pounds of bananas for $12.08. Which is the better buy? Explain.

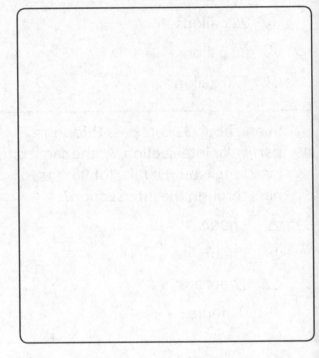

9. Mount Everest is 8,850 meters tall. About how many feet tall is Mount Everest?

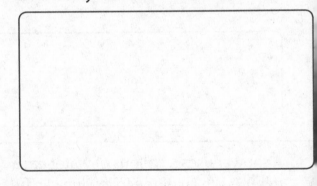

10. A loaf of bread weighs about 1 pound. Choose all the metric measures that are less than 1 pound.

- ☐ 1 kg
- ☐ 0.5 kg
- ☐ 500 g
- ☐ 450 g
- ☐ 100 g

Name _____

Julia is helping her family plan a trip to the northern California coast. She is in charge of planning the routes.

• Route 1 is 630 miles and provides more views of the countryside.
• Route 2 is 540 miles and is less scenic than Route 1.
• The family will stop to rest at hotels during the drive.

1. Regardless of the route they choose, the family wants to travel 186 miles in 3 hours.

   Part A

   At what constant speed would they need to travel?

   Part B

   About how many hours would it take to drive each of the two routes?

2. Julia's father is considering driving the total trip distance in 3 days and wants to drive the same number of miles each day. How many miles will the family need to drive each day for each route?

3. The family's car can travel 384 miles on 12 gallons of gas. How many more gallons of gas will they need to drive Route 1 than Route 2? Explain how you know.

4. If 12 gallons of gas cost an average of $45.00, about how much will the family spend on gas for each of the two routes? Explain how you can use a unit rate to solve the problem.

5. Which route would you recommend that the family travel? Explain how each factor contributed to your recommendation.

6. Julia's family will stay in a hotel on Thursday night, Friday night, and Saturday night. Julia found the following rates for hotels in the area. At which hotel should the family stay? Use unit rates to explain your reasoning.

- Hotel A – $89.99 per night
- Hotel B – $75.25 per night for Sunday through Thursday; $109 per night for Friday or Saturday
- Hotel C – $264.90 for any three nights

Ratio Concepts: Percent

Essential Questions: What is the meaning of percent? How can percent be estimated and found?

Digital Resources

Solve Learn Glossary Practice Buddy

Tools Assessment Help Games

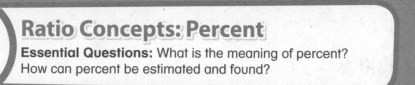

Your bones continue to grow during your teen years. And they grow rapidly.

Calcium is a mineral. A healthy diet provides calcium needed to grow strong bones.

Our bodies need calcium for many reasons. We're talking about health! Here's a project about your Dietary Reference Intake (DRI) and percents.

Math and Science Project: Nutrition

Do Research Use the Internet or other sources to learn more about the role of calcium in the human body and to find your DRI, or estimated average daily requirement for calcium.

Journal: Write a Report Include what you found. Also in your report:

- List the foods and beverages you might consume in one day. Include the amount consumed of each item.

- Find the amount of calcium in each item.

- What percent of your DRI for calcium is met?

- What other healthy foods can you add to your diet if you do not meet 100% of your DRI for calcium?

Review What You Know

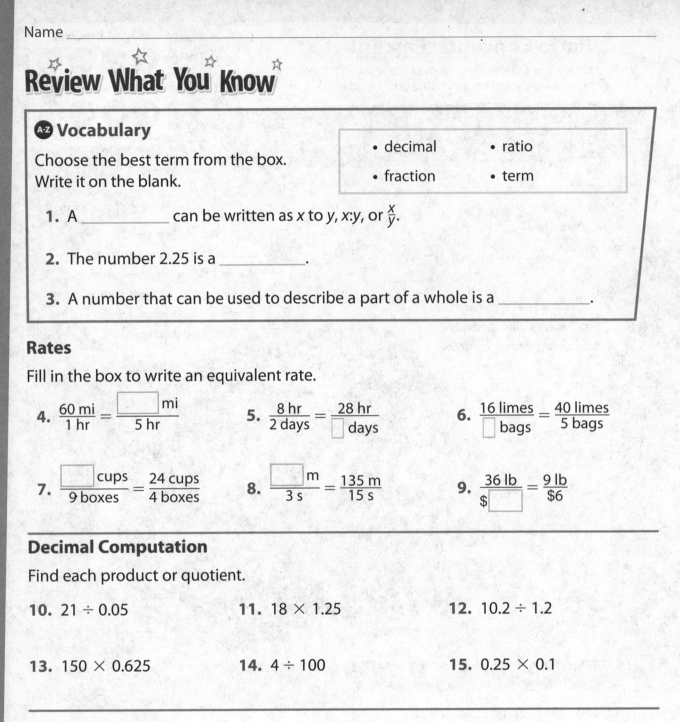

Vocabulary

Choose the best term from the box.
Write it on the blank.

- decimal
- ratio
- fraction
- term

1. A _____ can be written as x to y, x:y, or $\frac{x}{y}$.

2. The number 2.25 is a _____.

3. A number that can be used to describe a part of a whole is a _____.

Rates

Fill in the box to write an equivalent rate.

4. $\dfrac{60 \text{ mi}}{1 \text{ hr}} = \dfrac{\boxed{} \text{ mi}}{5 \text{ hr}}$

5. $\dfrac{8 \text{ hr}}{2 \text{ days}} = \dfrac{28 \text{ hr}}{\boxed{} \text{ days}}$

6. $\dfrac{16 \text{ limes}}{\boxed{} \text{ bags}} = \dfrac{40 \text{ limes}}{5 \text{ bags}}$

7. $\dfrac{\boxed{} \text{ cups}}{9 \text{ boxes}} = \dfrac{24 \text{ cups}}{4 \text{ boxes}}$

8. $\dfrac{\boxed{} \text{ m}}{3 \text{ s}} = \dfrac{135 \text{ m}}{15 \text{ s}}$

9. $\dfrac{36 \text{ lb}}{\$ \boxed{}} = \dfrac{9 \text{ lb}}{\$6}$

Decimal Computation

Find each product or quotient.

10. $21 \div 0.05$

11. 18×1.25

12. $10.2 \div 1.2$

13. 150×0.625

14. $4 \div 100$

15. 0.25×0.1

Equivalent Ratios

16. What are two different ways to find an equivalent ratio for $\frac{10}{25}$?

My Word Cards

Use the example for the word on the front of the card to help complete the definition on the back.

A-Z Glossary

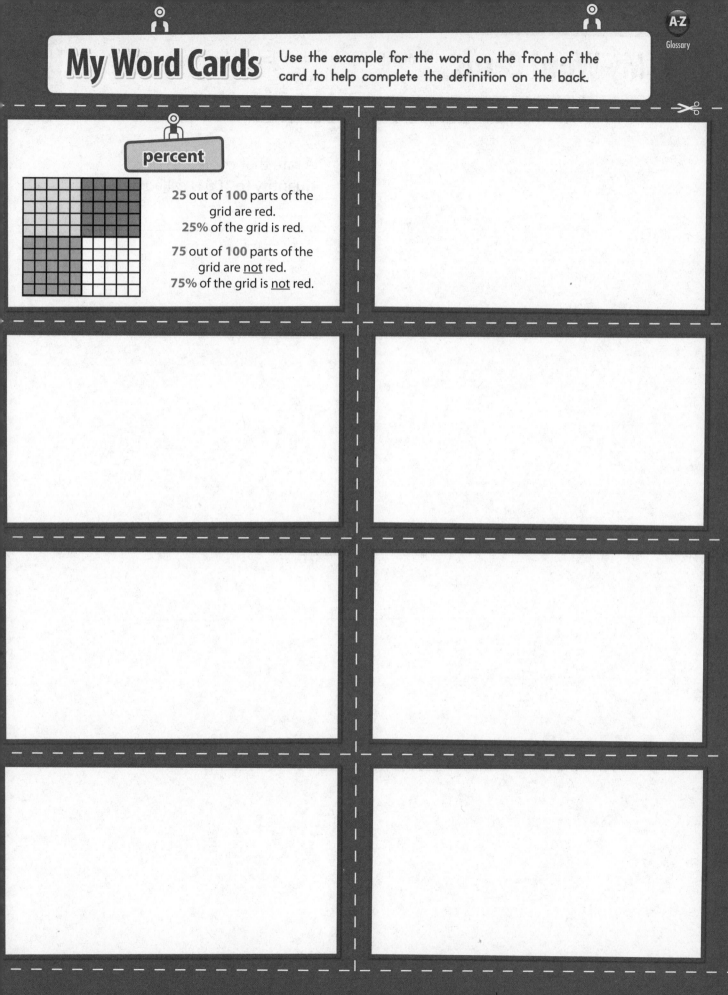

percent

25 out of **100** parts of the grid are red.
25% of the grid is red.

75 out of **100** parts of the grid are <u>not</u> red.
75% of the grid is <u>not</u> red.

My Word Cards

Complete the definition. Extend learning by writing your own definition.

A rate that compares one quantity to 100 is called a

_____.

Name _____

Solve & Share

Patrick's family ate a whole vegetable pizza for dinner. Each person ate 1 slice of the pizza. If each slice was exactly the same size, show how the pizza was cut for four people. What fraction of the pizza did each person have? **Solve this problem any way you choose.**

I can ...
represent and find the percent of a whole.

© Content Standard 6.RP.A.3c
Mathematical Practices MP.1, MP.2, MP.3, MP.4, MP.7

You can model with math to represent part of a whole.

Look Back! © **MP.2 Reasoning** Suppose one person ate half of the pizza. How can you write this fraction in another way to represent part of the whole pizza?

Essential Question: How Does Percent Relate to the Whole?

A

A percent is a rate in which the first term is compared to 100. The percent is the number of hundredths that represents the part of the whole.

What percent of people prefer Bright White Toothpaste?

You can use the % symbol to represent a percent. Fifty percent can be written as $\frac{50}{100} = 50\%$.

Seven out of ten people prefer Bright White Toothpaste.

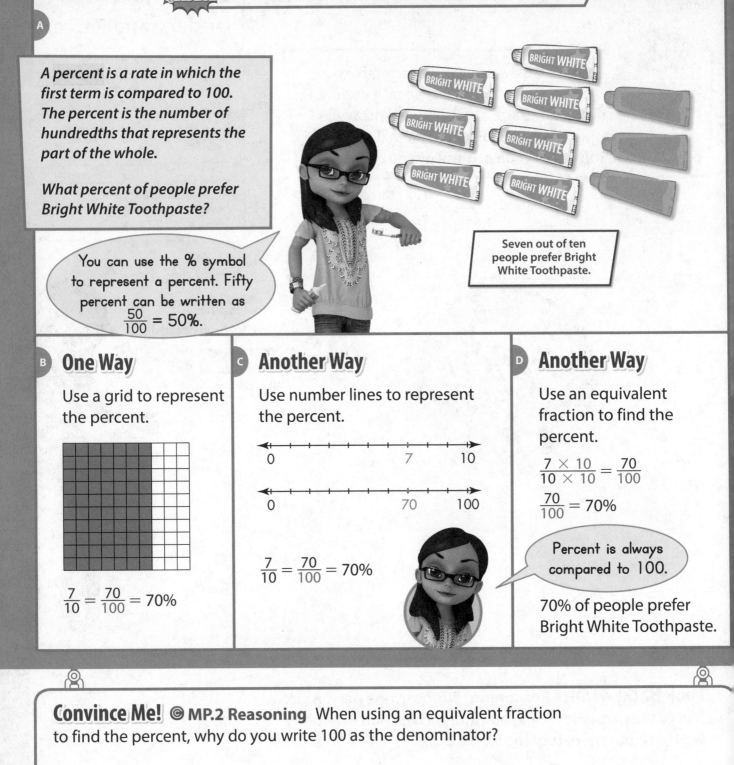

B ### One Way

Use a grid to represent the percent.

$$\frac{7}{10} = \frac{70}{100} = 70\%$$

C ### Another Way

Use number lines to represent the percent.

$$\frac{7}{10} = \frac{70}{100} = 70\%$$

D ### Another Way

Use an equivalent fraction to find the percent.

$$\frac{7 \times 10}{10 \times 10} = \frac{70}{100}$$

$$\frac{70}{100} = 70\%$$

Percent is always compared to 100.

70% of people prefer Bright White Toothpaste.

Convince Me! © MP.2 Reasoning When using an equivalent fraction to find the percent, why do you write 100 as the denominator?

Another Example

Each line segment represents 100%, but is a different length. Use equivalent rates to find the percent, or part of each line segment that points A and B represent.

You can write an equivalent rate with 100 as the denominator.

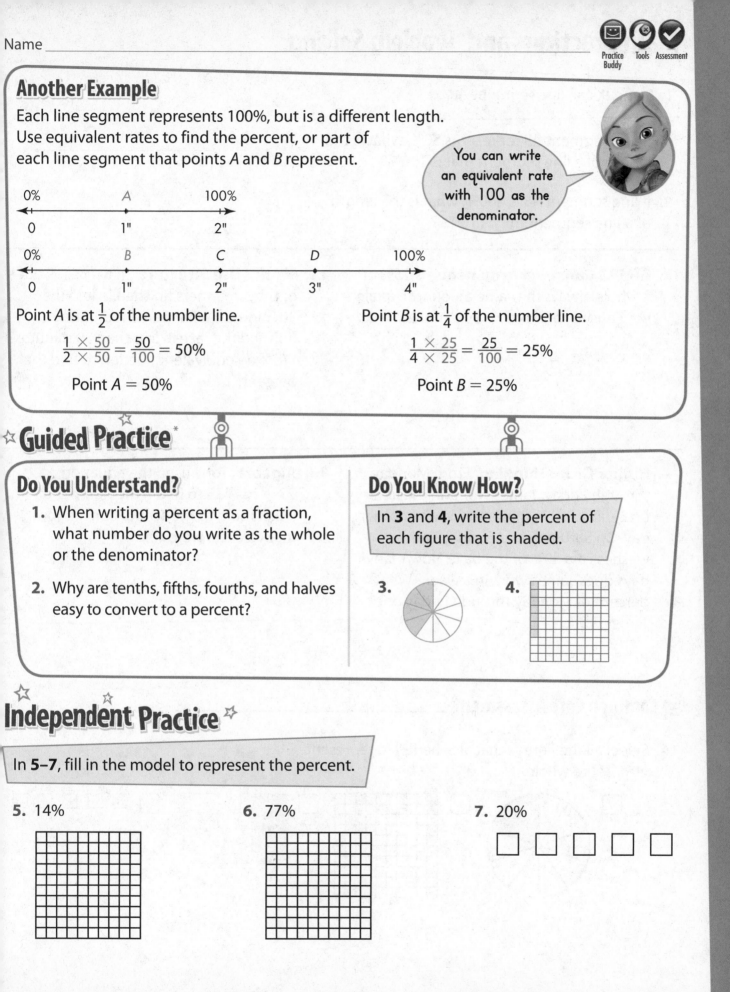

Point A is at $\frac{1}{2}$ of the number line.

$$\frac{1 \times 50}{2 \times 50} = \frac{50}{100} = 50\%$$

Point A = 50%

Point B is at $\frac{1}{4}$ of the number line.

$$\frac{1 \times 25}{4 \times 25} = \frac{25}{100} = 25\%$$

Point B = 25%

☆ Guided Practice ☆

Do You Understand?

1. When writing a percent as a fraction, what number do you write as the whole or the denominator?

2. Why are tenths, fifths, fourths, and halves easy to convert to a percent?

Do You Know How?

In **3** and **4**, write the percent of each figure that is shaded.

3.

4.

☆ Independent Practice ☆

In **5–7**, fill in the model to represent the percent.

5. 14%

6. 77%

7. 20%

Math Practices and Problem Solving

In **8** and **9**, use line segment *AB*.

8. If line segment *AB* represents 50%, what is the length of a line segment that is 100%?

A •————————————————————————• B

3 in.

9. If line segment *AB* is 300%, what is the length of a line segment that is 100%?

---

10. © **MP.3 Construct Arguments** Is 25% of a whole always the same amount? Explain your answer and provide examples.

11. © **MP.7 Use Structure** In a race, 19 out of the 50 runners finished in less than 30 minutes. What percent of runners finished the race in less than 30 minutes? Write an equivalent fraction to find the percent.

12. **Higher Order Thinking** From Monday through Friday, James works in the library on 2 days and in the cafeteria on another day. On Saturday and Sunday, James washes cars 50% of the days. How many days does James work in a week? What percent of Monday through Friday does James work?

13. **Algebra** Tony used the equation $23 + t = 435$ to find t, the number of tickets sold to the school dance. How many tickets were sold?

© **Common Core Assessment**

14. Select all the figures that are shaded to represent 20% of the whole.

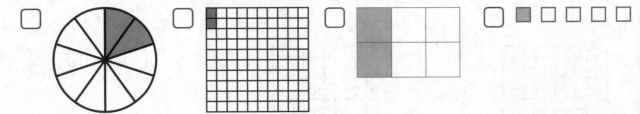

Help Practice Tools Games
      Buddy

Another Look!

What percent of each figure is shaded?

> If the second term of the rate is not 100, you can write an equivalent rate with 100 as the denominator.

> A percent is a rate that compares a part to a whole. The second term in the rate is always 100. The whole is 100%.

The circle has 1 of 10 parts shaded.

$$\frac{1 \times 10}{10 \times 10} = \frac{10}{100}$$

$$\frac{10}{100} = 10\%$$

So, 10% of the circle is shaded.

The grid has 60 of 100 squares shaded.

$$\frac{60}{100} = 60\%$$

So, 60% of the grid is shaded.

In **1–3**, write the percent of each figure that is shaded.

1.

2.
0   5   10   15   20

3.

In **4–6**, shade each model to represent the given percent.

4. 3%

5. 80%
0   6   12   18   24   30

6. 30%

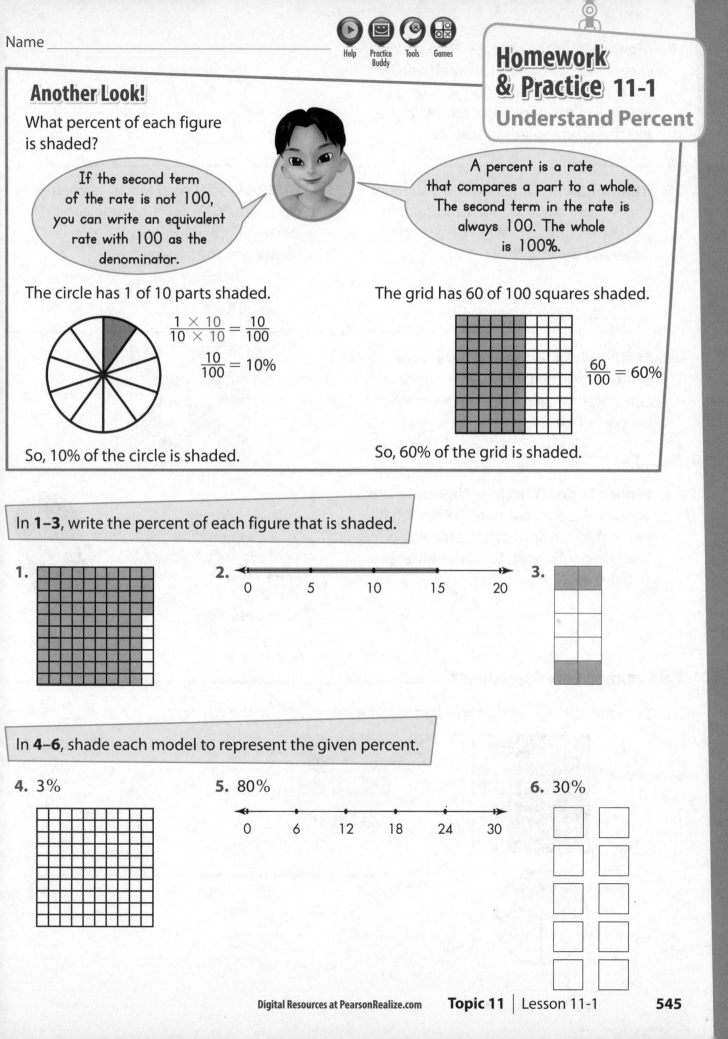

7. **Algebra** The zoo charges $1 to park your car and $3 per person for admission into the park. Use the equation $y = 3x + 1$, where x = the number of admissions to the zoo, to complete the table.

x	2	3	4
y			

8. **Number Sense** Jana divided a sheet of paper into 5 equal sections and colored 2 of the sections red. What percent of the paper did she color?

9. © **MP.4 Model with Math** Water makes up about 60% of the average adult's body weight. Represent this percent by shading in the squares.

10. © **MP.1 Make Sense and Persevere** Ally wants to tile her laundry room floor with checkered ceramic tile as shown. What percent of Ally's floor will be white?

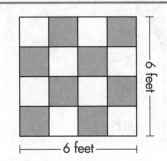

6 feet

6 feet

11. **Higher Order Thinking** Ally buys a box of blue tiles that will cover 18 ft². What percent of the floor can she tile using this box? Does Ally need to buy another box of blue tiles? Explain.

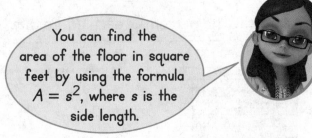

You can find the area of the floor in square feet by using the formula $A = s^2$, where s is the side length.

© **Common Core Assessment** _____

12. Select all the figures that are shaded to represent 75% of the whole.

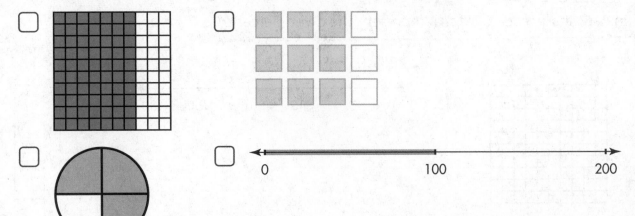

Name _____

Solve & Share

The grid is shaded with blue, orange, and yellow. What part of the grid is shaded blue? What part is shaded orange? What part of the grid is shaded? Write each answer as a fraction, decimal, and percent. *Solve this problem any way you choose.*

I can ...
write equivalent values as fractions, decimals, or percents.

Content Standard 6.RP.A.3c
Mathematical Practices MP.1, MP.2, MP.3, MP.7

You can make sense of the problem by using a drawing.

Look Back! MP.2 Reasoning How are the decimal and percent alike and how are they different?

Essential Question: How Are Fractions, Decimals, and Percents Related?

A

Each portion of time Teddy spends on homework is shown in the bar diagram. He spends 30% of his time reading, $\frac{3}{5}$ of his time doing math problems, and 0.10, or one tenth, of his time doing research for science.

Fractions, decimals, and percents are three ways to show parts of a whole. Write 30% as a fraction and a decimal, and write 0.10 as a fraction and percent.

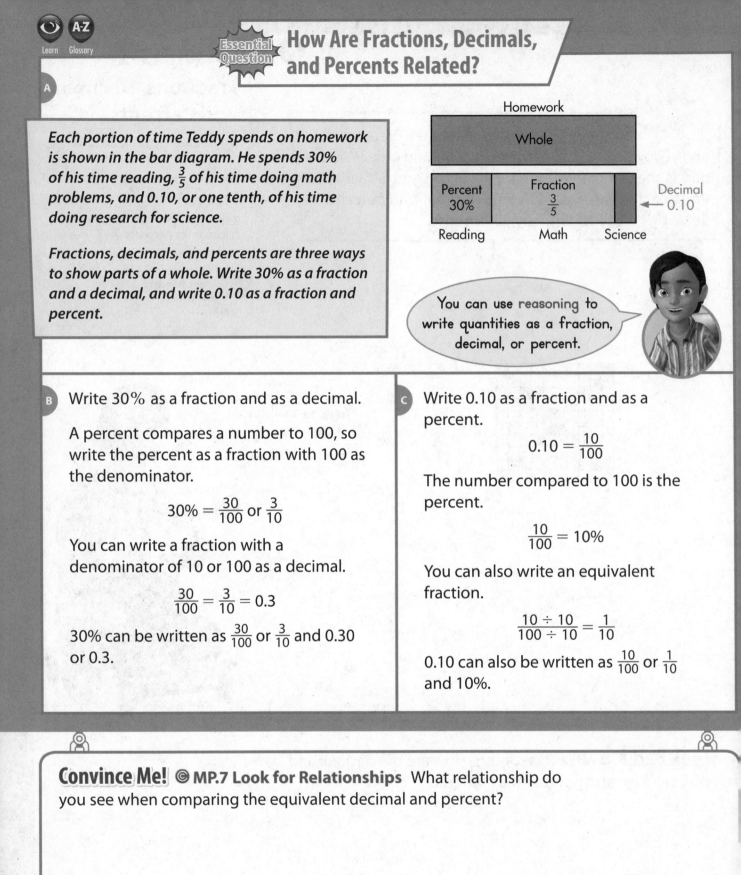

Homework

Whole

| Percent 30% | Fraction $\frac{3}{5}$ | Decimal ← 0.10 |

Reading   Math   Science

You can use reasoning to write quantities as a fraction, decimal, or percent.

B Write 30% as a fraction and as a decimal.

A percent compares a number to 100, so write the percent as a fraction with 100 as the denominator.

$$30\% = \frac{30}{100} \text{ or } \frac{3}{10}$$

You can write a fraction with a denominator of 10 or 100 as a decimal.

$$\frac{30}{100} = \frac{3}{10} = 0.3$$

30% can be written as $\frac{30}{100}$ or $\frac{3}{10}$ and 0.30 or 0.3.

C Write 0.10 as a fraction and as a percent.

$$0.10 = \frac{10}{100}$$

The number compared to 100 is the percent.

$$\frac{10}{100} = 10\%$$

You can also write an equivalent fraction.

$$\frac{10 \div 10}{100 \div 10} = \frac{1}{10}$$

0.10 can also be written as $\frac{10}{100}$ or $\frac{1}{10}$ and 10%.

Convince Me! © **MP.7 Look for Relationships** What relationship do you see when comparing the equivalent decimal and percent?

Another Example

Write $\frac{3}{5}$ as a decimal and as a percent.

If the denominator of a fraction is not 100, how can you change it to a decimal and percent?

Use division.
Write the fraction as a division problem. Then divide.

$$\begin{array}{r} 0.6 \\ 5)\overline{3.0} \\ -3\,0 \\ \hline 0 \end{array}$$

$\frac{3}{5}$ can be written as 0.6 or 0.60.

Write an equivalent rate.
A percent compares a number to 100.

$$\frac{3}{5} = \frac{x}{100}$$

$$\frac{3 \times 20}{5 \times 20} = \frac{60}{100}$$

$\frac{3}{5}$ can be written as $\frac{60}{100}$ or 60%.

☆ Guided Practice*

Do You Understand?

1. © MP.2 Reasoning Why can a fraction, a decimal, or a percent be written in equivalent forms?

Do You Know How?

In **2–4**, write each number in two equivalent forms as a fraction, decimal, or percent.

2. 27%   3. 0.91   4. $\frac{6}{100}$

Independent Practice*

In **5–10**, write each number in two equivalent forms as a fraction, decimal, or percent.

5. 0.25

6. $\frac{2}{2}$

7. 7%

8. 38%

9. $\frac{7}{8}$

10. 0.04

Math Practices and Problem Solving

11. Math and Science Many chemical elements can be found in the Earth's atmosphere. What fraction of Earth's atmosphere is made up of nitrogen?

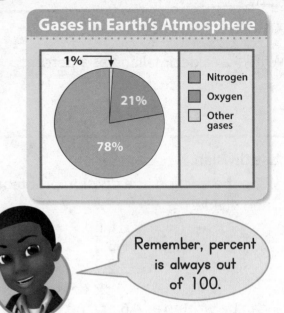

Gases in Earth's Atmosphere

1%

21%

78%

Nitrogen
Oxygen
Other gases

12. What part of Earth's atmosphere is made up of oxygen? Write the part as a decimal.

13. What percent of gases in Earth's atmosphere does the whole circle graph represent?

Remember, percent is always out of 100.

14. Number Sense Explain how you would use mental math to express $\frac{16}{25}$ as a percent.

15. Higher Order Thinking Ms. Rose bought a package of star stickers. Out of every 10 stars, 4 are gold. If there are 60 stars in the pack, what fraction of the stars in the pack is gold? What percent of the stars in the pack are gold?

16. © **MP.3 Construct Arguments** Films play continuously at the museum. If both films shown in the table to the right begin to play at the same time at 8 A.M., what time will it be before they begin playing together again? Explain.

DATA

Museum Film Schedule	
Film Title	**Length**
Introduction to the Museum	2 minutes
Profiles of Artists	10 minutes

© **Common Core Assessment**

17. Draw lines to match each fraction, decimal, or percent on the right to the equivalent fraction, decimal, or percent on the left.

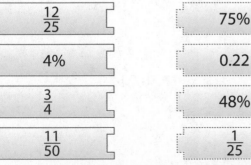

$\frac{12}{25}$	75%
4%	0.22
$\frac{3}{4}$	48%
$\frac{11}{50}$	$\frac{1}{25}$

Help Practice Tools Games
     Buddy

Another Look!

Fractions, decimals, and percents all name parts of a whole. How can you represent the shaded part of the whole?

Remember, when a fraction is not out of 100, you can divide the numerator by the denominator to find the decimal equivalent.

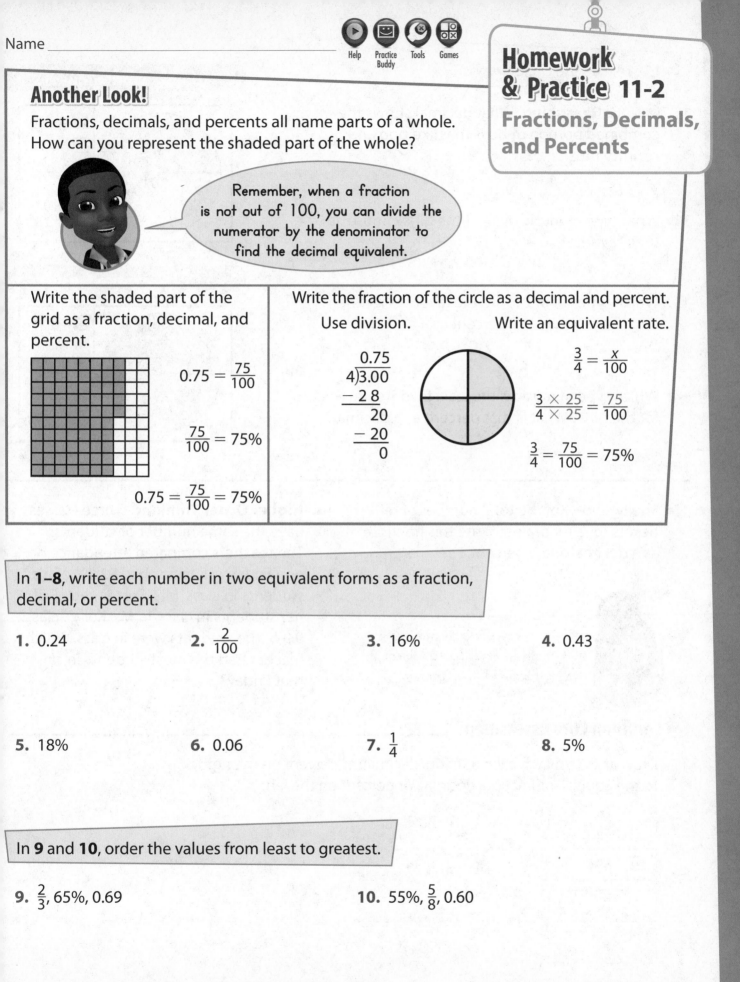

Write the shaded part of the grid as a fraction, decimal, and percent.

$0.75 = \frac{75}{100}$

$\frac{75}{100} = 75\%$

$0.75 = \frac{75}{100} = 75\%$

Write the fraction of the circle as a decimal and percent. Use division. Write an equivalent rate.

$$\begin{array}{r} 0.75 \\ 4\overline{)3.00} \\ -2\,8 \\ \hline 20 \\ -20 \\ \hline 0 \end{array}$$

$\frac{3}{4} = \frac{x}{100}$

$\frac{3 \times 25}{4 \times 25} = \frac{75}{100}$

$\frac{3}{4} = \frac{75}{100} = 75\%$

In **1–8**, write each number in two equivalent forms as a fraction, decimal, or percent.

1. 0.24

2. $\frac{2}{100}$

3. 16%

4. 0.43

5. 18%

6. 0.06

7. $\frac{1}{4}$

8. 5%

In **9** and **10**, order the values from least to greatest.

9. $\frac{2}{3}$, 65%, 0.69

10. 55%, $\frac{5}{8}$, 0.60

In **11–14**, use the circle graphs.

11. © MP.2 Reasoning What decimal shows the combined portion of boys that like pop and country music?

12. What type of music did $\frac{1}{5}$ of the girls choose as their favorite?

13. Which types of music are the favorites for the most boys? Write the percent as a fraction.

14. Which type of music is the least favorite music for the girls? What is that percent as a decimal?

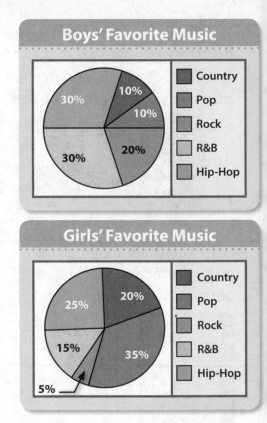

Boys' Favorite Music

30% 10% 10% 20% 30%

Country
Pop
Rock
R&B
Hip-Hop

Girls' Favorite Music

20% 25% 15% 35% 5%

Country
Pop
Rock
R&B
Hip-Hop

15. Shelly sold $\frac{8}{25}$ of the total number of raffle tickets for a fundraiser. Write this fraction as a decimal and a percent.

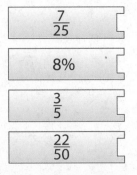

Try using mental math to find the equivalent forms of the fraction.

16. **Higher Order Thinking** Three classes have the same number of students. The teachers compared attendance on one Friday. Mr. Lopez had 92.5% of his students in class. Mrs. Foster had $\frac{19}{20}$ of her students in class. In Ms. Kelly's class, 0.9 of the students were in class. Which teacher had the most students in class that Friday?

© **Common Core Assessment**

17. Draw lines to match each fraction, decimal, or percent on the right to the equivalent fraction, decimal, or percent on the left.

$\frac{7}{25}$ 60%

8%   0.44

$\frac{3}{5}$ $\frac{2}{25}$

$\frac{22}{50}$ 28%

© Pearson Education, Inc. 6

Name _____

Solve & Share

Marci, Bobby, and Max began their homework at the same time. Marci finished her homework in 60 minutes. Bobby finished his homework in 50% of Marci's time. Max finished his homework in 150% of Marci's time. How long did each of them work? Use the number lines to help you.

I can ...
write percents that are greater than 100 or less than 1.

© Content Standard 6.RP.A.3c
Mathematical Practices MP.2, MP.3, MP.4

You can model with math to show a part that is greater than a whole.

Marci ⟵————|————|————|————⟶

Bobby ⟵————|————|————|————⟶

Max ⟵————|————|————|————⟶

Look Back! © MP.2 Reasoning Did Max spend more or less time on his homework than Marci?

A

Jan and Kim built model cars for a science project. Kim's car traveled 140% as far as Jan's car. How can you write 140% as a fraction and as a decimal?

START

Jan

Kim

0%   100%   140%

The distance Jan's car traveled represents the whole or 100%.

B Write 140% as a fraction compared to 100.

$$140\% = \frac{140}{100}$$

Use division to write an equivalent fraction.

$$140\% = \frac{140 \div 20}{100 \div 20} = \frac{7}{5}$$

140% can be written as $\frac{140}{100}$ or $\frac{7}{5}$.

The fraction equivalent of a percent greater than 100 has a numerator greater than the denominator.

C You can use reasoning or division to write 140% as a decimal.

Use reasoning.   Use division.

$$140\% = \frac{140}{100}$$
$$= \frac{14}{10}$$
$$= 1.4$$

$$
\begin{array}{r}
1.4 \\
100\overline{)140.0} \\
-100 \\
\hline
400 \\
-400 \\
\hline
0
\end{array}
$$

140% can be written as 1.4.

A decimal value greater than 1 will always be a percent greater than 100%.

Convince Me! © **MP.2 Reasoning** How would you write 1.75 as a percent? Give an example of when you would use a percent that is greater than 100.

Another Example

Write $\frac{1}{2}$% as a fraction and as a decimal.

> A percent less than 1 is less than $\frac{1}{100}$ of the whole.

Use the definition of percent to write $\frac{1}{2}$% as a fraction. Percent means *out of 100*, so you can divide $\frac{1}{2}$ by 100.

$$\frac{1}{2}\% = \frac{1}{2} \div 100$$

$$= \frac{1}{2} \times \frac{1}{100} \quad \text{Multiply by the reciprocal, } \frac{1}{100}.$$

$$= \frac{1}{200}$$

$\frac{1}{2}$% can be written as $\frac{1}{200}$.

Use the definition of percent to write $\frac{1}{2}$% as a decimal.

$$\frac{1}{2}\% = 0.5\% \qquad \text{Write } \frac{1}{2} \text{ as the decimal 0.5.}$$

$$= \frac{0.5}{100} \qquad \text{Write 0.5\% as a fraction.}$$

$$= \frac{5}{1,000} = 0.005 \quad \text{Use equivalent fractions and reasoning to write a decimal.}$$

$\frac{1}{2}$% can be written as 0.005.

☆ Guided Practice *

Do You Understand?

1. **© MP.2 Reasoning** Explain why 140% is greater than 1.

2. Explain the difference between $\frac{1}{2}$ and $\frac{1}{2}$%.

Do You Know How?

In **3–6**, write each percent as a fraction and as a decimal.

3. 150%

4. 0.2%

5. 325%

6. $\frac{3}{10}$%

☆ Independent Practice ☆

In **7–10**, write each percent as a fraction and as a decimal.

7. $\frac{2}{5}$%

8. 322%

9. .54%

10. 210%

Math Practices and Problem Solving

11. **ⓒ MP.2 Reasoning** How do you express 200% as a fraction and as a decimal?

The *Queen Mary* 2 is more than 200% longer than the Washington Monument is high.

Washington Monument

12. **Number Sense** About $\frac{3}{4}$ of the staterooms on the *Queen Mary 2* have balconies. How would you express this number as a decimal and as a percent?

13. The fastest boat can reach speeds over 710% as fast as the *Queen Mary 2*. How would you express this number as a fraction and as a decimal?

14. The weight of the Washington Monument is about 105% as much as the *Queen Mary 2*. Write this percent as a fraction and a decimal.

15. **ⓒ MP.3 Critique Reasoning** Nathan set his computer to print at 50% of the 8.5 in. × 11 in. page he normally uses. Allen thinks a document 50% its size will look huge. Is Allen correct about Nathan's printed report? Explain.

16. **Higher Order Thinking** A photo of a mosquito in a science book is increased to 635% as large as the actual size. If the mosquito is 16 millimeters, what is the size of the mosquito in the picture?

ⓒ Common Core Assessment

17. Cooper weighs 20 pounds. When he is an adult dog, he will weigh about 315% as much as his current weight.

Write 315% as a fraction and as a decimal.

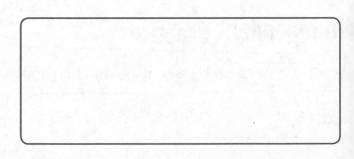

Name _____

Help   Practice Buddy   Tools   Games

Another Look!

Write 275% and $\frac{1}{5}$% as fractions and as decimals.

You can use what you know about percents to express percents greater than 100 or less than 1 in equivalent forms.

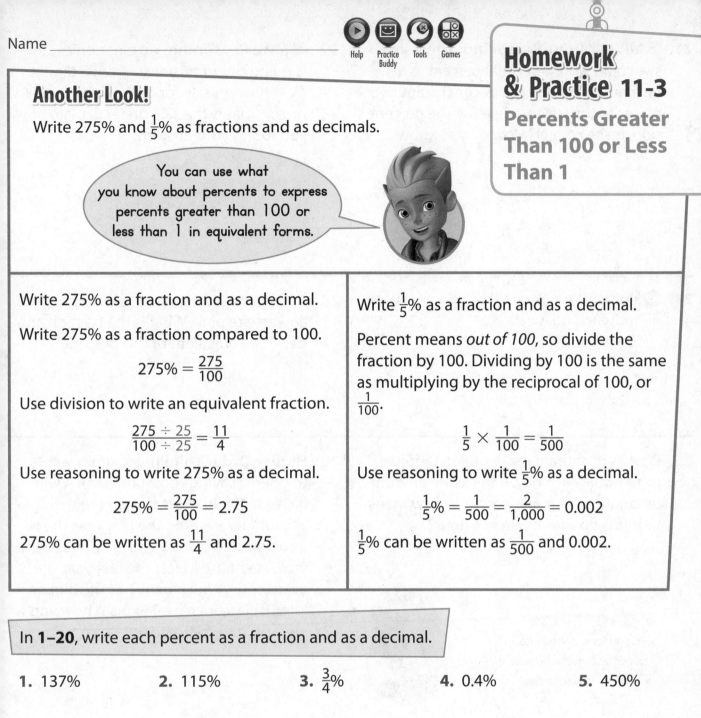

Write 275% as a fraction and as a decimal.

Write 275% as a fraction compared to 100.

$$275\% = \frac{275}{100}$$

Use division to write an equivalent fraction.

$$\frac{275 \div 25}{100 \div 25} = \frac{11}{4}$$

Use reasoning to write 275% as a decimal.

$$275\% = \frac{275}{100} = 2.75$$

275% can be written as $\frac{11}{4}$ and 2.75.

Write $\frac{1}{5}$% as a fraction and as a decimal.

Percent means *out of 100*, so divide the fraction by 100. Dividing by 100 is the same as multiplying by the reciprocal of 100, or $\frac{1}{100}$.

$$\frac{1}{5} \times \frac{1}{100} = \frac{1}{500}$$

Use reasoning to write $\frac{1}{5}$% as a decimal.

$$\frac{1}{5}\% = \frac{1}{500} = \frac{2}{1,000} = 0.002$$

$\frac{1}{5}$% can be written as $\frac{1}{500}$ and 0.002.

In **1–20**, write each percent as a fraction and as a decimal.

1. 137% 2. 115% 3. $\frac{3}{4}$% 4. 0.4% 5. 450%

6. 101% 7. $\frac{9}{25}$% 8. 0.22% 9. 810% 10. $\frac{3}{10}$%

11. 0.25% 12. 160% 13. 120% 14. 90% 15. 45%

16. 0.35% 17. 725% 18. 100.5% 19. 1,000% 20. 198%

21. **© MP.3 Critique Reasoning** Jamie said she could write a decimal percent as a decimal by moving the decimal point two places to the left and deleting the percent sign. Is she correct? How do you know?

22. **© MP.2 Reasoning** An electronics store is going out of business. A $458 digital TV is now on sale for 60% off the regular price. What is the sale price? Explain how you found your answer.

23. **A-Z Vocabulary** A rate that compares one quantity to 100 is called a _____.

24. At the botanical gardens $\frac{3}{5}$% of the flowers are pink. What is the fraction and decimal equivalent of this percent?

25. David's restaurant makes 1,860 taquitos in 12 hours each day. If the same amount of taquitos are made per hour, how many taquitos do they make in 1 hour?

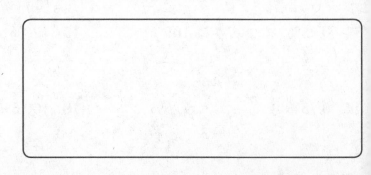

You are reasoning quantitatively when you find a unit rate.

26. **Higher Order Thinking** Lauren wants to open a savings account. Bank A will increase the interest rate on the savings account by $\frac{1}{4}$% after the first year she is a customer. Bank B offers an interest rate increase of 0.2% after the first year she is a customer. Which bank has the higher interest rate increase? Explain how you were able to compare the rates.

© Common Core Assessment

27. The image of a plant cell in a science book is enlarged to show the detail of its layers. The actual size of a plant cell is $\frac{1}{8}$% of the picture.

Write $\frac{1}{8}$% as a fraction and as a decimal.

Name _____

☆ ☆
Solve & Share

Sarah needs to correctly answer 78% of the questions on her next math test. The test has 40 questions. About how many questions must Sarah answer correctly on the test? *Solve this problem any way you choose.*

I can ...
estimate the percent of a number using equivalent fractions and compatible numbers.

© **Content Standard** 6.RP.A.3c
Mathematical Practices MP.1, MP.2, MP.7

You can use reasoning to understand how fractions relate to percents.

Look Back! © **MP.7 Use Structure** On her last test, Sarah answered 82% of 60 questions correctly. About how many questions did she answer correctly? Use estimation.

A

This graph shows the eye colors among 500 students at a school. About how many students have brown eyes? blue eyes?

You can use what you know about percents and their fraction equivalents to estimate.

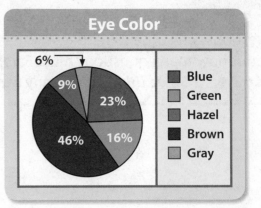

Eye Color

6%

9%

23%

46%

16%

- Blue
- Green
- Hazel
- Brown
- Gray

B

According to the graph, 46% of the students have brown eyes.

Estimate 46% of 500.

$46\% \approx 50\%$ and $50\% = \frac{1}{2}$

So, 46% of 500 is about $\frac{1}{2}$ of 500.

$$\frac{1}{2} \text{ of } 500 = 250$$

About 250 students have brown eyes.

C

According to the graph, 23% of the students have blue eyes.

Estimate 23% of 500.

$23\% \approx 25\%$ and $25\% = \frac{1}{4}$

So, 23% of 500 is about $\frac{1}{4}$ of 500.

$$\frac{1}{4} \text{ of } 500 = 125$$

About 125 students have blue eyes.

Convince Me! © **MP.7 Use Structure** Suppose the graph shows the percent of eye color among 118 students in a 6th-grade class. About how many 6th-grade students would have green eyes? Explain how you can use estimation to find the answer.

Name _____

☆ Guided Practice ☆*

Do You Understand?

1. © **MP.2 Reasoning** Explain how to estimate 32% of 212.

2. © **MP.7 Use Structure** Out of 195 students, 9% of the students have hazel eyes. How can you estimate the number of students with hazel eyes?

Do You Know How?

In **3** and **4**, estimate the percent of each number.

3. 47% of 77

   47% ≈ _____   77 ≈ _____

   _____ of _____ = 40

4. 18% of 48

   18% ≈ _____   48 ≈ _____

   _____ of _____ = 10

You can estimate using compatible numbers.

☆ Independent Practice ☆

In **5–16**, estimate the percent of each number.

5. 74% of 63

6. 18% of 96

7. 47% of 183

8. 8% of 576

9. 34% of 55

10. 27% of 284

11. 67% of 866

12. 4% of 802

13. 47% of 78

14. 33% of 238

15. 65% of 89

16. 6% of 489

*For another example, see Set D on page 586.

Math Practices and Problem Solving

17. There are about 300 million residents in the U.S. If 36% of them live in the South, estimate how many live in other areas of the U.S.

18. There are 13 students who play the trumpet and 15 who play the drums. What do the ratios 15:13 and 15:28 represent?

19. Number Sense If 10% of 60 is 6, what is 5% of 60? Explain how you found your answer.

20. © MP.1 Make Sense and Persevere Roland has 180 coins in his collection. Approximately 67% of the coins are quarters. About how much money does he have in quarters?

21. Higher Order Thinking Lea spent 25% of x hours at her part-time job. What is x if 25% of x is about 30 hours? Explain how you estimated and which property of equality you used to find x.

22. © MP.2 Reasoning Vanessa scored 78% on a test with 120 questions. What benchmark fraction would you use to estimate the number of questions that Vanessa answered correctly? Explain your reasoning.

© Common Core Assessment

23. Josie received an 84% on her last math test. The test had 50 questions.

What is the approximate number of questions Josie answered correctly?

Name _____

Another Look!

Using fraction equivalents can help you estimate the percent of a number.

You can also use compatible numbers to estimate.

Estimate 8% of 300,000.

$8\% \approx 10\%$ and $10\% = \frac{1}{10}$

$\frac{1}{10}$ of 300,000 = 30,000

8% of 300,000 is about 30,000.

Estimate 27% of 297.

$297 \approx 300$

$27\% \approx 25\%$ and $25\% = \frac{1}{4}$

$\frac{1}{4}$ of 300 = 75

27% of 297 is about 75.

Leveled Practice In **1–3**, fill in the blanks to estimate the percent of each number.

1. 24% of 94

   24% ≈ ____

   94 ≈ ____

   ____ of ____ = 25

2. 54% of 489

   54% ≈ ____

   489 ≈ ____

   ____ of ____ = 250

3. 8% of 212

   8% ≈ ____

   212 ≈ ____

   ____ of ____ = 20

In **4–12**, estimate the percent of each number.

4. 35% of 102

5. 42% of 307

6. 79% of 13

7. 84% of 897

8. 13% of 97

9. 28% of 95

10. 61% of 211

11. 19% of 489

12. 48% of 641

13. Tonya bought 13 tickets to a concert for $852.15. What was the cost of each ticket?

14. **Number Sense** If 10% of a number is 100, what is 15% of that number? Explain how you determined your answer.

15. With a full ink cartridge, the printer can print 2,500 pages. The printer cartridge is now 37% full. What is the best estimate of the number of pages the printer can still print?

16. **© MP.2 Reasoning** On a rainy day, 76% of the students in the school brought umbrellas. There are 600 students in the school. About how many students brought umbrellas?

17. **Higher Order Thinking** Marcus spent 20% of y dollars to pay for his car to be repaired. What is y if 20% of y is about $40? Explain how you estimated and which property of equality you used to find y.

18. **© MP.1 Make Sense and Persevere** Amanda's dog Zazau ate almost 18% of the 4 dozen cookies she baked. Estimate the number of cookies Zazau ate.

Remember, there are 12 cookies in a dozen.

© Common Core Assessment

19. At a middle school with 720 students, 78% of the students said they prefer rock music.

    About how many students prefer rock music?

Name _____

☆ ☆
Solve & Share

Lauren bought a jacket that was on sale. She paid 40% of the original price of $75. How much did Lauren pay for the jacket? *Solve this problem any way you choose.*

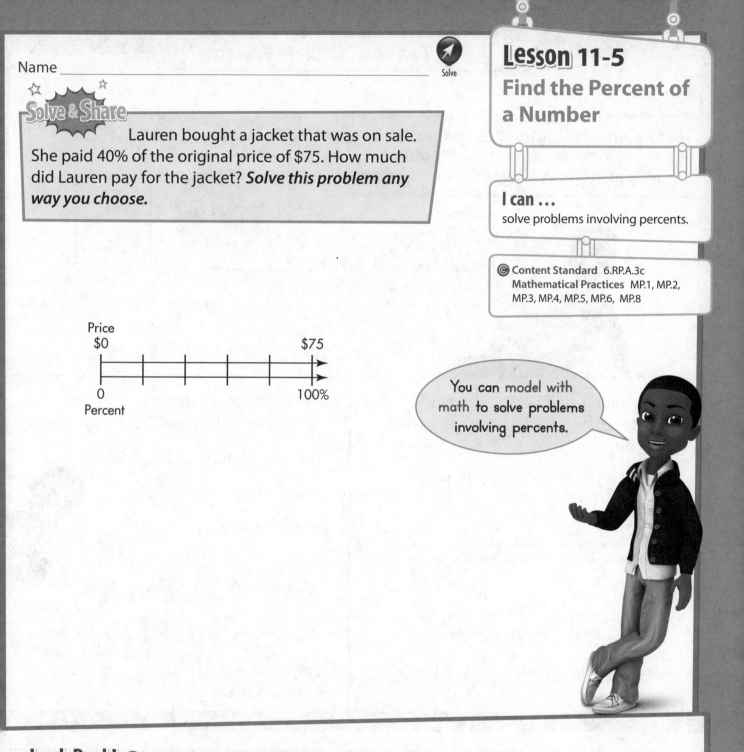

Price
$0 $75

0   100%
Percent

You can model with math to solve problems involving percents.

Look Back! © **MP.8 Generalize** When finding the percent of a number, how can you tell if your answer is reasonable? Will the answer be greater than or less than the original amount? Explain.

Essential Question **How Can You Calculate Percents?**

A

The fourth, fifth, and sixth graders at Great Oaks School are taking a field trip. Of the 575 students attending the field trip, how many are sixth graders?

Students Attending Field Trip

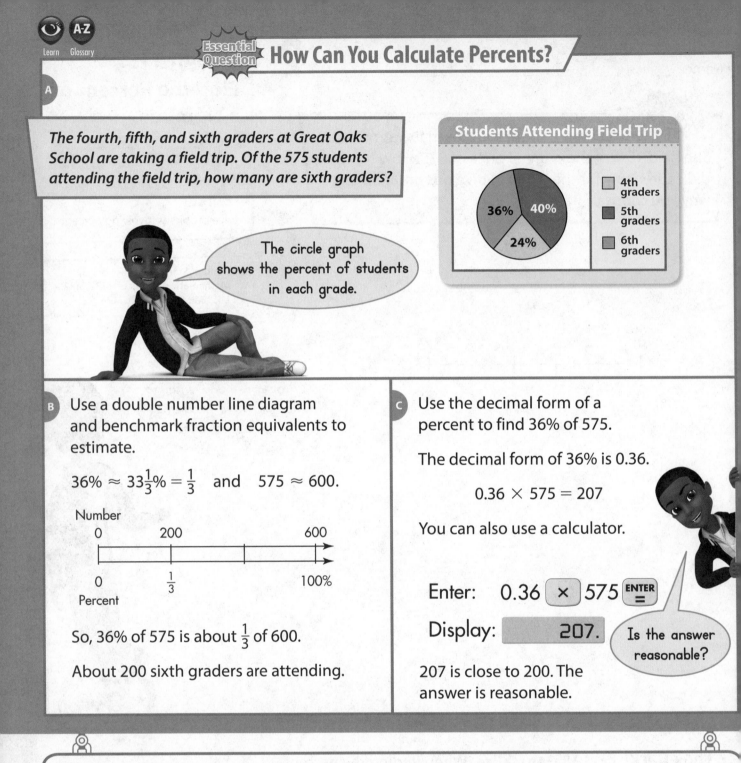

36% 40%

24%

☐ 4th graders
■ 5th graders
☐ 6th graders

The circle graph shows the percent of students in each grade.

B Use a double number line diagram and benchmark fraction equivalents to estimate.

$36\% \approx 33\frac{1}{3}\% = \frac{1}{3}$ and $575 \approx 600$.

Number

0   200   600

0        $\frac{1}{3}$ 100%
Percent

So, 36% of 575 is about $\frac{1}{3}$ of 600.

About 200 sixth graders are attending.

C Use the decimal form of a percent to find 36% of 575.

The decimal form of 36% is 0.36.

$0.36 \times 575 = 207$

You can also use a calculator.

Enter: 0.36 ⨯ 575 **ENTER =**

Display: 207.

Is the answer reasonable?

207 is close to 200. The answer is reasonable.

Convince Me! © MP.4 Model with Math Suppose 68% of the students attending the field trip were boys. How can you use the double number line shown above to help you find the number of boys and check for reasonableness?

Another Example

You can solve problems that involve finding the part or a percent.

> You can model with math by writing an equation to solve a problem.

What is 4.5% of 60?

Write an equation.

Let x = the unknown part.

$x = 0.045 \cdot 60$ ← Write 4.5% as a decimal.

$x = 2.7$

So, 2.7 is 4.5% of 60.

What percent of 92 is 11.5?

Write an equation.
Let p = the percent value.

$p \cdot 92 = 11.5$

$92p = 11.5$ Commutative Property

$\dfrac{92p}{92} = \dfrac{11.5}{92}$ Division Property of Equality

$p = 0.125 = 12.5\%$

So, 12.5% of 92 is 11.5.

☆ Guided Practice ☆

Do You Understand?

1. **© MP.6 Be Precise** In the expression 34% of 60, what operation does the word "of" mean?

2. **© MP.5 Use Appropriate Tools** How can you use a calculator to find what percent of 180 is 108?

Do You Know How?

In **3**, find the part.

3. What is 26% of 50?

In **4**, find the percent.

4. What percent of 315 is 126?

Independent Practice ☆

In **5–7**, find each part or each percent.

5. What is 35% of 10?

6. What percent of 75 is 33?

7. What is 2.25% of 24?

Math Practices and Problem Solving

8. © **MP.4 Model with Math** How can you use the double number line diagram to find what percent 270 is of 450?

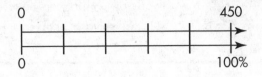

9. Nikki has rowing lessons every 4 days and tennis lessons every 7 days. If she had both lessons on the last day of the previous month, when will she have both lessons on the same day of the current month?

10. © **MP.6 Be Precise** Miguel collected aluminum cans for recycling. He collected a total of 150 cans. If 58% of the cans he collected were soda cans, how many other cans did he collect?

11. An electronics store donated a percent of every sale to charity. The total sales were $7,150 so the store donated $429. What percent of $7,150 was donated to charity?

12. © **MP.1 Make Sense and Persevere** Martina painted her bedroom walls with two different colors. She painted part of the room purple and another part pink. If the surface area of the walls in her room is 320 ft^2 and she painted 96 ft^2 purple, what percent of the room did she paint pink?

13. Higher Order Thinking Thomas has an album that holds 600 baseball cards. Each page of the album holds 6 cards. If 45% of the album is empty, how many pages are filled with baseball cards?

© Common Core Assessment

14. Ava's aquarium is 95% filled with water. The tank holds 1,120 gallons of water.

Select the remaining number of gallons of water needed to fill the aquarium to the top.

 Ⓐ 1,120 gallons

 Ⓑ 1,010 gallons

 Ⓒ 101 gallons

 Ⓓ 56 gallons

Help Practice Tools Games
      Buddy

Another Look!

When reading math expressions like "18% of 80", the word "of" means multiply.

What number is 12% of 6.75?

Write an equation.

Let x = the unknown part.

$x = 0.12 \cdot 6.75$ ← Write 12% as a decimal.

$x = 0.81$

0.81 is 12% of 6.75.

What percent of 64 is 4.8?

Write an equation.
Let p = the percent value.

$p \cdot 64 = 4.8$

$64p = 4.8$ Commutative Property

$\frac{64p}{64} = \frac{4.8}{64}$ Division Property of Equality

$p = 0.075 = 7.5\%$

4.8 is 7.5% of 64.

In **1–9**, find each part.

1. What is 8% of 200?

2. What is 12% of 800?

3. What is 12.8% of 312.5?

4. What is 46% of 388?

5. What is 86% of 20?

6. What is 300% of 24?

7. What is 99% of 100?

8. What is 110% of 333?

9. What is 4.75% of 2,000?

In **10–18**, find each percent.

10. What percent of 186 is 93?

11. What percent of 28 is 7?

12. What percent of 250 is 182?

13. What percent of 88 is 77?

14. What percent of 965 is 193?

15. What percent of 2,160 is 270?

16. What percent of 1,000 is 195?

17. What percent of 95 is 19?

18. What percent of 116 is 435?

In **19–21**, use the table.

19. © **MP.2 Reasoning** James has saved $200 to purchase some skateboarding equipment. Can he spend less than 50% of his savings on skateboarding shoes and knee pads? Explain.

Equipment Price List
Skateboard: $100
Skateboarding Shoes: $60
Knee Pads: $30
Elbow Pads: $20
Wrist Guards: $20
Helmet: $50
Ramp: $115

20. Which item or combination of items can James buy with 25% of his savings?

21. © **MP.3 Construct Arguments** James has 75% of his savings left. Can he buy a skateboard and shoes? Explain.

22. **Higher Order Thinking** Katrina has a bookcase that holds 200 books. She can put 20 books on each shelf. If 20% of the bookcase is empty, how many shelves are filled with books?

23. © **MP.4 Model with Math** A 50-pound bag of horse feed is a mixture of corn and oats. If 70% of the bag is oats, how many pounds of corn are in a bag? Draw a double number line diagram to show how to find the answer.

© Common Core Assessment

24. Pamela's house has 3,996 ft² of walls. She hired a contractor to paint 2,997 ft² of the walls.

    Select the percent of Pamela's house that did **NOT** get painted.

    Ⓐ 25%

    Ⓑ 40%

    Ⓒ 75%

    Ⓓ 80%

Name _____

Solve & Share

A school soccer team won 80% of its matches. Out of all the matches played, the team won 40 matches. How many matches did the soccer team play? *Solve this problem any way you choose.*

I can ...
find the whole amount when given a part and the percent.

© Content Standard 6.RP.A.3c
Mathematical Practices MP.2, MP.3, MP.4, MP.6, MP.7

You can model with math by creating a double number line diagram to analyze the relationship between the quantities.

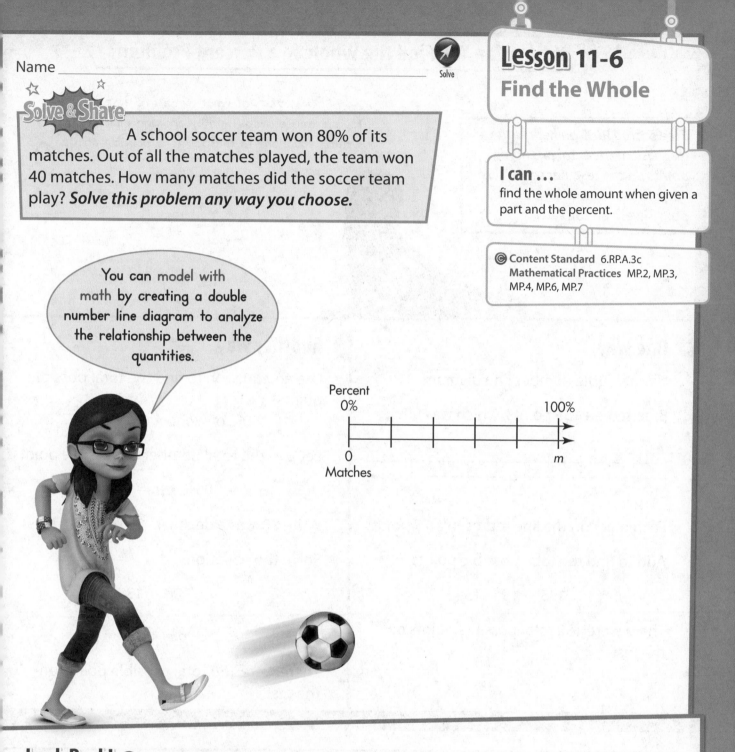

Percent
0%   100%

0   m
Matches

Look Back! © **MP.4 Model with Math** Write an equation to find the total number of matches played by the soccer team. Let *m* represent the total number of matches.

Essential Question **How Can You Find the Whole in a Percent Problem?**

A

Bree scored 90% on her math test. Out of the total possible points on the test, her score was 135 points. How many possible points were on the test?

Think, 90% of what number is 135? You can model with math by drawing pictures and writing equations to find the total possible points.

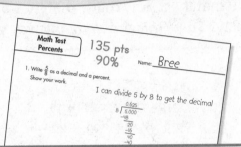

Math Test
Percents

135 pts
90%   Name: Bree

1. Write $\frac{5}{8}$ as a decimal and a percent.
Show your work.

I can divide 5 by 8 to get the decimal

```
    0.625
8 | 5.000
    -48
     20
    -16
     40
    -40
```

B **One Way**

Use a double number line diagram.

Bree scored 135 points, which was 90%.

```
0%                              90% 100%
|—|—|—|—|—|—|—|—|—|—|—→
0                              135  p
```

Each mark on the line represents 15 points.

Add to find the total possible points, p.

$$135 + 15 = 150$$

There were 150 total possible points on the test.

C **Another Way**

Use an equation to find the total possible points.

90% of *what number* is 135?

Let p = the total number of possible points.

$$90\% \cdot p = 135$$

Write 90% as a decimal. $90\% = \frac{90}{100} = 0.90$

Solve the equation.

$$0.90p = 135$$
$$p = 135 \div 0.90$$
$$p = 150$$

There were 150 total possible points on the test.

Convince Me! © **MP.4 Model with Math** Bree took another math test and scored 152 points, which was 95% of the total possible points on the test. Write and solve an equation to find the total number of possible points, p, on the test.

Name _____

Another Example

200% of what number is 40?

Is 200% the same as 2 times 100%?

One Way

Use a double number line diagram.

0%   100%   200%

0   n   40

$40 \div 10 = 4$

Each mark represents an increase of 4.
So, 100% is 20. 200% of 20 is 40.

Another Way

Write an equation.

$$200\% \cdot n = 40$$
$$2n = 40$$
$$\frac{2n}{2} = \frac{40}{2}$$
$$n = 20$$

200% of 20 is 40.

200% is the same as 2 times 100%.

☆ Guided Practice *

Do You Understand?

1. © MP.6 Be Precise Tony participated in 6 races, or 10% of the events. Do the 6 races represent the part, the percent, or the whole? Tell what the others represent.

Do You Know How?

2. 40% of what number is 80?

0%   40%   100%

0   80   n

☆ Independent Practice ☆

In 3–8, find each whole.

3. 35% of what number is 91?

4. 125% of what number is 45?

5. 10% of what number is 57?

6. 700% of what number is 1,540?

7. 34% of what number is 170?

8. 56% of what number is 14?

Math Practices and Problem Solving

9. **Algebra** The record for a city's greatest 1-day rainfall is 6.64 inches. Write an inequality to represent a rainfall that would break this record.

10. © **MP.2 Reasoning** Carrie gave her hair stylist a $4.20 tip. The tip was 15% of the cost of the haircut. Write an equation to find h, the cost of the haircut.

11. © **MP.7 Use Structure** Solve each of the number sentences and describe the pattern.

80% of what number is 80?
60% of what number is 60?
127% of what number is 127?

12. © **MP.4 Model with Math** Lynn walks 25% of the way to school and then takes a bus the rest of the way. The bus stop is 0.5 mile from her house. How many miles does Lynn live from school? Use a double number line diagram to help you solve.

13. © **MP.4 Make Sense and Persevere** Sydney completed 60% of the math problems assigned for homework. She has 4 more problems to finish. How many math problems were assigned for homework?

14. **Higher Order Thinking** An hour before show time, only 105 people are seated for a concert. According to ticket sales, 95% of the people have yet to arrive. How many tickets were sold for the concert? Explain your thinking.

© **Common Core Assessment**

15. People use water to cook, clean, and drink every day. An estimate of 16.8% of the water used each day is for cleaning. If a family uses 67.2 gallons of water a day for cleaning, how many gallons do they use every day?

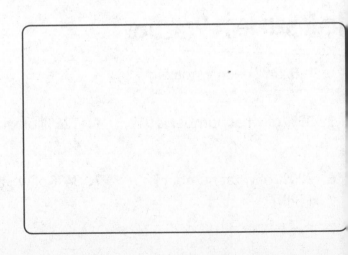

Another Look!

How can you find the whole when given a part and a percent?

You can use a double number line diagram or an equation to help you.

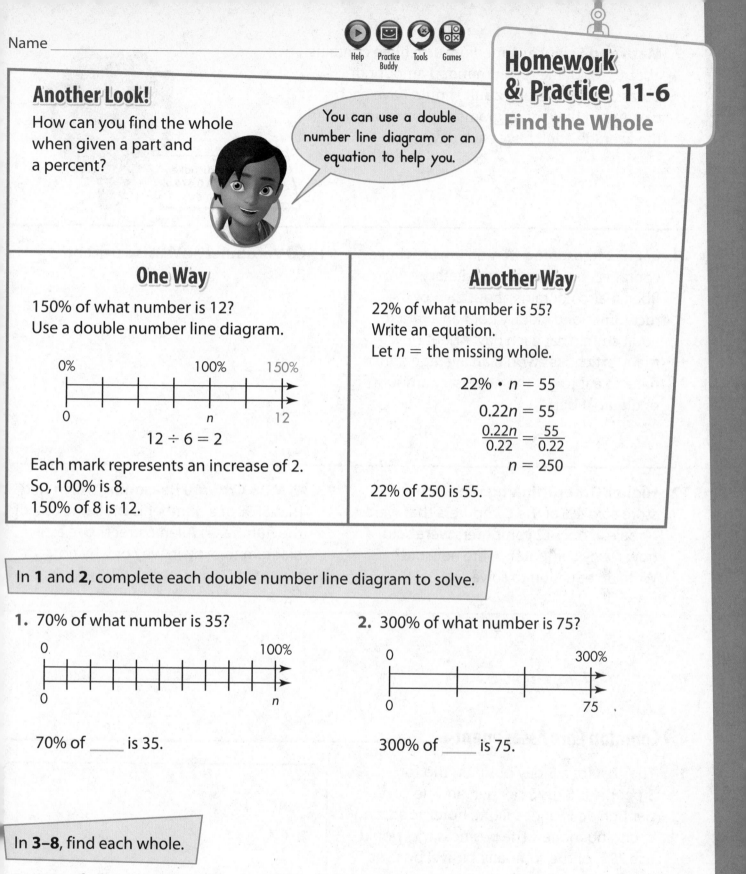

One Way

150% of what number is 12?
Use a double number line diagram.

0%   100%   150%

0   n   12

$12 \div 6 = 2$

Each mark represents an increase of 2.
So, 100% is 8.
150% of 8 is 12.

Another Way

22% of what number is 55?
Write an equation.
Let $n =$ the missing whole.

$$22\% \cdot n = 55$$
$$0.22n = 55$$
$$\frac{0.22n}{0.22} = \frac{55}{0.22}$$
$$n = 250$$

22% of 250 is 55.

In **1** and **2**, complete each double number line diagram to solve.

1. 70% of what number is 35?

0   100%

0   n

70% of _____ is 35.

2. 300% of what number is 75?

0   300%

0   75

300% of _____ is 75.

In **3–8**, find each whole.

3. 25% of what number is 2?   **4.** 150% of what number is 48?   **5.** 100% of what number is 6?

6. 50% of what number is 15?   **7.** 300% of what number is 51?   **8.** 200% of what number is 42?

9. **Math and Science** A medium artichoke contains about 13% of the recommended amount of potassium an average adult should have each day. About how many grams of potassium should the average adult have each day?

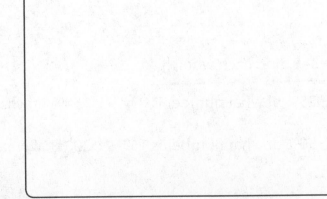

A medium artichoke contains about 0.474 g of potassium.

10. © **MP.2 Reasoning** A medium artichoke contains about 7 grams of dietary fiber. It also contains about 28% of the recommended dietary fiber an average adult should eat each day. About how many artichokes would an average adult have to eat to get the necessary amount of dietary fiber?

11. A-Z **Vocabulary** What is a percent?

12. **Higher Order Thinking** An electronics store sold 4% of the computers that were on sale. If only 12 computers were sold, how many computers were not sold? Write an equation to solve.

13. © **MP.3 Critique Reasoning** Allen said that 80% of a number is the same as $\frac{4}{5}$ of the number. Is Allen correct? Use a diagram to explain why or why not.

© **Common Core Assessment**

14. The cost for a 5-day business trip for 3 people is $1,975 per person. The cost per person includes flight, hotel, food, and spending money. The business trip would use 79% of the company's travel budget.

Find the total amount of money the company has budgeted for travel. Explain how you found the answer.

Name _____

Solve

Solve & Share

VideoLand is offering to pay 40% of the original price of any video game you bring to trade. Use a strategy to find the trade-in value for each of these games.

Original Prices:

Super Sam:	$30.00
Maze Maker II:	$45.00
Hippo Pat:	$24.00

I can ...
use what I know about percents to solve real-world problems.

© **Mathematical Practices** MP.8, MP.1, MP.2, MP.4, MP.6, MP.7
Content Standard 6.RP.A.3c

Thinking Habits

Be a good thinker!
These questions can help you.

- Are any calculations repeated?

- Can I generalize from examples?

- What shortcuts do I notice?

Look Back! © **MP.8 Generalize** A friend arrives at VideoLand with a video that originally cost $50.00. Explain to your friend the pattern you noticed for how to find the trade-in value.

Essential Question

How Do You Use Repeated Reasoning When Calculating Percentages?

A

The student council is selling items at a school fundraiser. They charge 150% of the cost of each item. What is the selling price of each item?

Original Cost of Each Fundraiser Item

Water bottle:	$6.00
T-shirt:	$7.00
Backpack:	$12.50

What do I need to do to solve this problem?

I have to use a strategy to find the selling price of an item and apply the strategy to find the selling prices of the other items.

Here's my thinking...

B

How can I make a generalization using repeated reasoning?

I can

- look at examples and see relationships.

- make a generalization based on what I know about finding percents.

- test whether my generalization works for other numbers.

C

Break apart the percent into two percents to solve mentally.

$$150\% = 100\% + 50\%$$

Water bottle ($6.00): $6.00 + $3.00
Water bottle selling price is $9.00.

Then apply this strategy to the other problems.

T-shirt ($7.00): $7.00 + $3.50   Backpack ($12.50): $12.50 + $6.25
T-shirt selling price is $10.50.   Backpack selling price is $18.75.

Then I justify that this strategy will work in any situation.

The percent of a number can be calculated as a single percent or you can break the percent apart into percents you can find mentally.

150% of 6 = 9   100% of 6 + 50% of 6 = 6 + 3 = 9

They are equal.

Convince Me! © MP.8 Generalize Your bank is advertising a monthly interest rate of $1\frac{1}{2}$%. If you deposit $120.00, how much will you earn after one month? Explain your reasoning.

☆ Guided Practice*

© MP.8 Generalize

The bicycles at a shop are on sale for 20% off. Henry is considering a bicycle that costs $150.00. How much will Henry save by purchasing the bicycle on sale?

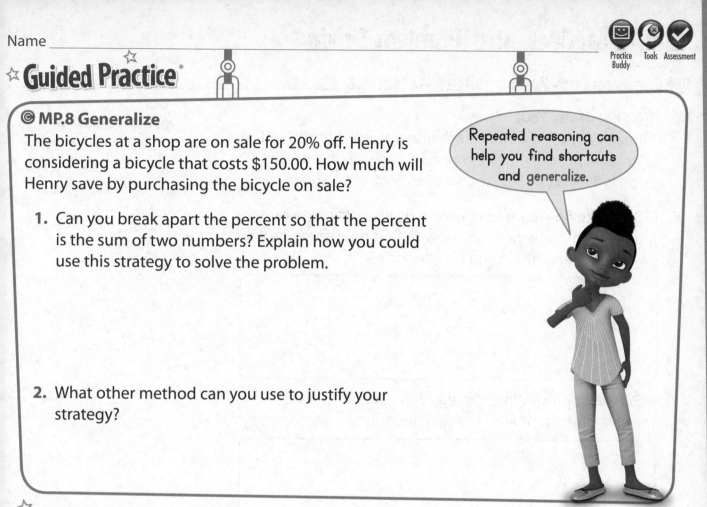

Repeated reasoning can help you find shortcuts and generalize.

1. Can you break apart the percent so that the percent is the sum of two numbers? Explain how you could use this strategy to solve the problem.

2. What other method can you use to justify your strategy?

☆ Independent Practice ☆

© MP.8 Generalize

Lena has $350.00 in a savings account. The bank offers 3% annual interest. How much interest will Lena's account earn in one year?

When you generalize and use repeated reasoning you notice patterns in calculations.

3. How can you use repeated reasoning to make a generalization about 3% of $350?

4. Test your generalization. Find 3% of $350.

5. What other way can you calculate the annual interest to show that your strategy will work when solving similar problems? Justify your reasoning.

For another example, see Set F on page 586.

Topic 11 | Lesson 11-7

Math Practices and Problem Solving

Common Core Performance Assessment

Big Sale of the Year

Tillman's Sporting Goods is offering a storewide 30%-off sale. Jesse has a 20%-off coupon he can use on the sale price. Is 20% off of 30% the same as 50% off? Explain.

6. **MP.1 Make Sense and Persevere** If Jesse wants to buy a tent, what does he need to know to find how much he will pay for the tent after using his coupon?

7. **MP.2 Reasoning** What strategy can you use to find the cost of the tent after the two discounts?

8. **MP.6 Be Precise** How much will Jesse pay for the tent using his coupon while it is on sale? Show your work.

You are using structure when you analyze patterns to make generalizations.

9. **MP.7 Use Structure** Compare the result of using a 20%-off coupon during a 30%-off sale to 50% off. Are the two sale prices the same? Use an example or counterexample to justify your answer.

Help Practice Buddy Tools Games

Another Look!

A smartphone is on sale for 40% off. What will you pay for the smartphone if its regular price is $120?

Tell how you can use repeated reasoning to find the sale price of the smartphone.

- I can make a generalization based on what I know about finding percents.

- I can test whether the generalization works for this problem.

Use what you know about finding percents to make a generalization. Test the generalization and justify your answer.

I can find 10% of the original price of the phone. Then I can use it to find the 40% discount or the sale price of 60% of the original price.

10% of $120.00 is $12.00.

The discount is $12.00 × 4 = $48.00.

The sale price of the phone is $120.00 − $48.00 = $72.00.

If the discount is 40% off, then the sale price is 60% of the original price. The sale price of the phone is $12.00 × 6 = $72.00. So, 40% off of $120 is the same as 60% of $120.

© MP.8 Generalize

Justine is buying art supplies. She has a 25% employee discount at an art supply store. What will Justine pay for the supplies?

1. What do you know about finding 25% of a number that can help you solve this problem?

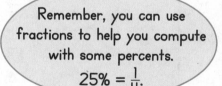

Art Store Prices:

Easel:	$84.00
Canvas:	$40.00
Oil Paints:	$120.00

2. Test your generalization. Find Justine's total cost for the canvas and oil paints. Show your work.

Remember, you can use fractions to help you compute with some percents. $25\% = \frac{1}{4}$.

3. Can you use the same strategy to find how much Justine would pay for an easel? Justify your reasoning.

Cross Country Training

Anthony is preparing for a 5K race. His best time is 20 minutes. The coach thinks Anthony can cut his time by 10%. Anthony sets a personal goal of cutting his time by 15%. What is the difference in time between the goal that the coach set and the goal that Anthony set?

4. **MP.4 Model with Math** Complete the double number line diagram to represent the goal that the coach set for Anthony. Explain the diagram.

5. **MP.7 Use Structure** Explain how you can use the diagram to determine the coach's goal time for Anthony.

6. **MP.8 Generalize** Explain how you can use repeated reasoning to find the goal that Anthony set for himself. Complete the double number line diagram to support your answer.

7. **MP.6 Be Precise** What is the difference in time between the two goals?

Name _____

Point & Tally

Find a partner. Get paper and a pencil. Each partner chooses a different color: light blue or dark blue.

Partner 1 and Partner 2 each point to a black number at the same time. Both partners multiply the numbers.

If the answer is on your color, you get a tally mark. Work until one partner has twelve tally marks.

I can ...
multiply multi-digit decimals.

© **Content Standard** 6.NS.B.3

Partner 1					Partner 2
12.3	4.412	36.972	17.1936	13.284	**2.5**
110.3	0.3792	0.492	0.6618	0.05688	**0.04**
63.2	0.0738	246.48	275.75	47.97	**1.08**
9.48	62.088	430.17	39.8	119.124	**3.9**
15.92	23.7	0.09552	2.528	0.6368	**0.006**
	30.75	68.256	158	10.2384	

Tally Marks for Partner 1

Tally Marks for Partner 2

Word List

- compatible numbers
- decimal
- equivalent fractions
- fraction
- percent
- ratio

Understand Vocabulary

Choose the best term from the Word List. Write it on the blank.

1. A ratio of a quantity to 100 is a _____.

2. A _____ compares two numbers or the number of items in two groups.

3. _____ are numbers that are easier to compute mentally.

Draw a line to match each *fraction*, *decimal*, or *percent* in Column A to the equivalent number in Column B.

Column A

4. $\frac{40}{50}$

5. 13%

6. 1.75

7. 155%

Column B

$1\frac{3}{4}$

$1\frac{11}{20}$

0.13

80%

Write *always*, *sometimes*, or *never*.

8. *Fractions* can _____ be written as decimals.

9. The *percent* of a whole is _____ less than the whole.

10. You can _____ find *compatible numbers* by rounding.

Use Vocabulary in Writing

11. Out of 230 students surveyed, 11% chose gymnastics as their favorite sport. Explain how you can estimate the number of students who chose gymnastics. Use at least 2 words from the Word List in your explanation.

Set A pages 541–546

Write the percent represented by the shaded part of the grid.

$\frac{54}{100}$ parts shaded = 54%

Write the percent of the number line that is shaded.

$\frac{2}{4} = \frac{2 \times 25}{4 \times 25} = \frac{50}{100} = 50\%$

Remember that *percent* means "of a hundred."

Write the percent of each figure that is shaded.

1.   2.

3.

Reteaching

Set B pages 547–552

Write 37% as a fraction and a decimal.

37% means 37 "of a hundred," or $\frac{37}{100}$.

$\frac{37}{100} = 37 \div 100 = 0.37$

Remember that you can use ratio reasoning to write equivalent forms of decimals, percents, and fractions.

Write each value in two other ways.

1. 0.16   2. $\frac{63}{100}$

3. 27%   4. $\frac{7}{8}$

5. 0.55   6. 7%

Set C pages 553–558

Write 221% as a fraction and a decimal.

Fraction as part of 100: $\frac{221}{100}$

Decimal: $\frac{221}{100} = 221 \div 100 = 2.21$

Write $\frac{1}{4}$% as a fraction and a decimal.

Fraction: $\frac{1}{4}\% = \frac{1}{4} \times \frac{1}{100} = \frac{1}{400}$

Decimal: $\frac{1}{4}\% = 0.25\% = \frac{0.25}{100}$

$= \frac{25}{10,000} = 0.0025$

Remember that percents less than 1% are less than $\frac{1}{100}$, and that percents greater than 100% are more than one whole.

Write each percent as a fraction and as a decimal.

1. 140%   2. $\frac{7}{10}$%

3. 375%   4. 0.33%

5. 0.5%   6. 250%

Set D pages 559–564

Estimate 24% of 83.

$24\% \approx 25\% = \frac{1}{4}$ and $83 \approx 80$

$\frac{1}{4} \times 80 = 20$

24% of 83 is about 20.

Remember that you can use benchmark fractions and compatible numbers to estimate percents.

Estimate the percent of each number.

1. 22% of 96

2. 38% of 58

Set E pages 565–570, 571–576

- Find 16% of 73.

  Change the percent to a decimal and multiply: $0.16 \times 73 = 11.68$.

  16% of 73 is 11.68

- What percent of 20 is 8?

  Write an equation: $x(20) = 8$.

  $x = 8 \div 20 = 0.4$ or 40%. 8 is 40% of 20.

- 80% of what number is 96?

  Change the percent to a decimal, and write an equation: $0.8n = 96$.

  $n = 96 \div 0.8 = 120$. 80% of 120 is 96.

Remember that you can write an equation to find the part, whole, or percent.

Find each part, percent, or whole.

1. 9% of 124

2. What percent of 20 is 3?

3. 80% of what number is 120?

4. 40% of what number is 10?

5. 43% of 82

6. What percent of 30 is 24?

Set F pages 577–582

Think about these questions to help you use **repeated reasoning** when solving percent problems.

Thinking Habits

- Are any calculations repeated?

- Can I generalize from examples?

- What shortcuts do I notice?

Remember that repeated reasoning can help you find a general method for solving problems.

A dive shop advertises a sale for 30% off. Carey wants to buy a wetsuit and scuba gear. Tags show the original prices: gear $180; wet suit $320.

1. What generalization can you make about the sales price of the scuba equipment?

2. How can you test and justify your strategy?

Name _____

1. Alicia and her father are painting a wall in their basement. She shaded a grid to show how much of the wall they have painted so far. What percent of the grid is shaded?

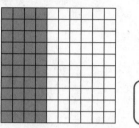

2. Margaret is saving money for her summer vacation. She calculates that her starting amount is 0.4% of the total amount she wants to save. What is 0.4% written as a decimal?

Ⓐ 0.0004

Ⓑ 0.004

Ⓒ 0.04

Ⓓ 0.4

3. Most U.S. households spend about 5% of their income on entertainment. Which of the following are equivalent to 5%? Choose all equivalent expressions.

☐ $\frac{1}{20}$

☐ $\frac{1}{5}$

☐ $\frac{5}{100}$

☐ $\frac{1}{2}$

☐ 0.05

☐ 0.005

4. The population of Gilbert increased 275%. Which of the following are equivalent to 275%?

4a. 275   ○ Yes ○ No

4b. $27\frac{1}{2}$ ○ Yes ○ No

4c. $2\frac{3}{4}$ ○ Yes ○ No

4d. $\frac{11}{4}$ ○ Yes ○ No

4e. 2.75   ○ Yes ○ No

5. A study found that 9% of dog owners brush their dog's teeth. Of 578 dog owners, about how many would be expected to brush their dog's teeth? Show your work.

6. Paula weeded 40% of her garden in 8 minutes. How many minutes will it take her to weed all of her garden? Explain how you solved the problem.

7. The circle graph shows the distribution of students at an elementary school.

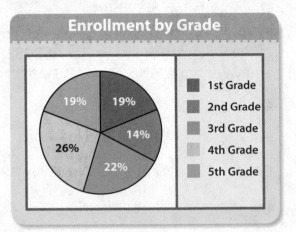

Enrollment by Grade

1st Grade
2nd Grade
3rd Grade
4th Grade
5th Grade

Part A

If there are 205 students in the school, about how many are in the 5th grade?

Part B

Explain how you made your estimate.

8. All but 4 state capitals have an interstate highway serving them. What percent of 50 is 4?

9. Draw lines to match each fraction, decimal, or percent on the right to an equivalent number on the left.

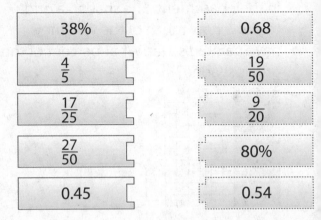

38%	0.68
$\frac{4}{5}$	$\frac{19}{50}$
$\frac{17}{25}$	$\frac{9}{20}$
$\frac{27}{50}$	80%
0.45	0.54

10. A coat and boots are on sale for 20% off. The regular price of the coat is $225. The regular price of the boots is $130.

Part A

Find the sale price of the coat. Show your work and explain your reasoning.

Part B

Ken wants to buy both the coat and the boots. How much will he pay if he buys them during the sale?

Name _____

Ed wants to borrow $20,000 from a bank to open a small gym. Three banks charge different interest rates.

1. The table shows the interest rates for each of the three options.

Table A

Bank	Annual Interest Rate	Repayment Period	Total Interest	Loan Plus Interest	Monthly Payment
First	7.5%	1 year			
City	8.2%	1 year			
Star	9%	1 year			

Part A

To find the total interest Ed must pay with each option, multiply the amount borrowed by the annual interest rate. Describe a strategy that you can use to find the total interest for the first option. Apply the strategy to find the total interest for all three options. Enter this in **Table A**.

Part B

For each option, find the total amount Ed must pay back (the loan amount plus the interest). Enter this in **Table A**.

Part C

Ed will have to make a payment each month. Calculate the amount and complete **Table A**.

2. To help decide the best loan option, Ed wants to know the percent profit he will make each month.

Part A

Total monthly expenses include the cost to run the gym, $5,000 per month, and the monthly loan repayment. Find Ed's total monthly expenses for each loan option. Enter this in **Table B**.

Table B

Bank	Repayment Period	Average Monthly Sales	Total Monthly Expenses	Average Monthly Profit	Estimated Percent Profit
First	1 year	$7,500			
City	1 year	$7,500			
Star	1 year	$7,500			

Part B

Ed expects to average $7,500 in sales per month the first year. Find Ed's average monthly profit. Explain how to find the monthly profit. Then complete **Table B**.

Part C

Explain how you found the estimated percent profit.

3. Ed's goal is to make the most profit. Which bank's loan do you think Ed should use to achieve his goal? Explain your choice.

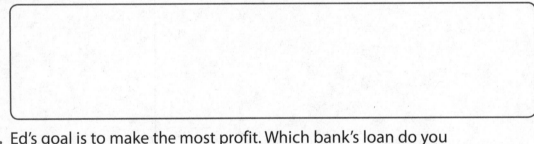

TOPIC 12

Divide Fractions by Fractions

Essential Question: What are standard procedures for estimating and finding quotients of fractions and mixed numbers?

Digital Resources

Solve | Learn | Glossary | Practice Buddy

Tools | Assessment | Help | Games

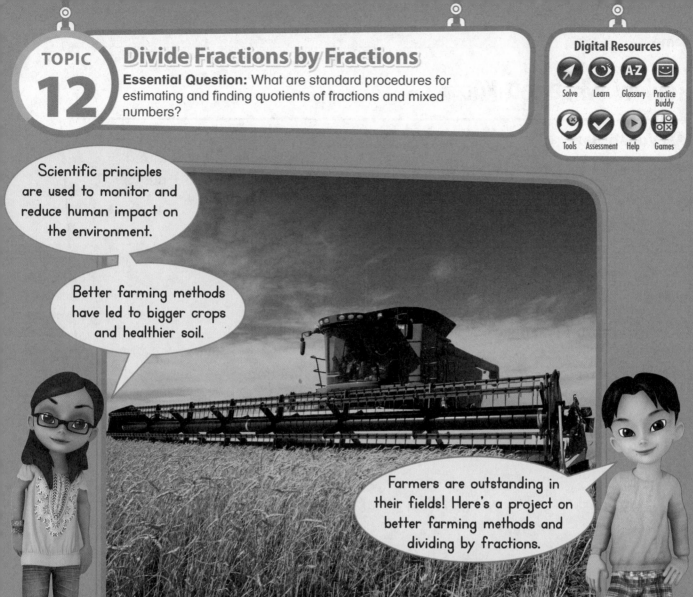

Scientific principles are used to monitor and reduce human impact on the environment.

Better farming methods have led to bigger crops and healthier soil.

Farmers are outstanding in their fields! Here's a project on better farming methods and dividing by fractions.

Math and Science Project: Farming by Fractions

Do Research Use the Internet or other sources to learn about three-field crop rotation. Also, research the benefits of using this method to farm.

Journal: Write a Report Include what you found. Also in your report:

- Calculate the number of fields that can be formed on a farm that is $3\frac{3}{5}$ acres.

- Plan a three-field crop rotation for the farm. Create a map to show what is planted in each field in turn.

- Describe how rotating crops reduces human impact on the environment.

Name _____

Review What You Know

Vocabulary

Choose the best term from the box.
Write it on the blank.

• dividend   • mixed number
• divisor
• equivalent expressions   • quotient

1. The result of a division problem is a(n) _____ .

2. The number used to divide is the _____ .

3. Expressions that have the same value are _____ .

4. A number that combines a whole number and a fraction is called a(n) _____ .

Solving Equations

Solve each equation.

5. $g \div 7 = 45$

6. $r + 312 = 487$

7. $\frac{k}{3} = 15$

8. $6m = 252$

9. $538 = a - 108$

10. $5w = 210$

Mixed Numbers and Fractions

Write each mixed number as a fraction. Write each fraction as a mixed number.

11. $8\frac{1}{3}$

12. $5\frac{3}{5}$

13. $2\frac{5}{8}$

14. $3\frac{4}{9}$

15. $\frac{24}{7}$

16. $\frac{43}{9}$

17. $\frac{59}{8}$

18. $\frac{32}{5}$

Verbal Expressions

19. How are the expressions "$\frac{1}{4}$ of 12" and "12 divided by 4" related?

Name _____

Lesson 12-1
Understand Division of Fractions

I can ...
use models to divide with fractions.

© Content Standard 6.NS.A.1
Mathematical Practices MP.2, MP.4

Solve & Share

Suppose it takes a $\frac{2}{3}$-foot length of leather strap to make one watchband. How many watchbands can be made from a 4-foot length of leather strap?

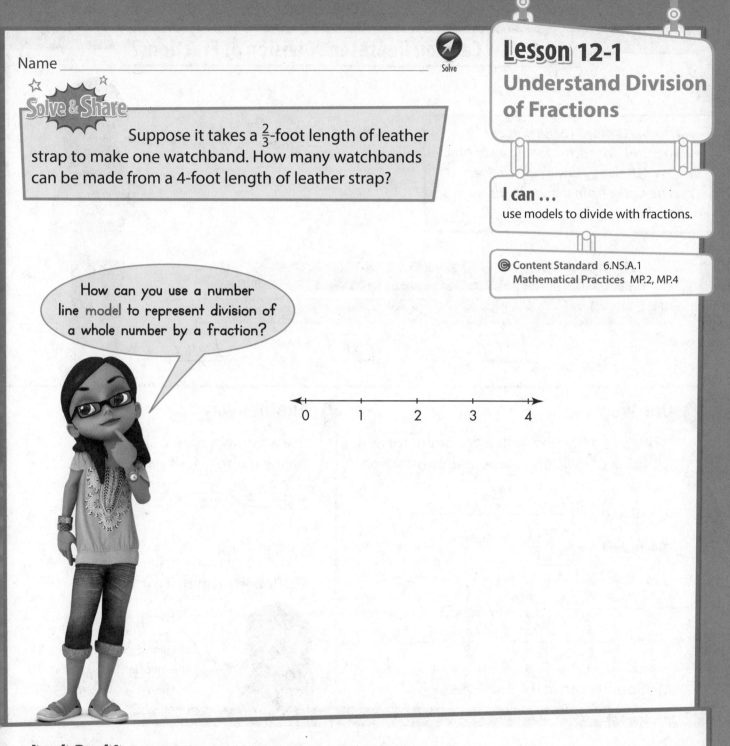

How can you use a number line model to represent division of a whole number by a fraction?

Look Back! © MP.4 Model with Math Write an equation that represents the problem and gives the solution.

Essential Question **How Can You Represent Division of Fractions?**

A

Mr. Roberts plans to use pieces of wood that are each $\frac{3}{4}$ foot long to build a set of shelves. How many shelves can he make from a board that is 3 feet long?

Think! How many $\frac{3}{4}$s are in 3?

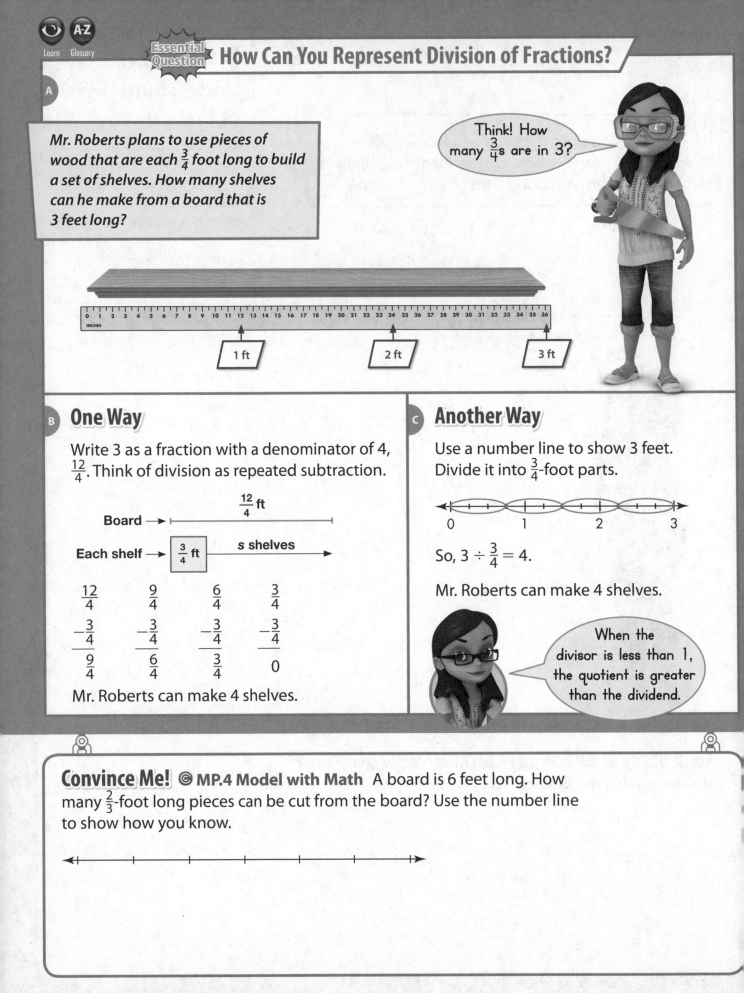

1 ft   2 ft   3 ft

B **One Way**

Write 3 as a fraction with a denominator of 4, $\frac{12}{4}$. Think of division as repeated subtraction.

$\frac{12}{4}$ ft

Board →

Each shelf → $\frac{3}{4}$ ft   s shelves

$\begin{array}{r}\frac{12}{4}\\-\frac{3}{4}\\\hline\frac{9}{4}\end{array}$ $\begin{array}{r}\frac{9}{4}\\-\frac{3}{4}\\\hline\frac{6}{4}\end{array}$ $\begin{array}{r}\frac{6}{4}\\-\frac{3}{4}\\\hline\frac{3}{4}\end{array}$ $\begin{array}{r}\frac{3}{4}\\-\frac{3}{4}\\\hline 0\end{array}$

Mr. Roberts can make 4 shelves.

C **Another Way**

Use a number line to show 3 feet. Divide it into $\frac{3}{4}$-foot parts.

0   1   2   3

So, $3 \div \frac{3}{4} = 4$.

Mr. Roberts can make 4 shelves.

When the divisor is less than 1, the quotient is greater than the dividend.

Convince Me! © **MP.4 Model with Math** A board is 6 feet long. How many $\frac{2}{3}$-foot long pieces can be cut from the board? Use the number line to show how you know.

Name _____

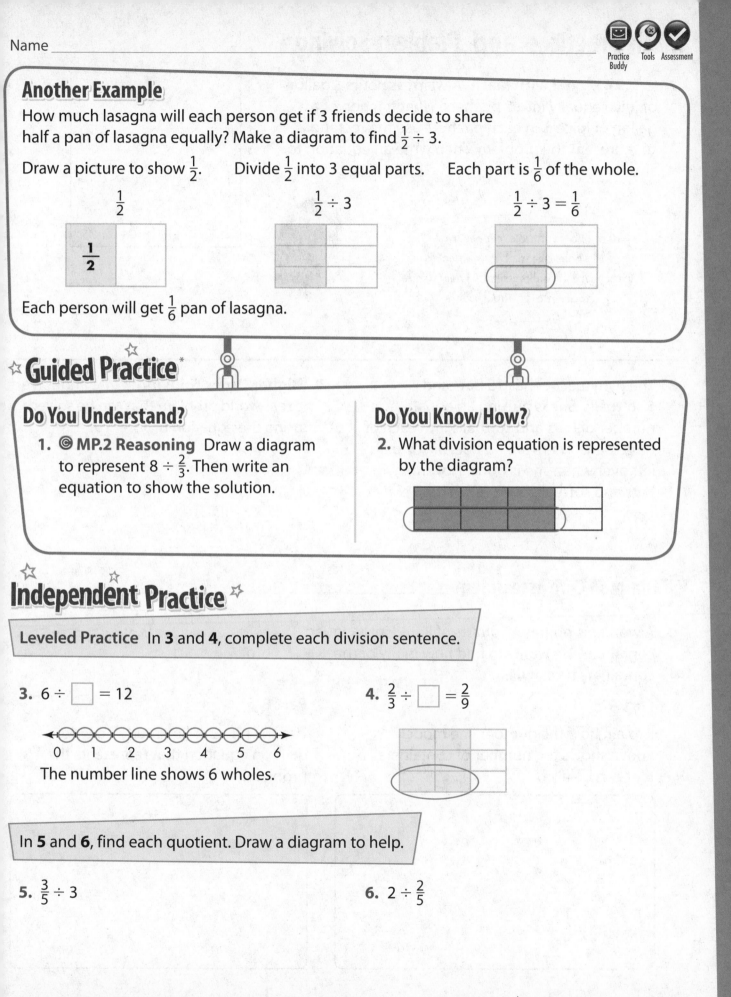

Another Example

How much lasagna will each person get if 3 friends decide to share half a pan of lasagna equally? Make a diagram to find $\frac{1}{2} \div 3$.

Draw a picture to show $\frac{1}{2}$.   Divide $\frac{1}{2}$ into 3 equal parts.   Each part is $\frac{1}{6}$ of the whole.

$\frac{1}{2}$ $\frac{1}{2} \div 3$ $\frac{1}{2} \div 3 = \frac{1}{6}$

Each person will get $\frac{1}{6}$ pan of lasagna.

Guided Practice

Do You Understand?

1. ⓒ **MP.2 Reasoning** Draw a diagram to represent $8 \div \frac{2}{3}$. Then write an equation to show the solution.

Do You Know How?

2. What division equation is represented by the diagram?

Independent Practice

Leveled Practice In **3** and **4**, complete each division sentence.

3. $6 \div \boxed{} = 12$

The number line shows 6 wholes.

4. $\frac{2}{3} \div \boxed{} = \frac{2}{9}$

In **5** and **6**, find each quotient. Draw a diagram to help.

5. $\frac{3}{5} \div 3$

6. $2 \div \frac{2}{5}$

For another example, see Set A on page 649.

Math Practices and Problem Solving

7. **MP.4 Model with Math** A waitress pours $\frac{3}{4}$ gallon of juice equally into 5 pitchers. What fraction of a gallon of juice is in each pitcher? Use the rectangle to represent the problem. Then write an equation to show the solution.

The rectangle represents 1 whole gallon. Draw lines to represent $\frac{3}{4}$ gallon first. Then divide that into 5 equal parts.

8. The gym teacher has 15 bats and 6 softballs. She is putting an equal number of bats and softballs into each of three bags. There are no bats or softballs left over when she is done. How many bats and softballs are in each bag?

9. **Higher Order Thinking** Write and solve a real-world problem that can be solved using the equation $8 \div \frac{4}{5} = 10$.

Common Core Assessment

10. A worker is pouring 3 quarts of liquid into $\frac{3}{8}$-quart containers. He wants to find how many of the containers he can fill.

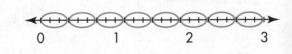

Part A

Explain how the number line model above shows the number of containers that can be filled.

Part B

Use the number line model to write a division equation that represents the problem.

Help Practice Buddy Tools Games

Another Look!

Find $\frac{3}{8} \div 4$.

Make an area model to show $\frac{3}{8}$.

| $\frac{1}{8}$ | $\frac{1}{8}$ | $\frac{1}{8}$ | $\frac{1}{8}$ | $\frac{1}{8}$ | $\frac{1}{8}$ | $\frac{1}{8}$ | $\frac{1}{8}$ |

The divisor is 4, so divide the area model into fourths.

So, $\frac{3}{8} \div 4 = \frac{3}{32}$.

Find $4 \div \frac{2}{3}$.

Use a number line to show 4 units.

Divide it into $\frac{2}{3}$-unit parts.

So, $4 \div \frac{2}{3} = 6$.

In **1** and **2**, complete each division sentence.

1. $\frac{2}{3} \div \square = \square = \square$

2. $3 \div \square = \square$

In **3–6**, find each quotient. Draw a diagram to help.

3. $\frac{3}{5} \div 2$

4. $4 \div \frac{2}{5}$

5. $4 \div \frac{4}{5}$

6. $\frac{5}{6} \div 2$

7. **MP.2 Reasoning** A team is practicing on a $\frac{3}{8}$-acre field. The coach divides the field into two equal parts for the practice. What fraction of an acre is each part?

8. **MP.4 Model with Math** A canal is 10 miles long. It has a lock every $\frac{2}{3}$ mile. How many locks are on the canal? Draw a number line to represent the problem.

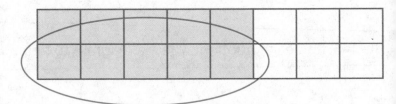

Draw a number line from 0 to 10 to represent the whole, 10 miles.

9. At a store, water bottles are sold in packs of 12, and juice bottles are sold in packs of 8. Elizabeth wants to buy the least number of packs that will provide an equal number of bottles of water and bottles of juice. How many packs of each should she buy?

10. **Higher Order Thinking** Olivia divided a fraction by $\frac{3}{4}$. The quotient was a whole number. Was the dividend less than $\frac{3}{4}$? Explain your reasoning.

© Common Core Assessment

11. Helen uses $\frac{5}{8}$ pound of ground beef to make two equal-sized hamburger patties. She wants to find out how much each patty weighs.

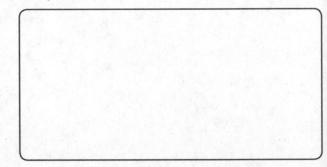

Part A

Explain how the area model above shows how much each patty weighs.

Part B

Write a division equation that represents the problem.

Name _____

☆ ⭐ ☆
Solve & Share

Find the value of each expression on the sign below. Then write two equations that show the values you found. *Solve this problem any way you choose.*

I can ...
divide whole numbers by fractions.

© Content Standard 6.NS.A.1
Mathematical Practices MP.1, MP.2, MP.4, MP.7

Use reasoning to decide what the numbers and symbols in these expressions mean.

$$3 \div \frac{1}{2}$$

$$3 \times \frac{2}{1}$$

Look Back! © MP.7 **Look for Relationships** Compare the two equations you wrote. How are they the same? How are they different?

Essential Question: How Can You Divide a Whole Number by a Fraction?

A

Look at the division and multiplication sentences on the right. Find a pattern that can help you divide. Then use the pattern to find the quotient for $4 \div \frac{2}{3}$.

$8 \div \frac{4}{1} = 2$	$8 \times \frac{1}{4} = 2$
$6 \div \frac{2}{1} = 3$	$6 \times \frac{1}{2} = 3$
$5 \div \frac{1}{2} = 10$	$5 \times \frac{2}{1} = 10$
$3 \div \frac{3}{4} = 4$	$3 \times \frac{4}{3} = 4$

Look for relationships between the multiplication and division statements.

B Two numbers whose product is 1 are called reciprocals of each other. If a nonzero number is named as a fraction $\frac{a}{b}$, then its reciprocal is $\frac{b}{a}$.

Notice that when you divide by a fraction, you have the same results as when you multiply by its reciprocal.

C To find $4 \div \frac{2}{3}$, rewrite the problem as a multiplication problem.

$$4 \div \frac{2}{3} = 4 \times \frac{3}{2}$$
$$= \frac{4}{1} \times \frac{3}{2}$$
$$= \frac{12}{2}$$

Write the quotient as a whole number or mixed number.

$$\frac{12}{2} = 6$$

Convince Me! © MP.7 Use Structure Use the pattern for dividing by a fraction to find $8 \div \frac{3}{4}$.

☆ Guided Practice *

Do You Understand?

1. **⊚ MP.2 Reasoning** Is $4 \div \frac{3}{2}$ the same as $4 \div \frac{2}{3}$? Explain.

2. How can you write any nonzero whole number as a fraction?

3. **⊚ MP.7 Look for Relationships** How does the quotient compare to the dividend when the divisor is a fraction less than 1?

Do You Know How?

In **4–7**, find each reciprocal.

4. $\frac{3}{5}$

5. $\frac{1}{6}$

6. 9

7. $\frac{7}{4}$

In **8–11**, find each quotient.

8. $6 \div \frac{2}{3}$

9. $12 \div \frac{3}{8}$

10. $2 \div \frac{1}{2}$

11. $3 \div \frac{1}{4}$

☆ Independent Practice ☆

In **12–19**, find each reciprocal.

12. $\frac{3}{10}$

13. 6

14. $\frac{1}{15}$

15. 3

16. $\frac{7}{12}$

17. $\frac{11}{5}$

18. 12

19. $\frac{22}{5}$

In **20–31**, find each quotient.

20. $4 \div \frac{4}{7}$

21. $2 \div \frac{3}{8}$

22. $5 \div \frac{2}{3}$

23. $9 \div \frac{4}{5}$

24. $36 \div \frac{3}{4}$

25. $7 \div \frac{3}{4}$

26. $18 \div \frac{2}{3}$

27. $20 \div \frac{1}{2}$

28. $9 \div \frac{3}{5}$

29. $5 \div \frac{2}{7}$

30. $12 \div \frac{1}{3}$

31. $8 \div \frac{3}{8}$

*For another example, see Set A on page 649.

Math Practices and Problem Solving

In **32–35**, use the given information.

A tortoise can move 600 ft in $\frac{2}{3}$ h.

A snail can move 120 ft in $\frac{3}{4}$ h.

A sloth can move 250 ft in $\frac{5}{8}$ h.

32. Higher Order Thinking Without doing any calculations, how can you use the information given to tell which animal moves the fastest?

33. © MP.2 Reasoning The quotient $250 \div \frac{5}{8}$ tells about how far a sloth may move in one hour. How far can a sloth go in 90 minutes? Justify your reasoning.

34. The quotient $600 \div \frac{2}{3}$ tells about how far a tortoise may move in one hour. Find that distance.

35. © MP.4 Model with Math Write and solve an equation to find how far a snail can go in one hour.

36. Nancy saves 30% of the money she earns from babysitting. How much will she save from a babysitting job that pays her $15?

© Common Core Assessment

37. Select all of the equations that are true.

- [ ] $14 \div \frac{7}{10} = 14 \times \frac{10}{7}$
- [ ] $12 \div \frac{2}{3} = \frac{1}{12} \times \frac{2}{3}$
- [ ] $10 \div \frac{3}{5} = 10 \times \frac{5}{3}$
- [ ] $20 \div 4 = 20 \times \frac{1}{4}$
- [ ] $16 \div \frac{4}{5} = \frac{1}{16} \times \frac{4}{5}$

Help Practice Buddy Tools Games

Another Look!

To divide a whole number by a fraction, you can multiply the whole number by the reciprocal of the fraction.

Find $14 \div \frac{4}{7}$.

The reciprocal of $\frac{4}{7}$ is $\frac{7}{4}$.

Step 1

Rewrite the division as multiplication using the reciprocal of the divisor.

$$14 \div \frac{4}{7} = 14 \times \frac{7}{4}$$

Step 2

Write 14 as a fraction. Then multiply.

$$\frac{14}{1} \times \frac{7}{4} = \frac{98}{4} = \frac{49}{2}$$

Step 3

Write the quotient as a whole number or mixed number.

$$\frac{49}{2} = 24\frac{1}{2}$$

In **1–3**, find each reciprocal.

1. $\frac{5}{9}$

2. 8

3. $\frac{7}{3}$

The product of a number and its reciprocal is 1.

In **4–15**, find each quotient.

4. $8 \div \frac{2}{5}$

5. $4 \div \frac{1}{6}$

6. $18 \div \frac{3}{8}$

7. $12 \div \frac{1}{2}$

8. $42 \div \frac{7}{9}$

9. $10 \div \frac{5}{6}$

10. $20 \div \frac{3}{4}$

11. $22 \div \frac{5}{6}$

12. $7 \div \frac{2}{3}$

13. $9 \div \frac{1}{8}$

14. $15 \div \frac{1}{3}$

15. $6 \div \frac{1}{5}$

16. **Math and Science** Honeybees get the nectar they need to make honey from flowers. In the process, bees carry pollen from one plant to another. This results in the pollination necessary for fruits and vegetables to grow. This helping relationship is called *symbiosis*. Write 80% as a decimal and as a fraction.

Honeybees pollinate about 80% of food crops.

17. © **MP.1 Make Sense and Persevere** It is estimated that one honeybee can make about $\frac{1}{12}$ teaspoon of honey in its lifetime. How many honeybees will it take to make 2 tablespoons of honey?

18. © **MP.2 Reasoning** A store sells honey in $\frac{3}{8}$-quart jars. If the store has 24 quarts of honey available on a shelf, how many jars of honey are on the shelf?

Remember, 1 tbsp = 3 tsp

19. A recording of the current weather conditions lasts $\frac{3}{4}$ minute. If the recording plays continuously, how many times could the recording be played in 1 hour?

20. **Higher Order Thinking** Which is a better buy, $\frac{1}{2}$ gallon of orange juice for $3.99 or $\frac{1}{4}$ gallon for $1.79? Explain.

21. **Number Sense** How many $\frac{3}{8}$-pound burgers can be made from 3 pounds of ground turkey?

22. In the number 5.78342, which digit is in the ten-thousandths place?

© **Common Core Assessment**

23. Select all of the number statements that are true.

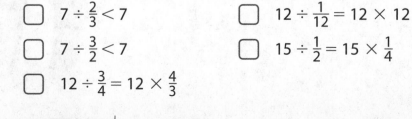

☐ $7 \div \frac{2}{3} < 7$ ☐ $12 \div \frac{1}{12} = 12 \times 12$

☐ $7 \div \frac{3}{2} < 7$ ☐ $15 \div \frac{1}{2} = 15 \times \frac{1}{4}$

☐ $12 \div \frac{3}{4} = 12 \times \frac{4}{3}$

Name _____

Lesson 12-3
Use Models to Divide Fractions

Solve & Share

Model $\frac{3}{4} \div \frac{1}{8}$ to find how many $\frac{1}{8}$-quart servings can be poured from a $\frac{3}{4}$-quart container of apple juice. **Solve this problem any way you choose.**

I can ...
make and use a model to divide a fraction by a fraction.

© Content Standard 6.NS.A.1
Mathematical Practices MP.1, MP.2, MP.4, MP.5

You can use fraction strips or other tools to help perform operations with fractions.

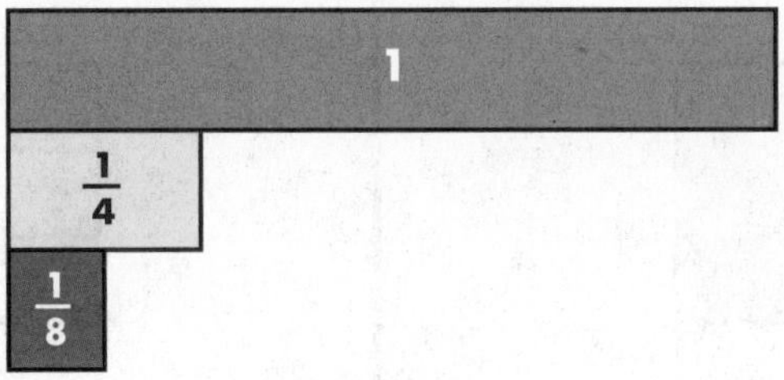

1

$\frac{1}{4}$

$\frac{1}{8}$

Look Back! © MP.1 Make Sense and Persevere How can you check that your answer makes sense?

Essential Question

How Can You Model Dividing a Fraction by a Fraction?

A

Simon buys $\frac{1}{2}$ yard of material. He uses $\frac{1}{6}$ yard of the material to make a footbag. How many footbags can Simon make? Find $\frac{1}{2} \div \frac{1}{6}$.

$\frac{1}{6}$ yard of material for each footbag

You can use an area model to show division.

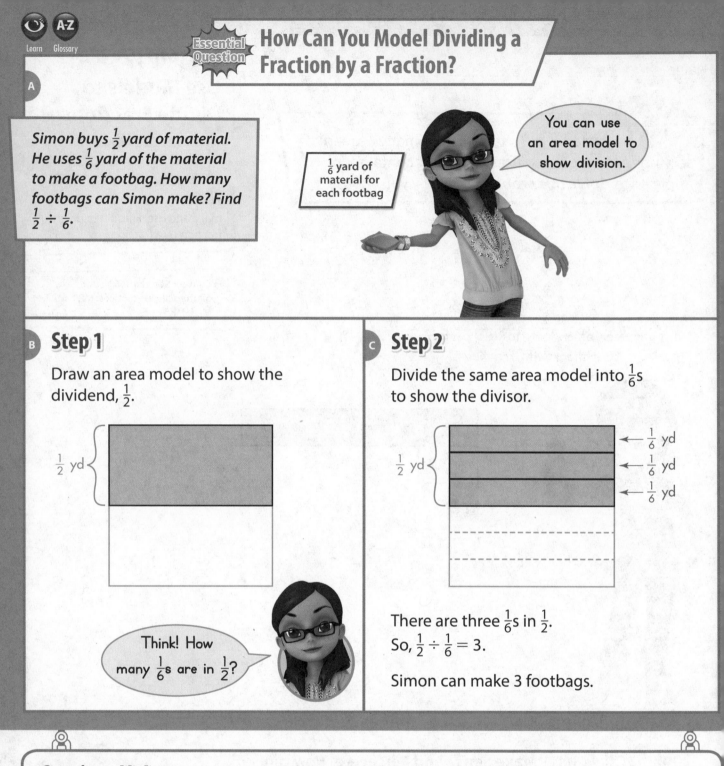

B ## Step 1

Draw an area model to show the dividend, $\frac{1}{2}$.

$\frac{1}{2}$ yd

Think! How many $\frac{1}{6}$s are in $\frac{1}{2}$?

C ## Step 2

Divide the same area model into $\frac{1}{6}$s to show the divisor.

$\frac{1}{2}$ yd

$\leftarrow \frac{1}{6}$ yd
$\leftarrow \frac{1}{6}$ yd
$\leftarrow \frac{1}{6}$ yd

There are three $\frac{1}{6}$s in $\frac{1}{2}$.
So, $\frac{1}{2} \div \frac{1}{6} = 3$.

Simon can make 3 footbags.

Convince Me! © **MP.5 Use Appropriate Tools** Use the number line below to model $\frac{1}{6} \times 3 = \frac{1}{2}$. Then write an equivalent division sentence also shown by your model.

0 ———————————————— 1

Name _____

Practice Buddy Tools Assessment

Another Example

How much of a $\frac{3}{4}$-cup serving is in $\frac{2}{3}$ cup of yogurt? Find $\frac{2}{3} \div \frac{3}{4}$.

Step 1

Draw area strips to show $\frac{2}{3}$ and $\frac{3}{4}$.

Step 2

Use the common unit of twelfths to compare $\frac{2}{3}$ and $\frac{3}{4}$.

Notice that $\frac{2}{3}$ is 8 parts when $\frac{3}{4}$ is divided into 9 equal parts. So, $\frac{2}{3}$ cup is $\frac{8}{9}$ of a $\frac{3}{4}$-cup serving.

☆ Guided Practice *

Do You Understand?

1. **© MP.2 Reasoning** If you divide $\frac{9}{10}$ by $\frac{3}{5}$, will the quotient be greater than or less than $\frac{3}{5}$?

Do You Know How?

2. Write a division sentence to represent the model.

0   $\frac{1}{5}$ $\frac{2}{5}$ $\frac{3}{5}$ $\frac{4}{5}$ 1

☆ Independent Practice ☆

In **3** and **4**, complete each division sentence using the models provided.

3. $\frac{1}{3} \div \frac{1}{12} = \square$

0   $\frac{1}{3}$

4. $\frac{2}{5} \div \frac{1}{10} = \square$

$\frac{2}{5}$ {   ← $\frac{1}{10}$ ← $\frac{1}{10}$ ← $\frac{1}{10}$ ← $\frac{1}{10}$

In **5–8**, make a model to find each quotient.

5. $\frac{2}{3} \div \frac{1}{3}$

6. $\frac{1}{2} \div \frac{1}{16}$

7. $\frac{1}{4} \div \frac{1}{12}$

8. $\frac{6}{7} \div \frac{3}{7}$

*For another example, see Set B on page 649.

Topic 12 | Lesson 12-3   607

Math Practices and Problem Solving

9. **©MP.4 Model with Math** A cafeteria uses $\frac{1}{6}$ pound of coffee to fill a large coffee dispenser. The cafeteria has $\frac{2}{3}$ pound of coffee to use.

   a. Complete the model at the right to find how many coffee dispensers the cafeteria can fill.
   b. Write a division sentence that describes the model and tells how many dispensers can be filled.

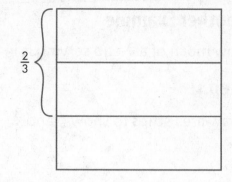

10. **©MP.4 Model with Math** A full load for a small truck to haul is $\frac{2}{3}$ ton of gravel. The truck is hauling $\frac{1}{2}$ ton of gravel.

   a. Complete the model below to find how much of a full load the truck is hauling.
   b. Write a division sentence that describes the model and tells how much of a full load the truck is hauling.

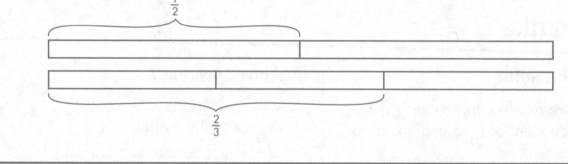

11. Blueberries are being shipped in boxes that hold 24 plastic containers of blueberries. How many boxes are needed to ship 1,060 containers of blueberries?

12. **Higher Order Thinking** Write a problem that could be solved by finding $\frac{2}{5} \div \frac{5}{8}$.

©Common Core Assessment

13. Which division sentence is shown by the model at the right?

   Ⓐ $\frac{2}{3} \div \frac{1}{9} = 6$

   Ⓑ $\frac{1}{9} \div \frac{2}{3} = \frac{1}{6}$

   Ⓒ $6 \div \frac{1}{9} = 54$

   Ⓓ $6 \div \frac{2}{3} = 9$

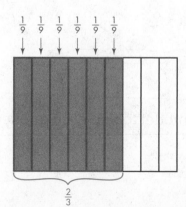

Name _____

Another Look!

Find $\frac{1}{3} \div \frac{1}{6}$.

You can use fraction strips to divide fractions.

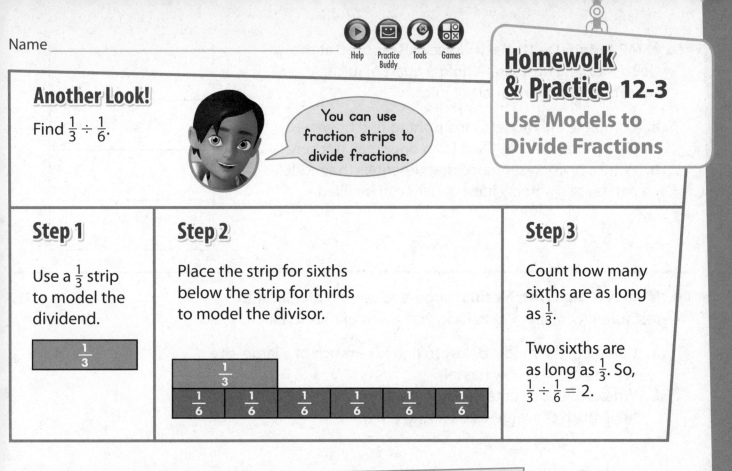

Step 1

Use a $\frac{1}{3}$ strip to model the dividend.

| $\frac{1}{3}$ |

Step 2

Place the strip for sixths below the strip for thirds to model the divisor.

Step 3

Count how many sixths are as long as $\frac{1}{3}$.

Two sixths are as long as $\frac{1}{3}$. So, $\frac{1}{3} \div \frac{1}{6} = 2$.

In **1–4**, complete each division sentence using the models provided.

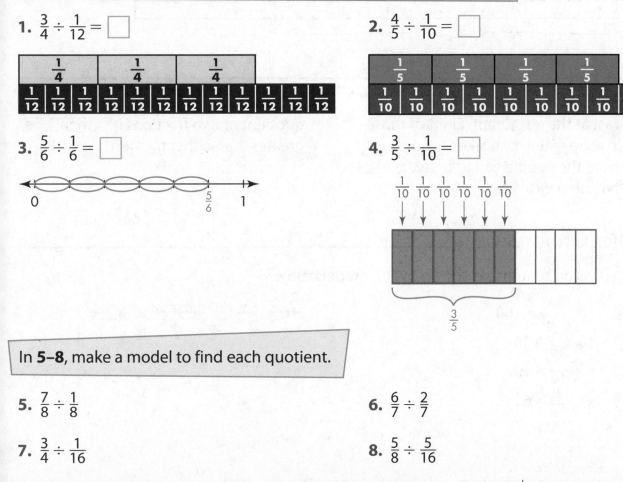

1. $\frac{3}{4} \div \frac{1}{12} = \square$

2. $\frac{4}{5} \div \frac{1}{10} = \square$

3. $\frac{5}{6} \div \frac{1}{6} = \square$

4. $\frac{3}{5} \div \frac{1}{10} = \square$

In **5–8**, make a model to find each quotient.

5. $\frac{7}{8} \div \frac{1}{8}$

6. $\frac{6}{7} \div \frac{2}{7}$

7. $\frac{3}{4} \div \frac{1}{16}$

8. $\frac{5}{8} \div \frac{5}{16}$

9. © **MP.4 Model with Math** Juice glasses used at the Good Morning Restaurant hold $\frac{1}{8}$ quart of juice. A small pitcher holds $\frac{3}{4}$ quart of juice.

$\frac{3}{4}$ {

a. Complete the model at the right to find how many juice glasses can be filled from one small pitcher.

b. Write a division sentence that describes the model and tells how many juice glasses can be filled.

---

10. © **MP.4 Model with Math** A large-size serving of milk at the restaurant contains $\frac{3}{4}$ pint. Ricky has $\frac{1}{2}$ pint of milk left in his glass.

a. Complete the model below to find how much of a large-size serving of milk Ricky has left.

b. Write a division sentence that describes the model and tells how much of a large-size serving is left.

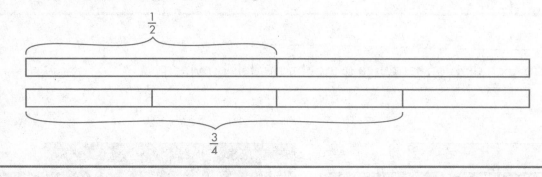

$\frac{1}{2}$

$\frac{3}{4}$

---

11. One morning, 32 people were eating breakfast at the restaurant. Eight of those people were eating pancakes. What percent of the people eating breakfast were having pancakes?

12. **Higher Order Thinking** When will the quotient of two fractions less than 1 be greater than either fraction?

© **Common Core Assessment**

13. Which division sentence is shown by the model below?

Ⓐ $10 \div \frac{1}{16} = 160$

Ⓑ $10 \div \frac{5}{8} = 16$

Ⓒ $\frac{5}{8} \div \frac{1}{16} = 10$

Ⓓ $\frac{5}{8} \div \frac{1}{10} = 6\frac{1}{4}$

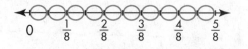

$0 \quad \frac{1}{8} \quad \frac{2}{8} \quad \frac{3}{8} \quad \frac{4}{8} \quad \frac{5}{8}$

Name _____

★ ☆ ★
Solve & Share

A granola bar was cut into 6 equal pieces. Someone ate part of the granola bar so that $\frac{2}{3}$ of the original bar remains. How many $\frac{1}{6}$ parts are left? Complete the picture to find $\frac{2}{3} \div \frac{1}{6}$.

Solve

Lesson 12-4
Divide Fractions

I can ...
divide a fraction by another fraction.

© Content Standard 6.NS.A.1
Mathematical Practices MP.1, MP.2, MP.3, MP.4, MP.6, MP.7

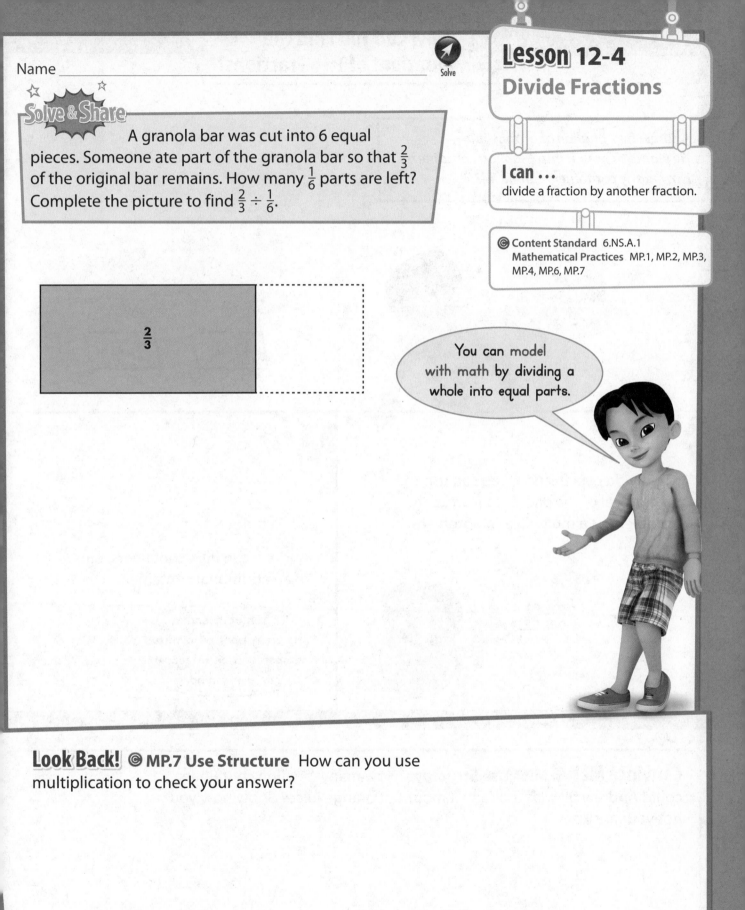

$\frac{2}{3}$

You can model with math by dividing a whole into equal parts.

Look Back! © MP.7 Use Structure How can you use multiplication to check your answer?

Essential Question: How Can You Find the Quotient of Two Fractions?

A

Andrew has $\frac{3}{4}$ gallon of orange juice. He wants to pour it into $\frac{1}{6}$-gallon containers. How many containers can he fill?

Divide to find equal parts.

$\frac{3}{4}$ gallon $\frac{1}{6}$ gallon

B Find $\frac{3}{4} \div \frac{1}{6}$.

To divide by a fraction, you can use the reciprocal of the divisor to rewrite the problem as a multiplication problem.

$\frac{6}{1}$ is the reciprocal of $\frac{1}{6}$.

C

$$\frac{3}{4} \div \frac{1}{6} = \frac{3}{4} \times \frac{6}{1}$$

$$= \frac{18}{4}$$

$$= 4\frac{1}{2}$$

Andrew can fill 4 containers, plus $\frac{1}{2}$ of an additional container.

Sometimes the fraction part of a mixed number can be interpreted as a remainder.

Convince Me! © **MP.7 Use Structure** How many $\frac{1}{8}$-gallon containers could Andrew fill with the same amount of orange juice? Show how you got your answer.

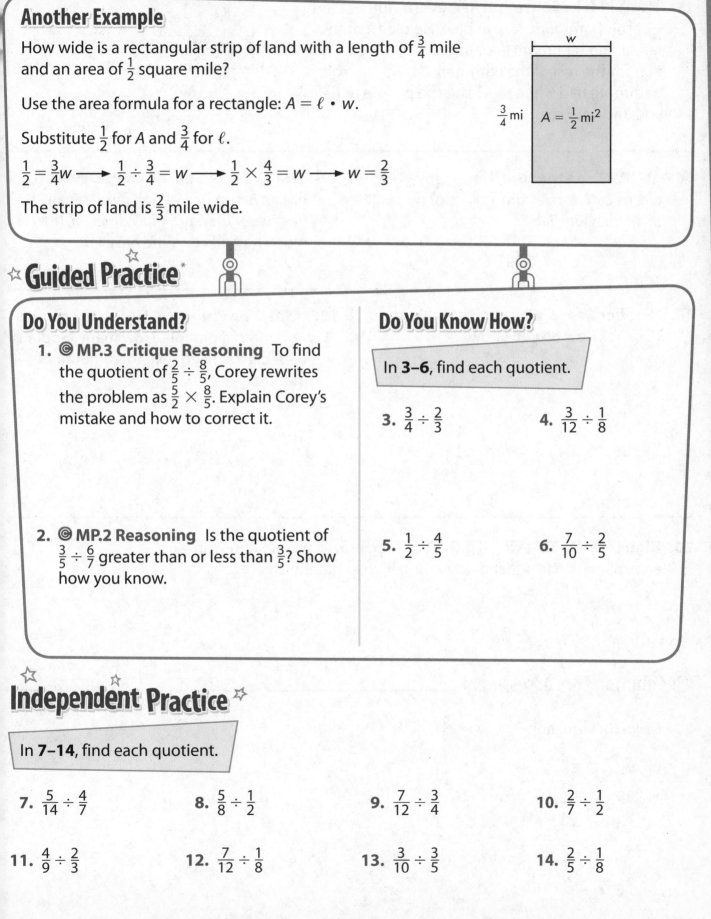

Another Example

How wide is a rectangular strip of land with a length of $\frac{3}{4}$ mile and an area of $\frac{1}{2}$ square mile?

Use the area formula for a rectangle: $A = \ell \cdot w$.

Substitute $\frac{1}{2}$ for A and $\frac{3}{4}$ for ℓ.

$\frac{1}{2} = \frac{3}{4}w \longrightarrow \frac{1}{2} \div \frac{3}{4} = w \longrightarrow \frac{1}{2} \times \frac{4}{3} = w \longrightarrow w = \frac{2}{3}$

The strip of land is $\frac{2}{3}$ mile wide.

$\frac{3}{4}$ mi $\quad A = \frac{1}{2}$ mi^2

☆ Guided Practice *

Do You Understand?

1. © MP.3 Critique Reasoning To find the quotient of $\frac{2}{5} \div \frac{8}{5}$, Corey rewrites the problem as $\frac{5}{2} \times \frac{8}{5}$. Explain Corey's mistake and how to correct it.

2. © MP.2 Reasoning Is the quotient of $\frac{3}{5} \div \frac{6}{7}$ greater than or less than $\frac{3}{5}$? Show how you know.

Do You Know How?

In **3–6**, find each quotient.

3. $\frac{3}{4} \div \frac{2}{3}$

4. $\frac{3}{12} \div \frac{1}{8}$

5. $\frac{1}{2} \div \frac{4}{5}$

6. $\frac{7}{10} \div \frac{2}{5}$

☆ Independent Practice ☆

In **7–14**, find each quotient.

7. $\frac{5}{14} \div \frac{4}{7}$

8. $\frac{5}{8} \div \frac{1}{2}$

9. $\frac{7}{12} \div \frac{3}{4}$

10. $\frac{2}{7} \div \frac{1}{2}$

11. $\frac{4}{9} \div \frac{2}{3}$

12. $\frac{7}{12} \div \frac{1}{8}$

13. $\frac{3}{10} \div \frac{3}{5}$

14. $\frac{2}{5} \div \frac{1}{8}$

Math Practices and Problem Solving

15. **MP.1 Make Sense and Persevere** Tomas tiled $\frac{1}{2}$ of this bathroom floor in blue. He tiled $\frac{2}{3}$ of the remaining bathroom floor in green. He used white tiles for the rest of the bathroom. How much of the bathroom had white tiles? Use the picture to help you find your solution.

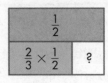

16. **MP.7 Use Structure** How many $\frac{1}{4}$–inch pieces can be cut from a piece of metal $\frac{5}{8}$ of an inch long?

17. **MP.1 Make Sense and Persevere** Luis has an 8-cup bag of trail mix to share. If he gives 9 friends $\frac{2}{3}$ of a cup each, how much trail mix does he have left?

18. **Number Sense** Which fraction is greater, $\frac{6}{10}$ or $\frac{10}{15}$? How do you know?

19. **MP.6 Be Precise** A large bag contains $\frac{12}{15}$ pound of granola. How many $\frac{1}{3}$-pound bags can be filled with this amount of granola?

20. **Higher Order Thinking** Find $\frac{3}{4} \div \frac{2}{3}$. Then draw a picture and write an explanation to a friend describing how to get the answer.

Common Core Assessment

21. Solve the equation $\frac{13}{16} \div n = 2\frac{1}{6}$.

   (A) $n = \frac{4}{9}$

   (B) $n = \frac{3}{8}$

   (C) $n = \frac{4}{7}$

   (D) $n = \frac{5}{8}$

Help | Practice Buddy | Tools | Games

Another Look!

To divide by a fraction, you can multiply by its reciprocal.

Find $\frac{4}{5} \div \frac{3}{10}$.

A fraction and its reciprocal multiply to 1. The reciprocal of $\frac{3}{10}$ is $\frac{10}{3}$ because $\frac{3}{10} \cdot \frac{10}{3} = \frac{30}{30} = 1$.

Rewrite the division as multiplication using the reciprocal of the divisor. The reciprocal of $\frac{3}{10}$ is $\frac{10}{3}$. $\frac{4}{5} \div \frac{3}{10} = \frac{4}{5} \times \frac{10}{3}$	Multiply the fractions. $\frac{4}{5} \times \frac{10}{3} = \frac{40}{15} = \frac{8}{3}$	When the numerator is greater than the denominator, write the answer as a mixed number. $\frac{8}{3} = 2\frac{2}{3}$

Leveled Practice In **1–18**, find each quotient.

1. $\frac{1}{2} \div \frac{3}{4} = \frac{1}{2} \times \frac{\square}{\square} = \frac{4}{\square} = \frac{\square}{3}$

2. $\frac{4}{5} \div \frac{2}{9} = \frac{\square}{5} \times \frac{\square}{\square} = \frac{36}{\square} = 3\frac{\square}{\square}$

3. $\frac{1}{3} \div \frac{1}{2}$

4. $\frac{2}{5} \div \frac{2}{3}$

5. $\frac{5}{8} \div \frac{7}{10}$

6. $\frac{3}{7} \div 3$

7. $\frac{1}{3} \div \frac{8}{9}$

8. $\frac{5}{6} \div \frac{1}{8}$

9. $\frac{5}{9} \div \frac{1}{2}$

10. $\frac{3}{5} \div \frac{3}{4}$

11. $\frac{3}{4} \div \frac{5}{6}$

12. $\frac{9}{10} \div \frac{4}{5}$

13. $\frac{1}{3} \div \frac{3}{8}$

14. $\frac{4}{7} \div \frac{3}{4}$

15. $\frac{11}{12} \div \frac{2}{3}$

16. $\frac{8}{9} \div \frac{3}{4}$

17. $\frac{1}{4} \div \frac{6}{7}$

18. $\frac{1}{7} \div \frac{1}{5}$

19. **© MP.1 Make Sense and Persevere** Lisette covered $\frac{1}{3}$ of her garden with lilies. She covered $\frac{3}{5}$ of the remaining garden with daisies. She used marigolds for the rest of the garden. How much of the garden was covered with marigolds? Use the picture to help you find your solution.

| $\frac{1}{3}$ | $\frac{3}{5} \times \frac{2}{3}$ |
| | ? |

---

20. **Algebra** Simplify $(2 \times 5)^2 \div 2$.

21. **© MP.6 Be Precise** Brenda makes wooden coasters. She cuts small round posts into $\frac{2}{3}$-inch thick discs of wood. How many coasters can she get from a post that measures $\frac{1}{2}$ foot in length?

---

22. **Number Sense** Which fraction is greater, $\frac{7}{12}$ or $\frac{11}{20}$? How do you know?

23. **© MP.4 Model with Math** A $\frac{5}{6}$-yard piece of fencing is made of boards that are $\frac{1}{12}$ yard wide. How many boards make up the fence? Draw a picture to help you solve.

---

24. **Higher Order Thinking** Write a problem that can be solved be dividing $\frac{9}{10}$ by $\frac{1}{4}$. Solve the problem.

© Common Core Assessment _____

25. Solve the equation $\frac{17}{20} \div n = 4\frac{1}{4}$.

     Ⓐ $n = \frac{2}{3}$

     Ⓑ $n = \frac{2}{5}$

     Ⓒ $n = \frac{1}{3}$

     Ⓓ $n = \frac{1}{5}$

Name _____

★ ☆ ★
Solve & Share

Kareem is putting $12\frac{1}{8}$ pounds of trail mix into containers to take on a hike. About how many containers can he fill if he puts $2\frac{3}{4}$ pounds in each container? **Solve this problem any way you choose.**

I can ...
use rounding or compatible numbers to estimate quotients with mixed numbers.

© Content Standard 6.NS.A.1
Mathematical Practices MP.2, MP.3, MP.4, MP.6, MP.7, MP.8

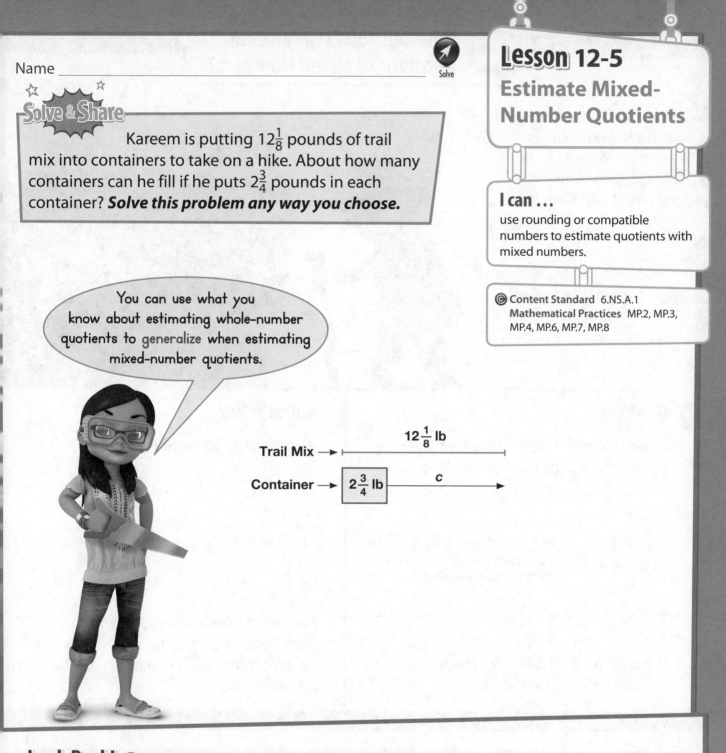

You can use what you know about estimating whole-number quotients to generalize when estimating mixed-number quotients.

Trail Mix → $12\frac{1}{8}$ lb

Container → $2\frac{3}{4}$ lb c

Look Back! © **MP.3 Construct Arguments** Is there enough trail mix to fill the number of containers you estimated? Explain how you can use your estimate to check that the quotient is reasonable.

How Can You Estimate the Quotient of Mixed Numbers?

A

Lillian and her friends can hike an average of $3\frac{5}{8}$ miles per hour. About how many hours will it take them to hike the trail?

Estimate the quotient $15\frac{5}{6} \div 3\frac{5}{8}$ to find out.

HIKING TRAIL
$15\frac{5}{6}$ MILES

B ## One Way

Round to the nearest whole number by comparing the fractions to $\frac{1}{2}$.

$15\frac{5}{6} \div 3\frac{5}{8}$

$\downarrow \quad\quad \downarrow$

$16 \div 4 = 4$

Both $\frac{5}{6}$ and $\frac{5}{8}$ are greater than $\frac{1}{2}$, so round both mixed numbers up to the nearest whole number.

So $15\frac{5}{6} \div 3\frac{5}{8} \approx 4$.

It will take Lillian and her friends about 4 hours to finish their hike.

C ## Another Way

Use compatible numbers.

$15\frac{5}{6} \div 3\frac{5}{8}$ $15\frac{5}{6} \div 3\frac{5}{8}$

$\downarrow \quad\quad \downarrow$ $\downarrow \quad\quad \downarrow$

$16 \div 4 = 4$ $15 \div 3 = 5$

So $15\frac{5}{6} \div 3\frac{5}{8} \approx 4$.   So $15\frac{5}{6} \div 3\frac{5}{8} \approx 5$.

Both examples are easy to compute and close to the actual dividend and divisor. So, an estimate of 4 or 5 hours for the hike is reasonable.

Convince Me! © MP.3 Construct Arguments Estimate the amount of time it would take Lillian and her friends to hike $23\frac{1}{4}$ miles. Explain how you estimated.

© Pearson Education, Inc. 6

Other Examples

Estimate $55\frac{1}{3} \div 6\frac{1}{4}$.

Use compatible numbers.

$$55\frac{1}{3} \div 6\frac{1}{4}$$

$$54 \div 6 = 9$$

$$55\frac{1}{3} \div 6\frac{1}{4} \approx 9$$

Estimate $7\frac{3}{4} \div 1\frac{7}{8}$.

Use rounding.

$$7\frac{3}{4} \div 1\frac{7}{8}$$

$$8 \div 2 = 4$$

$$7\frac{3}{4} \div 1\frac{7}{8} \approx 4$$

Estimate $26\frac{3}{4} \div 5\frac{1}{4}$.

Use compatible numbers.

$$26\frac{3}{4} \div 5\frac{1}{4}$$

$$25 \div 5 = 5$$

$$26\frac{3}{4} \div 5\frac{1}{4} \approx 5$$

☆ Guided Practice*

Do You Understand?

1. Ⓒ **MP.3 Construct Arguments** Explain how to use rounding to estimate $8\frac{5}{9} \div 3\frac{3}{8}$.

2. Ⓒ **MP.2 Reasoning** If you wanted to estimate $18\frac{3}{4} \div 3\frac{1}{3}$, would you use rounding or compatible numbers? Why?

Do You Know How?

In **3–10**, estimate each quotient.

3. $35\frac{1}{3} \div 6\frac{2}{3}$

4. $11\frac{3}{8} \div 3\frac{7}{9}$

5. $24\frac{5}{8} \div 5\frac{4}{7}$

6. $24\frac{3}{5} \div 5\frac{9}{10}$

7. $8\frac{1}{12} \div 4\frac{1}{10}$

8. $44\frac{4}{5} \div 8\frac{2}{3}$

9. $78\frac{1}{9} \div 9\frac{3}{4}$

10. $23\frac{8}{9} \div 3\frac{1}{2}$

☆ Independent Practice ☆

In **11–26**, estimate each quotient.

11. $39\frac{4}{5} \div 9\frac{1}{2}$

12. $35\frac{2}{9} \div 5\frac{8}{9}$

13. $3\frac{7}{8} \div 1\frac{1}{12}$

14. $19\frac{2}{3} \div 6\frac{7}{8}$

15. $13\frac{7}{9} \div 2\frac{1}{3}$

16. $87\frac{4}{7} \div 7\frac{3}{4}$

17. $60\frac{5}{9} \div 11\frac{1}{2}$

18. $23\frac{3}{10} \div 2\frac{4}{5}$

19. $32\frac{1}{3} \div 7\frac{2}{3}$

20. $40\frac{1}{4} \div 5\frac{1}{9}$

21. $23\frac{4}{5} \div 11\frac{2}{3}$

22. $49\frac{6}{7} \div 4\frac{2}{3}$

23. $27\frac{2}{3} \div 13\frac{5}{6}$

24. $99\frac{2}{9} \div 4\frac{3}{4}$

25. $74\frac{7}{8} \div 24\frac{2}{5}$

26. $55\frac{2}{3} \div 27\frac{5}{6}$

For another example, see Set C on page 649.

Math Practices and Problem Solving

27. © **MP.6 Be Precise** What is the perimeter of the parallelogram below?

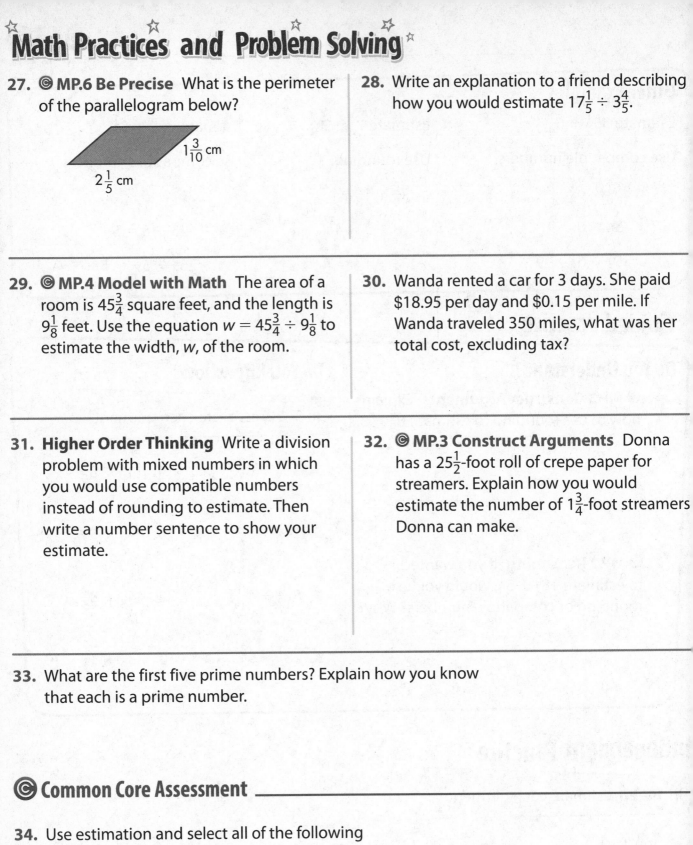

$1\frac{3}{10}$ cm

$2\frac{1}{5}$ cm

28. Write an explanation to a friend describing how you would estimate $17\frac{1}{5} \div 3\frac{4}{5}$.

29. © **MP.4 Model with Math** The area of a room is $45\frac{3}{4}$ square feet, and the length is $9\frac{1}{8}$ feet. Use the equation $w = 45\frac{3}{4} \div 9\frac{1}{8}$ to estimate the width, w, of the room.

30. Wanda rented a car for 3 days. She paid $18.95 per day and $0.15 per mile. If Wanda traveled 350 miles, what was her total cost, excluding tax?

31. **Higher Order Thinking** Write a division problem with mixed numbers in which you would use compatible numbers instead of rounding to estimate. Then write a number sentence to show your estimate.

32. © **MP.3 Construct Arguments** Donna has a $25\frac{1}{2}$-foot roll of crepe paper for streamers. Explain how you would estimate the number of $1\frac{3}{4}$-foot streamers Donna can make.

33. What are the first five prime numbers? Explain how you know that each is a prime number.

© **Common Core Assessment**

34. Use estimation and select all of the following comparisons that are true.

☐ $13\frac{5}{7} \div 2\frac{1}{3} > 9$

☐ $11\frac{5}{7} \div 3\frac{1}{5} < 3$

☐ $39\frac{8}{9} \div 3\frac{7}{8} > 9$

☐ $26\frac{1}{6} \div 4\frac{9}{10} < 6$

Help Practice Buddy Tools Games

Another Look!

You can use rounding or compatible numbers to estimate quotients with mixed numbers.

Always consider how the quantities are related when deciding which method makes the most sense.

Use rounding when the nearest whole numbers are easy to divide.

Estimate $23\frac{5}{6} \div 8\frac{3}{7}$.

$$24 \div 8 = 3$$

So, $23\frac{5}{6} \div 8\frac{3}{7} \approx 3$.

Use compatible numbers when they are easier to divide than the nearest whole numbers.

Estimate $31\frac{1}{6} \div 4\frac{5}{8}$.

$$30 \div 5 = 6$$

So, $31\frac{1}{6} \div 4\frac{5}{8} \approx 6$.

Think: $31\frac{1}{6} \div 4\frac{5}{8}$ are close to 30 and 5.

In **1** and **2**, identify the estimation method.

1. $29\frac{2}{3} \div 14\frac{8}{9}$

$$30 \div 15 = 2$$
$$29\frac{2}{3} \div 14\frac{8}{9} \approx 2$$

2. $67\frac{3}{4} \div 10\frac{1}{12}$

$$70 \div 10 = 7$$
$$67\frac{3}{4} \div 10\frac{1}{12} \approx 7$$

In **3–18**, estimate each quotient.

3. $11\frac{1}{2} \div 6\frac{1}{4}$

4. $19\frac{1}{3} \div 3\frac{2}{3}$

5. $41\frac{7}{9} \div 7\frac{1}{5}$

6. $35\frac{1}{8} \div 5\frac{4}{5}$

7. $62\frac{2}{7} \div 8\frac{7}{9}$

8. $72\frac{2}{9} \div 7\frac{7}{8}$

9. $86\frac{3}{4} \div 10\frac{5}{6}$

10. $26\frac{9}{10} \div 2\frac{5}{8}$

11. $11\frac{2}{7} \div 3\frac{3}{5}$

12. $7\frac{9}{10} \div 2\frac{3}{10}$

13. $47\frac{6}{10} \div 7\frac{1}{12}$

14. $60\frac{5}{8} \div 5\frac{4}{5}$

15. $40\frac{9}{10} \div 20\frac{1}{6}$

16. $35\frac{2}{9} \div 5\frac{8}{9}$

17. $3\frac{7}{8} \div 1\frac{1}{5}$

18. $21\frac{2}{3} \div 6\frac{4}{5}$

19. © **MP.7 Use Structure** The area of this rectangle is $257\frac{1}{4}$ in^2. Estimate side length w.

Remember, $A = \ell \times w$.

$257\frac{1}{4}$ in^2 $10\frac{1}{2}$ in.

w

20. © **MP.8 Generalize** What estimation method did you use to find the length of side w? Explain your reasoning.

21. © **MP.2 Reasoning** On Monday, John hiked for $26\frac{1}{2}$ miles along the Appalachian Trail. On Tuesday, he covered only $6\frac{3}{4}$ miles. About how many times farther did John hike on Monday than on Tuesday?

22. **Higher Order Thinking** Anh-Tuan wants to cut strips of paper that are $2\frac{1}{4}$ in. wide. His sheet of paper is $11\frac{1}{2}$ in. wide. He estimates that $11\frac{1}{2} \div 2\frac{1}{4} \approx 6$, so he can cut 6 strips from each sheet of paper. Is his estimate an overestimate or an underestimate? Explain.

23. © **MP.4 Model with Math** What is the value of the expression $x(7 + x) - 22$ if $x = 8$?

24. A factory makes oatmeal raisin cookies in which $2\frac{1}{4}$ cups of raisins and $9\frac{2}{5}$ cups of flour and oatmeal are needed for a batch. About how many cups of flour and oatmeal are there for every cup of raisins?

© **Common Core Assessment**

25. Use estimation and select all of the following comparisons that are true.

☐ $23\frac{5}{7} \div 3\frac{4}{5} < 7$ ☐ $31\frac{3}{10} \div 5\frac{3}{5} > 6$

☐ $34\frac{8}{9} \div 6\frac{1}{8} < 5$ ☐ $19\frac{4}{7} \div 4\frac{2}{9} > 4$

Name _____

Solve & Share

A jeweler has a $5\frac{1}{2}$-inch strip of silver wire that she is cutting into $1\frac{3}{8}$-inch pieces. How many pieces will she make? *Solve this problem any way you choose.*

I can ...
find the quotient of mixed numbers.

© **Content Standard** 6.NS.A.1
Mathematical Practices MP.1, MP.6, MP.7, MP.8

You can generalize. How can you use what you know about solving problems with fractions to help?

Look Back! © **MP.8 Generalize** Explain how to use estimation to check your answer for reasonableness.

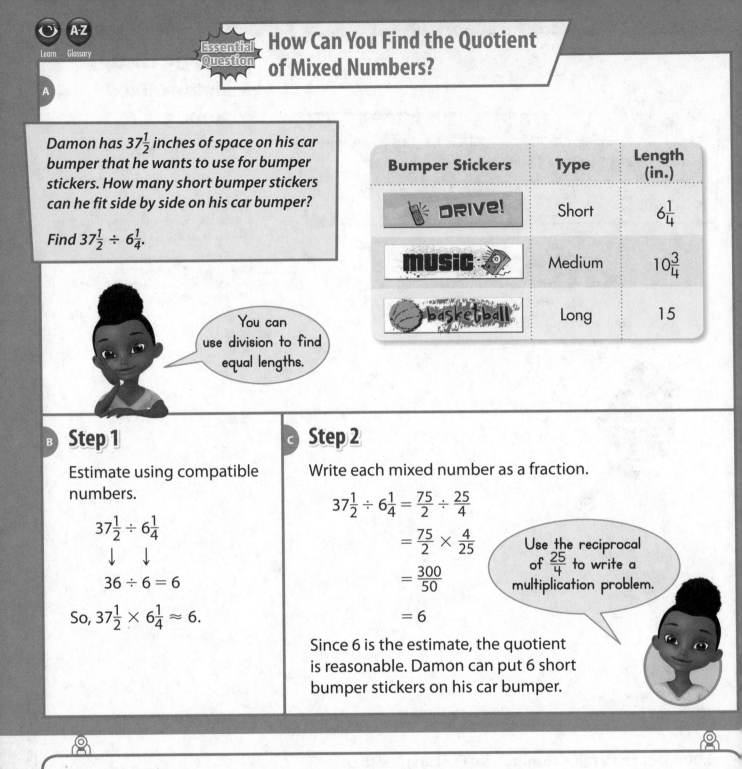

Essential Question

How Can You Find the Quotient of Mixed Numbers?

A

Damon has $37\frac{1}{2}$ inches of space on his car bumper that he wants to use for bumper stickers. How many short bumper stickers can he fit side by side on his car bumper?

Find $37\frac{1}{2} \div 6\frac{1}{4}$.

Bumper Stickers	Type	Length (in.)
DRIVE!	Short	$6\frac{1}{4}$
music	Medium	$10\frac{3}{4}$
basketball	Long	15

You can use division to find equal lengths.

B ## Step 1

Estimate using compatible numbers.

$$37\frac{1}{2} \div 6\frac{1}{4}$$
$$\downarrow \qquad \downarrow$$
$$36 \div 6 = 6$$

So, $37\frac{1}{2} \times 6\frac{1}{4} \approx 6$.

C ## Step 2

Write each mixed number as a fraction.

$$37\frac{1}{2} \div 6\frac{1}{4} = \frac{75}{2} \div \frac{25}{4}$$
$$= \frac{75}{2} \times \frac{4}{25}$$
$$= \frac{300}{50}$$
$$= 6$$

Use the reciprocal of $\frac{25}{4}$ to write a multiplication problem.

Since 6 is the estimate, the quotient is reasonable. Damon can put 6 short bumper stickers on his car bumper.

Convince Me! © MP.7 Look for Relationships How many medium bumper stickers can Damon fit side by side on his car bumper? Find $37\frac{1}{2} \div 10\frac{3}{4}$.

Practice Buddy   Tools   Assessment

☆ Guided Practice *

Do You Understand?

1. © **MP.8 Generalize** When dividing mixed numbers, why is it important to estimate the quotient first?

2. © **MP.6 Be Precise** In the problem on page 624, how many long bumper stickers can Damon fit side by side on his car bumper? Will there be uncovered space? Explain.

Do You Know How?

In **3–10**, find each quotient.

3. $18 \div 3\frac{2}{3}$

4. $4\frac{1}{3} \div 2\frac{4}{5}$

5. $5 \div 6\frac{2}{5}$

6. $6\frac{5}{9} \div 1\frac{7}{9}$

7. $2\frac{1}{2} \div 4\frac{1}{10}$

8. $8\frac{1}{5} \div 3\frac{3}{4}$

9. $4\frac{8}{9} \div 2\frac{1}{3}$

10. $10\frac{1}{12} \div 2\frac{6}{7}$

☆ Independent Practice ☆

In **11–22**, find each quotient.

> Remember! Estimate to check your answers for reasonableness.

11. $1\frac{3}{8} \div 4\frac{1}{8}$

12. $2\frac{5}{6} \div 6\frac{1}{3}$

13. $3\frac{1}{4} \div 4\frac{2}{7}$

14. $5\frac{1}{2} \div 7\frac{2}{5}$

15. $1 \div 8\frac{5}{9}$

16. $3\frac{5}{6} \div 9\frac{5}{6}$

17. $4\frac{1}{3} \div 3\frac{1}{4}$

18. $8 \div 2\frac{2}{3}$

19. $6\frac{3}{4} \div 1\frac{7}{8}$

20. $2\frac{5}{8} \div 13$

21. $3\frac{6}{7} \div 6\frac{3}{4}$

22. $9\frac{7}{9} \div 8\frac{1}{4}$

For another example, see Set C on page 649.

Math Practices and Problem Solving

In **23** and **24**, use the picture. The larger room is twice as long as the smaller room.

23. **Number Sense** How long is the larger room?

24. If the length of the smaller room is divided into 4 equal parts, how long is each part?

$20\frac{4}{5}$ feet

?

25. ⓒ **MP.1 Make Sense and Persevere** Luis has 3 pounds of ground turkey to make turkey burgers. He uses $\frac{3}{8}$ pound per burger to make 6 burgers. How many $\frac{1}{4}$-pound burgers can Luis make with the remaining turkey?

26. **Higher Order Thinking** If $9 \times \frac{n}{5} = 9 \div \frac{n}{5}$, then what does n equal? Explain.

27. Margaret uses $1\frac{3}{4}$ teaspoons of vanilla to make 12 vanilla cupcakes. She wants to make 30 cupcakes. How much vanilla will Margaret use?

28. ⓒ **MP.7 Use Structure** The biggest diamond ever found weighed about $1\frac{1}{2}$ pounds uncut. If this diamond were cut into 6 equal pieces, how much would each piece weigh?

ⓒ Common Core Assessment

29. A restaurant has $15\frac{1}{5}$ pounds of ground beef to make meat loaves.

Part A

Each meat loaf requires $2\frac{3}{8}$ pounds of ground beef. How many meat loaves can be made? Show how you got your answer.

Part B

The restaurant could make a smaller size meat loaf that uses $1\frac{3}{5}$ pounds of ground bee How many more smaller meat loaves can be made than the larger size meat loaves? Explain your answer.

Help Practice Tools Games
Buddy

Another Look!

Find $5\frac{1}{3} \div 1\frac{1}{3}$.

You can follow these steps.

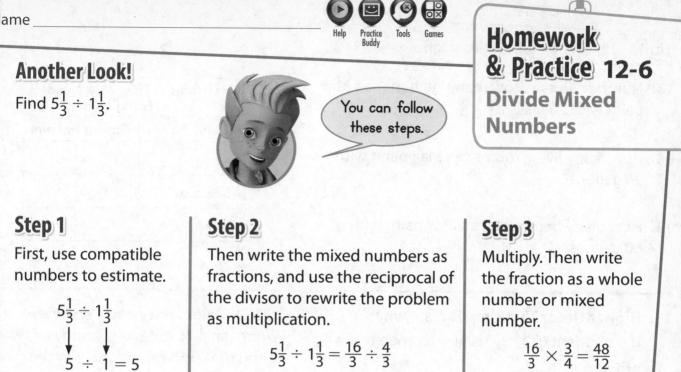

Step 1

First, use compatible numbers to estimate.

$$5\frac{1}{3} \div 1\frac{1}{3}$$

$$5 \div 1 = 5$$

Step 2

Then write the mixed numbers as fractions, and use the reciprocal of the divisor to rewrite the problem as multiplication.

$$5\frac{1}{3} \div 1\frac{1}{3} = \frac{16}{3} \div \frac{4}{3}$$

$$= \frac{16}{3} \times \frac{3}{4}$$

Step 3

Multiply. Then write the fraction as a whole number or mixed number.

$$\frac{16}{3} \times \frac{3}{4} = \frac{48}{12}$$

$$= 4$$

Compare the quotient to your estimate: 4 is close to 5. The answer is reasonable.

In **1–12**, find each quotient.

1. $2\frac{2}{3} \div 3\frac{1}{4}$

2. $1\frac{3}{4} \div 4\frac{1}{8}$

3. $2\frac{1}{5} \div 2\frac{1}{3}$

4. $5\frac{1}{4} \div 3$

5. $2\frac{1}{4} \div 1\frac{1}{2}$

6. $3\frac{1}{2} \div 2\frac{1}{4}$

7. $3\frac{3}{4} \div 2$

8. $1\frac{1}{2} \div 2\frac{1}{4}$

9. $2\frac{3}{8} \div 8\frac{9}{10}$

10. $8\frac{4}{5} \div 1\frac{1}{4}$

11. $7\frac{1}{3} \div 8\frac{11}{12}$

12. $5\frac{1}{7} \div 3$

In **13–15**, use the table at the right.

13. **Number Sense** How many kitchens can Max paint with 20 gallons?

Gallons of Paint Max Needs for Each Room	
Room	Gallons of Paint
Kitchen	$2\frac{1}{2}$
Bedroom	$3\frac{3}{4}$
Living room	$4\frac{1}{3}$

14. How many living rooms can Max paint with 26 gallons?

15. How many bedrooms can Max paint with 60 gallons?

16. **Higher Order Thinking** Explain why the quotient of $3\frac{7}{8} \div \frac{1}{8}$ is greater than the product of $3\frac{7}{8} \times \frac{1}{8}$.

17. © **MP.1 Make Sense and Persevere** Tyrone ran 4.26 miles on Saturday. Every day he runs 0.15 mile more than the day before. On which day will Tyrone run more than 5 miles for the first time?

18. © **MP.6 Be Precise** Esther's garden is $18\frac{1}{2}$ feet long. She divides it into 5 equal sections. How long is each section to the nearest tenth of an inch?

19. **A-Z Vocabulary** Write the *reciprocal* of $\frac{11}{12}$.

© **Common Core Assessment**

20. Franco has decorating ribbon that is $18\frac{3}{4}$ feet long to be used for gift packages.

Part A

Each package requires $2\frac{1}{2}$ feet of ribbon. How many packages can Franco decorate with his ribbon? Show how you got your answer.

Part B

Suppose that $1\frac{1}{4}$ feet of ribbon is needed to decorate a smaller package. How many more smaller packages could Franco decorate than large packages? Explain your answer.

Name _____

Solve & Share

Patricia is making cookies. She has $2\frac{1}{2}$ cups of flour. She uses the expression $2\frac{1}{2} \div f$ to find the number of batches she can make when the recipe calls for f cups of flour. If she has plenty of other ingredients, how many batches of the Yummy Cookie Recipe can she make? **Solve this problem any way you choose.**

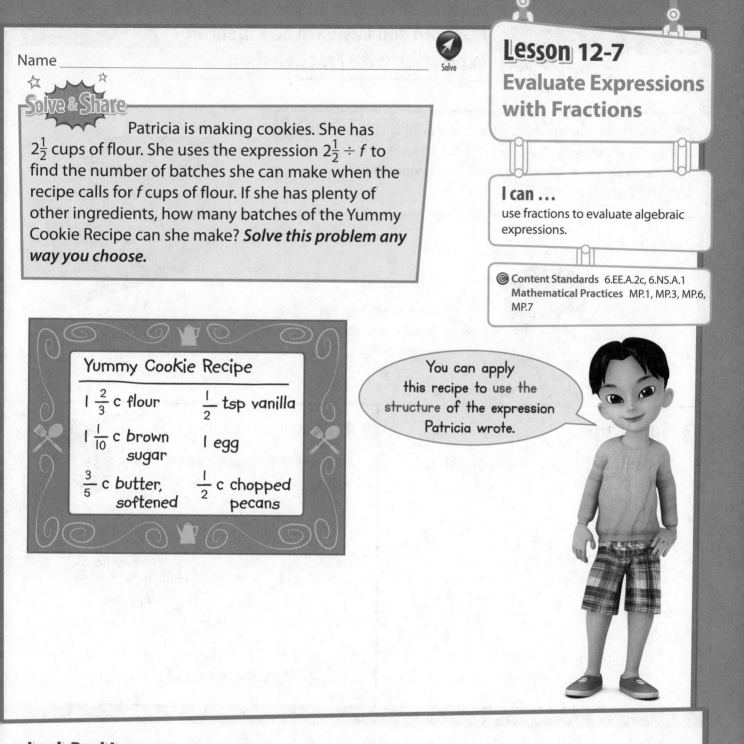

Yummy Cookie Recipe

$1\frac{2}{3}$ c flour $\frac{1}{2}$ tsp vanilla

$1\frac{1}{10}$ c brown sugar   1 egg

$\frac{3}{5}$ c butter, softened $\frac{1}{2}$ c chopped pecans

You can apply this recipe to use the structure of the expression Patricia wrote.

Look Back! © MP. 1 Make Sense and Persevere How can you check that your answer is reasonable and makes sense?

How Can You Evaluate an Algebraic Expression with Fractions?

Essential Question

A

Mr. Grant wants to tile a 27 square foot area with square tiles. Let $s =$ the side length, in feet, of a square tile. Use the expression $27 \div s^2$ to find the number of tiles Mr. Grant needs to buy.

Tile

You can substitute fractions for variables in an expression.

$s = \frac{1}{3}$ ft

B ## Substitute

Substitute $\frac{1}{3}$ for s in the expression $27 \div s^2$.

$$27 \div s^2$$
$$= 27 \div \left(\frac{1}{3} \cdot \frac{1}{3}\right)$$
$$= 27 \div \frac{1}{9}$$

C ## Evaluate

Evaluate the expression.

$$27 \div \frac{1}{9}$$
$$= 27 \cdot \frac{9}{1}$$
$$= 243$$

To divide by $\frac{1}{9}$, multiply by the reciprocal.

Mr. Grant needs to buy 243 tiles.

Convince Me! © **MP. 7 Use Structure** Suppose Mr. Grant decides to buy square tiles that have side lengths of $\frac{3}{4}$ foot. How many of these tiles will he need to buy? Use area reasoning to evaluate an algebraic expression and show how you found the answer.

Another Example

Use order of operations to evaluate the expression $x^2 + 3x - \frac{3}{4}$ for $x = \frac{1}{2}$.

Substitute $\frac{1}{2}$ for the variable x.　　　　　$\left(\frac{1}{2}\right)^2 + 3 \cdot \frac{1}{2} - \frac{3}{4}$

Evaluate powers.　　　　　　　　　　$= \frac{1}{4} + 3 \cdot \frac{1}{2} - \frac{3}{4}$

Multiply and divide from left to right.　　$= \frac{1}{4} + 1\frac{1}{2} - \frac{3}{4}$

Add and subtract from left to right.　　　$= 1\frac{3}{4} - \frac{3}{4} = 1$

☆ Guided Practice*

Do You Understand?

1. How is evaluating an expression with fractions like evaluating an expression with whole numbers? How is it different?

Do You Know How?

In **2** and **3**, evaluate each expression for the given variable value.

2. $x \div 12; x = \frac{2}{3}$　　　　3. $\frac{3}{4} + 4y \div 3; y = 1\frac{1}{2}$

☆ Independent Practice ☆

In **4–11**, evaluate each expression for the given variable value.

4. $j + \frac{3}{8}; j = \frac{3}{4}$

5. $8 - g \div \frac{7}{8}; g = \frac{5}{6}$

6. $3m \div \frac{2}{5}; m = \frac{2}{3}$

7. $w + \left(\frac{11}{12} - \frac{2}{3}\right) \cdot 4;$
   $w = \frac{3}{4}$

8. $k \div 5; k = 4\frac{1}{6}$

9. $1\frac{3}{8} + 2m^2; m = \frac{3}{4}$

10. $12 \div p; p = \frac{3}{4}$

11. $\frac{n}{3} - \frac{n}{6}; n = 2$

In **12** and **13**, complete each table by evaluating the expression for each value of the variable.

Remember to use the order of operations!

12.

i	$\frac{1}{2}$	$\frac{4}{5}$	$1\frac{3}{4}$
$2i + \frac{3}{5}$			

13.

n	$\frac{2}{3}$	$1\frac{1}{5}$	$2\frac{1}{4}$
$3 \div n - \frac{5}{6}$			

*For another example, see Set D on page 650.　　　　**Topic 12** | Lesson 12-7　　**631**

Math Practices and Problem Solving

In **14–17**, use the bin at the right.

14. ⓒ **MP. 1 Make Sense and Persevere** The formula $w = V \div (\ell \cdot h)$ can be used to find the width of the bin shown. Find the width, w, of the bin if the length, ℓ, is 2 feet, the height, h, is 2 feet, and the volume, V, is as shown at the right.

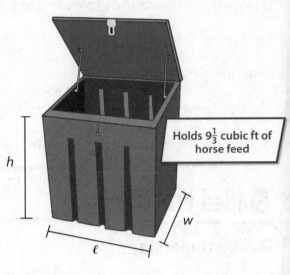

Holds $9\frac{1}{3}$ cubic ft of horse feed

15. ⓒ **MP. 7 Look for Relationships** How much feed does the bin hold:

   a. When it is half full?

   b. When it is three-quarters full?

16. ⓒ **MP. 3 Construct Arguments** The expression $9\frac{1}{3} \div d$, where d is the amount of food a horse can eat each day, can be used to find how many days of feed the bin holds. Explain how to use the expression to find the days of feed for a horse that eats $\frac{1}{6}$ cubic foot of feed each day.

17. **Higher Order Thinking** The formula $V = s^3$ can be used to find the volume of a bin in the shape of a cube. Use the formula to find the volume, V, of a cube-shaped bin with side length s of $\frac{2}{3}$ yard.

18. 🅰🆉 **Vocabulary** What is the *coefficient* in $4x^2$?

ⓒ Common Core Assessment

19. For which value of n does the expression $\frac{9}{n}$ have the greatest value?

   Ⓐ $n = \frac{3}{10}$

   Ⓑ $n = \frac{3}{5}$

   Ⓒ $n = \frac{3}{4}$

   Ⓓ $n = \frac{3}{2}$

Help Practice Tools Games
Buddy

Another Look!

Evaluate $n \cdot \frac{6}{7} - \frac{2}{7}$ for $n = 1\frac{5}{6}$.

Follow the same steps as evaluating expressions with whole numbers.

Step 1

Replace the variable with the given value.

$$1\frac{5}{6} \cdot \frac{6}{7} - \frac{2}{7}$$

Write the mixed-number value as a fraction.

$$\frac{11}{6} \cdot \frac{6}{7} - \frac{2}{7}$$

Step 2

Follow the order of operations. Multiply before subtracting.

$$\frac{11}{6} \cdot \frac{6}{7} - \frac{2}{7}$$
$$= \frac{11}{7} - \frac{2}{7}$$
$$= \frac{9}{7}$$

Step 3

Write the fraction as a mixed number.

$$\frac{9}{7} = 1\frac{2}{7}$$

Leveled Practice In **1–7**, evaluate each expression for the given variable value.

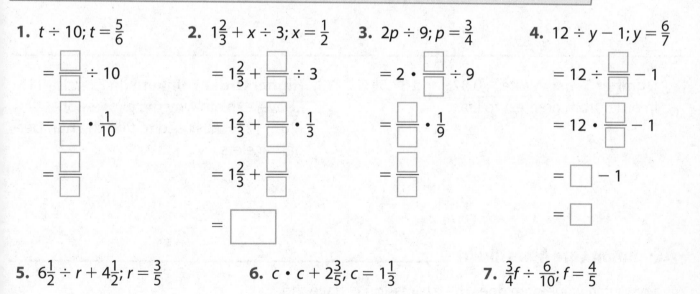

1. $t \div 10; t = \frac{5}{6}$

$$= \frac{\square}{\square} \div 10$$

$$= \frac{\square}{\square} \cdot \frac{1}{10}$$

$$= \frac{\square}{\square}$$

2. $1\frac{2}{3} + x \div 3; x = \frac{1}{2}$

$$= 1\frac{2}{3} + \frac{\square}{\square} \div 3$$

$$= 1\frac{2}{3} + \frac{\square}{\square} \cdot \frac{1}{3}$$

$$= 1\frac{2}{3} + \frac{\square}{\square}$$

$$= \boxed{}$$

3. $2p \div 9; p = \frac{3}{4}$

$$= 2 \cdot \frac{\square}{\square} \div 9$$

$$= \frac{\square}{\square} \cdot \frac{1}{9}$$

$$= \frac{\square}{\square}$$

4. $12 \div y - 1; y = \frac{6}{7}$

$$= 12 \div \frac{\square}{\square} - 1$$

$$= 12 \cdot \frac{\square}{\square} - 1$$

$$= \square - 1$$

$$= \square$$

5. $6\frac{1}{2} \div r + 4\frac{1}{2}; r = \frac{3}{5}$

6. $c \cdot c + 2\frac{3}{5}; c = 1\frac{1}{3}$

7. $\frac{3}{4}f \div \frac{6}{10}; f = \frac{4}{5}$

8. Complete the table by evaluating the expression for each value of the variable.

h	$\frac{2}{3}$	$\frac{4}{5}$	$\frac{7}{8}$	$4\frac{1}{5}$
$3h - \frac{1}{3}$				

9. **© MP.6 Be Precise** The diagram at the right shows the floor size of a square bedroom. What is the area of the floor in square feet?

$s = 3\frac{2}{3}$ yd

10. **© MP. 1 Make Sense and Persevere** Margaret wants to cover a tabletop with rectangular tiles. She wants to order the tile that has the greater area. Her choices are:

   • Tile A is $1\frac{3}{8}$ inches wide and $2\frac{5}{8}$ inches long.

   • Tile B is $1\frac{3}{4}$ inches wide and $2\frac{1}{2}$ inches long.

   Which tile should she order? Explain how you know.

11. Salina has 20 feet of ribbon. She is going to cut the ribbon into equal-sized lengths to make bracelets. Let b = the length of each bracelet in inches. Evaluate the expression $(20 \cdot 12) \div b$.

   a. How many $7\frac{1}{2}$-in. bracelets can Salina make?

   b. How many $6\frac{3}{4}$-in. bracelets can Salina make?

12. **Number Sense** Write $\frac{3}{8}$, 0.375 and 37.5% in order from greatest to least.

13. **Higher Order Thinking** In Exercise 11 above, explain why the expression $(20 \cdot 12) \div b$ is used to find the number of bracelets.

© **Common Core Assessment**

14. For which value of m does the expression $\frac{6}{m}$ have the least value?

   Ⓐ $m = \frac{5}{9}$

   Ⓑ $m = \frac{5}{8}$

   Ⓒ $m = \frac{5}{7}$

   Ⓓ $m = \frac{5}{6}$

Name _____

☆ ☆
Solve & Share

Gayle gave some of her baseball cards to her brother. Now she has 22 cards left. The number of cards left is $\frac{2}{3}$ of the number, n, she had at the start. Gayle wrote the equation shown below to show this situation. How many cards did she start with? *Solve this problem any way you choose.*

I can ...
use fractions to solve equations.

© Content Standards 6.EE.B.7, 6.NS.A.1
Mathematical Practices MP.1, MP.2, MP.3, MP.4

Use reasoning to decide how a variable is related to other terms in an equation or expression.

$$\frac{2}{3} \cdot n = 22$$

Look Back! © **MP.2 Reasoning** Suppose Gayle had used x to represent the number of cards she had at the start. How would that change the solution?

How Can You Solve Algebraic Equations with Fractions?

A

Marcus has carved $3\frac{3}{8}$ feet of a totem. He says that the totem is $\frac{3}{4}$ complete. How tall will the totem be?

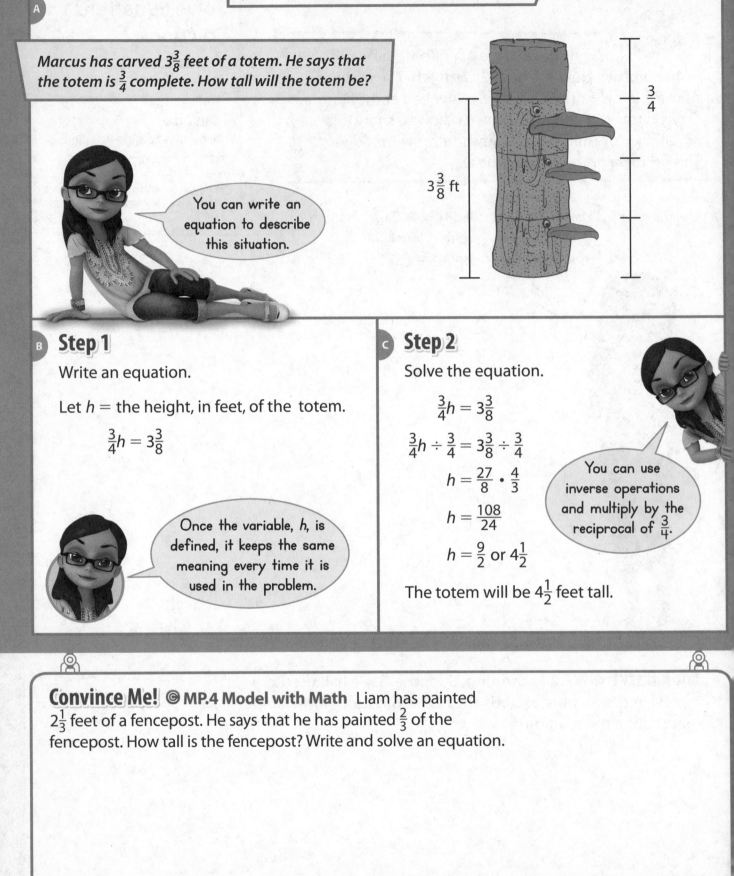

$3\frac{3}{8}$ ft

$\frac{3}{4}$

You can write an equation to describe this situation.

B ## Step 1

Write an equation.

Let h = the height, in feet, of the totem.

$$\frac{3}{4}h = 3\frac{3}{8}$$

Once the variable, h, is defined, it keeps the same meaning every time it is used in the problem.

C ## Step 2

Solve the equation.

$$\frac{3}{4}h = 3\frac{3}{8}$$

$$\frac{3}{4}h \div \frac{3}{4} = 3\frac{3}{8} \div \frac{3}{4}$$

$$h = \frac{27}{8} \cdot \frac{4}{3}$$

$$h = \frac{108}{24}$$

$$h = \frac{9}{2} \text{ or } 4\frac{1}{2}$$

The totem will be $4\frac{1}{2}$ feet tall.

You can use inverse operations and multiply by the reciprocal of $\frac{3}{4}$.

Convince Me! © MP.4 Model with Math Liam has painted $2\frac{1}{3}$ feet of a fencepost. He says that he has painted $\frac{2}{3}$ of the fencepost. How tall is the fencepost? Write and solve an equation.

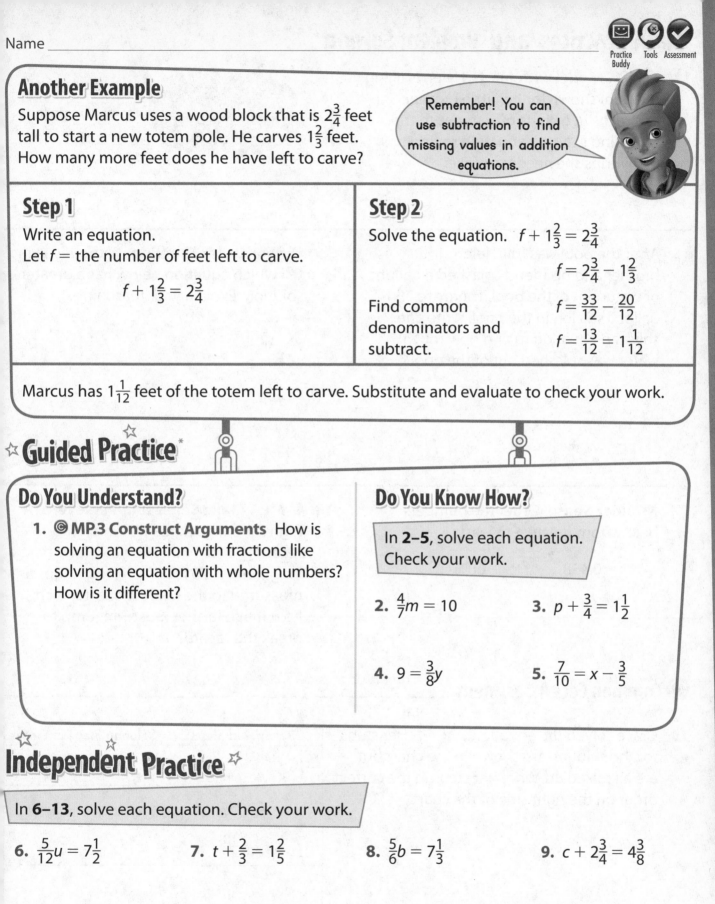

Another Example

Suppose Marcus uses a wood block that is $2\frac{3}{4}$ feet tall to start a new totem pole. He carves $1\frac{2}{3}$ feet. How many more feet does he have left to carve?

Remember! You can use subtraction to find missing values in addition equations.

Step 1

Write an equation.
Let f = the number of feet left to carve.

$$f + 1\frac{2}{3} = 2\frac{3}{4}$$

Step 2

Solve the equation. $f + 1\frac{2}{3} = 2\frac{3}{4}$

$$f = 2\frac{3}{4} - 1\frac{2}{3}$$

Find common denominators and subtract.

$$f = \frac{33}{12} - \frac{20}{12}$$
$$f = \frac{13}{12} = 1\frac{1}{12}$$

Marcus has $1\frac{1}{12}$ feet of the totem left to carve. Substitute and evaluate to check your work.

☆ Guided Practice*

Do You Understand?

1. Ⓒ MP.3 **Construct Arguments** How is solving an equation with fractions like solving an equation with whole numbers? How is it different?

Do You Know How?

In **2–5**, solve each equation. Check your work.

2. $\frac{4}{7}m = 10$

3. $p + \frac{3}{4} = 1\frac{1}{2}$

4. $9 = \frac{3}{8}y$

5. $\frac{7}{10} = x - \frac{3}{5}$

Independent Practice ☆

In **6–13**, solve each equation. Check your work.

6. $\frac{5}{12}u = 7\frac{1}{2}$

7. $t + \frac{2}{3} = 1\frac{2}{5}$

8. $\frac{5}{6}b = 7\frac{1}{3}$

9. $c + 2\frac{3}{4} = 4\frac{3}{8}$

10. $\frac{3}{8} = z \div \frac{4}{9}$

11. $z + 2\frac{3}{10} = 5\frac{1}{5}$

12. $2\frac{2}{3}x = 2\frac{8}{9}$

13. $1\frac{1}{6} = 5\frac{1}{4}v$

*For another example, see Set E on page 650.

Math Practices and Problem Solving

14. © **MP.4 Model with Math** Helen is filling the pool shown for her little brother. She can carry $1\frac{7}{8}$ gallons of water each trip. Write and solve an equation to find how many trips she needs to make.

Holds $10\frac{1}{2}$ gallons

---

15. After the pool was full, Helen's little brother and his friend splashed g gallons of water out of the pool. There are $7\frac{7}{8}$ gallons still left in the pool. Write and solve an equation to find how much water was splashed out of the pool.

16. **Higher Order Thinking** Without solving, tell which equation below has a greater solution. Explain your reasoning.

$$\frac{5}{8}m = 2\frac{3}{4} \qquad \frac{5}{9}m = 2\frac{3}{4}$$

---

17. **Number Sense** Order the numbers below from greatest to least.

$$0.458 \qquad \frac{5}{9} \qquad 60\%$$

18. © **MP.1 Make Sense and Persevere** A high school track team's long jump record is 21 ft $2\frac{1}{4}$ in. This year, Tim's best long jump is 20 ft $9\frac{1}{2}$ in. If long jumps are measured to the nearest quarter inch, how much farther must Tim jump to break the record?

© **Common Core Assessment**

19. Grace solved the equation $2\frac{1}{2}y = \frac{5}{8}$. Her steps for the solution are shown in the chart but are all mixed up. Write her steps in the correct order on the right side of the chart.

Scrambled Steps	Solution Steps in Order
$y = \frac{1}{4}$	
$2\frac{1}{2}y = \frac{5}{8}$	
$y = \frac{10}{40}$	
$\frac{5}{2}y = \frac{5}{8}$	
$y = \frac{5}{8} \cdot \frac{2}{5}$	

Name _____

Another Look!

Solve $\frac{8}{10}f = 2\frac{1}{4}$.

Remember, division and multiplication have an inverse relationship.

Step 1	**Step 2**	**Step 3**
Write mixed numbers as fractions before performing operations. $$\frac{8}{10}f = \frac{9}{4}$$	Solve for f. Multiply by the reciprocal of the coefficient. $$f = \frac{9}{4} \times \frac{10}{8}$$ $$f = \frac{90}{32}$$	Write fractions as mixed numbers, if necessary. $$f = \frac{90}{32} = \frac{45}{16}$$ $$f = 2\frac{13}{16}$$

Leveled Practice In **1–14**, solve each equation. Check your work.

Use inverse operations when finding unknown values in equations.

1. $\frac{3}{4}x = 2$

$\frac{4}{3} \cdot \dfrac{\square}{\square}x = \square \cdot \frac{4}{3}$

$x = \dfrac{\square}{\square} \cdot \frac{4}{3}$

$x = \frac{8}{3} = \square$

2. $\frac{8}{9}y = 3\frac{1}{12}$

$\frac{9}{8} \cdot \dfrac{\square}{\square}y = \square \cdot \frac{9}{8}$

$y = \dfrac{\square}{\square} \cdot \frac{9}{8}$

$y = \dfrac{\square}{96} = \square$

3. $z \div \frac{2}{3} = 1\frac{1}{8}$

4. $t - \frac{2}{3} = \frac{5}{6}$

5. $v + 4\frac{3}{4} = 5\frac{2}{5}$

6. $\frac{7}{10}c = 4\frac{1}{5}$

7. $2\frac{1}{3} = d + \frac{4}{9}$

8. $1\frac{1}{2}b = 6\frac{3}{4}$

9. $m - \frac{5}{6} = 2\frac{2}{3}$

10. $n + 5\frac{7}{10} = 9\frac{3}{5}$

11. $1\frac{1}{4}p = 4\frac{1}{2}$

12. $\frac{4}{5}s = 6$

13. $q \div \frac{7}{9} = 1\frac{2}{7}$

14. $\frac{1}{2} = 8\frac{3}{4}r$

15. © **MP.4 Model with Math** Hugo is painting a rectangular mural on a wall. The area and height of the mural are shown at the right. Write and solve an equation to find the length of the mural.

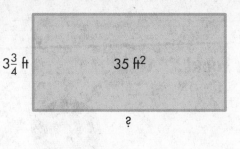

$3\frac{3}{4}$ ft   35 ft^2

?

16. Tian is hiking in a park at a rate of $\frac{3}{50}$ km per minute. If he keeps this pace, how many minutes will it take him to hike a $1\frac{1}{2}$ km trail?

17. © **MP.4 Model with Math** Alejandra is biking to visit a friend. The total distance to her friend's house is $1\frac{3}{4}$ miles. Alejandra has gone $\frac{3}{10}$ of a mile. Write and solve an equation to find how far Alejandra has left to bike.

18. **Higher Order Thinking** Which equations in the table do you think will have a solution greater than 2 and which will have a solution less than 2? Complete the table to check your predictions.

Equation	$\frac{2}{5}x = 2$	$\frac{4}{5}x = 2$	$\frac{6}{5}x = 2$	$\frac{8}{5}x = 2$
Solution				

© **Common Core Assessment**

19. Aaron solved the equation $x + 3\frac{7}{8} = 5\frac{2}{3}$. His steps for the solution are shown in the chart but are all mixed up. Write his steps in the correct order on the right side of the chart.

Scrambled Steps	Solution Steps in Order
$x = 5\frac{16}{24} - 3\frac{21}{24}$	
$x = 4\frac{40}{24} - 3\frac{21}{24}$	
$x = 5\frac{2}{3} - 3\frac{7}{8}$	
$x = 1\frac{19}{24}$	
$x + 3\frac{7}{8} = 5\frac{2}{3}$	

Name _____

Solve & Share

Three members of a local club are making snowflake ornaments using salt dough. Each member brought $2\frac{1}{2}$ cups of flour and $\frac{1}{2}$ cup of salt. How many snowflake ornaments can they make?

Salt Dough Ornament Recipe

Makes 25 snowflake ornaments.

$3\frac{1}{4}$ cups flour

1 cup salt

$1\frac{1}{2}$ cups water

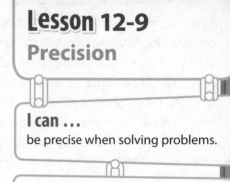

I can ...
be precise when solving problems.

© Mathematical Practices MP.6, MP.1, MP.2, MP.3
Content Standard 6.NS.A.1

Thinking Habits

Be a good thinker!
These questions can help you.

- Am I using numbers, units, and symbols appropriately?

- Am I using the correct definitions?

- Am I calculating accurately?

- Is my answer clear?

Look Back! © **MP.6 Be Precise** If you had only 1 cup of flour and adjusted the recipe accordingly, about how many snowflake ornaments could you make? Explain.

Essential Question **How Can You Be Precise When You Solve Math Problems?**

A

A farmer is building the small horse-riding arena. The fencing around the arena is built using three rows of wood planks. The farmer decided to use wood planks that are $8\frac{1}{2}$ feet long, so he ordered 130 of these wood planks from a local lumberyard. Did he order enough wood planks to build the arena? Explain.

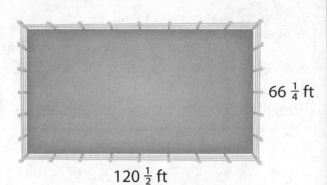

$66\frac{1}{4}$ ft

$120\frac{1}{2}$ ft

What do I need to do to solve the problem?

I need to be precise. I will find the perimeter of the arena and find the number of wood planks needed to build the fencing.

Here's my thinking...

B **How can I be precise in solving this problem?**

I can

- correctly use the information given.

- calculate accurately.

- interpret remainders correctly.

- use appropriate units.

- be sure my answer is clear and appropriate.

C I have to find the perimeter of the arena.

$P = 2 \cdot 120\frac{1}{2} + 2 \cdot 66\frac{1}{4} = 241 + 132\frac{1}{2} = 373\frac{1}{2}$ ft

The farmer needs enough wood planks for 3 times the perimeter.

$3 \cdot 373\frac{1}{2} = 1{,}120\frac{1}{2}$ ft

Now divide to find how many $8\frac{1}{2}$-ft-long planks are needed.

$1{,}120\frac{1}{2} \div 8\frac{1}{2} = \frac{2{,}241}{2} \div \frac{17}{2}$

$= \frac{2{,}241}{2} \cdot \frac{2}{17} = \frac{4{,}482}{34} = 131\frac{14}{17}$

The farmer needs at least 132 wood planks to build the fencing. He did not order enough wood planks.

Convince Me! © **MP.6 Be Precise** The farmer decided that he ordered enough planks for an arena that measured $115\frac{1}{4}$ ft by $63\frac{1}{2}$ ft. Is he correct? Be precise in your explanation.

Name _____

☆ Guided Practice ☆

© MP.6 Be Precise

A $26\frac{1}{5}$-mile marathon is being planned. Water stations and medic tents must be placed along the route.

> You can be precise by calculating accurately when you solve problems.

1. Water stations are being set every $2\frac{1}{2}$ miles along the marathon route and at the finish line. How many water stations are needed?

2. There are 5 medic tents equally spaced along the marathon route, including one at the starting line and one at the finish line. At which mile markers should the other 3 medic tents be placed?

Independent Practice ☆

© MP.6 Be Precise

Horse races are measured in furlongs. The Kentucky Derby is $1\frac{1}{4}$ miles long.

3. How long is the Kentucky Derby in furlongs?

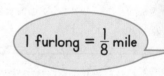

1 furlong = $\frac{1}{8}$ mile

4. The Indianapolis 500 is a 500-mile automobile race. If the Indianapolis-500 were a horse race, how would you describe its length in furlongs?

5. The Belmont Stakes is a 12-furlong horse race. How long is this race in miles?

Math Practices and Problem Solving

Common Core Performance Assessment

Bike Messengers

Companies in large cities sometimes use bike messengers to deliver important documents and other packages. A typical delivery trip takes less than 5 minutes.

Bike Messenger Rates	
Regular Rate	$12.00 per mile (includes pick up)
Rush Rate	$1\frac{1}{2}$ times regular rate
Sunday Rate	$2\frac{1}{2}$ times regular rate

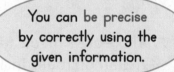

6. **MP.2 Reasoning** A bike messenger rides $\frac{3}{4}$ mile to pick up and deliver a package. How much does he earn on this trip?

You can be precise by correctly using the given information.

7. **MP.1 Make Sense and Persevere** A bike messenger is hired to make a delivery. He rode a total of 1 mile and charged the customer $30.00. What rate was the customer charged for the delivery? Explain how you know.

8. **MP.3 Construct Arguments** A bike messenger rode a total of $3\frac{1}{4}$ miles to deliver a package. She rode at a rate of $\frac{2}{5}$ mile per minute. Did she make the delivery within the typical delivery time? Construct an argument to justify your solution.

Help Practice Buddy Tools Games

Another Look!

Jenna feeds her cat twice a day.

She gives her cat $\frac{3}{4}$ can of cat food each time.

Jenna is having a friend take care of her cat for 5 days.

To prepare, she has bought 8 cans of cat food.

Did Jenna buy enough cat food? Explain.

Tell how you can be precise in your solution.

- I can correctly use the information given.

- I can calculate accurately.

- I can interpret remainders correctly.

- I can use appropriate units.

Solve the problem.

Jenna feeds her cat $\frac{3}{4} \cdot 2 = \frac{6}{4} = 1\frac{1}{2}$ cans of food per day.

$8 \div 1\frac{1}{2} = \frac{8}{1} \div \frac{3}{2} = \frac{8}{1} \cdot \frac{2}{3} = \frac{16}{3} = 5\frac{1}{3}$

Jenna has enough cat food for 5 days.

> You can be precise by using clear and concise notation to record your work.

© **MP.6 Be Precise**

A landscaper has $3\frac{2}{3}$ gallons of concentrated liquid lawn food. The instructions state to mix $\frac{1}{8}$ gallon of the lawn food with water to make 1 gallon of lawn food.

1. How many gallons of lawn food can the landscaper make?

2. The landscaper recommends that $\frac{1}{4}$ gallon of lawn food be used for 6,000 square feet of lawn. How many lawns of this size can the landscaper feed with the lawn food that he has? Explain.

Spirit Wear Fundraiser

Members of the student council are making headbands and cloth bracelets to sell at a fundraiser.

Spirit Wear	Amount of Fabric Needed (in yards)
Headband	$\frac{1}{2}$
Bracelet	$\frac{1}{5}$

3. **MP.6 Be Precise** The members decide that headbands should be made using red fabric and bracelets should be made from blue fabric. They have $8\frac{1}{2}$ yards of blue fabric left over from last year's fundraiser. How many bracelets can they make using this fabric?

4. **MP.2 Reasoning** The student council members want to make the same number of headbands as bracelets. Will the 10 yards of red fabric they have be enough to make the headbands?

5. **MP.1 Make Sense and Persevere** The bracelets will sell for $3 and the headbands will sell for $5. Suppose the council makes all of the bracelets and headbands with only the fabric they have and sells all of the spirit wear. How much money will they have raised?

6. **MP.6 Be Precise** The student council decides to make and sell 50 bracelets and 50 headbands. How much more of each fabric do they need to buy?

Find a Match

Work with a partner. Point to a clue. Read the clue.

Look below the clues to find a match. Write the clue letter in the box next to the match.

Find a match for every clue.

I can ...
divide multi-digit numbers.

© **Content Standard** 6.NS.B.2

Clues

A This quotient is the greatest of them all.

E The quotient is 194 more than the divisor.

U The divisor has the same digits as the quotient.

I Each digit of the quotient is less than 5.

Q The tens digit in the quotient is about $\frac{1}{3}$ the value of the ones digit.

O This quotient is the least of them all.

N The quotient is 3 less than 100.

T The quotient and the divisor are multiples of 9.

☐	☐	☐	☐
7,752 ÷ 34	7,645 ÷ 55	6,786 ÷ 78	12,834 ÷ 46
☐	☐	☐	☐
15,309 ÷ 81	11,931 ÷ 97	5,256 ÷ 72	8,051 ÷ 83

A-Z
Glossary

Word List

- dividend
- divisor
- evaluate
- mixed number
- order of operations
- quotient
- reciprocal

Understand Vocabulary

Choose the best term from the Word List. Write it on the blank.

1. To write a division expression as multiplication, you multiply by the _____ of the _____.

2. The _____ is the quantity to be divided.

3. The result of a division problem is called the _____.

Use the *order of operations* to *evaluate* each expression for $g = \frac{3}{5}$.

4. $3g \div \frac{2}{3}$

5. $9 + g^2 \div 9$

6. $\left(g + \frac{1}{10}\right) + 4g\left(\frac{3}{8}\right)$

Write T for *true* or F for *false*.

_____ 7. The *quotient* of two fractions is always less than the *dividend* and the *divisor*.

_____ 8. A *mixed number* can always be written as a fraction.

_____ 9. Dividing by x is the same as multiplying by $\frac{1}{x}$.

Use Vocabulary in Writing

10. Explain how to use multiplication to find the value of $\frac{1}{3} \div \frac{9}{5}$. Use at least 3 words from the Word List in your explanation.

Set A | pages 593–598, 599–604

Find $4 \div \frac{4}{5}$. Use a number line.

Divide 4 into $\frac{4}{5}$ parts.

$4 \div \frac{4}{5} = 5$

Remember that when the divisor is less than 1, the quotient is greater than the dividend.

1. $7 \div \frac{1}{2}$ 2. $6 \div \frac{2}{5}$

3. $2 \div \frac{1}{8}$ 4. $8 \div \frac{4}{9}$

Set B | pages 605–610, 611–616

Use a model to find $\frac{3}{4} \div \frac{1}{8}$.

There are six $\frac{1}{8}$ parts in $\frac{3}{4}$, so $\frac{3}{4} \div \frac{1}{8} = 6$.

Find $\frac{3}{4} \div \frac{5}{8}$.

$\frac{3}{4} \div \frac{5}{8} = \frac{3}{4} \times \frac{8}{5}$ — Rewrite the problem as a multiplication problem.

$\frac{3}{4} \times \frac{8}{5} = \frac{24}{20}$ or $1\frac{1}{5}$ — Multiply. Then write fraction quotients as mixed numbers.

Remember that the product of a number and its reciprocal is 1.

Use a model to find **1** and **2**.

1. $\frac{1}{2} \div \frac{1}{4}$ 2. $\frac{8}{10} \div \frac{1}{5}$

For **3–6**, find each quotient.

3. $\frac{5}{6} \div \frac{3}{8}$ 4. $\frac{1}{3} \div \frac{1}{2}$

5. $5 \div \frac{5}{16}$ 6. $\frac{7}{12} \div \frac{3}{4}$

Set C | pages 617–622, 623–628

Find $6\frac{1}{2} \div 1\frac{1}{6}$. Estimate first by rounding or using compatible numbers.

$6\frac{1}{2}$ is about 7. $1\frac{1}{6}$ is about 1.

$7 \div 1 = 7$

$6\frac{1}{2} \div 1\frac{1}{6} = \frac{13}{2} \div \frac{7}{6}$ — Write the mixed numbers as fractions.

$\frac{13}{2} \div \frac{7}{6} = \frac{13}{2} \times \frac{6}{7}$ — Then write the problem as a multiplication problem using the reciprocal of the divisor.

$\frac{13}{2} \times \frac{6}{7} = \frac{78}{14}$ or $5\frac{4}{7}$ — Multiply. Write fraction quotients as mixed numbers.

$5\frac{4}{7}$ is close to the estimate of 7.

Remember to estimate before solving the problem so you can check the reasonableness of your answer.

Estimate and find each quotient.

1. $6\frac{3}{8} \div 4\frac{1}{4}$ 2. $9 \div 2\frac{2}{7}$

3. $3\frac{3}{5} \div 1\frac{1}{5}$ 4. $5\frac{1}{2} \div 3\frac{3}{8}$

5. $3\frac{2}{5} \div 1\frac{1}{5}$ 6. $12\frac{1}{6} \div 3$

Set D pages 629–634

Use substitution to evaluate the expression for $r = \frac{1}{5}$.

$10 \div r$

$10 \div \frac{1}{5}$ **Substitute $\frac{1}{5}$ for r.**

$10 \cdot \frac{5}{1}$ **Find the reciprocal of $\frac{1}{5}$ and change the division to multiplication.**

$\frac{50}{1} = 50$ **Write fractions as whole or mixed numbers.**

Remember you can use the order of operations to evaluate expressions for a specified value of a variable.

Evaluate each expression for $b = \frac{5}{6}$.

1. $b \div 20$ **2.** $7b \div 2$

3. $b \div \frac{1}{5}$ **4.** $6\frac{3}{4} \div 3b$

Set E pages 635–640

Solve for the value of q.

$\frac{3}{4}q = 4\frac{1}{2}$

$q = 4\frac{1}{2} \cdot \frac{4}{3}$ **Multiply by the reciprocal of the coefficient.**

$q = \frac{9}{2} \cdot \frac{4}{3}$ **Change mixed numbers to fractions.**

$q = 6$ **Solve.**

Remember that you can use inverse operations to solve each equation.

Solve each equation.

1. $\frac{5}{6}h = 22$ **2.** $\frac{1}{3}i = 15$

3. $4\frac{5}{8} + e = 6\frac{3}{4}$ **4.** $j \div 4\frac{1}{2} = \frac{3}{8}$

Set F pages 641–646

Think about these questions to help you **be precise** when you solve problems.

Thinking Habits

- Am I using numbers, units, and symbols appropriately?

- Am I using the correct definitions?

- Am I calculating accurately?

- Is my answer clear?

Remember to use the given information to solve the problem.

Daisy has a cucumber that is 8 inches long. She cuts the cucumber into $\frac{3}{8}$-inch thick slices and adds them to a salad. How many $\frac{3}{8}$-inch thick slices did she make?

1. Write an equation to represent the problem. Let $s =$ the number of slices.

2. Explain how to use the equation to solve the problem. Solve. Then explain your answer.

1. Raven is making pillows. Each pillow requires $\frac{3}{5}$ yard of fabric. Raven has 6 yards of fabric. Use the number line to find $6 \div \frac{3}{5}$, the number of pillows Raven can make.

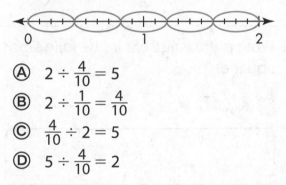

Ⓐ 10 pillows

Ⓑ 6 pillows

Ⓒ 5 pillows

Ⓓ 3 pillows

2. Look at the number line below.

Part A

Which number sentence is represented by the number line?

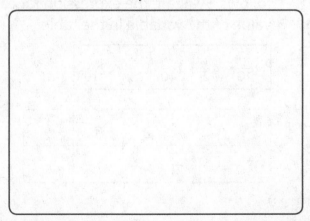

Ⓐ $2 \div \frac{4}{10} = 5$

Ⓑ $2 \div \frac{1}{10} = \frac{4}{10}$

Ⓒ $\frac{4}{10} \div 2 = 5$

Ⓓ $5 \div \frac{4}{10} = 2$

Part B

Explain how the number line shows the number sentence you chose.

3. Which expression has the same value as $3 \div \frac{5}{9}$?

Ⓐ $3 \times \frac{5}{9}$

Ⓑ $\frac{1}{3} \div \frac{5}{9}$

Ⓒ $3 \div \frac{9}{5}$

Ⓓ $3 \times \frac{9}{5}$

4. Holly is displaying a postcard collection on a bulletin board that is $35\frac{3}{4}$ inches wide. Each postcard is $5\frac{7}{8}$ inches wide. Holly estimates the number of postcards she can display in each row is 7. Is this the best estimate? Explain your reasoning.

5. A model train is $15\frac{3}{4}$ inches long. Each car on this train is $2\frac{5}{8}$ inches in length. How many cars are on the train?

Ⓐ 3 cars

Ⓑ 4 cars

Ⓒ 5 cars

Ⓓ 6 cars

6. Mr. Sanchez is making pancakes. Each batch of pancakes uses $\frac{3}{4}$ cup of milk. There are 16 cups in 1 gallon.

Part A

How many full batches can he make with $\frac{1}{2}$ gallon of milk? Explain how you know.

Part B

How many more cups would Mr. Sanchez need to make 12 batches of pancakes? Show how you know.

7. Find the quotient. Use the diagram to help.

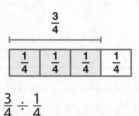

$$\frac{3}{4} \div \frac{1}{4}$$

8. How many $\frac{1}{8}$-pint tubes can be filled from a $\frac{3}{4}$-pint bottle of hydrogen peroxide?

9. Evaluate each expression for the value of the variable shown. Draw a line to match each expression in Column A with its value in Column B.

Column A	Column B
$2\frac{1}{6} \div d, \ d = \frac{2}{3}$	$\frac{5}{6}$
$3\frac{1}{3} \div a, \ a = 4$	$13\frac{1}{3}$
$2\frac{1}{6} \div b, \ b = \frac{1}{2}$	$3\frac{1}{4}$
$3\frac{1}{3} \div c, \ c = \frac{1}{4}$	$4\frac{1}{3}$

10. Which of the following tells the number of $\frac{3}{4}$-foot long pieces of ribbon that can be cut from a ribbon that is $7\frac{3}{8}$ feet long?

Ⓐ $4\frac{5}{6}$ pieces   Ⓒ $9\frac{1}{3}$ pieces

Ⓑ $5\frac{17}{32}$ pieces   Ⓓ $9\frac{5}{6}$ pieces

11. What is the value of t in the following equation?

$$t + \frac{1}{4} = 2\frac{7}{12}$$

12. Choose the correct numbers from the box below to complete the table that follows. Evaluate the expression for each value of the variable in the table.

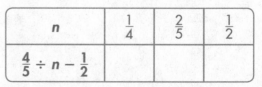

$$1\frac{1}{10} \quad 1\frac{1}{2} \quad 1\frac{7}{10} \quad 2\frac{1}{2} \quad 2\frac{7}{10}$$

n	$\frac{1}{4}$	$\frac{2}{5}$	$\frac{1}{2}$
$\frac{4}{5} \div n - \frac{1}{2}$			

Name _____

This is Anna's recipe for vegetable bean soup.

Vegetable Bean Soup
Serves 8

$1\frac{1}{4}$ cups navy beans   1 cup carrots $\frac{2}{3}$ cup onions

$1\frac{3}{4}$ pounds cabbage $\frac{7}{8}$ cup turnips $1\frac{1}{8}$ teaspoons of thyme

$1\frac{1}{2}$ cups potatoes

1. Anna is using a $\frac{1}{4}$-cup measuring cup.

   Part A
   How many times will she need to fill the measuring cup to measure
   $\frac{7}{8}$ cup of turnips? Show your work.

   Part B
   How many times will she need to fill the measuring cup
   to measure $1\frac{1}{4}$ cups of navy beans? Show your work.

2. If Anna divides the ingredients equally into 4 pots, how many cups
   of onions will she need in each pot?

3. Anna has 14 pounds of cabbage. To find how many batches of the recipe she
   can make with that amount of cabbage, she wrote the equation $1\frac{3}{4}t = 14$.

   Part A
   Explain how the numbers in the equation relate to the situation and
   what the variable in Anna's equation represents. Then solve to find the
   number of batches she can make.

Part B

Use the equation $1\frac{3}{4}t = c$. Let $t = 10$ batches and solve to find how many pounds of cabbage, c, Anna will need to serve soup to 80 people.

4. Sam has the ingredients listed below. He wants to make as many batches of vegetable bean soup as he can. Estimate the greatest number of servings he can make with the ingredients he has if he makes whole batches. Explain your answer.

   • 6 cups navy beans
   • 6 pounds cabbage
   • 4 cups each of potatoes, carrots, and turnips
   • 3 cups onions
   • 5 teaspoons thyme

Solve Area Problems

Essential Question: How can the area of certain shapes be found?

Digital Resources

Solve   Learn   Glossary   Practice Buddy

Tools   Assessment   Help   Games

Scientists must have a clear set of goals and limits to evaluate solutions to problems.

Using scientific principles to manage storm water helps increase water supplies while reducing pollution.

Managing storm water sure covers a lot of ground! Here's a project on storm water solutions and area.

Math and Science Project: Just Passing Through the Area

Do Research Use the Internet or other sources to learn about what pervious concrete is, what it does, and how much it costs per square foot to use. Locate a map of your school that shows parking lots and sidewalks and has a scale for finding distances.

Journal: Write a Report Include what you found. Also in your report:

- Decide on a total project cost for installing pervious concrete.

- Calculate the areas in square feet of parking lots, sidewalks, and patio areas around your school. Draw shapes on your map to support your calculations.

- Write a plan for which areas to replace with pervious concrete based on your budget.

Name _____

Review What You Know

A-Z Vocabulary

Choose the best term from the box.
Write it on the blank.

• parallel   • perpendicular
• parallelogram   • polygon

1. A triangle is an example of a three-sided _____.

2. _____ lines form a right angle.

3. A _____ has opposite sides that are parallel and the same length.

Evaluate Expressions

Find the value of each expression when $a = 12$, $b = 3$, $c = 4$, and $d = 9$.

4. ac

5. $\frac{1}{2}b$

6. bd

7. $0.5a$

8. $\frac{3}{4}(ad)$

9. $ab + cd$

Multiply Decimals

Find each product.

10. 3.14×12

11. 45.8×5

12. 0.8×2.7

13. 35×12.8

14. 64.9×5.8

15. 7.75×3.4

Geometry

16. How are parallelograms and rectangles similar and how are they different?

My Word Cards

Use the example for the word on the front of the card to help complete the definition on the back.

kite

My Word Cards

Complete the definition. Extend learning by writing your own definition.

A quadrilateral with two pairs of adjacent sides that are equal in length is a

_____

Name _____

Solve & Share

Connect point *A* to *B*, *B* to *C*, *C* to *D*, and *D* to *A*. Then find the area of the shape and explain how you found it. Using the same grid, move points *B* and *C* four units to the right. Connect the points to make a new parallelogram *ABCD*. What is the area of this shape? **Solve this problem any way you choose.**

I can ...
use what I know about areas of rectangles to find the areas of parallelograms and rhombuses.

© **Content Standards** 6.G.A.1, 6.EE.A.2c
Mathematical Practices MP.2, MP.3, MP.4, MP.6, MP.7, MP.8

You can use structure by finding relationships between rectangles and parallelograms.

Look Back! © **MP. 8 Generalize** How do you think you can find the area of any parallelogram?

How Can You Use the Formula for the Area of a Rectangle to Find the Area Formula of a Parallelogram?

A

Look at the parallelogram below. If you move the triangle to the opposite side, you form a rectangle with the same area as the parallelogram. How can you find the formula to find the area of the parallelogram?

To compose the rectangle, you first decompose the parallelogram into a triangle and a trapezoid.

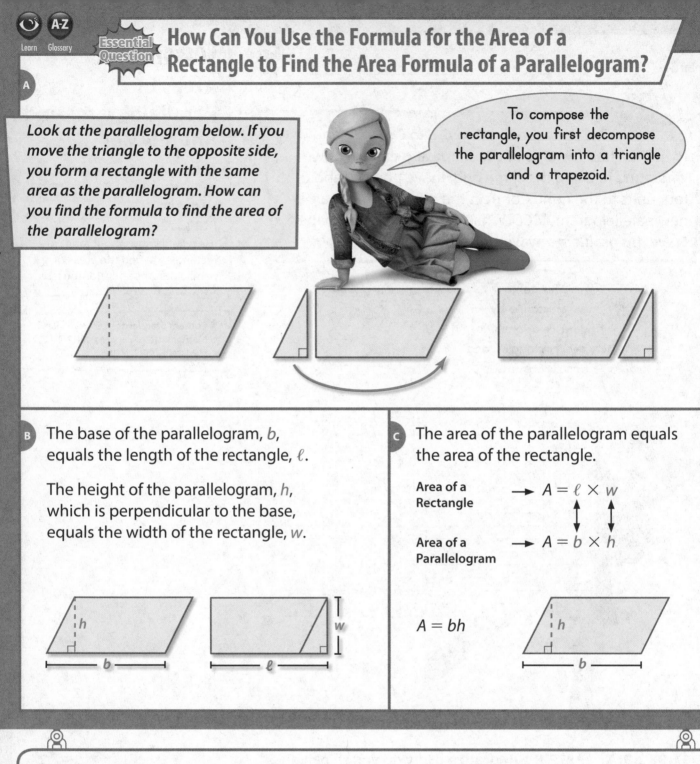

B The base of the parallelogram, b, equals the length of the rectangle, ℓ.

The height of the parallelogram, h, which is perpendicular to the base, equals the width of the rectangle, w.

C The area of the parallelogram equals the area of the rectangle.

Area of a Rectangle → $A = \ell \times w$

Area of a Parallelogram → $A = b \times h$

$A = bh$

Convince Me! © **MP.6 Be Precise** What is the area of a parallelogram if the base, b, is 7 centimeters and the height, h, is 4.5 centimeters? Write an equation to show how you know.

Practice Buddy   Tools   Assessment

Another Example

How do you find the area of a rhombus?

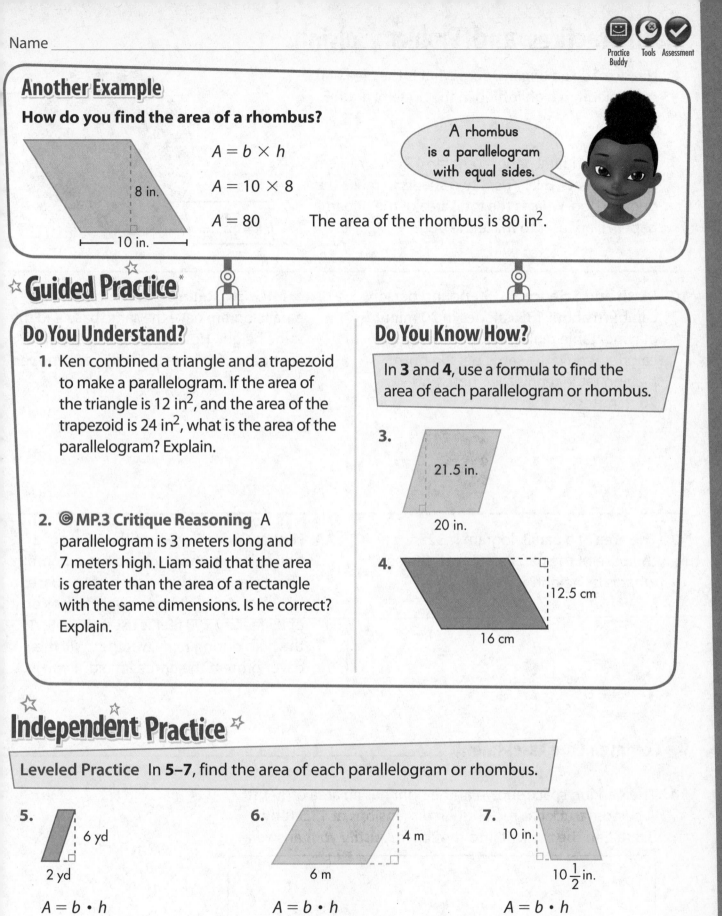

$A = b \times h$

$A = 10 \times 8$

$A = 80$ The area of the rhombus is 80 in².

8 in.

10 in.

A rhombus is a parallelogram with equal sides.

☆ Guided Practice*

Do You Understand?

1. Ken combined a triangle and a trapezoid to make a parallelogram. If the area of the triangle is 12 in², and the area of the trapezoid is 24 in², what is the area of the parallelogram? Explain.

2. ⓒ **MP.3 Critique Reasoning** A parallelogram is 3 meters long and 7 meters high. Liam said that the area is greater than the area of a rectangle with the same dimensions. Is he correct? Explain.

Do You Know How?

In **3** and **4**, use a formula to find the area of each parallelogram or rhombus.

3.

21.5 in.

20 in.

4.

12.5 cm

16 cm

Independent Practice ☆

Leveled Practice In **5–7**, find the area of each parallelogram or rhombus.

5.

6 yd

2 yd

$A = b \cdot h$

$= \underline{\quad} \cdot 6$

$= \underline{\quad}$ yd²

6.

4 m

6 m

$A = b \cdot h$

$= \underline{\quad} \cdot \underline{\quad}$

$= 24$ m²

7.

10 in.

$10\frac{1}{2}$ in.

$A = b \cdot h$

$= \underline{\quad} \cdot \underline{\quad}$

$= \underline{\quad}$ in²

Math Practices and Problem Solving

8. Hilary made an origami dog. What is the area of the parallelogram highlighted in the origami figure?

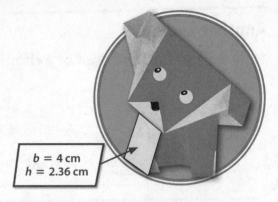

9. A type of origami paper comes in 15 cm by 15 cm square sheets. Hilary uses two sheets to make the origami dog. What is the total area of the origami paper Hilary uses to make the dog?

$b = 4$ cm
$h = 2.36$ cm

10. **Math and Science** A 150-pound person can burn about 135 calories in 30 minutes playing table tennis. About how many calories would the same person burn playing table tennis for 1 hour and 20 minutes?

11. © **MP.2 Reasoning** A rectangle and a parallelogram have the same base and the same height. How are their areas related? Provide an example to justify your answer.

12. The area of a parallelogram is 325 ft². If the base of the parallelogram is 25 feet, what is its height?

13. **Higher Order Thinking** The infield of a baseball diamond is shaped like a rhombus. The distance between each of the bases is 90 feet. An infield cover with dimensions of 85 feet by 100 feet is used to protect the field during rainy weather. Will the cover protect the entire infield? Explain.

© **Common Core Assessment**

14. The parking space shown at the right has an area of 171 ft². A custom truck has rectangular dimensions of 13.5 ft by 8.5 ft. Can the truck fit into the space? Justify your answer.

19 ft

b ft

Name _____

Another Look!

Remember to write areas in square units (units^2).

Find the area of the parallelogram.

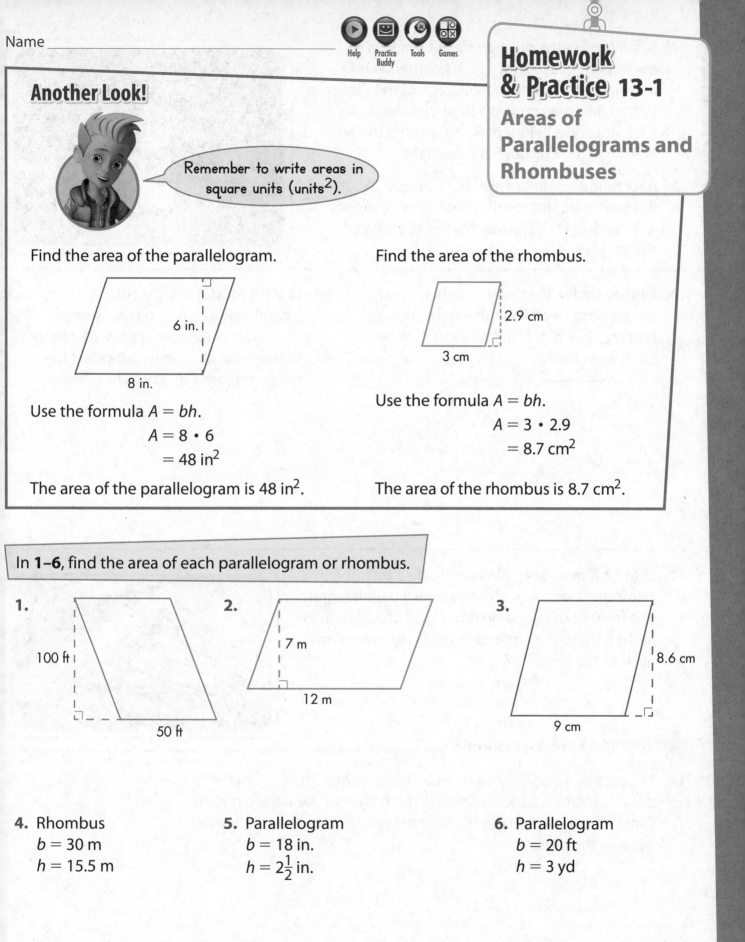

6 in.

8 in.

Use the formula $A = bh$.

$A = 8 \cdot 6$

$= 48 \text{ in}^2$

The area of the parallelogram is 48 in^2.

Find the area of the rhombus.

2.9 cm

3 cm

Use the formula $A = bh$.

$A = 3 \cdot 2.9$

$= 8.7 \text{ cm}^2$

The area of the rhombus is 8.7 cm^2.

In **1–6**, find the area of each parallelogram or rhombus.

1.

100 ft

50 ft

2.

7 m

12 m

3.

8.6 cm

9 cm

4. Rhombus
$b = 30$ m
$h = 15.5$ m

5. Parallelogram
$b = 18$ in.
$h = 2\frac{1}{2}$ in.

6. Parallelogram
$b = 20$ ft
$h = 3$ yd

7. Sarah applies the pearl guitar fret markers to her fret board as shown. Each fret marker is in the shape of a parallelogram. Each of the three bottom fret markers has a base that measures 52.5 mm and a height of 6 mm. What is the area of each of the bottom fret markers?

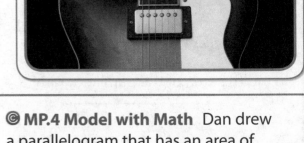

8. A rectangular guitar case has a unique sticker printed on its surface that measures 20 inches long and 45 inches wide. What is the area of the sticker?

9. **Higher Order Thinking** Tony says that he does not have enough information to find the area of this parallelogram. Is he correct? Explain.

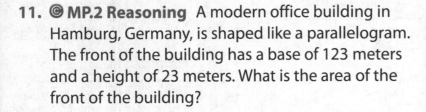

7.2 cm

14.5 cm

10. ⓒ **MP.4 Model with Math** Dan drew a parallelogram that has an area of 144 square inches to represent a section of sidewalk. Draw an example of the parallelogram Dan could have drawn.

11. ⓒ **MP.2 Reasoning** A modern office building in Hamburg, Germany, is shaped like a parallelogram. The front of the building has a base of 123 meters and a height of 23 meters. What is the area of the front of the building?

ⓒ **Common Core Assessment**

12. The area of a parallelogram is 42 square inches. The base of the parallelogram is 6 inches. What is the height of the parallelogram? Explain how you can use the formula for the area of a parallelogram to solve the problem.

Name _____

Lesson 13-2
Areas of Triangles

Solve & Share

Connect point *A* to *B*, *B* to *C*, *C* to *D*, and *D* to *A*. Then draw a diagonal line connecting opposite vertices in the figure and find the area of each triangle formed. **Solve this problem any way you choose.**

I can ...
find the areas of triangles.

© Content Standards 6.G.A.1, 6.EE.A.2c
Mathematical Practices MP.1, MP.2, MP.3, MP.7, MP.8

You can look for and make use of structure when evaluating relationships between the areas of parallelograms and triangles.

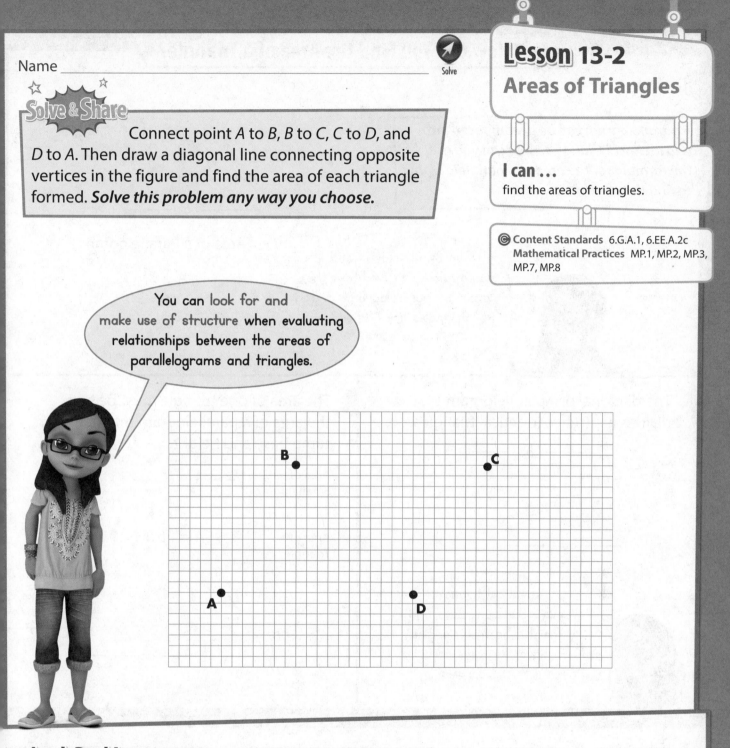

Look Back! © **MP.8 Generalize** What is a rule for finding the area of any triangle?

Essential Question How Can You Find the Area of a Triangle?

A

A parallelogram can be decomposed into two identical triangles. How can you use the formula for the area of a parallelogram to find the area of a triangle?

Reason abstractly and quantitatively to find how the areas of parallelograms and triangles are related.

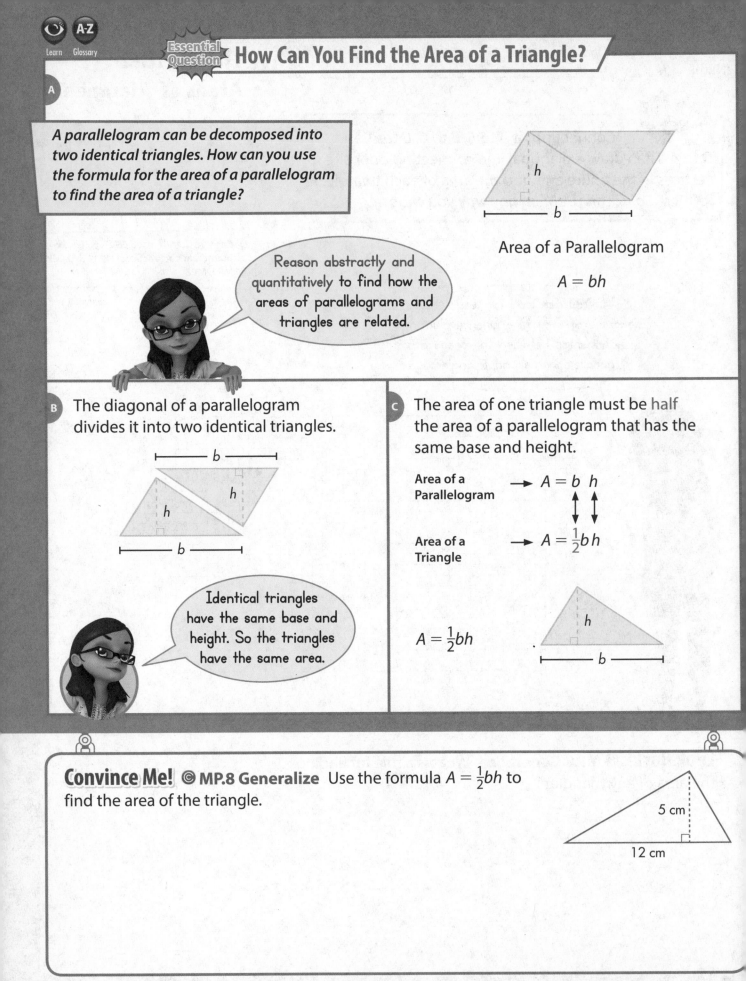

Area of a Parallelogram

$$A = bh$$

B The diagonal of a parallelogram divides it into two identical triangles.

Identical triangles have the same base and height. So the triangles have the same area.

C The area of one triangle must be half the area of a parallelogram that has the same base and height.

Area of a Parallelogram → $A = b\ h$

Area of a Triangle → $A = \frac{1}{2}bh$

$A = \frac{1}{2}bh$

Convince Me! © MP.8 Generalize Use the formula $A = \frac{1}{2}bh$ to find the area of the triangle.

5 cm

12 cm

Another Example

Kaylan drew the triangle shown below. Find the area of the triangle.

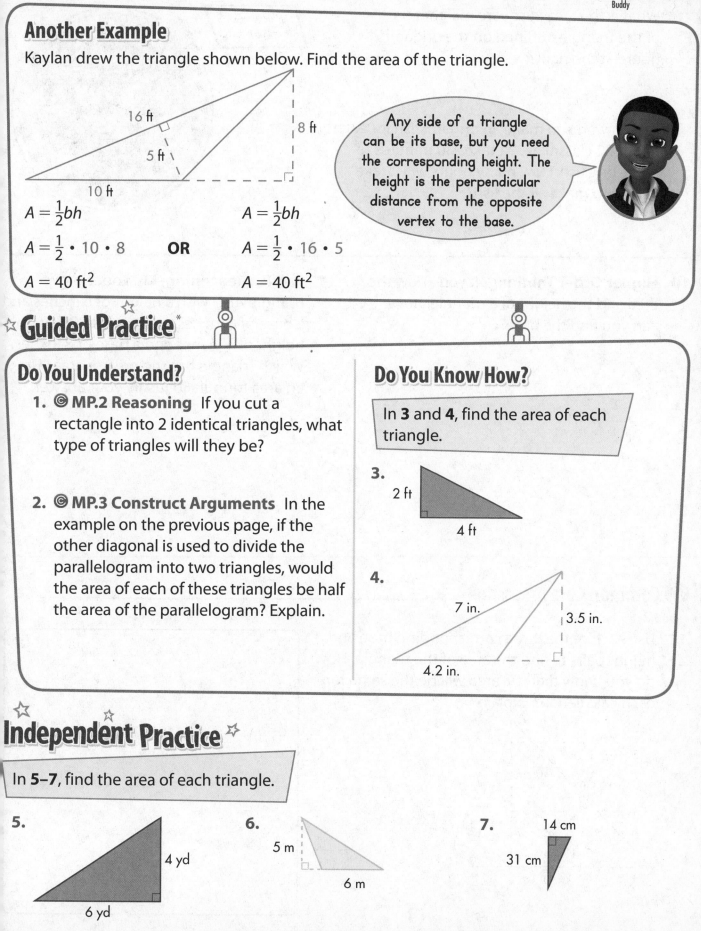

16 ft
8 ft
5 ft
10 ft

$A = \frac{1}{2}bh$

$A = \frac{1}{2} \cdot 10 \cdot 8$

$A = 40 \text{ ft}^2$

OR

$A = \frac{1}{2}bh$

$A = \frac{1}{2} \cdot 16 \cdot 5$

$A = 40 \text{ ft}^2$

Any side of a triangle can be its base, but you need the corresponding height. The height is the perpendicular distance from the opposite vertex to the base.

Guided Practice *

Do You Understand?

1. ⓒ **MP.2 Reasoning** If you cut a rectangle into 2 identical triangles, what type of triangles will they be?

2. ⓒ **MP.3 Construct Arguments** In the example on the previous page, if the other diagonal is used to divide the parallelogram into two triangles, would the area of each of these triangles be half the area of the parallelogram? Explain.

Do You Know How?

In **3** and **4**, find the area of each triangle.

3.
2 ft
4 ft

4.
7 in.
3.5 in.
4.2 in.

Independent Practice *

In **5–7**, find the area of each triangle.

5.
4 yd
6 yd

6.
5 m
6 m

7.
14 cm
31 cm

Math Practices and Problem Solving

8. What is the area in square millimeters of the triangle outlined on the origami figure at the right?

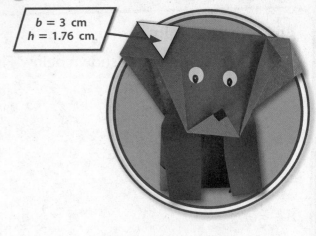

b = 3 cm
h = 1.76 cm

9. Fawzia wants to make an origami fish for each of her 22 classmates. It takes 30 minutes to make one fish. How many hours will it take Fawzia to make all the fish?

---

10. Higher Order Thinking If you know the area and the height of a triangle, how can you find the base?

11. © MP.2 Reasoning Ms. Lopez drew triangle *ABC*, with a height of 6 inches and a base of 6 inches, and triangle *RST*, with a height of 4 inches and a base of 8 inches. Which triangle has the greater area? Use an area formula to justify your answer.

© Common Core Assessment

12. Use each of the three corresponding base and height pairs to find the area of the triangle. How do you know that the area will be the same for each calculation? Explain.

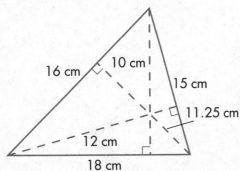

16 cm
10 cm
15 cm
11.25 cm
12 cm
18 cm

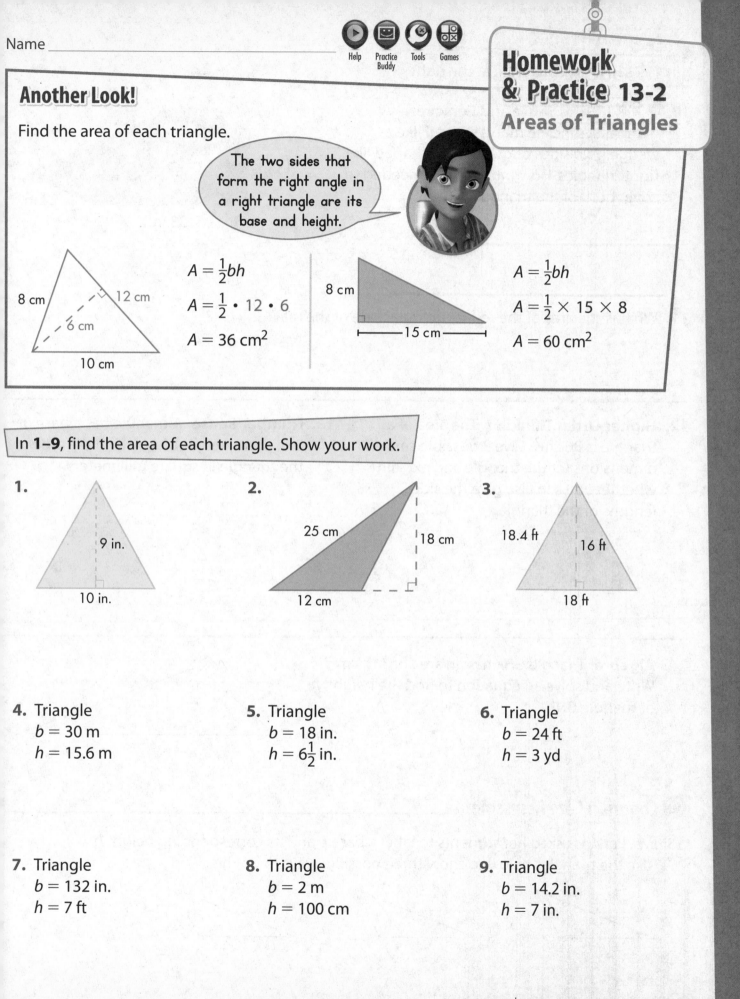

Help   Practice   Tools   Games
       Buddy

Another Look!

Find the area of each triangle.

The two sides that form the right angle in a right triangle are its base and height.

8 cm   12 cm

6 cm

10 cm

$A = \frac{1}{2}bh$

$A = \frac{1}{2} \cdot 12 \cdot 6$

$A = 36 \text{ cm}^2$

8 cm

15 cm

$A = \frac{1}{2}bh$

$A = \frac{1}{2} \times 15 \times 8$

$A = 60 \text{ cm}^2$

In **1–9**, find the area of each triangle. Show your work.

1.

9 in.

10 in.

2.

25 cm

18 cm

12 cm

3.

18.4 ft   16 ft

18 ft

4. Triangle
   $b = 30$ m
   $h = 15.6$ m

5. Triangle
   $b = 18$ in.
   $h = 6\frac{1}{2}$ in.

6. Triangle
   $b = 24$ ft
   $h = 3$ yd

7. Triangle
   $b = 132$ in.
   $h = 7$ ft

8. Triangle
   $b = 2$ m
   $h = 100$ cm

9. Triangle
   $b = 14.2$ in.
   $h = 7$ in.

10. © **MP.1 Make Sense and Persevere** A gymnastics incline mat is shaped like a wedge. Two sides of the mat are shaped like right triangles. How much vinyl is needed to cover both of the triangular sides?

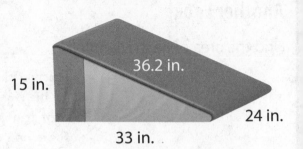

15 in.

36.2 in.

24 in.

33 in.

11. What is the area of the red rectangular side of the mat?

12. **Higher Order Thinking** The area of a triangle is 36 cm^2. Give 3 possible sets of dimensions for the triangle and explain whether you can also give the side lengths of the triangle.

13. **Number Sense** A triangle has a base of 2 m and a height of 4 m. Find the area of the triangle in square millimeters.

14. **Algebra** Triangle *GHK* has an area of 117 cm^2. Write and solve an equation to find the height, *h*, of triangle *GHK*.

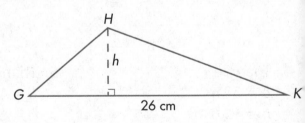

H

h

G

26 cm

K

© **Common Core Assessment**

15. Ms. Perkins asked her students to label a base *b* and its corresponding height *h*. Use the triangles below to show three possible ways to do this.

Name _____

☆ ☆
Solve & Share

The European basketball key was changed from a trapezoid shape to a rectangle in 2010. The diagram shows the shape of the key before 2010 outlined in blue. How could you decompose this shape to find its area? *Solve this problem any way you choose.*

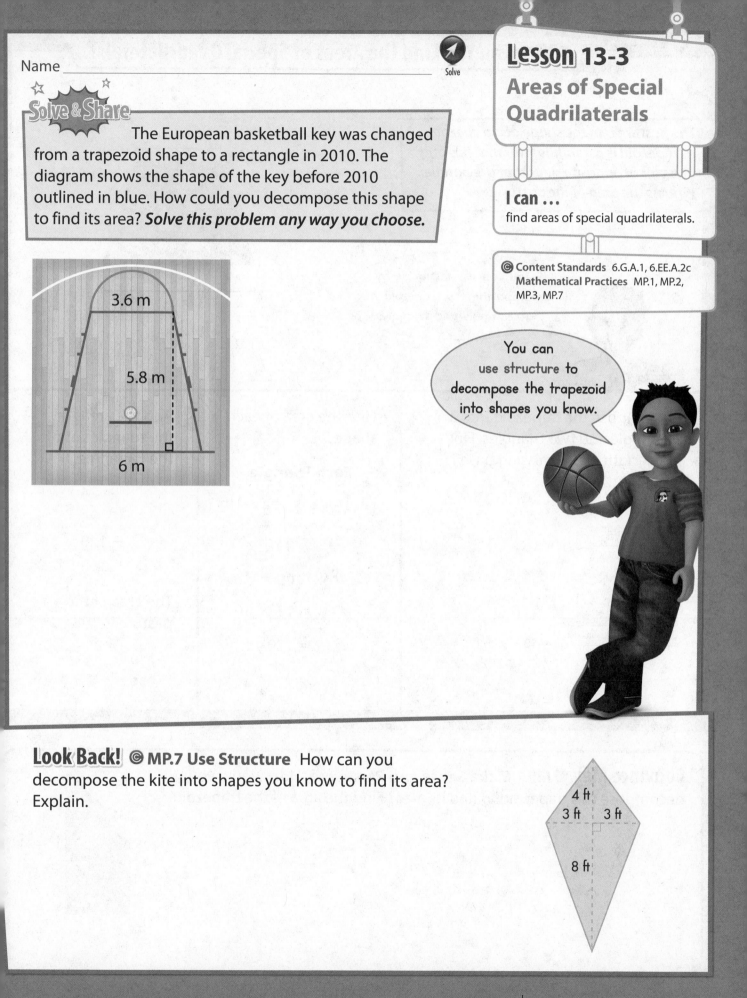

3.6 m

5.8 m

6 m

Lesson 13-3
Areas of Special Quadrilaterals

I can ...
find areas of special quadrilaterals.

© **Content Standards** 6.G.A.1, 6.EE.A.2c
Mathematical Practices MP.1, MP.2, MP.3, MP.7

You can use structure to decompose the trapezoid into shapes you know.

Look Back! © **MP.7 Use Structure** How can you decompose the kite into shapes you know to find its area? Explain.

4 ft
3 ft   3 ft

8 ft

A

The pasture is in the shape of a trapezoid. A trapezoid is a quadrilateral that has only one pair of opposite sides that are parallel. What is the area of the pasture?

10 yd

12 yd

4 yd

18 yd

You can use structure by decomposing the trapezoid into a rectangle and triangles.

B Decompose the trapezoid into a rectangle and two triangles. Find the length of any missing base or height.

10 yd

12 yd

4 yd   10 yd   4 yd   ◄— $18 - (4 + 10) = 4$

18 yd

C Find the area of each shape.

Each Triangle

$A = \frac{1}{2}bh = \frac{1}{2} \times 4 \times 12$

$= 24 \text{ yd}^2$

Rectangle

$A = \ell w = 12 \times 10$

$= 120 \text{ yd}^2$

D Add the areas of the triangles and the rectangle.

```
   24
   24
+ 120
  168
```

The area of the pasture is 168 yd².

Convince Me! © **MP.1 Make Sense and Persevere** How would you decompose this trapezoid to find its area? Find the area of the trapezoid.

11.25 ft

6.25 ft

5 ft

Another Example

Jackson has a rectangular piece of cloth that has an area of 298 cm². Does he have enough cloth to make the kite shown?

A **kite** is a quadrilateral with two pairs of adjacent sides that are equal in length.

Find the area of the kite by dividing it into two identical triangles.

$A = \frac{1}{2}bh$

$A = \frac{1}{2} \cdot 30 \cdot 10$

$A = 150 \text{ cm}^2$

The area is $2 \times 150 = 300 \text{ cm}^2$.
Jackson does not have enough cloth to make the kite.

5 cm
10 cm
25 cm
30 cm

⭐ Guided Practice ⭐

Do You Understand?

1. Draw a line to divide the pasture on the previous page into two triangles. What are the measures of the bases and the heights of the two triangles?

2. © MP.3 **Construct Arguments** In Another Example, how could you use 4 triangles to find the kite's area?

Do You Know How?

In **3** and **4**, find the area of each shape.

3.

6 m
8 m
12 m

4.

6 ft
8 ft
6 ft 9 ft

⭐ Independent Practice ⭐

In **5–7**, find the area of each shape.

When you decompose a trapezoid into a rectangle and two triangles, the triangles may not be identical.

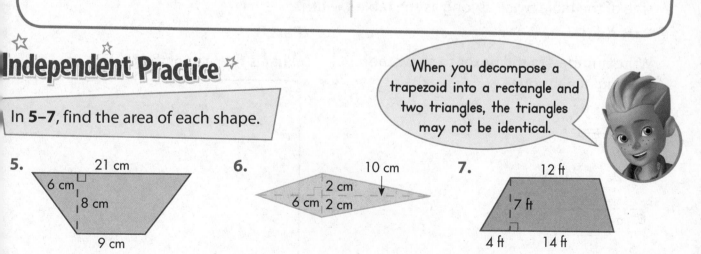

5.
21 cm
6 cm
8 cm
9 cm

6.
10 cm
2 cm
6 cm 2 cm

7.
12 ft
7 ft
4 ft   14 ft

Math Practices and Problem Solving

8. **© MP.2 Reasoning** Mary is creating a pattern using 14 of the tiles shown. What is the area of the entire pattern?

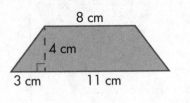

8 cm

4 cm

3 cm   11 cm

9. **© MP.7 Use Structure** Sam and Sandy made 2 pizzas and cut each pizza into 8 equal-sized slices. Together they ate $\frac{5}{8}$ of the pizza slices. How many slices of pizza are left? Explain how you know.

10. **Higher Order Thinking** A craftsman wants to build this fiddle. He needs to know the area of the face of the fiddle. How could he use the measurements shown to find the area? Use your strategy to find the area of the face of the fiddle.

77 mm

326 mm

216 mm

© Common Core Assessment

11. Marique is making a large table in the shape of a trapezoid. She needs to calculate the area of the table. She is making the longest side of the table twice as long as the table's width.

Part A

Write numbers in the boxes to show the missing dimensions.

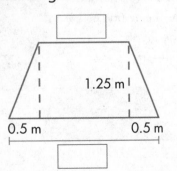

1.25 m

0.5 m   0.5 m

Part B

What is the area of the table?

© Pearson Education, Inc. 6

Name _____

Another Look!

Find the area of the trapezoid.

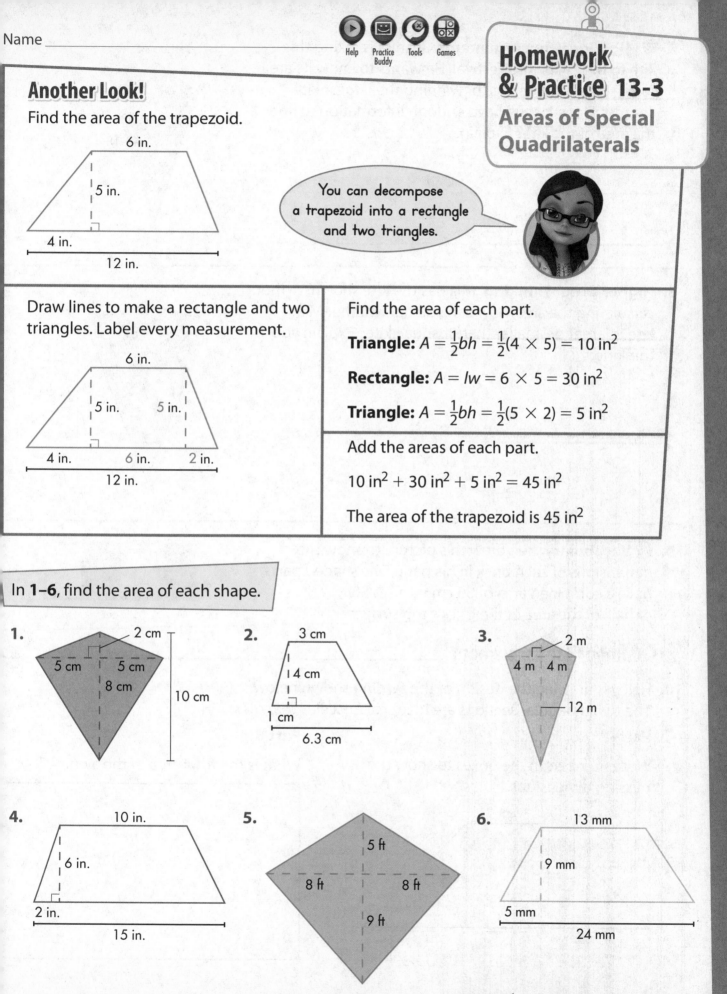

6 in.

5 in.

4 in.

12 in.

You can decompose a trapezoid into a rectangle and two triangles.

Draw lines to make a rectangle and two triangles. Label every measurement.

6 in.

5 in.   5 in.

4 in.   6 in.   2 in.

12 in.

Find the area of each part.

Triangle: $A = \frac{1}{2}bh = \frac{1}{2}(4 \times 5) = 10$ in²

Rectangle: $A = lw = 6 \times 5 = 30$ in²

Triangle: $A = \frac{1}{2}bh = \frac{1}{2}(5 \times 2) = 5$ in²

Add the areas of each part.

10 in² + 30 in² + 5 in² = 45 in²

The area of the trapezoid is 45 in²

In **1–6**, find the area of each shape.

1.
2 cm
5 cm   5 cm
8 cm
10 cm

2.
3 cm
4 cm
1 cm
6.3 cm

3.
2 m
4 m 4 m
12 m

4.
10 in.
6 in.
2 in.
15 in.

5.
5 ft
8 ft   8 ft
9 ft

6.
13 mm
9 mm
5 mm
24 mm

7. **© MP.3 Construct Arguments** Joshua is taking this
kite to the Zilker Kite Festival. He wants to know its area
to see if he has a chance of winning the largest kite
contest. Does Joshua have enough information to find
the area of the kite? Explain.

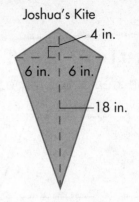

Joshua's Kite
4 in.
6 in. | 6 in.
18 in.

8. **Higher Order Thinking** Mia has the kite shown. Without
calculating the area, how can you tell whether Mia's
kite is larger or smaller than Joshua's kite? Explain your
thinking.

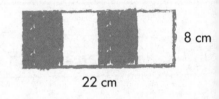

Mia's Kite
2 cm
8 cm | 8 cm
20 cm
22 cm

9. **A-Z Vocabulary** Ben drew this picture to show the
dimensions of each brick in his patio. The shaded parts
have a combined area of 88 cm². This is 50 _____,
or half, of the area of the brick's top surface.

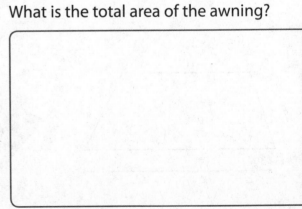

8 cm
22 cm

© Common Core Assessment

10. Haley is drawing the design of the awning shown below.
    The two triangular sections are identical isosceles triangles.

Part A

Write numbers in the boxes to show the
missing dimensions.

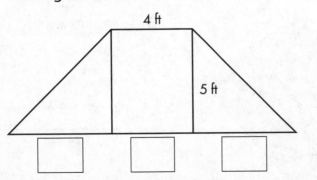

4 ft
5 ft

Part B

What is the total area of the awning?

Name _____

Solve & Share

Gabrielle wants to use felt material to cover the floors of a room and a hallway in her dollhouse. She measured the room and hallway and sketched it below. How many 8.5 in. × 11 in. pieces of felt does Gabrielle need for the room and hallway? **Solve this problem any way you choose.**

I can ...
find the areas of polygons.

© Content Standards 6.G.A.1, 6.EE.A.2c
Mathematical Practices MP.1, MP.4, MP.6, MP.7

Make sense of the problem by decomposing the sketch into shapes you know.

5 in.

22 in.

15 in.

10 in.

Look Back! © MP.7 Use Structure Show how you can find the area of the polygon in another way.

Essential Question ## How Can You Find the Areas of Polygons?

A

Denise is building a patio in her backyard as shown in the diagram. What is the area of the patio?

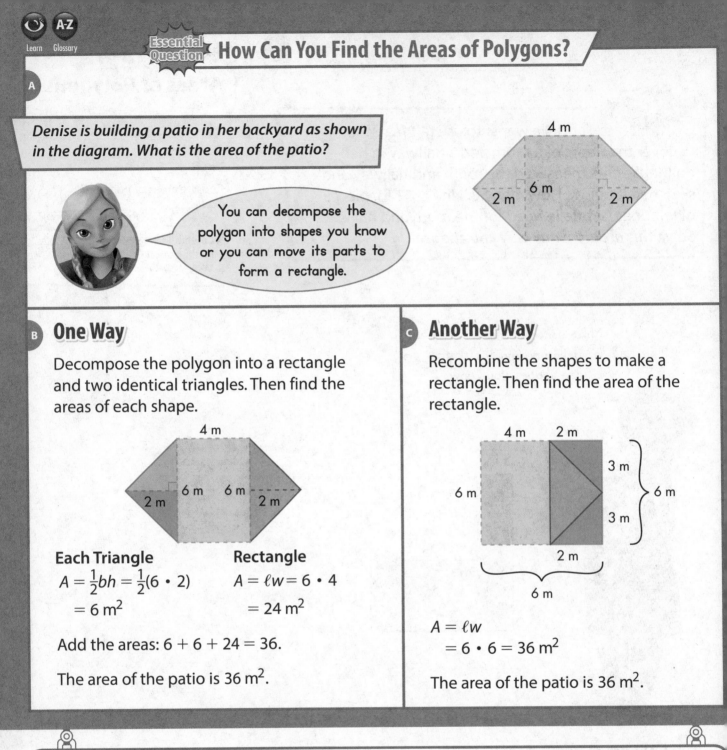

You can decompose the polygon into shapes you know or you can move its parts to form a rectangle.

4 m
6 m
2 m   2 m

B ## One Way

Decompose the polygon into a rectangle and two identical triangles. Then find the areas of each shape.

4 m
6 m   6 m
2 m   2 m

Each Triangle
$A = \frac{1}{2}bh = \frac{1}{2}(6 \cdot 2)$
$= 6 \text{ m}^2$

Rectangle
$A = \ell w = 6 \cdot 4$
$= 24 \text{ m}^2$

Add the areas: $6 + 6 + 24 = 36$.

The area of the patio is 36 m^2.

C ## Another Way

Recombine the shapes to make a rectangle. Then find the area of the rectangle.

4 m   2 m
3 m
6 m   6 m
3 m
2 m
6 m

$A = \ell w$
$= 6 \cdot 6 = 36 \text{ m}^2$

The area of the patio is 36 m^2.

Convince Me! © **MP.4 Model with Math** Shari found the area of the patio by drawing a rectangle around the polygon then subtracting the areas of the 4 small triangles formed at each corner. Show how Shari found the area of the patio.

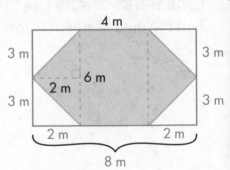

4 m
3 m   3 m
6 m
2 m
3 m   3 m
2 m   2 m
8 m

Practice Buddy   Tools   Assessment

☆ Guided Practice *

Do You Understand?

1. Look at the arrow in Exercise 3. How can you decompose the arrow into known shapes to find its area?

2. Describe a way you can use subtraction to find the area of the shape in Exercise 4.

Do You Know How?

In **3** and **4**, find the area of each shape.

3.

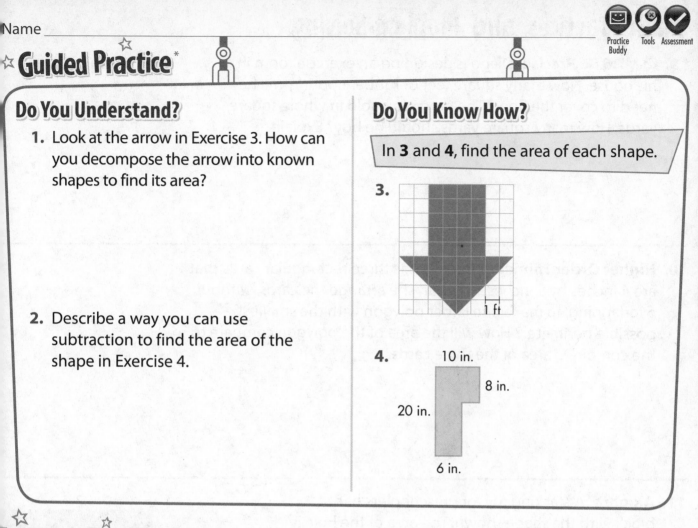

1 ft

4.

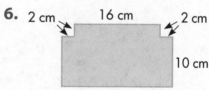

10 in.

8 in.

20 in.

6 in.

☆ Independent Practice ☆

In **5–8**, find the area of each polygon.

5.

26 ft

15 ft

5 ft →

3 ft

4 ft

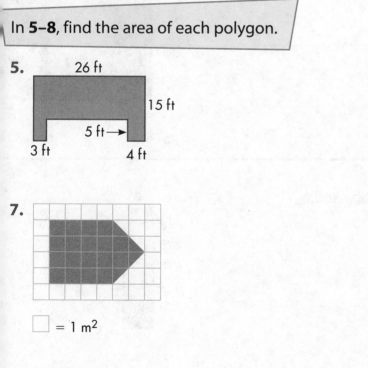

6. 2 cm   16 cm   2 cm

10 cm

7.

☐ = 1 m²

8.

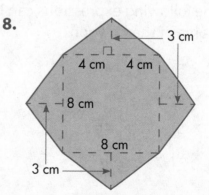

3 cm

4 cm   4 cm

8 cm

8 cm

3 cm

9. **MP.6 Be Precise** Diego is designing an exercise room in his house. How many square feet of rubber flooring will he need to cover the floor? The product is sold in whole square yards. How many square yards should he buy? Explain.

15 ft

9 ft

8 ft

14 ft

10. **Higher Order Thinking** Isabella has three rectangular cards that are 4 inches by 5 inches. How can she arrange the cards, without overlapping, to make one larger polygon with the smallest possible perimeter? How will the area of the polygon compare to the combined area of the three cards?

11. **Algebra** A stacking toy for preschoolers has a block with the shape shown. The area of the hole is 12.56 in². Write an equation to find the area, *A*, of the top surface of the block.

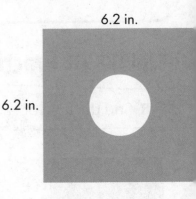

6.2 in.

6.2 in.

12. Which of the following expressions can be used to find the area of the polygon?

    Ⓐ $(2 \times 5) + (6 \times 4)$

    Ⓑ $(5 \times 2) + 2 \cdot \frac{1}{2}(3 \times 4)$

    Ⓒ $(6 \times 5) - (3 \times 4)$

    Ⓓ $(6 \times 9) - (3 \times 4)$

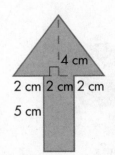

4 cm

2 cm 2 cm 2 cm

5 cm

Name _____

Another Look!

A path around a garden measures 8 meters by 7 meters. The garden measures 4 meters by 3 meters. What is the area of the path?

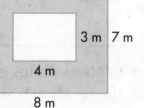

3 m 7 m

4 m

8 m

You can decompose shapes in more than one way to check your answer.

Step 1

Find the area of the garden and the path together.

Path and garden together:
$A = \ell w$
$A = 8 \times 7$
$A = 56 \text{ m}^2$

Step 2

Find the area of the garden, then subtract.

Garden:
$A = \ell w$
$A = 4 \times 3$
$A = 12 \text{ m}^2$

The area of the path is $56 - 12 = 44 \text{ m}^2$.

In **1–4**, find the area of each polygon.

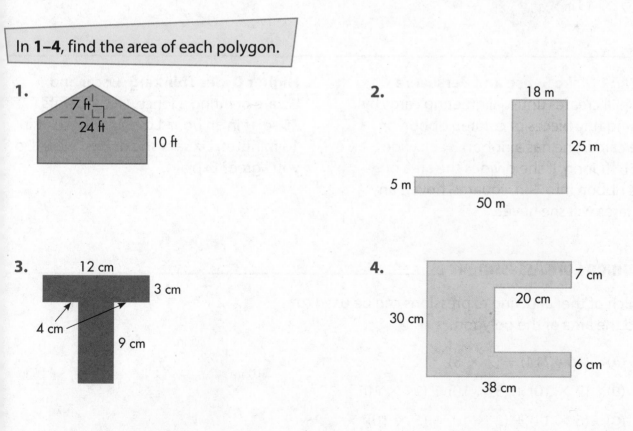

1.

7 ft
24 ft
10 ft

2.

18 m
25 m
5 m
50 m

3.

12 cm
3 cm
4 cm
9 cm

4.

7 cm
20 cm
30 cm
6 cm
38 cm

5. © **MP.6 Be Precise** Jasmine and her dad are landscaping their backyard. There will be grass and a fish pond in one corner. What is the area of the grass? Justify your answer.

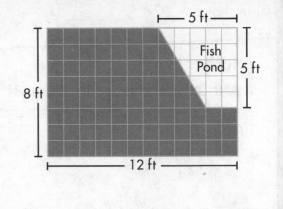

6. Math and Science The city engineer plans to insert a storm water drain within a public garden space. The green garden space will be filled with rock and plants that help to purify the water. What is the area of the space that will be filled with plants and rock?

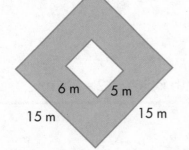

7. © **MP.4 Model with Math** Carlos is tiling a countertop that has identical holes cut out for double sinks, as shown below. Write an equation you could use to find the area, *A*, that Carlos will tile. Then find the area.

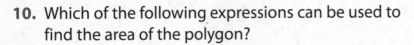

8. © **MP.1 Make Sense and Persevere** Amelia creates unusual greeting cards by gluing tiny pieces of colored ribbon on the cards. She has a ribbon $3\frac{1}{2}$ in. wide by $1\frac{1}{2}$ ft long. If she divides the area of the ribbon into $\frac{1}{2}$-in. squares, how many squares will she have?

9. Higher Order Thinking Oscar and Liz are painting a fence. Oscar paints 75 sq. ft in an hour. Liz paints 18 sq. ft in 15 minutes. Liz says she paints faster. Do you agree? Explain.

© **Common Core Assessment**

10. Which of the following expressions can be used to find the area of the polygon?

 Ⓐ $(10 \times 14) - (7 \times 5)$

 Ⓑ $(2 \times 10) + (5 \times 10) + (14 \times 10)$

 Ⓒ $(6 \times 14) + (2 \times 10) + (5 \times 10)$

 Ⓓ $(10 \times 4) + (2 \times 4) + (5 \times 4)$

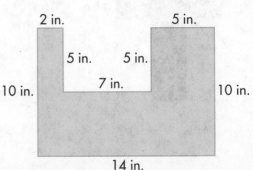

Name _____

Solve & Share

A landscaping plan is sketched on a coordinate plane. Each unit represents 1 foot. The grassy area of the plan is shaped like a pentagon with vertices (4, 1), (1, 1), (−1, −1), (1, −5), and (3, −4). If 80 grams of seed are planted per square foot, how much grass seed does the landscaper need to buy?

I can ...
find the areas of polygons on a coordinate plane.

© **Content Standards** 6.G.A.3, 6.G.A.1, 6.NS.C.6c, 6.NS.C.8
Mathematical Practices MP.1, MP.2, MP.4, MP.7

You can model with math by plotting the vertices on a coordinate plane. Then use what you know about polygons to solve the problem.

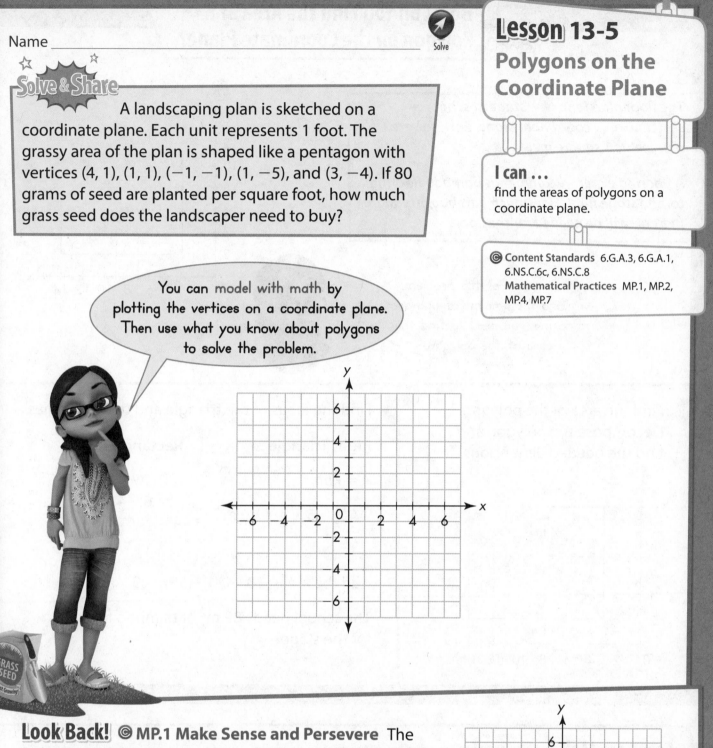

Look Back! © **MP.1 Make Sense and Persevere** The polygon at the right was decomposed into three triangles as shown. Can you use these triangles to find the area of the purple space? Explain.

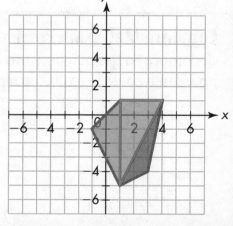

How Can You Find the Area of a Polygon on the Coordinate Plane?

A

The floor plan for a new stage at school is sketched on a coordinate plane. Each square represents 1 square meter.

A flooring expert recommends bamboo flooring for the stage floor. How much bamboo, in square meters, will be needed for the floor?

Make sense of the problem. To find the amount of bamboo flooring, you need to find the area of the polygon.

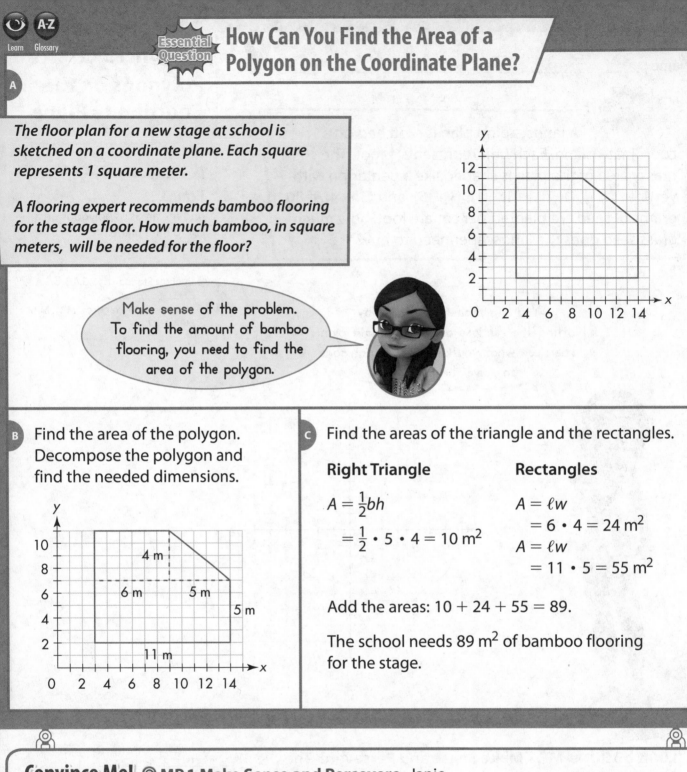

B Find the area of the polygon. Decompose the polygon and find the needed dimensions.

C Find the areas of the triangle and the rectangles.

Right Triangle

$A = \frac{1}{2}bh$

$= \frac{1}{2} \cdot 5 \cdot 4 = 10 \text{ m}^2$

Rectangles

$A = \ell w$

$= 6 \cdot 4 = 24 \text{ m}^2$

$A = \ell w$

$= 11 \cdot 5 = 55 \text{ m}^2$

Add the areas: $10 + 24 + 55 = 89$.

The school needs 89 m^2 of bamboo flooring for the stage.

Convince Me! © MP.1 Make Sense and Persevere Janie decomposed the polygon into a rectangle and a trapezoid. Show how Janie could use this drawing to find the area of the stage.

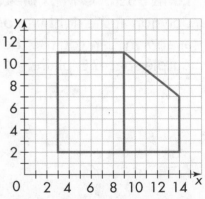

☆ Guided Practice *

Do You Understand?

1. Look back at the landscaping plan in Solve and Share. How can you use absolute value to find the height of the figure?

2. ⓒ **MP.4 Model with Math** Describe another way to break the floor plan on the previous page into a trapezoid and a rectangle. Use coordinates to describe the line you can draw.

Do You Know How?

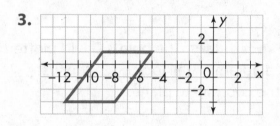

In **3** and **4**, find the area of each polygon in square units.

3.
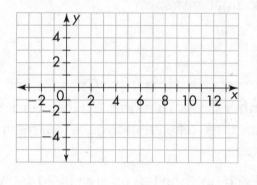

4. A polygon with vertices at (6, 2), (9, 5), (12, 2), (12, −4), and (6, −4)

☆ Independent Practice ☆

In **5–7**, find the area of each polygon in square units.

5.
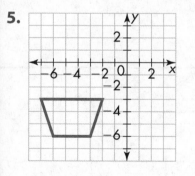

6.
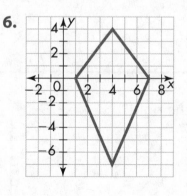

7. A polygon with vertices at (16, 1), (14, 1), (14, −5), (12, −5), (12, 1), (10, 1), (10, 3), and (16, 3)

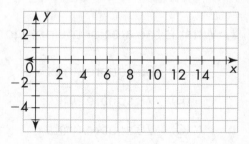

Math Practices and Problem Solving

In **8–10**, use the diagram at the right.

8. David drew this diagram of a picture frame he is going to make. Each square represents 1 square inch. What is the area of the picture frame?

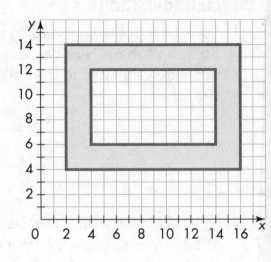

9. (A-Z) **Vocabulary** The points David plotted to make his diagram are all located in the first _____ of the coordinate plane.

10. © **MP.7 Use Structure** How could you find the area of the picture frame without decomposing the frame into smaller shapes?

11. **Higher Order Thinking** On the coordinate plane, draw three different polygons that meet these criteria.

- Each polygon has an area of 20 square units.
- One polygon has two of its vertices at (2, 2) and (−3, −2).
- One polygon is a triangle.
- One polygon is a parallelogram.

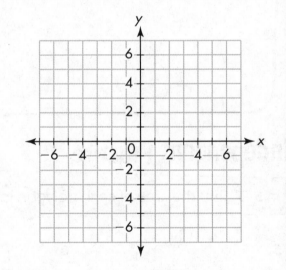

© **Common Core Assessment**

12. What is the area of the polygon at the right?

Ⓐ 86 square units

Ⓑ 78 square units

Ⓒ 70 square units

Ⓓ 68 square units

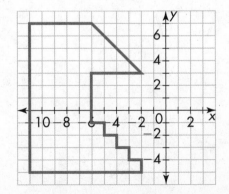

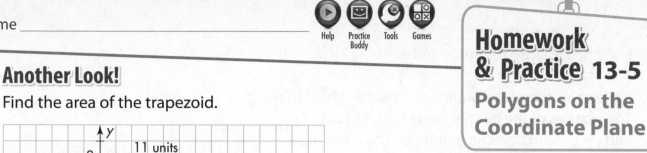

Help   Practice   Tools   Games
        Buddy

Homework
& Practice 13-5
Polygons on the
Coordinate Plane

Another Look!

Find the area of the trapezoid.

How can you compose the trapezoid into a rectangle or decompose the trapezoid into triangles and rectangles?

The trapezoid is decomposed into 2 right triangles and a rectangle.

You can compose the polygon into a rectangle by moving one of the triangles to the opposite side of the figure. Then you can count squares or use the area formula to find the area of the rectangle.

$A = \ell \cdot w$
$\ \ \ = 14 \cdot 6 = 84$

The area of the trapezoid is 84 square units.

You can also use formulas to find the areas of the triangles and the rectangle.

Areas of the Right Triangles
$A = \frac{1}{2}bh$
$\ \ \ = \frac{1}{2} \cdot 3 \cdot 6 = 9$ square units

Area of the Rectangle
$A = \ell w$
$\ \ \ = 11 \cdot 6 = 66$ square units

Add the areas: $9 + 9 + 66 = 84$.

The area of the trapezoid is 84 square units.

In **1** and **2**, find the area of each polygon in square units.

1.

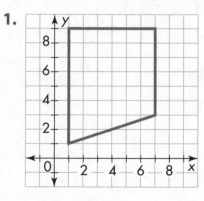

2.

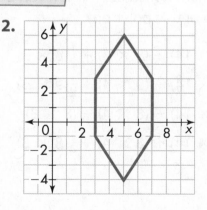

3. Abriana sketched the outline of a banner she is making. The vertices of the banner are at $(-3, 5)$, $(3, 5)$, $(3, -1)$, and $(-3, -6)$. Draw the banner on the coordinate plane. What is the area of the drawing of the banner?

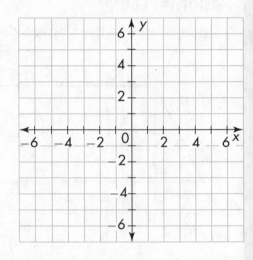

4. © **MP.2 Reasoning** Abriana wants the top edge of the banner to measure 3 feet. Use the same scale to find the length of the longest side of the banner. Show your work.

5. **Higher Order Thinking** Mrs. Via needs to buy grass seed for her yard. She drew a diagram of her yard. Each square represents 1 square yard. Five pounds of seed is enough to plant 100 square yards of grass. Grass seed is sold in 2-pound bags. How many bags of grass seed does Mrs. Via need?

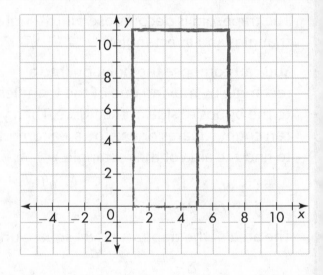

© **Common Core Assessment**

6. A polygon has vertices $(-4, 8)$, $(5, 8)$, $(5, 2)$, $(9, 2)$, $(12, -6)$, and $(-4, -6)$. Graph the polygon on the coordinate plan. Which expression can be used to find the area of this polygon?

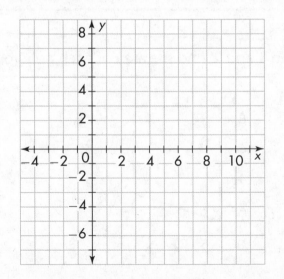

Ⓐ $(9 \times 14) + (8 \times 4) + \frac{1}{2}(8 \times 3)$

Ⓑ $(8 \times 14) + (9 \times 4) + \frac{1}{2}(9 \times 3)$

Ⓒ $(9 \times 14) + (8 \times 4) + (8 \times 3)$

Ⓓ $(9 \times 14) + (8 \times 4) + \frac{1}{4}(8 \times 3)$

Name _____

Solve & Share

The points $A(0, -2)$ and $B(0, 4)$ are shown on the coordinate plane. Locate and plot the coordinates of two points, C and D, so that both triangle ABC and triangle ABD have an area of 18 square units. Explain how you found each point.

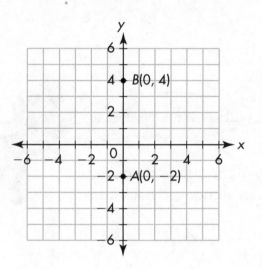

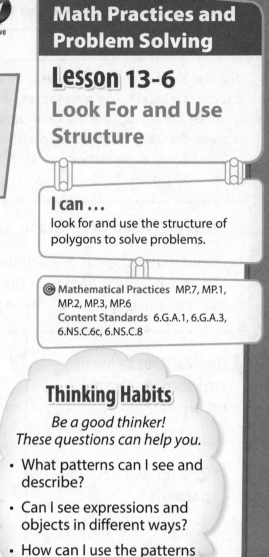

Math Practices and Problem Solving

Lesson 13-6
Look For and Use Structure

I can ...
look for and use the structure of polygons to solve problems.

Ⓒ **Mathematical Practices** MP.7, MP.1, MP.2, MP.3, MP.6
Content Standards 6.G.A.1, 6.G.A.3, 6.NS.C.6c, 6.NS.C.8

Thinking Habits

Be a good thinker!
These questions can help you.

• What patterns can I see and describe?

• Can I see expressions and objects in different ways?

• How can I use the patterns to solve problems?

Look Back! Ⓒ **MP.7 Use Structure** Use the structure of the coordinate plane and the triangles to find a point E so that the triangle ABE also has an area of 18 square units.

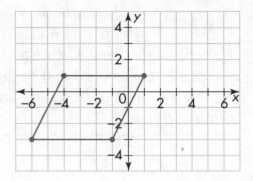
Essential Question — How Can You Look For and Use Structure?

A

The shape of a regional park is shown on the coordinate plane. The planners ask the designer for another parallelogram design that has the same area and uses as many of the original vertices shown as possible. What are the coordinates of the vertices of the new parallelogram design?

What do I need to do to solve the problem?

I need to use the structure of the coordinate plane to find a parallelogram with the same area using as many of the original vertices as possible.

Here's my thinking...

B **How can I make use of structure to solve the problem?**

I can

- look for and describe patterns.

- describe how objects are related.

- use the features of the pattern to generate or extend a pattern.

C

I know that a parallelogram can be decomposed into two triangles and then composed back into a different parallelogram.

I can use triangles to make a new parallelogram as shown.

The original design and the new design are both parallelograms.

The coordinates of the vertices of the new parallelogram design are (1, 1), (6, 1), (−1, −3), and (−6, −3).

Convince Me! © **MP.7 Use Structure** The regional park planning team is worried about the budget. The planners ask the designer for another parallelogram design that has half the area of the original design and uses as many of the original vertices shown as possible. What are the coordinates of the vertices of the new parallelogram design?

© Pearson Education, Inc. 6

☆ **Guided Practice** *

© **MP.7 Use Structure**

Mr. Lin is designing his garden. He started with a rectangle. He wants to change the shape of his garden to a parallelogram with the same area but no right angles. He wants to use three of the original vertices. What could be the coordinates of the vertices of the new parallelogram design?

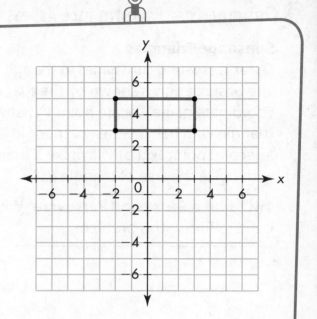

1. What do you know about the structure of rectangles and parallelograms that can help you solve this problem?

2. How can you use structure to find the coordinates of the parallelogram?

Independent Practice ☆

© **MP.7 Use Structure**

Diane is constructing a rectangular patio that has twice the area of the triangle shown. What could be the coordinates of her new patio if she uses as many vertices of the triangle as possible?

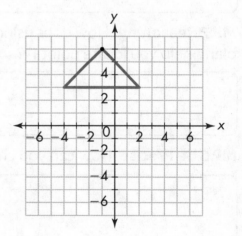

3. What do you know about triangles and their structure that can help you solve this problem?

4. How can you use structure to form a rectangle and find the coordinates?

Math Practices and Problem Solving

© Common Core Performance Assessment

Sunshade Triangles

Oscar is creating sunshades in triangle shapes. The basic design is shown by the triangle on the coordinate plane. Locate point *V* that will make a triangle with half the area of triangle *RST*. Locate a second point *W* that will make a triangle *RSW* with twice the area of triangle *RST*.

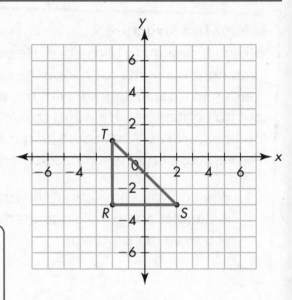

5. **MP.1 Make Sense and Persevere** What do you need to find in this problem?

6. **MP.7 Use Structure** How can you use the formula for the area of a triangle to help you decide where to place point *V*?

You attend to precision when you apply formulas correctly.

7. **MP.2 Reasoning** How does using the coordinate plane help you locate point *W*?

8. **MP.6 Be Precise** How can you check your answers?

Help Practice Buddy Tools Games

Another Look!

A rectangle is shown on the coordinate plane. Using two vertices of the rectangle and one point in the first quadrant, make a triangle with the same area as the rectangle.

How can you look for and make use of structure?

- I can locate shapes on the coordinate plane and describe them.

- I can use the features of the coordinate plane to extend the drawing and solve the problem.

Explain how you can use structure to solve the problem.

- I can draw the diagonal of the rectangle from $(-5, 5)$ to $(-1, -1)$ to decompose the rectangle into two triangles with equal areas.

- The point at $(3, 5)$ along with $(-5, 5)$ and $(-1, -1)$ creates a triangle with an area equal to the area of the original rectangle.

© **MP.7 Use Structure**

Use the rectangle shown to make an isosceles triangle that has an area of 12 square units.

1. How can you use the relationship of rectangles and triangles to help solve the problem?

2. How can you use the structure of the coordinate plane to find a triangle that has an area of 12 square units?

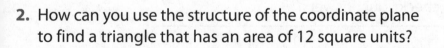

Reconstruction A contractor needs to change the configuration of the entryway to a building. He wants the area of the new triangular entryway to be 15 ft². The triangle on the coordinate plane shows the entryway now. Each square represents 1 square foot. Use the diagram to find one way to make a new entryway.

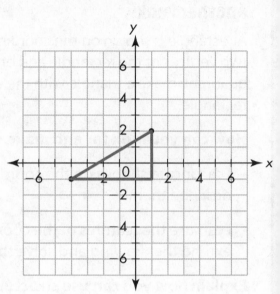

3. **MP.1 Make Sense and Persevere** How can you use the diagram to explore possible solutions to the problem?

4. **MP.3 Construct Arguments** Will the new entryway have an area that is greater than or less than the area of the current entryway? Explain how you know.

5. **MP.7 Use Structure** Find coordinates for one possible new entryway. Explain how you can use the shape and dimensions of the current entryway to help you locate these coordinates.

6. **MP.6 Be Precise** How can you check your answers?

Name _____

Follow the Path

Shade a path from **START** to **FINISH**.
Follow the sums and differences in which the digit in the tenths place is greater than the digit in the hundredths place. You can only move up, down, right, or left.

I can ...
add and subtract multi-digit decimals.

© Content Standard 6.NS.B.3

Start				
$3.13 + 7.404$	$30.6 - 0.79$	$3.443 - 0.92$	$6.2 + 3.13$	$13.2 - 4.94$
$5.01 - 1.45$	$1.081 + 22.2$	$5.34 - 1.7$	$4.37 + 3.809$	$0.91 + 1.98$
$16 - 7.324$	$1.12 + 0.09$	$9.4 + 3.03$	$26 - 1.85$	$7.1 - 6.32$
$10 - 2.754$	$8.28 - 7.43$	$30 + 1.04$	$12.16 + 8.03$	$1.2 + 6.02$
$9.4 - 3.18$	$1.262 + 4.05$	$2.34 + 13.2$	$15.03 - 9.487$	$0.4 + 7.35$

Finish

Word List

- area
- base
- height
- kite
- parallelogram
- rhombus
- trapezoid
- triangle

Understand Vocabulary

Choose the best term from the Word List. Write it on the blank.

1. A _____ has opposite sides parallel and all sides equal in length.

2. A quadrilateral with only one pair of parallel sides is a _____.

3. The perpendicular distance from the base of a polygon to an opposite vertex is the _____ of the polygon.

4. A _____ has two pairs of adjacent sides that are equal in length.

5. Write *always, sometimes,* or *never.*

   Area is _____ measured in square units.

   A *parallelogram* _____ has a right angle.

   The *height* of a triangle is _____ greater than the *base.*

In **6–8**, refer to the parallelogram. Write T for *true* or F for *false.*

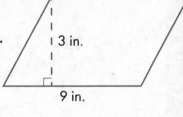

_____ 6. The *height* of the parallelogram is perpendicular to its *base.*

_____ 7. The *area* of the parallelogram is 13.5 in^2.

_____ 8. The *base* of the parallelogram measures 9 inches.

3 in.

9 in.

Use Vocabulary in Writing

9. Describe how to find the area of the quadrilateral. Use at least 5 words from the Word List.

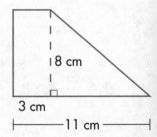

8 cm

3 cm

11 cm

Set A pages 659–664, 665–670 _____ **Reteaching**

Use these formulas to find the area of each figure.

Parallelogram and Rhombus: $A = bh$

Triangle: $A = \frac{1}{2}bh$

$A = bh$
$A = 12 \cdot 8$
$A = 96$ ft^2

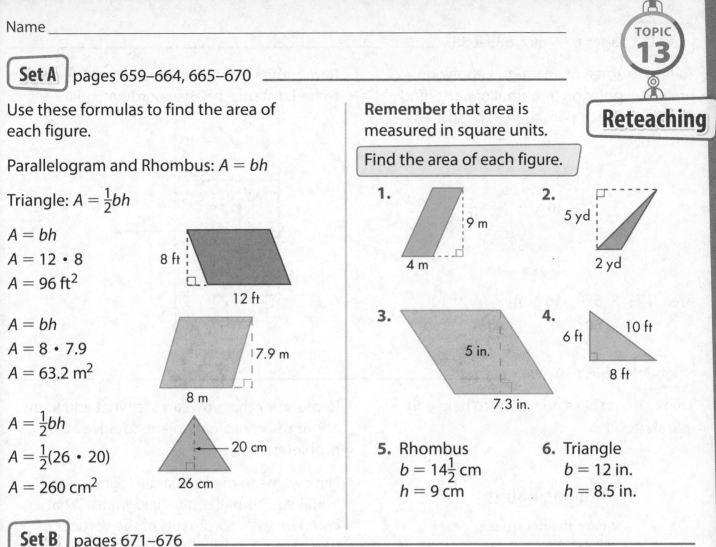

8 ft
12 ft

$A = bh$
$A = 8 \cdot 7.9$
$A = 63.2$ m^2

7.9 m
8 m

$A = \frac{1}{2}bh$
$A = \frac{1}{2}(26 \cdot 20)$
$A = 260$ cm^2

20 cm
26 cm

Remember that area is measured in square units.

Find the area of each figure.

1.
9 m
4 m

2.
5 yd
2 yd

3.
5 in.
7.3 in.

4.
6 ft
10 ft
8 ft

5. Rhombus
$b = 14\frac{1}{2}$ cm
$h = 9$ cm

6. Triangle
$b = 12$ in.
$h = 8.5$ in.

Set B pages 671–676 _____

A trapezoid is a quadrilateral that has only one pair of sides that are parallel. You can find the area of a trapezoid by dividing it into a rectangle and triangles.

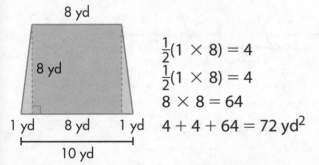

8 yd
8 yd
1 yd   8 yd   1 yd
10 yd

$\frac{1}{2}(1 \times 8) = 4$
$\frac{1}{2}(1 \times 8) = 4$
$8 \times 8 = 64$
$4 + 4 + 64 = 72$ yd^2

A kite is a quadrilateral with 2 pairs of adjacent sides that are equal in length. You can find the area of a kite by dividing it into 2 triangles that have the same area.

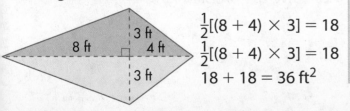

8 ft   3 ft
4 ft
3 ft

$\frac{1}{2}[(8 + 4) \times 3] = 18$
$\frac{1}{2}[(8 + 4) \times 3] = 18$
$18 + 18 = 36$ ft^2

Remember that you can decompose figures into rectangles and triangles to find the area.

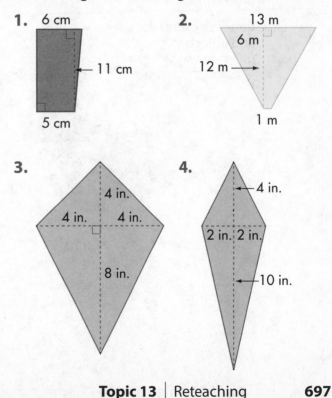

1.
6 cm
11 cm
5 cm

2.
13 m
6 m
12 m
1 m

3.
4 in.
4 in.   4 in.
8 in.

4.
4 in.
2 in. 2 in.
10 in.

To find the area of an irregular polygon, break the polygon into smaller parts, find the area of each part, then add the areas together.

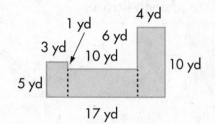

Area = $(3 \times 5) + (10 \times 4) + (4 \times 10)$
     = $15 + 40 + 40 = 95$ yd^2

Remember that you can use absolute values to find distance on the coordinate plane.

1.

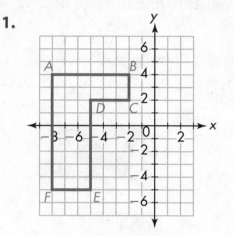

Think about these questions to help you **use structure**.

Thinking Habits

- What patterns can I see and describe?

- How can I use the patterns to solve the problem?

- Can I see expressions and objects in different ways?

Remember that you can use what you know about the coordinate plane to solve area problems.

Nina wants to make a parallelogram into two equal-sized smaller parallelograms. What could be the coordinates of the vertices of one of the new parallelograms?

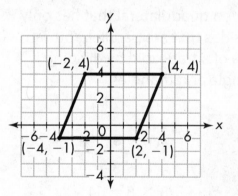

1. What patterns do you see?

2. Solve the problem.

1. Caroline is making a triangular flag with a base of 10 inches and a height of 8 inches. What is the area of the flag?

Ⓐ 18 in²

Ⓑ 40 in²

Ⓒ 80 in²

Ⓓ 160 in²

2. Two figures are arranged as shown. Which of the following can be used to find the area of the yellow figure?

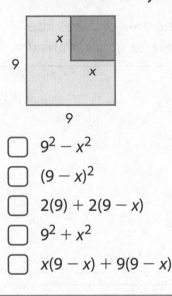

☐ $9^2 - x^2$

☐ $(9 - x)^2$

☐ $2(9) + 2(9 - x)$

☐ $9^2 + x^2$

☐ $x(9 - x) + 9(9 - x)$

3. Adrian found the area of the figure. Which expression could he have used? Choose all that apply.

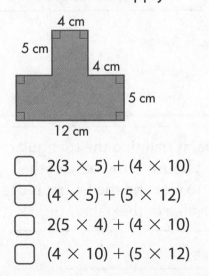

☐ $2(3 \times 5) + (4 \times 10)$

☐ $(4 \times 5) + (5 \times 12)$

☐ $2(5 \times 4) + (4 \times 10)$

☐ $(4 \times 10) + (5 \times 12)$

4. Which equation can be used to find A, the area of the parallelogram shown?

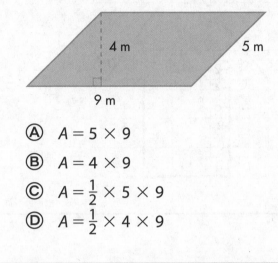

Ⓐ $A = 5 \times 9$

Ⓑ $A = 4 \times 9$

Ⓒ $A = \frac{1}{2} \times 5 \times 9$

Ⓓ $A = \frac{1}{2} \times 4 \times 9$

5. Use the points shown as vertices of a right triangle with an area of 28 square units. Identify one possible third vertex of the triangle. Justify your answer.

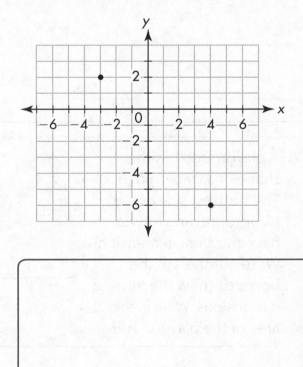

6. Lisa drew an arrow on the coordinate plane as shown. What is the area of the arrow? Show your work.

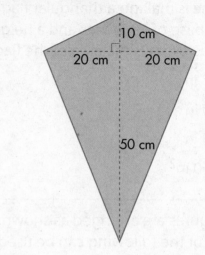

7. A playground has the shape of a trapezoid. The shortest side of the playground and its width have the same dimension. Write numbers in the boxes to show the missing dimensions. What is the area of the playground?

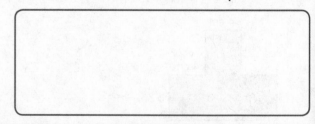

8. Jake drew the sketch below of a kite that he wants to make.

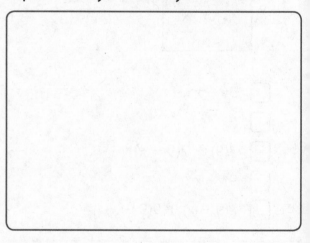

Part A

What will be the area of Jake's kite? Explain how you found your answer.

Part B

Could you have used a different strategy to find the area of the kite? Explain.

9. Mr. Aufleger is painting the triangular gable of his house. If the base of the triangle is 16 feet and the height is 6 feet, what is the area of the gable?

The Mural

Rafael is painting a mural on one wall of a community center.
The wall is rectangular and measures 14 feet high and 32 feet long.
He drew a design of his mural on the coordinate plane.

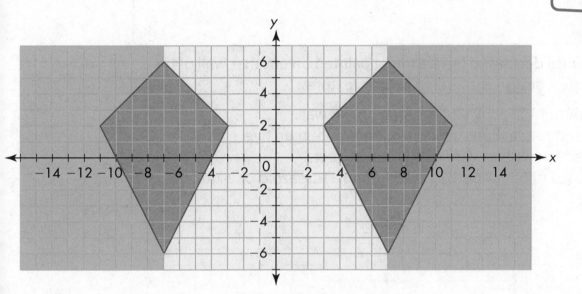

1. Rafael needs to find the area of each section of the
mural in order to determine how much paint he needs.

Section of Mural	Area (ft²)
Green	
Purple	
Yellow	

Part A

Describe the strategy you will use to find the total area
of the sections painted with each color.

Part B

Find the total area of the sections painted with each color. Complete the
table above. Show your work.

2. The community center will furnish the paint for the mural. Each can covers 32 square feet. How many cans of each color paint will Rafael need?

3. The city council decides to have a mural painted on another wall of the center. Create a design with the following features:

  • Fills the entire 14-foot by 32-foot rectangular wall.
  • Has at least three sections of color, but no more than five.
  • Has one section with an area of 100 square feet.
  • Uses at least 3 different polygons including a trapezoid or a kite.

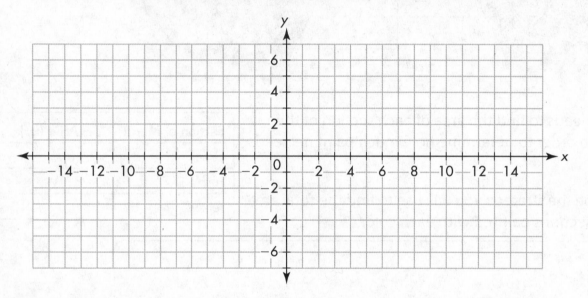

4. Complete the table to show the area for each section of your mural. Be sure to include the color of each section in the table.

Section of Mural	Area (square feet)

Solve Surface Area and Volume Problems

Essential Questions: What is the meaning of surface area and how can surface area be found? What is the meaning of volume and how can volume be found?

Digital Resources

Solve   Learn   Glossary   Practice Buddy

Tools   Assessment   Help   Games

The function of a cell is related to its size and shape.

The volume of water in plant cells helps keep stems and leaves from wilting.

I 'wilt' be sure to water my plants at home! Here's a project on cells, surface area, and volume.

Math and Science Project: Cell Size

Do Research Use the Internet or other sources to learn about the shape of a plant cell. Research the range of lengths of a plant cell in micrometers or microns.

Journal: Write a Report Include what you found. Also in your report:

- Choose 3 values in the range of lengths that you found for a plant cell.
- Sketch a net of a plant cell's surface and label the lengths you chose.
- Calculate the surface area and volume of your cell.

Review What You Know

A-Z Vocabulary

Choose the best term from the box.
Write it on the blank.

| • area | • perimeter |
| • formula | • volume |

1. _____ is the distance around a figure.

2. The number of square units needed to cover a surface or figure is its _____.

3. _____ is the number of cubic units needed to fill a solid figure.

Area

Find the area of each shape.

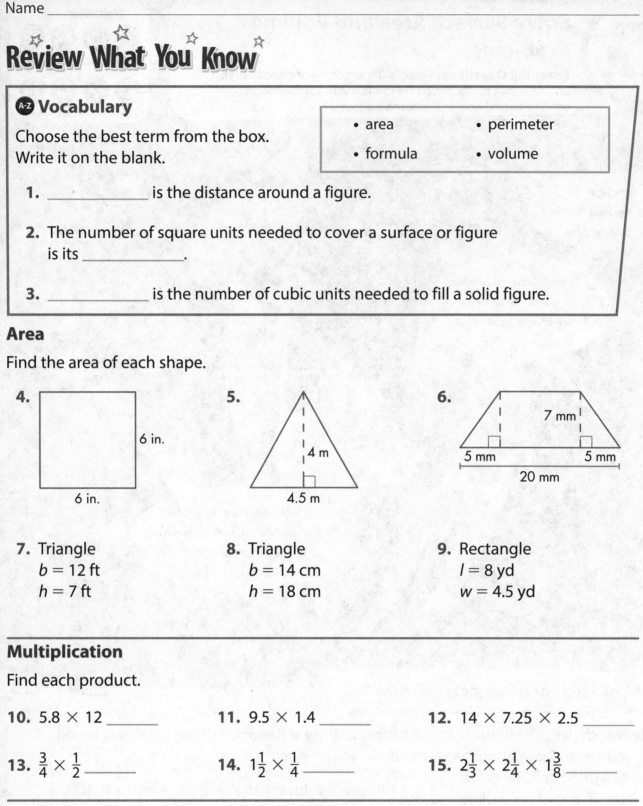

4.

6 in.

6 in.

5.

4 m

4.5 m

6.

7 mm

5 mm   5 mm

20 mm

7. Triangle
   $b = 12$ ft
   $h = 7$ ft

8. Triangle
   $b = 14$ cm
   $h = 18$ cm

9. Rectangle
   $l = 8$ yd
   $w = 4.5$ yd

Multiplication

Find each product.

10. 5.8×12 _____

11. 9.5×1.4 _____

12. $14 \times 7.25 \times 2.5$ _____

13. $\frac{3}{4} \times \frac{1}{2}$ _____

14. $1\frac{1}{2} \times \frac{1}{4}$ _____

15. $2\frac{1}{3} \times 2\frac{1}{4} \times 1\frac{3}{8}$ _____

Formulas

16. How are the formulas for the area of a rectangle and the area of a triangle alike and different? Explain.

My Word Cards

Use the examples for each word on the front of the card to help complete the definitions on the back.

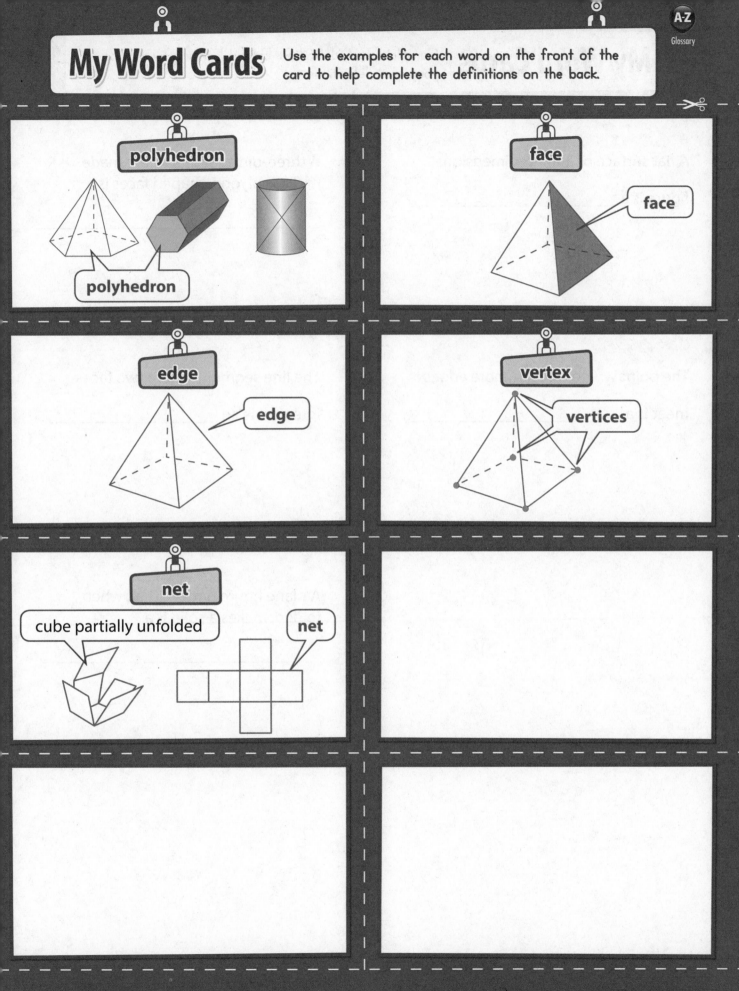

polyhedron

polyhedron

face

face

edge

edge

vertex

vertices

net

cube partially unfolded

net

My Word Cards

A flat surface of a three-dimensional figure is a _____.

A three-dimensional figure made of flat, polygon-shaped faces is a _____.

The point where three or more edges meet is a _____.

The line segment where two faces intersect is an _____.

A plane figure pattern that, when folded, makes a solid is a _____.

Name _____

Solve & Share

What would the unfolded and flat box of dog biscuits look like? Draw a diagram to represent the Dog-Eeze Biscuits box unfolded. Draw dotted lines where the box is folded and a solid outline around the outside of the figure. The side of each square on the grid below represents 1 inch.

I can ...
identify nets of solid figures.

© **Content Standard** 6.G.A.4
Mathematical Practices MP.2, MP.4, MP.6, MP.7, MP.8

You can model with math by using a diagram to represent a three-dimensional figure.

Dog-Eeze
Biscuits

12 inches

4 inches

16 inches

Look Back! © **MP.2 Reasoning** Describe how you could have drawn the diagram in a different way.

Essential Question How Do You Classify Solids?

A

A polyhedron is a three-dimensional figure made of flat polygon-shaped surfaces called *faces*. The line segment where two faces intersect is called an *edge*. The point where several edges meet is called a *vertex*.

How can you classify a polyhedron?

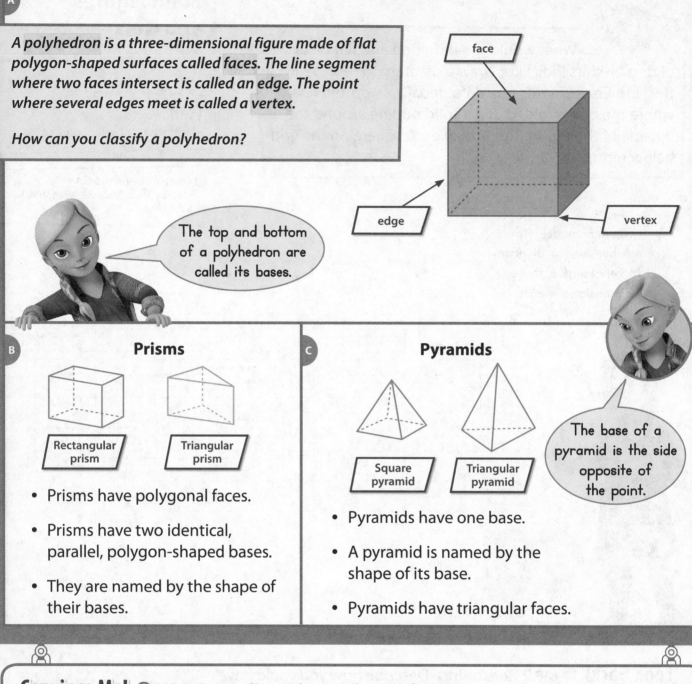

face

edge

vertex

The top and bottom of a polyhedron are called its bases.

B **Prisms**

Rectangular prism

Triangular prism

- Prisms have polygonal faces.

- Prisms have two identical, parallel, polygon-shaped bases.

- They are named by the shape of their bases.

C **Pyramids**

Square pyramid

Triangular pyramid

The base of a pyramid is the side opposite of the point.

- Pyramids have one base.

- A pyramid is named by the shape of its base.

- Pyramids have triangular faces.

Convince Me! © **MP.8 Generalize** What attributes of a solid figure should you identify in order to classify it as a polyhedron?

Another Example

A net is a plane figure pattern which, when folded, makes a solid. How can you identify a solid from its net?

The net shows three pairs of identical rectangular faces.

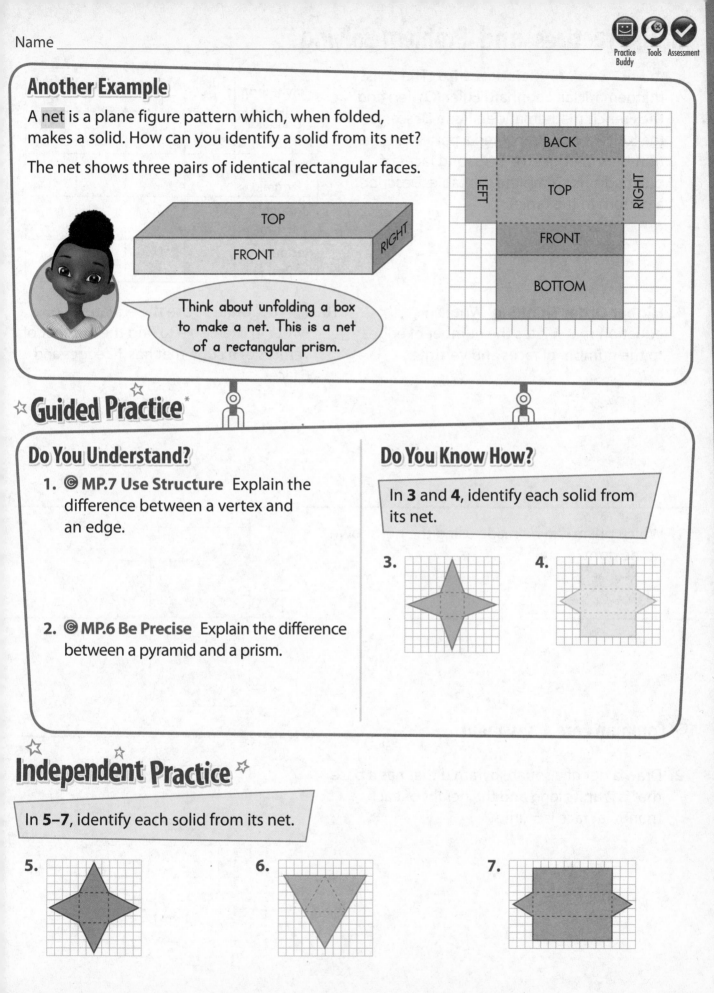

Think about unfolding a box to make a net. This is a net of a rectangular prism.

Guided Practice

Do You Understand?

1. **MP.7 Use Structure** Explain the difference between a vertex and an edge.

2. **MP.6 Be Precise** Explain the difference between a pyramid and a prism.

Do You Know How?

In **3** and **4**, identify each solid from its net.

3.

4.

Independent Practice

In **5–7**, identify each solid from its net.

5.

6.

7.

Math Practices and Problem Solving

8. **© MP.7 Look for Relationships** The Swiss mathematician Leonhard Euler (OY-ler) and the French mathematician Rene Descartes (dã KART) both discovered a pattern in the numbers of edges, vertices, and faces of polyhedrons. Complete the table. Describe a pattern in the table.

Polyhedron	Faces (F)	Vertices (V)	F + V	Edges (E)
Triangular Pyramid				
Rectangular Pyramid				
Triangular Prism				
Rectangular Prism				

9. **Higher Order Thinking** Write an equation that relates the number of edges to the number of faces and vertices.

10. **A-Z Vocabulary** Use the equation you wrote in Exercise 9 to find the number of *vertices* of a cube that has 12 edges and 6 faces.

---

11. Which prism can be made using the net shown at the right?

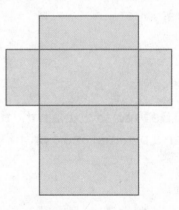

© Common Core Assessment

12. Draw a net of a square pyramid that has a base that is 2 units long and the height of each triangular face is 5 units.

© Pearson Education, Inc. 6

Help Practice Buddy Tools Games

Another Look!

How can you classify a polyhedron and draw its net? Faces of a polyhedron are the flat polygon-shaped surfaces. The faces intersect at the edge. Edges meet at the vertex.

A net represents a polyhedron when it is unfolded.

Polyhedron	Prisms	Pyramids
Bases	Two identical parallel polygon-shaped bases.	One polygon-shaped base.
Classified by	Shape of its bases.	Shape of its base.
Faces	Parallelograms	Triangles
Rectangular		
Triangular		
Examples of Nets	Triangular Prism	Triangular Pyramid

In **1–3**, identify each solid from its net.

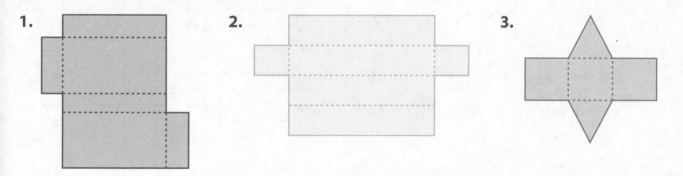

1.

2.

3.

4. Classify the polyhedron. Name all of the vertices, edges, and faces.

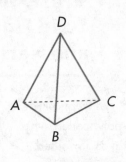

5. **Higher Order Thinking** If the top of a pencil box is 8 inches by 3 inches and the side is 3 inches by 2 inches, can you find the dimensions of the front of the box? Explain.

6. **MP.7 Use Structure** A solid may have several nets. The net at the right can be folded to make a solid. Identify the solid it forms. Then draw a different net of that solid.

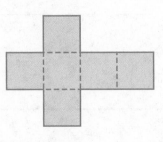

7. A square pyramid is 4 units long and the height of each triangular face is 3 units. Draw a net that represents this pyramid.

Name _____

Solve & Share

Marianne orders a pack of shipping boxes shaped like cubes. When they arrive, she finds flat pieces of cardboard as shown below. What is the least amount of cardboard needed to make each box? Explain how you know. **Solve this problem any way you choose.**

I can ...
find the surface area of prisms.

© **Content Standards** 6.G.A.4, 6.EE.A.2a, 6.EE.A.2c, 6.EE.B.6
Mathematical Practices MP.1, MP.2, MP.3, MP.5, MP.8

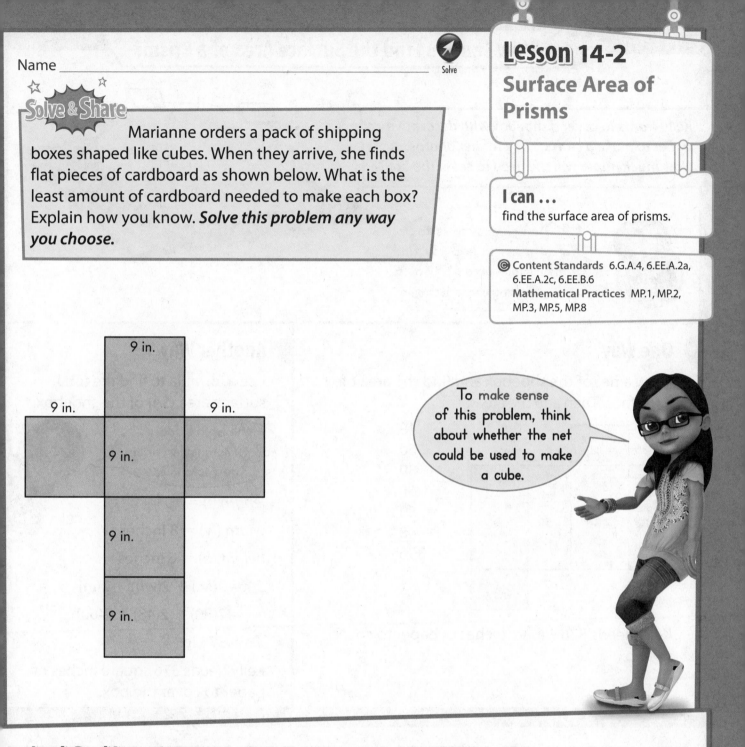

9 in.

9 in.   9 in.

9 in.

9 in.

9 in.

To make sense of this problem, think about whether the net could be used to make a cube.

Look Back! © **MP.1 Make Sense and Persevere** Suppose Marianne only has one large sheet of green paper that is 15 inches by 30 inches. Will she have enough paper to cover all the faces of the box? Explain how you know.

A

Kelly wants to cover a shoebox with decorative paper to make a storage box for her photos. How much paper will she need to cover the box?

You can use tools to draw a net to help you find the surface area (SA) of a rectangular prism.

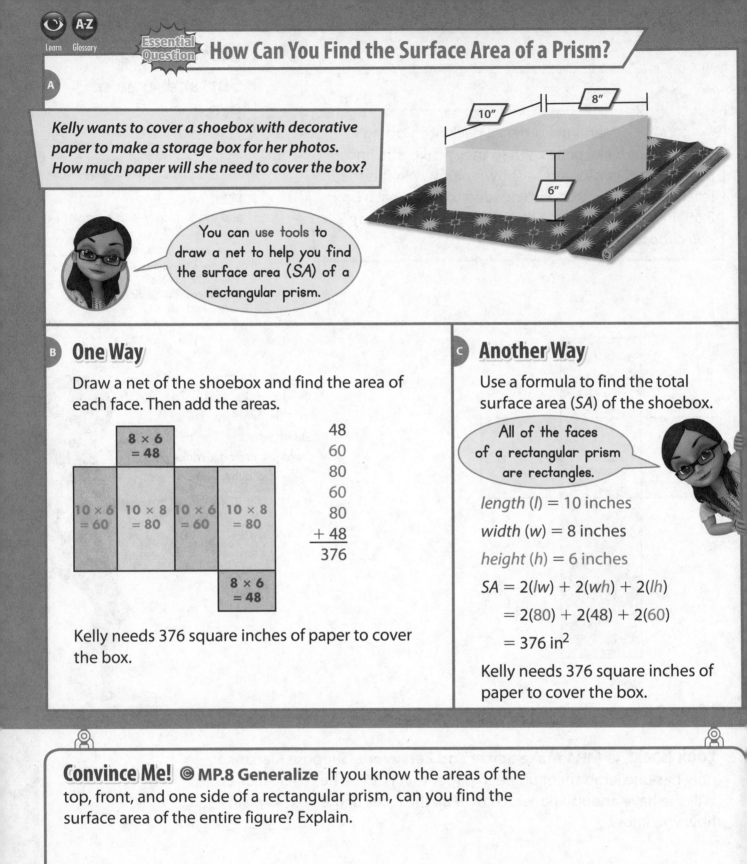

10"   8"

6"

B **One Way**

Draw a net of the shoebox and find the area of each face. Then add the areas.

8 × 6 = 48

10 × 6 = 60 | 10 × 8 = 80 | 10 × 6 = 60 | 10 × 8 = 80

8 × 6 = 48

$$
\begin{array}{r}
48 \\
60 \\
80 \\
60 \\
80 \\
+\ 48 \\
\hline
376
\end{array}
$$

Kelly needs 376 square inches of paper to cover the box.

C **Another Way**

Use a formula to find the total surface area (SA) of the shoebox.

All of the faces of a rectangular prism are rectangles.

length (l) = 10 inches

width (w) = 8 inches

height (h) = 6 inches

$SA = 2(lw) + 2(wh) + 2(lh)$

$= 2(80) + 2(48) + 2(60)$

$= 376 \text{ in}^2$

Kelly needs 376 square inches of paper to cover the box.

Convince Me! © **MP.8 Generalize** If you know the areas of the top, front, and one side of a rectangular prism, can you find the surface area of the entire figure? Explain.

Another Example

Draw a net of the triangular prism and find the areas of each face. Then add the areas.

How do you find the surface area of this triangular prism?

Area of the triangular bases
$$A = \frac{1}{2}bh = \frac{1}{2}(12)(9) = 54 \text{ cm}^2$$

Area of the bottom
$$A = \ell w = 12(18) = 216 \text{ cm}^2$$

Area of the back
$$A = \ell w = 9(18) = 162 \text{ cm}^2$$

Area of the sloped side
$$A = \ell w = 18(15) = 270 \text{ cm}^2$$

$$SA = 2(54) + 216 + 162 + 270 = 756 \text{ cm}^2$$

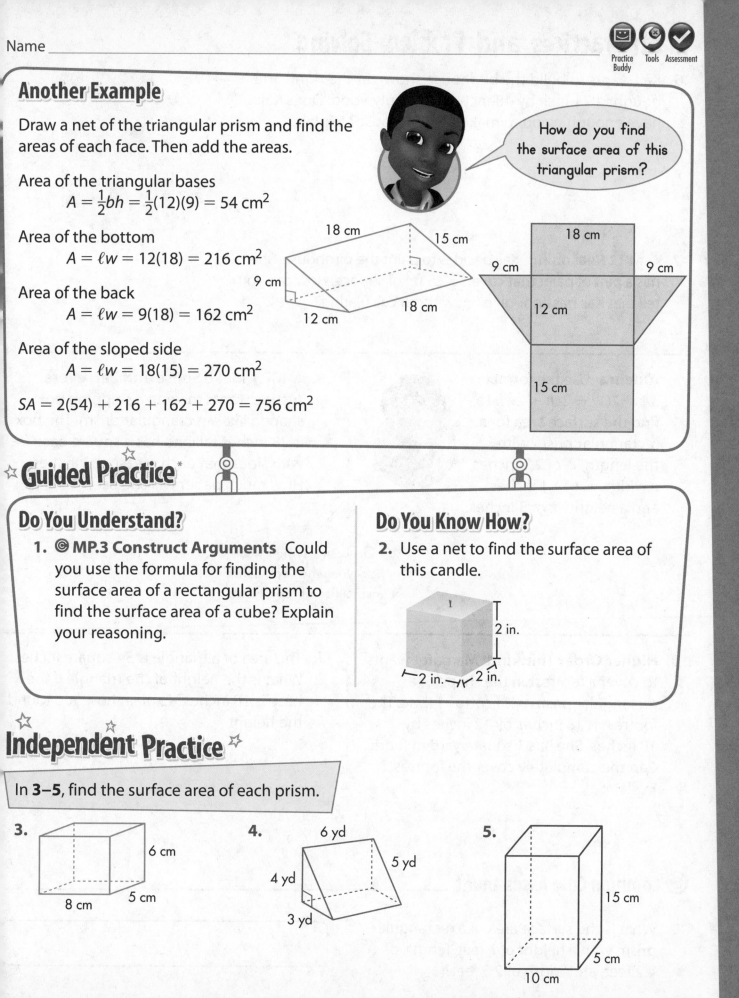

☆ Guided Practice *

Do You Understand?

1. **ⓒ MP.3 Construct Arguments** Could you use the formula for finding the surface area of a rectangular prism to find the surface area of a cube? Explain your reasoning.

Do You Know How?

2. Use a net to find the surface area of this candle.

2 in.
2 in. — 2 in.

☆ Independent Practice ☆

In **3–5**, find the surface area of each prism.

3.
6 cm
8 cm   5 cm

4.
6 yd
5 yd
4 yd
3 yd

5.
15 cm
10 cm   5 cm

Math Practices and Problem Solving

6. Kali wants to build the birdhouse shown at the right. She bought a 24-inch by 48-inch sheet of plywood. Does Kali have enough wood to make the birdhouse? Explain.

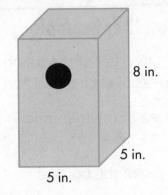

8 in.

5 in.

5 in.

7. © **MP.2 Reasoning** Kali decides to paint the birdhouse. She has a pint of paint that covers 32.5 ft² of surface. How can you tell that Kali has enough paint without calculating?

8. **Algebra** Use the formula $SA = 2\ell w + 2\ell h + 2wh$ to find the surface area for a rectangular prism with the length, ℓ, of 2.3 inches, a width, w, of 1.1 inches, and a height, h, of 3 inches.

Grouping symbols can help you when calculating multiple math operations.

9. © **MP.1 Make Sense and Persevere** Justine wants to wrap a shipping box shaped like a rectangular prism. The box is 28 inches tall and has a square base with sides that each measure 2 inches. How much paper will she use?

10. **Higher Order Thinking** Margaret wants to cover a footrest in the shape of a rectangular prism with cotton fabric. The footrest is 18 inches by 12 inches by 10 inches. She has 1 square yard of fabric. Can she completely cover the footrest? Explain.

11. The area of a triangle is 54 square inches. What is the height of the triangle if the base is 18 inches? Explain how you found the height.

© **Common Core Assessment**

12. What is the surface area of a rectangular prism with a height of 2 feet, length of 4.2 feet, and width of 2.5 feet?

Help Practice Buddy Tools Games

Another Look!

Use a net to find the surface area (SA) of each prism.

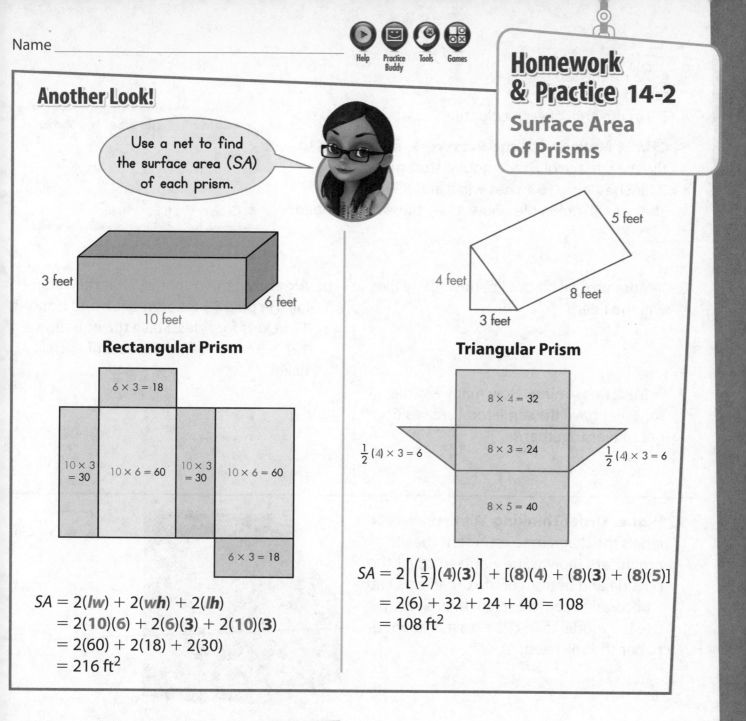

Rectangular Prism

$6 \times 3 = 18$

$10 \times 3 = 30$ $10 \times 6 = 60$ $10 \times 3 = 30$ $10 \times 6 = 60$

$6 \times 3 = 18$

$SA = 2(lw) + 2(wh) + 2(lh)$
$= 2(10)(6) + 2(6)(3) + 2(10)(3)$
$= 2(60) + 2(18) + 2(30)$
$= 216 \text{ ft}^2$

Triangular Prism

$8 \times 4 = 32$

$\frac{1}{2}(4) \times 3 = 6$ $8 \times 3 = 24$ $\frac{1}{2}(4) \times 3 = 6$

$8 \times 5 = 40$

$SA = 2\left[\left(\frac{1}{2}\right)(4)(3)\right] + [(8)(4) + (8)(3) + (8)(5)]$
$= 2(6) + 32 + 24 + 40 = 108$
$= 108 \text{ ft}^2$

In **1–3**, find the surface area of the prisms.

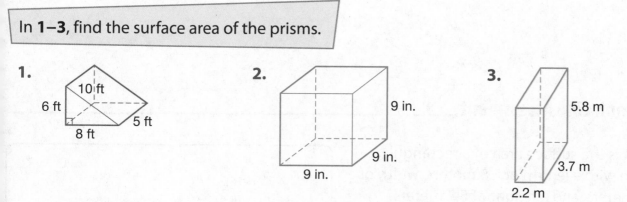

1.
10 ft
6 ft
5 ft
8 ft

2.
9 in.
9 in.
9 in.

3.
5.8 m
3.7 m
2.2 m

4. Fill in the area of each color tile.

5. © **MP.1 Make Sense and Persevere** Mora wants to tile the surface of a rectangular storage case that is 24 inches long, 16 inches wide, and 8 inches tall. If she uses all green tiles, how many tiles will she need?

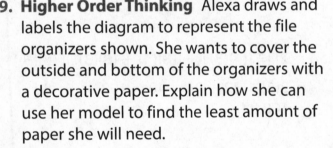

DATA	Color	Tile Size	Area
	Black	4 in. × 4 in.	
	Red	2 in. × 2 in.	
	Green	8 in. × 8 in.	

6. If Mora uses all black tiles, how many tiles will she need?

7. © **MP.2 Reasoning** How many red tiles together have the same total area as 6 green tiles together?

8. **Algebra** Emilio spent $21 at the state fair. He paid $3 for admission and bought 12 tickets for rides. Solve the equation $12t + 3 = 21$ to find the cost of each ticket.

9. **Higher Order Thinking** Alexa draws and labels the diagram to represent the file organizers shown. She wants to cover the outside and bottom of the organizers with a decorative paper. Explain how she can use her model to find the least amount of paper she will need.

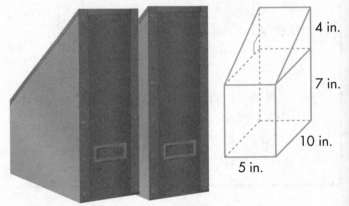

4 in.

7 in.

10 in.

5 in.

© **Common Core Assessment**

10. What is the surface area of a rectangular prism with a length of 2.8 meters, width of 4.3 meters, and a height of 6.2 meters?

Name _____

Solve & Share

The fence around Marci's house has decorative tops in the shape of square pyramids every 6 feet. She paints every side of each top a different color. How much total surface area does Marci need to paint? *Solve this problem any way you choose.*

I can ...
draw a net of a pyramid and find its surface area.

© **Content Standards** 6.G.A.4, 6.EE.A.2a, 6.EE.A.2c, 6.EE.B.6
Mathematical Practices MP.3, MP.4, MP.5, MP.6, MP.7

You can use tools, such as grid paper and a ruler, to make a net.

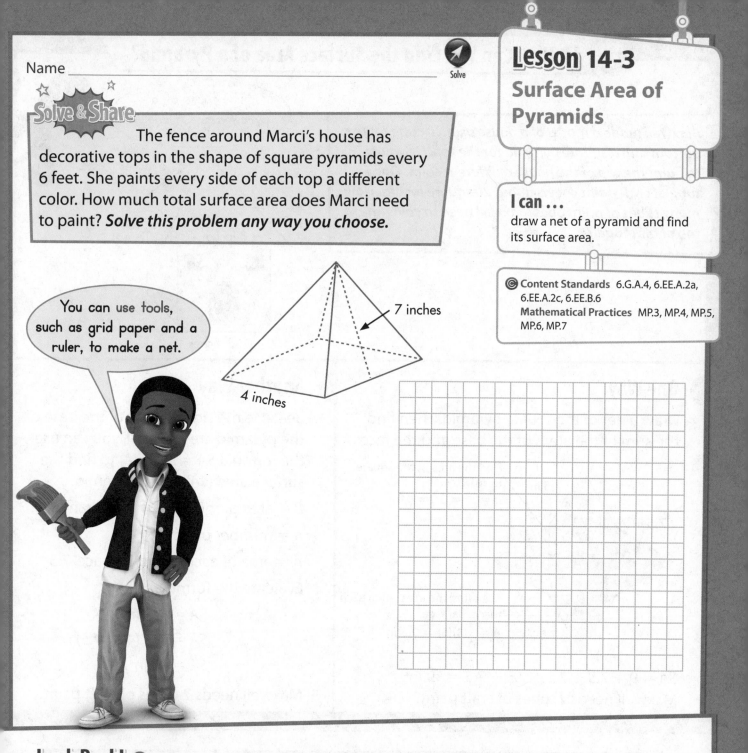

7 inches

4 inches

Look Back! © **MP.7 Use Structure** The fence in the back yard also has fence tops shaped like pyramids. They are 2 inches greater on each side of the square base and the triangular sides are 7 inches high. How much paint does Marci need to paint all of the sides of one of these fence tops?

A

Maxwell made a model of a house using a cube for the bottom and a square pyramid for the top. He wants to paint the top of the house a different color. One tube of craft paint covers about 20 square inches. How many tubes of paint does Maxwell need to cover the top of his model?

The faces of a pyramid are triangles.

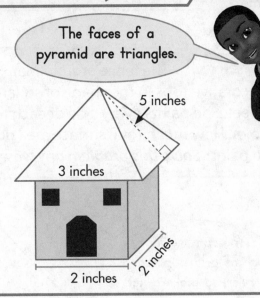

5 inches

3 inches

2 inches

2 inches

B **One Way**

Draw a net of the square pyramid. Then find the sum of the areas of the base and the faces.

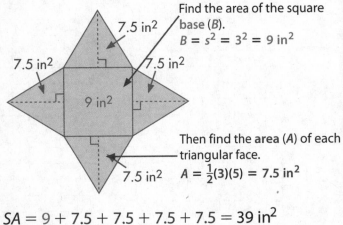

7.5 in²

7.5 in²

7.5 in²

9 in²

7.5 in²

Find the area of the square base (B).
$B = s^2 = 3^2 = 9$ in²

Then find the **area (A)** of each triangular face.
$A = \frac{1}{2}(3)(5) = 7.5$ in²

$SA = 9 + 7.5 + 7.5 + 7.5 + 7.5 = 39$ in²
Maxwell needs 2 tubes of craft paint.

C **Another Way**

Because the side lengths of the base of the pyramid are all equal, you can use the formula $SA = B + (nA)$ to find the surface area (SA) of this pyramid.

B = area of the base of the pyramid, 9

n = number of faces, 4

A = area of each triangular face, 7.5

Evaluate the formula.

$$SA = B + (n \times A)$$
$$SA = 9 + (4 \times 7.5)$$
$$SA = 39 \text{ in}^2$$

Maxwell needs 2 tubes of craft paint.

Convince Me! © **MP.6 Be Precise** Suppose Maxwell also wants to paint 5 of the 6 sides of the bottom of his model house. How many tubes of craft paint does he need to cover the model? Explain.

Another Example

How can you find the surface area of a pyramid that has an equilateral triangle as a base?

Draw a net.

Find the area of each **triangle** (T).

$T = \frac{1}{2}(5)(4.33) = 10.825 \text{ cm}^2$

Then find the surface area (SA) by multiplying the area of one triangle by 4.

$SA = 4T$

$SA = 4 \times 10.825 = 43.3$
$= 43.3 \text{ cm}^2$

> If you know the faces are equilateral triangles then you just find the area of one triangle and multiply by 4.

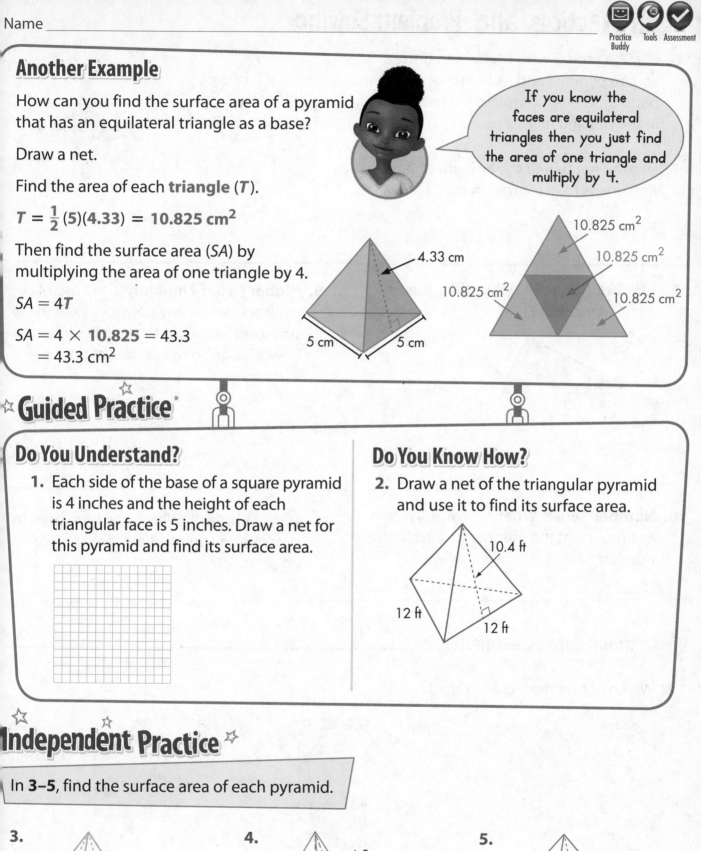

4.33 cm

5 cm   5 cm

10.825 cm²
10.825 cm²
10.825 cm²
10.825 cm²

☆ Guided Practice ⃰

Do You Understand?

1. Each side of the base of a square pyramid is 4 inches and the height of each triangular face is 5 inches. Draw a net for this pyramid and find its surface area.

Do You Know How?

2. Draw a net of the triangular pyramid and use it to find its surface area.

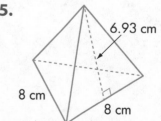

10.4 ft

12 ft

12 ft

☆ Independent Practice ☆

In **3–5**, find the surface area of each pyramid.

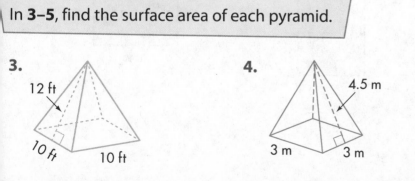

3.
12 ft
10 ft
10 ft

4.
4.5 m
3 m   3 m

5.
6.93 cm
8 cm
8 cm

Math Practices and Problem Solving

6. **© MP.4 Model with Math** Ken drew a square pyramid and its net to represent a patio umbrella. Complete the net by filling in the missing measures.

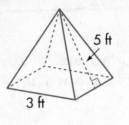

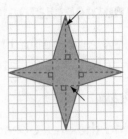

7. Use the net to find the amount of fabric Ken needs to make the umbrella.

8. **Algebra** The area of this triangle is 48 ft². What is the height?

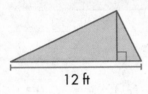

9. **Higher Order Thinking** The base of a pyramid can be any polygon. How many surfaces does a pentagonal pyramid have? Describe the shapes of the surfaces.

10. **Number Sense** What are two ways you can represent the number 125 using the number 5?

11. **A-Z Vocabulary** What is the term used to describe any point where three or more edges meet?

© Common Core Assessment

12. Which net represents a pyramid?

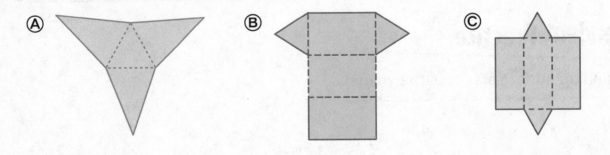

Ⓐ   Ⓑ   Ⓒ

Another Look!

Draw a net to represent the square pyramid below. Then use the net to find the surface area of the pyramid.

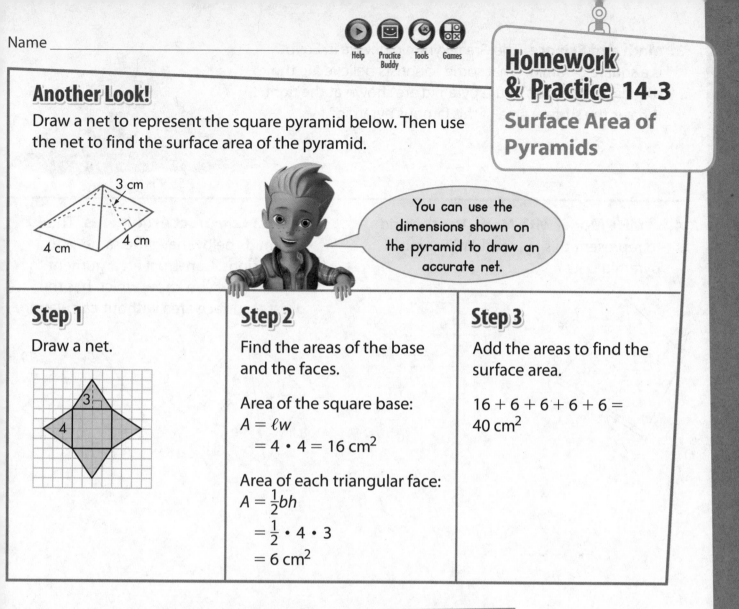

You can use the dimensions shown on the pyramid to draw an accurate net.

Step 1

Draw a net.

Step 2

Find the areas of the base and the faces.

Area of the square base:
$A = \ell w$
$\quad = 4 \cdot 4 = 16 \text{ cm}^2$

Area of each triangular face:
$A = \frac{1}{2}bh$
$\quad = \frac{1}{2} \cdot 4 \cdot 3$
$\quad = 6 \text{ cm}^2$

Step 3

Add the areas to find the surface area.

$16 + 6 + 6 + 6 + 6 =$
40 cm^2

In **1** and **2**, find the surface area of each pyramid by drawing its net.

1.

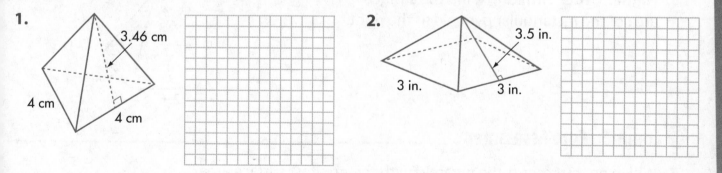

2.

3. Math and Science The Great Pyramid of Giza in Egypt is a square pyramid. What some scientists believe are the original dimensions of the pyramid are shown at the right. What is the surface area of this famous pyramid?

610 ft

755.9 ft

4. ⓒ **MP.4 Model with Math** Use the grid to represent this pyramid. What type of pyramid is it?

3 m

4 m

5. ⓒ **MP.3 Construct Arguments** The pyramids below have the same dimensions. Construct an argument to explain how you know which has the greater surface area without calculating.

6.9 ft

8 ft

8 ft

6.9 ft

8 ft

8 ft

6. Higher Order Thinking Find the surface area of the rectangular pyramid at the right.

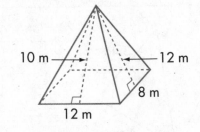

10 m   12 m

8 m

12 m

ⓒ **Common Core Assessment**

7. Which net represents the pyramid with the greatest surface area?

Ⓐ 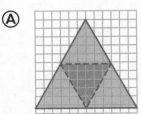   Ⓑ 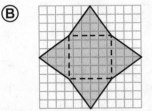   Ⓒ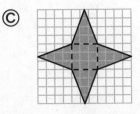

© Pearson Education, Inc. 6

Name _____

Solve & Share

A rectangular prism has the dimensions shown below. What is the volume of this rectangular prism? Use $\frac{1}{2}$-inch cubes to find the volume.

I can ...
find the volume of a rectangular prism with fractional edge lengths.

© **Content Standards** 6.G.A.2, 6.EE.A.2a, 6.EE.A.2c, 6.EE.B.6
Mathematical Practices MP.1, MP.2, MP.3, MP.6, MP.7, MP.8

You can use structure to fill the prism with layers of cubes to find its volume.

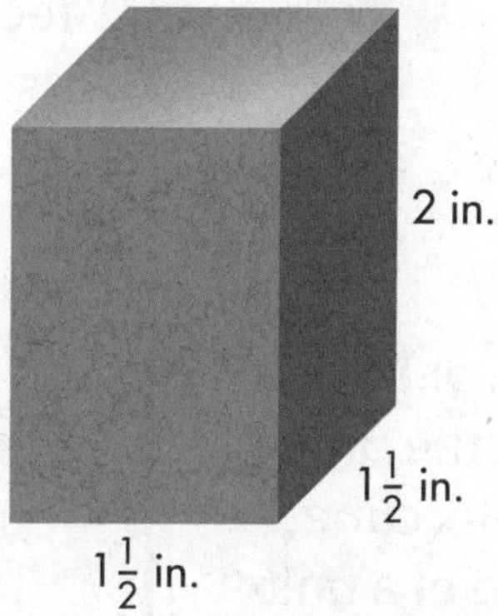

2 in.

$1\frac{1}{2}$ in.

$1\frac{1}{2}$ in.

Look Back! © **MP.2 Reasoning** You know how to use the formula $V = \ell w h$ to find the volume of a rectangular prism with whole-number edge lengths. Use the formula to find the volume of the prism above. How does this volume compare to the one you found from the model?

Essential Question

How Can You Find the Volume of a Rectangular Prism with Fractional Edge Lengths?

A

What is the volume of the rectangular prism?

$1\frac{1}{2}$ in.

$2\frac{1}{2}$ in. $2\frac{1}{2}$ in.

> Remember that volume is the number of cubic units needed to fill a solid figure.

B ## Step 1

Find the number of $\frac{1}{2}$-inch cubes that will fill the rectangular prism.

Five $\frac{1}{2}$-inch cubes fit along each $2\frac{1}{2}$-inch edge of the prism. So the bottom layer has 5×5, or 25 cubes.

The prism is 3 cubes high, so there are 25×3, or 75 cubes in the prism.

$\frac{1}{2}$ in.
$\frac{1}{2}$ in. $\frac{1}{2}$ in.

3 cubes

5 cubes

5 cubes

C ## Step 2

Find the volume of each smaller $\frac{1}{2}$-in. cube by using it to fill a unit cube.

There are 4 smaller cubes on the bottom layer of the unit cube, and the unit cube is 2 smaller cubes high.

$\frac{1}{2}$ in.
$\frac{1}{2}$ in. $\frac{1}{2}$ in.

1 in.

1 in.   1 in.

There are 4×2, or 8 smaller cubes in the unit cube. So each $\frac{1}{2}$-in. cube has $\frac{1}{8}$ the volume of a unit cube, or $\frac{1}{8} \times 1$ in^3 = $\frac{1}{8}$ in^3.

D ## Step 3

Find the volume of the prism.

Multiply the volume of each $\frac{1}{2}$-in. cube by the total number of cubes that fill the prism.

The volume of the rectangular prism is
$75 \times \frac{1}{8}$ in^3 = $\frac{75}{8}$ = $9\frac{3}{8}$ in^3.

> Be precise and use the correct units to describe area and volume.

Convince Me! © MP.8 Generalize Use the example above to show that you can also use the formula $V = \ell wh$ to find the volume of a rectangular prism with fractional edge lengths.

Name _____

Practice Buddy Tools Assessment

Do You Understand?

1. How is finding the volume of a rectangular prism with fractional edge lengths similar to finding the volume of a rectangular prism with whole number edge lengths?

2. © **MP.3 Construct Arguments** Explain how finding the number of $\frac{1}{2}$-inch cubes in a rectangular prism helps you find the number of unit cubes in a rectangular prism.

Do You Know How?

In **3** and **4**, tell how many of each size cube can fill a 1-inch cube.

3. Edge $= \frac{1}{3}$ inch

4. Edge $= \frac{1}{4}$ inch

In **5** and **6**, find the volume of each rectangular prism. Show your work.

5. 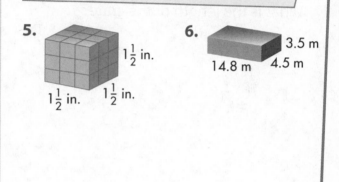 $1\frac{1}{2}$ in.

$1\frac{1}{2}$ in. $1\frac{1}{2}$ in.

6. 3.5 m

14.8 m   4.5 m

☆ **Independent Practice** ☆

In **7–10**, find the volume of each rectangular prism.

7.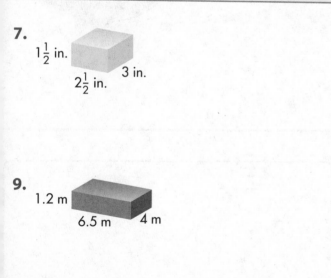

$1\frac{1}{2}$ in.

3 in.

$2\frac{1}{2}$ in.

8.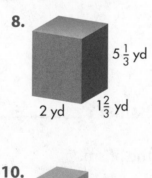

$5\frac{1}{3}$ yd

2 yd $1\frac{2}{3}$ yd

9.

1.2 m

6.5 m   4 m

10.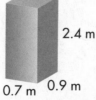

2.4 m

0.7 m   0.9 m

---

*For another example, see Set C on page 740.

Math Practices and Problem Solving

11. © **MP.7 Use Structure** Sandy has two boxes with the dimensions shown. She wants to use the box with the greater volume to ship a gift to her friend. Which box should Sandy use? Explain.

	Length	Width	Height
Box A	$7\frac{1}{2}$ in.	2 in.	$11\frac{1}{2}$ in.
Box B	9 in.	$2\frac{1}{4}$ in.	$8\frac{1}{2}$ in.

12. Algebra The volume of a large crate is 84 yd³. It is $2\frac{2}{3}$ yd wide and $4\frac{2}{3}$ yd high. What is the length of the crate?

13. Higher Order Thinking A box covers an area of $8\frac{3}{4}$ in² when resting on its base. The volume of the box is $74\frac{3}{8}$ in³. Can you find the surface area of the box? Explain your reasoning.

14. Math and Science A gold bar is similar in shape to a rectangular prism. A standard mint bar is approximately 7 in. × $3\frac{5}{8}$ in. × $1\frac{3}{4}$ in. If the value of gold is $1,313 per ounce, about how much is one gold bar worth? Use the formula $w \approx 11.15n$, where w is the weight in ounces and $n =$ volume in cubic inches, to find the weight in ounces. Explain how you found your answer.

© **Common Core Assessment**

15. Find the volume of the prism.

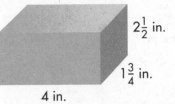

$2\frac{1}{2}$ in.

$1\frac{3}{4}$ in.

4 in.

© Pearson Education, Inc. 6

Name _____

Another Look!

What is the volume of the rectangular prism shown in the diagram?

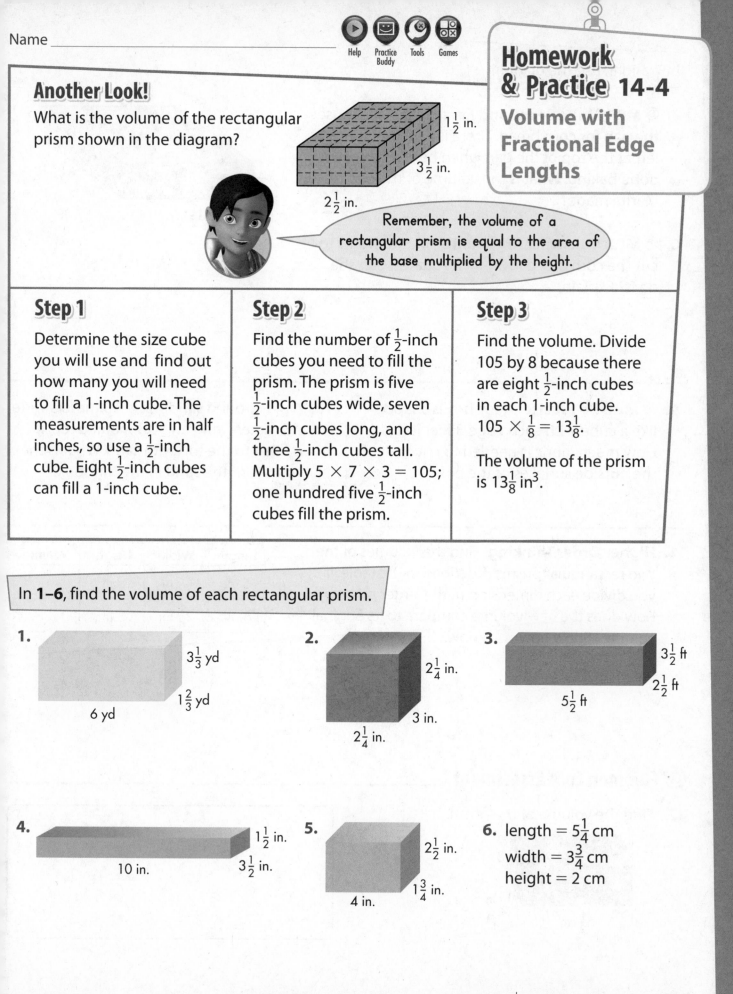

$1\frac{1}{2}$ in.

$3\frac{1}{2}$ in.

$2\frac{1}{2}$ in.

Remember, the volume of a rectangular prism is equal to the area of the base multiplied by the height.

Step 1

Determine the size cube you will use and find out how many you will need to fill a 1-inch cube. The measurements are in half inches, so use a $\frac{1}{2}$-inch cube. Eight $\frac{1}{2}$-inch cubes can fill a 1-inch cube.

Step 2

Find the number of $\frac{1}{2}$-inch cubes you need to fill the prism. The prism is five $\frac{1}{2}$-inch cubes wide, seven $\frac{1}{2}$-inch cubes long, and three $\frac{1}{2}$-inch cubes tall. Multiply $5 \times 7 \times 3 = 105$; one hundred five $\frac{1}{2}$-inch cubes fill the prism.

Step 3

Find the volume. Divide 105 by 8 because there are eight $\frac{1}{2}$-inch cubes in each 1-inch cube. $105 \times \frac{1}{8} = 13\frac{1}{8}$.

The volume of the prism is $13\frac{1}{8}$ in^3.

In **1–6**, find the volume of each rectangular prism.

1.

$3\frac{1}{3}$ yd

$1\frac{2}{3}$ yd

6 yd

2.

$2\frac{1}{4}$ in.

3 in.

$2\frac{1}{4}$ in.

3.

$3\frac{1}{2}$ ft

$2\frac{1}{2}$ ft

$5\frac{1}{2}$ ft

4.

$1\frac{1}{2}$ in.

$3\frac{1}{2}$ in.

10 in.

5.

$2\frac{1}{2}$ in.

$1\frac{3}{4}$ in.

4 in.

6. length = $5\frac{1}{4}$ cm
width = $3\frac{3}{4}$ cm
height = 2 cm

In **7** and **8**, use the diagram.

7. © **MP.1 Make Sense and Persevere** Marita uses the pan for corn bread. There is $\frac{3}{4}$ inch of space left at the top of the pan when her corn bread is done baking. What is the volume of the corn bread Marita made?

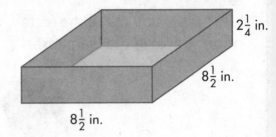

$2\frac{1}{4}$ in.

$8\frac{1}{2}$ in.

$8\frac{1}{2}$ in.

8. © **MP.3 Construct Arguments** Marita wants to cut the corn bread in $1\frac{1}{2}$-inch squares. Can she do it? Explain.

9. © **MP.6 Be Precise** A toy box is shaped like a cube with each edge 3 feet long. How much fabric is needed to cover all of the outside surfaces of the box?

10. A playground sandbox is 3.5 meters wide, 2.5 meters long and 0.3 meter deep. It is filled to the top with sand. What is the volume of the sand in the sandbox?

11. **Higher Order Thinking** Find the volumes of the two rectangular prisms described in the table. If you divide each dimension of the larger prism by 2, how does the new volume compare to its original volume? Show how you know.

Length	Width	Height	Volume
5 in.	$4\frac{1}{2}$ in.	6 in.	
$2\frac{1}{2}$ in.	$2\frac{1}{4}$ in.	3 in.	

© **Common Core Assessment**

12. Find the volume of the prism.

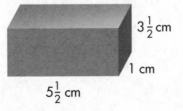

$3\frac{1}{2}$ cm

1 cm

$5\frac{1}{2}$ cm

Name _____

Solve & Share

The Power Hour game show has just posed a challenge: Design an environmentally friendly box that will hold 120 one-inch cubes. Design your box using as little cardboard as possible. Tell how much cardboard you will need to build your box.

Math Practices and Problem Solving

Lesson 14-5
Reasoning

I can ...
use reasoning to solve problems.

ⓒ Mathematical Practices MP.2, MP.3, MP.4, MP.7
Content Standards 6.G.A.2, 6.G.A.4, 6.EE.A.2a, 6.EE.A.2c, 6.EE.B.6

Thinking Habits

Be a good thinker!
These questions can help you.

• What do the numbers and symbols in the problem mean?

• How are the numbers or quantities related?

• How can I represent a word problem using pictures, numbers, or equations?

Look Back! ⓒ **MP.2 Reasoning** Molly builds a box with a base that is 2 inches by 5 inches. How can you use the base dimensions to find the minimum height Molly's box needs to be to hold 120 one-inch cubes?

Essential Question — How Can You Use Reasoning to Solve Problems?

A

> Amanda is building a house for her dog, Ralph. She has the roof completed but still needs to make the walls. She plans to use a leftover piece of wood measuring 6 feet by 4 feet to build the four sides. How might she cut the wood to make the walls of the doghouse?

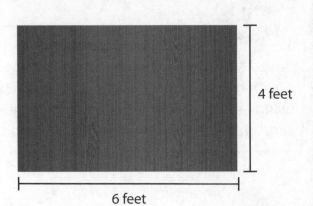

4 feet

6 feet

What do I need to do to solve this problem?

I need to find a way to cut the wood to make the walls of the doghouse.

Here's my thinking...

B How can I use reasoning to solve this problem?

I can

- identify the quantities I know.

- draw a picture to show relationships.

- consider the units involved.

- apply what I know about surface area and measuring.

C

I know that Amanda has a piece of wood measuring 6 feet by 4 feet. She will cut the wood to make four rectangular sides of a doghouse.

Each side should be of equal height. Opposite sides should have the same dimensions.

I can draw a picture to show one way to cut the wood.

Amanda can cut the wood into four pieces, each measuring 2 feet by 3 feet.

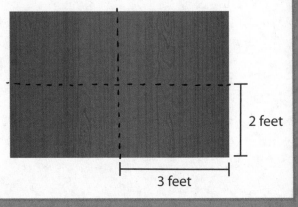

2 feet

3 feet

Convince Me! © **MP.2 Reasoning** If the side measurements Amanda used were 1 foot by 6 feet, how would the total surface area of the doghouse's walls change compared to the doghouse made above?

© Pearson Education, Inc. 6

Practice Buddy   Tools   Assessment

☆ Guided Practice*

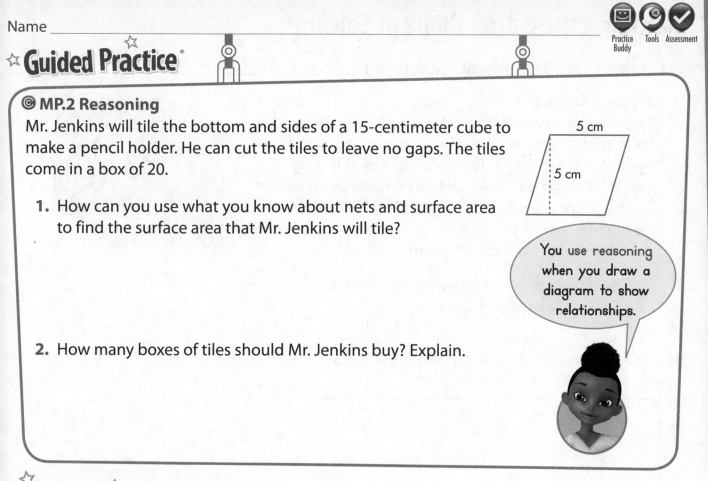

© **MP.2 Reasoning**

Mr. Jenkins will tile the bottom and sides of a 15-centimeter cube to make a pencil holder. He can cut the tiles to leave no gaps. The tiles come in a box of 20.

5 cm

5 cm

1. How can you use what you know about nets and surface area to find the surface area that Mr. Jenkins will tile?

You use reasoning when you draw a diagram to show relationships.

2. How many boxes of tiles should Mr. Jenkins buy? Explain.

Independent Practice ☆

© **MP.2 Reasoning**

Mia wants to cover a gift box that is 9 inches by 12 inches by 3 inches with colored construction paper. Each sheet of paper is 9 by 12 inches.

3. Draw a net to represent the gift box.

4. What is the least number of sheets of construction paper Mia can use to cover the box? Explain how you know.

Math Practices and Problem Solving

Shipping Shapes

Boltz Hardware has 60 boxes of product ready to pack in a shipping container. Each box is cube shaped, with edges measuring $\frac{1}{2}$ foot. To stay within the shipping budget, all 60 boxes must fit into a container with inside dimensions of 2 feet long, $1\frac{1}{2}$ feet wide, and $2\frac{1}{2}$ feet high. Use the rules below to decide how the boxes could be packed to match these container dimensions.

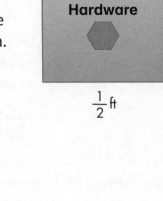

- The boxes can be arranged in 5 or 6 layers.
- Each layer can have 10 or 12 boxes.

5. **MP.7 Use Structure** How can looking for patterns help you solve this problem? Explain.

When you arrange numbers and objects in different ways to solve problems, you are using structure.

6. **MP.3 Construct Arguments** How can you decide whether the boxes should be arranged in 5 layers or 6 layers?

7. **MP.2 Reasoning** How could you pack the container to meet the shipping requirements? Is there more than one correct answer? Explain your reasoning.

Name _____

Another Look!

Mitch is making a square pyramid sculpture using a sheet of metal that is 1 foot wide and 3 feet long. Does he have enough sheet metal to make the pyramid sculpture shown? Explain how you know.

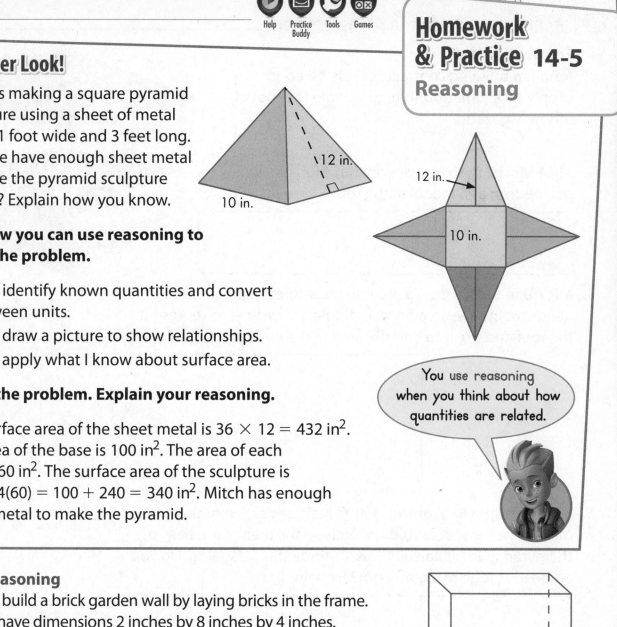

12 in.

10 in.

12 in.

10 in.

Tell how you can use reasoning to solve the problem.

- I can identify known quantities and convert between units.
- I can draw a picture to show relationships.
- I can apply what I know about surface area.

Solve the problem. Explain your reasoning.

The surface area of the sheet metal is $36 \times 12 = 432$ in^2. The area of the base is 100 in^2. The area of each face is 60 in^2. The surface area of the sculpture is $100 + 4(60) = 100 + 240 = 340$ in^2. Mitch has enough sheet metal to make the pyramid.

You use reasoning when you think about how quantities are related.

© **MP.2 Reasoning**

The Millers build a brick garden wall by laying bricks in the frame. The bricks have dimensions 2 inches by 8 inches by 4 inches.

1. Describe how to find the number of bricks needed to fill the bottom layer of the frame. Draw a picture to help.

$3\frac{1}{3}$ ft

1 ft

4 ft

2. How many bricks do the Millers need to build the wall?

Contracting Bid

John is a building contractor. He is asked to supply an estimate, or bid, to shingle the roof of this new gazebo.

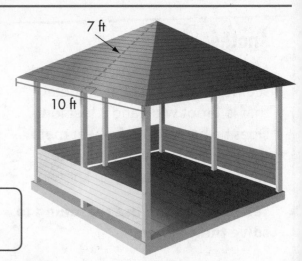

7 ft

10 ft

3. **MP.4 Model with Math** How can John use a polyhedron as a model of the roof?

4. **MP.7 Use Structure** To provide an accurate estimate, John needs to find the area he will shingle. Draw a net to represent the roof and use it to find the area that John will shingle.

$\dfrac{\text{KEY}}{2\text{ft}}$

5. **MP.3 Critique Reasoning** John's assistant says that there is a mistake because John did not include the area of the base of the pyramid in his calculations. Critique this reasoning. Do you agree that John made an error? Explain.

6. **MP.2 Reasoning** The shingles John uses come in bundles that cover 33 ft^2 and cost $29.25 each. Additional materials costs are estimated at $100. John also estimates labor charges at a rate of 2 times the cost of materials and adds a contractor's fee of 20% of the total job cost to finalize the estimate. What do you recommend John bid for this roofing job?

☆ ☆
Point & Tally

Find a partner. Get paper and a pencil. Each partner chooses a different color: light blue or dark blue.

Partner 1 and Partner 2 each point to a black number at the same time. Both partners divide the greater number by the lesser number.

If the answer is on your color, you get a tally mark. Work until one partner has twelve tally marks.

I can ...
divide multi-digit whole numbers.

© **Content Standard** 6.NS.B.2

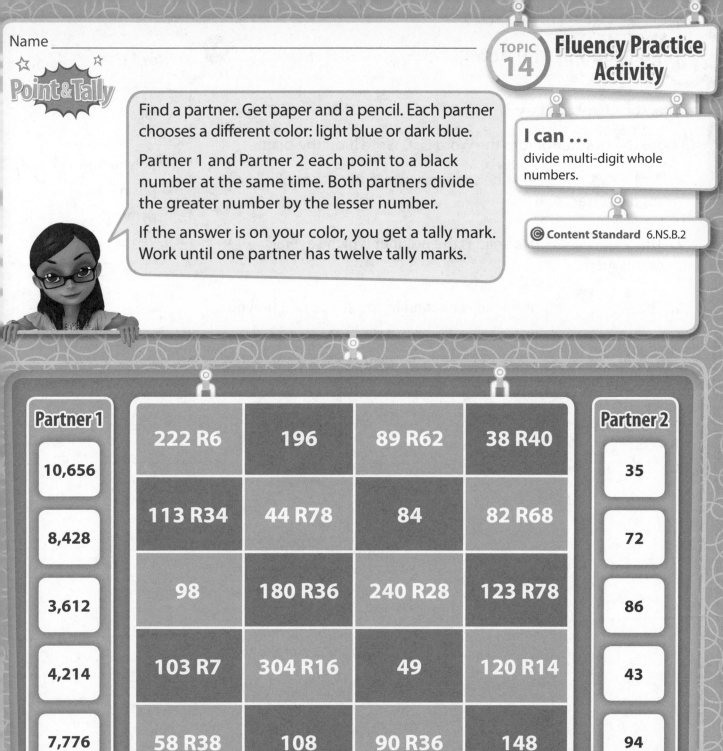

Partner 1

| 10,656 |
| 8,428 |
| 3,612 |
| 4,214 |
| 7,776 |

222 R6	196	89 R62	38 R40
113 R34	44 R78	84	82 R68
98	180 R36	240 R28	123 R78
103 R7	304 R16	49	120 R14
58 R38	108	90 R36	148
42	247 R35	117 R4	50 R12

Partner 2

| 35 |
| 72 |
| 86 |
| 43 |
| 94 |

Tally Marks for Partner 1

Tally Marks for Partner 2

Vocabulary Review

A-Z
Glossary

Word List

- edge
- face
- net
- polyhedron
- prism
- pyramid
- vertex

Understand Vocabulary

Choose the best term from the Word List. Write it on the blank.

1. A(n) _____ is a line segment where two faces of a solid intersect.

2. The _____ of a solid is the point at which several edges meet.

3. The _____ of a solid is flat and in the shape of a polygon.

Draw a line from each *net* in Column A to the name of the *polyhedron* it represents in Column B.

Column A   **Column B**

4.   square pyramid

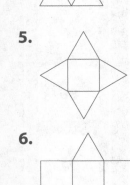

5.   triangular prism

6.   triangular pyramid

Use Vocabulary in Writing

7. Compare the two solids. Use at least 5 words from the Word List.

A   B

Set A · pages 707–712

To classify a polyhedron, first determine whether it is a prism or a pyramid. Then use the shape of its base to name it.

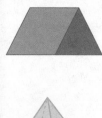

This figure has two congruent parallel bases, so it is a prism. The bases are triangles, so it is a **triangular prism**.

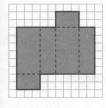

This figure has one base, and the edges are joined at a point outside the base, so it is a pyramid. The base is a square and the faces are triangles, so it is a **square pyramid**.

A **net** shows what a polyhedron would look like "unfolded," with all surfaces on the plane. This is a net of a rectangular prism.

Remember that a prism has two identical bases and a pyramid has one base.

Draw a net of the pyramid shown.

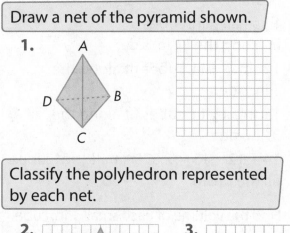

1.

Classify the polyhedron represented by each net.

2.   3.

Set B · pages 713–718, 719–724

To find the total surface area (SA) of a polyhedron, you can draw a net and then add the areas of each face.

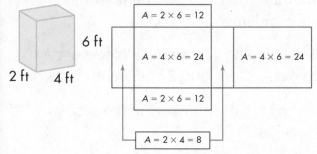

$SA = 12 + 8 + 24 + 12 + 24 + 8 = 88$ ft²

You can also use a formula.

$SA = 2(\ell w) + 2(wh) + 2(\ell h)$
$= 2(8) + 2(12) + 2(24)$
$= 16 + 24 + 48$
$= 88$ ft²

The surface area of the prism is 88 ft².

Remember that surface area is measured in square units.

Find the surface area of each solid.

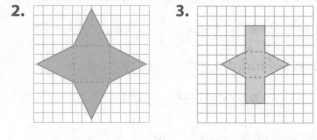

1.   5 ft   2.   5 m
     6 ft   3 ft   4 m   4 m

Find the surface area of each prism.

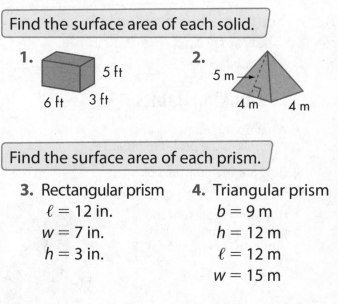

3. Rectangular prism
    $\ell = 12$ in.
    $w = 7$ in.
    $h = 3$ in.

4. Triangular prism
    $b = 9$ m
    $h = 12$ m
    $\ell = 12$ m
    $w = 15$ m

Find the volume of the rectangular prism.

Step 1 Find the number of small $\frac{1}{4}$-in. cubes that will fill the prism.

$3\frac{3}{4}$ in.

3 in.

$3\frac{1}{2}$ in.

14 small $\frac{1}{4}$-in. cubes fit along the $3\frac{1}{2}$ in. side.

12 small $\frac{1}{4}$-in. cubes fit along the 3 in. side.

15 small $\frac{1}{4}$-in. cubes fit along the $3\frac{3}{4}$ in. side.

$14 \cdot 12 \cdot 15 = 2{,}520$ small $\frac{1}{4}$-in. cubes fill the prism.

Step 2 Find the volume of each small $\frac{1}{4}$-in. cube.

$$V = \ell wh = \frac{1}{4} \cdot \frac{1}{4} \cdot \frac{1}{4} = \frac{1}{64} \text{ in}^3$$

Step 3 Find the volume of the prism.

$$2{,}520 \cdot \frac{1}{64} \text{ in}^3 = 39\frac{3}{8} \text{ in}^3$$

You can also use a formula.

$$V = \ell wh = 3\frac{1}{2} \text{ in.} \times 3 \text{ in.} \times 3\frac{3}{4} \text{ in.} = 39\frac{3}{8} \text{ in}^3$$

Remember that volume is measured in cubic units.

Find the volume of each rectangular prism.

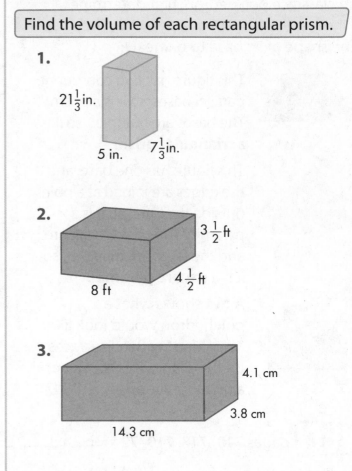

1.

$21\frac{1}{3}$ in.

5 in. $7\frac{1}{3}$ in.

2.

$3\frac{1}{2}$ ft

8 ft $4\frac{1}{2}$ ft

3.

4.1 cm

3.8 cm

14.3 cm

Think about these questions to help you **reason abstractly and quantitatively**.

Thinking Habits

• What do the numbers and symbols in the problem mean?

• How are the numbers or quantities related?

• How can I represent the problem using pictures, numbers, or equations?

Remember that you can use reasoning to solve problems.

Kylie is shipping 4 rectangular blocks of clay. Each block is 4 in. long, 3 in. wide, and 2 in. high.

1. How are the numbers in the problem related?

2. What is the least amount of cardboard Kylie needs to make the shipping box?

Name _____

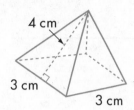

© **Assessment**

1. Which of the following can be used to find the volume of a rectangular prism with length 7.5 centimeters, width 2 centimeters, and height 4.2 centimeters?

   ☐ $V = 15 + 4.2$

   ☐ $V = 15 \times 4.2 \times 4.2$

   ☐ $V = 15 \times 4.2$

   ☐ $V = 7.5 \times 2 \times 4.2$

   ☐ $V = (7.5 + 2) \times 4.2$

2. What is the surface area of the triangular prism shown?

   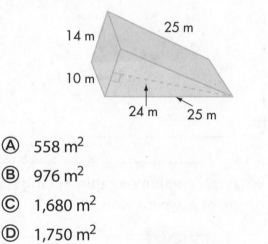

   Ⓐ 558 m²

   Ⓑ 976 m²

   Ⓒ 1,680 m²

   Ⓓ 1,750 m²

3. Small $\frac{1}{2}$-foot cubes will be packed into the prism below. How many small cubes are needed to completely fill the prism?

   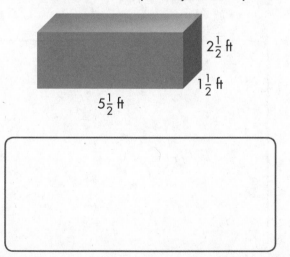

4. A square pyramid is shown below.

   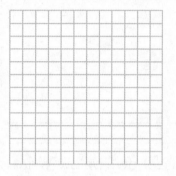

   Part A

   Draw a net that represents the pyramid.

   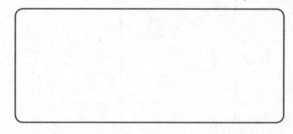

   Part B

   What is the surface area of the pyramid?

5. The net below represents a container. What solid figure does it show? How many vertices does the container have?

   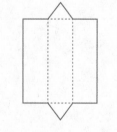

6. Find the height of a rectangular prism having the measurements listed below.

Volume: 383.04 m^3
Length: 10.5 m
Width: 7.6 m

7. A net of a box is shown below. What is the surface area of the box?

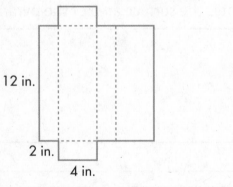

12 in.

2 in.

4 in.

8. Stephan has a piece of wood that measures 18 inches long and 12 inches wide. He wants to make a tray with sides 2 inches high. Maurice says he can make a tray that has a base measuring $10\frac{1}{2}$ inches by $10\frac{1}{2}$ inches. Is he correct? Explain your reasoning.

9. What is the volume of this rectangular prism? Show your work.

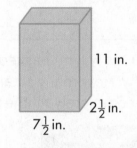

11 in.

$2\frac{1}{2}$ in.

$7\frac{1}{2}$ in.

Name _____

Bounce House

Katie works for a company that designs children's bounce houses. The diagram shows her design for a new bounce house.

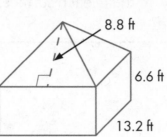

8.8 ft

6.6 ft

13.2 ft

13.2 ft

© **Performance Assessment**

1. A requirement for the bounce house is that it has a volume of at least 1,150 ft^3. Does Katie's bounce house meet the requirement? Justify your conclusion.

2. Katie needs to choose the material to cover each of the surfaces of her bounce house. Draw a net to show each of the surfaces of the bounce house.

3. Katie will use vinyl to make each surface. How much vinyl will she need for the bounce house?

4. Katie can select the color of the vinyl used to make the bounce house. Each side must be made from a solid 14 ft by 14 ft sheet of vinyl.

Color	Cost per Sheet
Yellow	$712.50
Blue	$716.00
Green	$716.00
Pink	$720.50
Purple	$720.50
Orange	$712.50
Silver	$725.00

Part A

How many pieces of vinyl will she need? Explain your reasoning.

Part B

The total budget for the vinyl is $5,000. What colors do you recommend she use for each piece? What is the total cost of the vinyl?

Measures of Center and Variability

Essential Questions: How can you describe a data distribution? How can data be described by a single number?

Interactions of sunlight and the atmosphere influence weather and climate.

Weather occurs in the troposphere. It's the lowest layer of the atmosphere.

Does that make Earth a little "under the weather"? Here's a project on the atmosphere and averages.

Math and Science Project: Atmospheric Temperatures

Do Research Use the Internet or other sources to find a graph that shows how temperature changes with altitude in the layers of Earth's atmosphere.

Journal: Write a Report Include what you found. Also in your report:

• Create a table of the high and low temperatures for each of the four layers closest to Earth's surface.

• Calculate the average of each pair of values. Then, calculate the average of the four average values.

• Describe how useful each average is for describing the data for each layer and for the atmosphere as a whole.

Name _____

Review What You Know

A-Z Vocabulary

Choose the best term from the box.
Write it on the blank.

- bar graph
- data
- survey
- tally chart

1. _____ are pieces of gathered information.

2. Collecting information by asking a number of people the same question and recording their answers is called a _____.

3. Use the lengths of bars to show and compare data in a _____.

Summarize Data

Use the data set below to answer the questions.

Number of Text Messages Henry Sent Each Day
6, 12, 2, 6, 3, 4, 2, 5, 6

4. What is the least value?

5. What is the greatest value?

6. What numbers are repeated?

7. How many text messages did Henry send in all?

Analyze Data

Use the graph to answer the questions about a student's test performance.

8. How many more points were earned on Test 3 than on Test 1?

9. Which two tests have the least difference in score? What is the difference?

10. What is the greatest difference between two scores? How do you know?

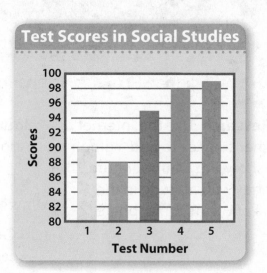

My Word Cards

Use the examples for each word on the front of the card to help complete the definitions on the back.

statistical question

How many pets does each of the students in my class own?

mean

7, 8, 4, 3, 6, 8

$7 + 8 + 4 + 3 + 6 + 8 = 36$

$36 \div 6 = 6$

The mean is 6.

> Find the sum. Divide by the number of values in the set.

median

10, 8, 4, 3, 6, 8

3, 4, 6, 8, 8, 10

The median is halfway between 6 and 8.

The median is 7.

> Order the numbers. Find the middle number.

mode

7, 8, 4, 3, 6, 8

There are two 8s. The other numbers occur only once.

The mode is 8.

> Find the number that occurs most often.

range

7, 8, 4, 3, 6, 8

$8 - 3 = 5$

The range is 5.

> Find the difference of the greatest and least values.

My Word Cards

Complete each definition. Extend learning by writing your own definitions.

You can calculate the _____ of a data set by finding the sum of all of the values and dividing by the number of values in the set.

A question that anticipates there will be a variety of different answers is called a _____.

The value that occurs most often in a data set is the _____.

The middle number in a set of ordered data is the _____.

The difference between the greatest and least values in a data set is the _____.

Name _____

Solve & Share

Ms. Jackson wrote a question on the board. Then she collected student responses to the question and recorded them in a tally chart. What question could she have asked? Is there more than one possible response to the question? Explain.

I can ...
identify and write statistical questions.

© Content Standards 6.SP.A.1, 6.SP.B.4
Mathematical Practices MP.1, MP.2, MP.8

Number of Books Read Last Month	
0	III
1	IIII
2	IIII I
3	IIII
4	II
5	I

You can make sense of the problem. Think about what you know and what you need to find out.

Look Back! © MP.2 Reasoning Suppose Ms. Jackson wants to know the amount of time her students spent outdoors the previous afternoon. What question might she ask each student in order to gather the data?

A

Mr. Borden asked his students a question and recorded the data in the table. Which of the following is a statistical question that Mr. Borden could have asked?

- What is the area of an $8\frac{1}{2}''\times 11''$ sheet of notebook paper?
- How many sheets of paper did you use last week?
- Did Bill use notebook paper to write his book report?

A statistical question anticipates that there will be a variety of answers.

Sheets of Paper Used Last Week	
Number of Sheets	Number of Students
5	I
10	I
15	II
20	IIII
25	ЖЖ I
30	ЖЖ

B

The question *How many sheets of paper did you use last week?* may be answered in various ways by Mr. Borden's students, so it is a statistical question.

The questions *What is the area of an $8\frac{1}{2}''\times 11''$ sheet of notebook paper?* and *Did Bill use notebook paper to write his book report?* have only one correct answer, so they are not statistical questions.

C

You can display the data in the tally chart in a bar graph.

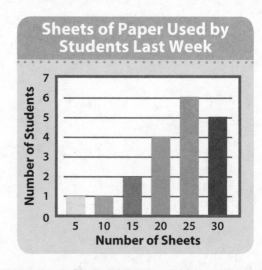

Sheets of Paper Used by Students Last Week

Convince Me! © **MP.8 Generalize** Is the question *What was the high temperature on March 8 of last year?* a statistical question? Explain.

☆Guided Practice*

Do You Understand?

1. Write a statistical question that involves movies your classmates saw last month. Then describe how to display the data.

2. © **MP.2 Reasoning** Mr. Borden wants to know how far his students live from school. What statistical question could he ask himself before gathering these data?

Do You Know How?

In **3–6**, tell whether each question is *statistical* or *not statistical*.

3. In which month is your birthday?

4. Does Sue wear glasses?

5. Who is the current President of the United States?

6. How tall are the students in Grade 6?

Independent Practice ☆

In **7** and **8**, write a statistical question you could ask to gather data on each topic.

7. Number of pets classmates own

8. Heights of different household plants

9. Kim asked her classmates, *How many siblings do you have?* She collected the following responses: 0, 1, 2, 1, 2, 0, 3, 1, 0, 5, 5, 1, 3, 1, 0, 2, 4, 1, 3, 0. Make a dot plot to display the data.

> A dot plot is a type of line plot that uses dots to represent data values above a number line.

Math Practices and Problem Solving

10. © **MP.1 Make Sense and Persevere** What statistical question could have been asked to collect the data shown in the dot plot?

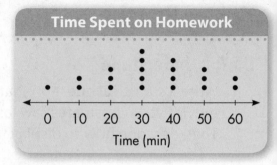

Time Spent on Homework

Time (min)

11. **Higher Order Thinking** If the data in the dot plot shows how many minutes students spent on homework the previous night, how many hours in all did these students spend doing homework? Did a typical student from this group spend more or fewer than 30 minutes on homework?

12. 🅰️🆉 **Vocabulary** Wyatt says that a *statistical question* must have a numerical answer. Do you agree with Wyatt? Explain.

© Common Core Assessment

13. Ms. Williams asked each student in her class these two questions:

    How many digits are in a phone number, including the area code? In a typical week, how many days do you spend some time watching television?

    Part A

    Which of the questions Ms. Williams asked is a statistical question? Explain.

    Part B

    The results of the statistical question Ms. Williams asked are shown below. Make a bar graph to display the data.

2	3	0	5	4	1	2	3	7	2
1	6	0	2	2	1	3	4	3	4

Name _____

Another Look!

How can you identify and write a statistical question, and then display the collected data?

To identify and write statistical questions, determine whether the question you want to ask a group of people has several different answers.

How many nickels are in a dollar? **Not statistical**

What former U.S. President appears on a nickel? **Not statistical**

How many nickels are in your backpack? **Statistical**

Good statistical questions anticipate a variety of different answers.

You can use a chart to keep track of the responses. Then make a dot plot or a bar graph to display the data.

Number of Nickels in Students' Backpacks	
Number of Nickels	Number of Students
0	I I
1	ⅬⅬⱦ
2	I I
3	I I
4	I I

Number of Nickels in Students' Backpacks

Number of Nickels

In **1** and **2**, tell whether each question is *statistical* or *not statistical*.

1. How long does it take sixth-grade students to eat lunch?

2. When does Carver Elementary School's summer break begin?

3. Write a statistical question you might ask to gather data on the cost of a restaurant meal.

4. Dean asked his classmates, *How many apples did you eat last week?* He got the following responses: 7, 5, 5, 5, 7, 3, 2, 1, 0, 0, 4, 3, 2, 1, 0, 7, 5, 6, 7, 0, 2, 2, 1, 4. Make a dot plot to display the data.

5. What statistical question might Tessa have asked her classmates to gather the data displayed in the bar graph?

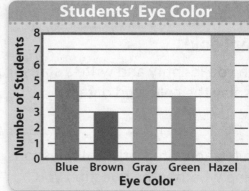

Students' Eye Color

6. Higher Order Thinking People with *heterochromia* have two different colored eyes. A new student in Tessa's class has heterochromia. How might you show that the student has one blue eye and one brown eye on the bar graph? Explain your reasoning.

Bar graphs and dot plots can help you analyze statistical data.

© Common Core Assessment

7. Charles asked each member of the basketball team these two questions:

How many inches tall are you?
How many points were scored in the last game?

Part A

Which of the questions Charles asked is a statistical question? Explain.

Part B

The results of the statistical question Charles asked are shown below. Make a dot plot to display the data.

68 70 73 74 72 74 75 76
70 71 73 72 73 70 73 74

Name _____

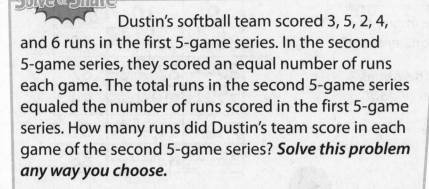

Solve & Share

Dustin's softball team scored 3, 5, 2, 4, and 6 runs in the first 5-game series. In the second 5-game series, they scored an equal number of runs each game. The total runs in the second 5-game series equaled the number of runs scored in the first 5-game series. How many runs did Dustin's team score in each game of the second 5-game series? *Solve this problem any way you choose.*

I can ...
find the mean of a data set and recognize its value as a measure of center.

ⓒ Content Standards 6.SP.A.3, 6.SP.B.5c
Mathematical Practices MP.2, MP.3, MP.6, MP.8

You can use reasoning to identify how the total number of runs scored and the number of games played are related.

Look Back! ⓒ **MP.8 Generalize** Antonio's basketball team scored 244 points in 4 games. Repeat the strategy you used above to find the average number of points Antonio's team scored each game.

How Can You Use a Single Number to Describe a Data Set?

A

Carla is in a bowling league. What is the mean, or average, final score of the five bowlers on her team?

The mean, or average, is the sum of all the values in a data set divided by the total number of data values in the set.

9	10	FINAL SCORE
86 ^{7} $_{2}$	95 ^{6} $_{3}$ –	95
80 ^{4} $_{2}$	87 ^{7} $_{0}$ –	87
77 ^{5} $_{1}$	84 ^{4} $_{3}$ –	84
74 ^{2} $_{4}$	81 ^{5} $_{2}$ –	81
75 ^{3} $_{3}$	83 ^{6} $_{2}$ –	83

The mean is a measure of center that can be used to summarize a data distribution.

B ## Step 1

Add the final scores in the data set.

Find the mean final score for the team.

$$\begin{array}{r} \overset{2}{95} \\ 87 \\ 84 \\ 81 \\ + 83 \\ \hline 430 \end{array}$$

The sum of the final scores for all five bowlers is 430.

C ## Step 2

Divide the sum by the number of values in the data set.

430 ÷ 5 scores

$$\begin{array}{r} 86 \\ 5)\overline{430} \\ -40 \\ \hline 30 \\ -30 \\ \hline 0 \end{array}$$

The mean, or average, final score is 86.

Convince Me! © **MP.6 Be Precise** The lowest scorer on Carla's team is sick the next week. Her replacement bowls a 151-point game. The other bowlers match their scores from the previous week. What is the new mean final score for the team? Show how you know.

Do You Understand?

1. Chester scored 84, 88, and 80 on his first 3 math tests. How can you find his mean, or average, score on these tests?

2. What is Chester's mean score?

3. © **MP.2 Reasoning** Suppose Chester scores a 90 on his next test. Without doing any calculations, will his mean score increase, decrease, or stay the same? Explain how you know.

Do You Know How?

In **4** and **5**, use the following data about the students in three classes.

Teacher	Boys	Girls
Ms. Green	15	14
Mr. Nesbit	12	12
Ms. Jackson	12	16

4. What is the mean number of boys in the three classes? What is the mean number of girls in the three classes?

5. What is the mean number of students in the three classes?

Independent Practice

In **6** and **7**, use the data shown in the table to find each mean.

6. Technical marks from judges

7. Presentation marks from judges

8. Find the combined marks, or total score, awarded by each of the 7 judges. Record your answers in the table.

A U.S. Figure Skater's Scores			
Judge	Technical Marks	Presentation Marks	Total Scores
A	5.9	5.4	
B	5.8	5.7	
C	5.8	5.6	
D	5.6	5.3	
E	5.9	5.5	
F	5.6	5.3	
G	6.0	5.7	

9. What is the mean total score awarded by the judges?

Math Practices and Problem Solving

In **10–13**, use the table.

10. **Math and Science** What is the average low temperature forecasted for the five days?

11. What is the average high temperature forecasted for the five days?

12. What percent of the forecasted high temperatures is greater than 50°F?

Forecasted Temperatures		
Day	Low (°F)	High (°F)
Monday	42	55
Tuesday	44	57
Wednesday	45	60
Thursday	34	45
Friday	40	50

13. **Higher Order Thinking** The forecast for Wednesday is later changed to a high of 70°F. Without calculating the new mean, describe how this changes the mean high temperature for the 5 days. How do you know?

14. **MP.3 Critique Reasoning** Maria says the mean of the scores 7, 8, 3, 0, 2 is 5, because she added the scores and divided by 4. Is she correct? Explain why or why not.

Common Core Assessment

15. In a–d, choose True or False for each statement. Use the data in the table.

Number of Cars Passing Through Intersection	
Hour	Cars
6 A.M.	15
7 A.M.	27
8 A.M.	37
9 A.M.	29
10 A.M.	12

a. The mean number of cars passing through the intersection each hour from 6 A.M. to 10 A.M. is 25.

○ True   ○ False

b. If the data for 10 A.M. is removed, the mean is increased by 3 cars.

○ True   ○ False

c. If 2 fewer cars had passed through the intersection between 6 A.M. and 10 A.M., it would decrease the mean by 2 cars.

○ True   ○ False

d. On another morning, the mean number of cars passing through the intersection was 22. This was a total of 10 fewer cars during these hours.

○ True   ○ False

Another Look!

Eduardo surveyed 7 of his friends to find out how many books each of them had read during the month. The table shows the data. What is the mean number of books read by Eduardo's friends?

Book Reading	
Friend	**Number of Books Read**
Jean	2
Raul	3
Sally	8
Jonathan	5
Haley	6
Kristen	3
Owen	1

The mean, or average, of a set of data is a way of describing the data with a single number.

Step 1 Add the number of books read by each friend.
$2 + 3 + 8 + 5 + 6 + 3 + 1 = 28$

Step 2 Divide the sum by the number of friends.
$28 \div 7 = 4$

The mean number of books read by the friends is 4.

In **1–4**, find the mean of the data given.

1. Number of pets in 6 families: 3, 0, 2, 4, 2, 1

2. Test scores: 89, 88, 82, 93

3. Number of apps on five friends' smart phones: 42, 42, 23, 75, 64

4. Number of students in 3 middle schools: 285, 336, 327

In **5** and **6**, use the data about the weekly salaries of employees at two small companies.

Company A: $500, $510, $530, $510, $550
Company B: $450, $440, $440, $470, $800

5. What is the mean weekly salary at each company?

6. Four of the 5 employees at Company B each received a raise of $40. After the raises, how much greater is the mean of the salaries for Company B than Company A? Explain how you solved the problem.

In **7–10**, use the table.

Money Each Student Has Raised for a Band Trip									
$24.50	$18.25	$5.75	$48.00	$32.50	$12.80	$22.90	$35.00	$18.75	$16.25

7. What is the mean amount raised by the students?

8. Higher Order Thinking How much more money do the 10 students need to raise to increase the mean to $25.00? Explain how you know.

9. Algebra The students want to raise $300. What percent, p, of the money have they raised so far? Write and solve an equation. Round your answer to the nearest whole percent.

10. Ⓒ **MP.2 Reasoning** Two students have not yet turned in their money. How much money would each of the two students need to raise in order to reach the goal of $300? Explain your thinking.

Ⓒ **Common Core Assessment**

11. In a–d, choose True or False for each statement. Use the data shown about the number of movies students in Ms. Joseph's class have watched.

Number of Movies Each Student Has Watched This Month									
3	9	2	3	1	0	4	2	4	2

a. The mean number of movies watched is 3.

○ True   ○ False

b. If the student who watched 0 movies had watched 3 movies instead, the class mean would be 3.

○ True   ○ False

c. If the teacher, who watched 10 movies, was included in the group, the mean would increase to 4.

○ True   ○ False

d. At the end of the month the class watched one more movie together. This increased the mean by 1.

○ True   ○ False

Name _____

⭐ ⭐
Solve & Share

Eight students were surveyed about the number of hours they spend each week reading for fun. Order their responses from least to greatest values. What is the middle value in the data set? What is the value that occurs most often?

I can ...
identify the median, mode, and range of a data set.

© Content Standards 6.SP.B.5c, 6.SP.A.3
Mathematical Practices MP.1, MP.3, MP.6, MP.7, MP.8

Reading For Fun Survey

Hours spent reading for
fun each week:

11, 4, 7, 13, 3, 7, 12, 5

You can look for relationships by ordering and analyzing numbers in a data set.

Look Back! © **MP.3 Critique Reasoning** Jamal says that the middle value in a data set can also be the number that occurs most often. Evan says he is wrong. Who is correct? Explain.

Essential Question How Can the Median, Mode, and Range Be Used to Summarize Data?

A

Trey is downloading songs to his personal music library. He lists each type of music and the total playing time in minutes for each. How can he summarize the entire data set with one number?

You can use quantitative measures like mean, median, mode, and range, to summarize a data set.

DATA

Trey's Music Library	
Music Type	**Minutes**
Blues	62
Classical	72
Country	61
Gospel	67
Jazz	67
Movie Soundtrack	63
Popular	59

B Find the **median.**

The median is the middle data value, so it is a measure of center.

List the data values in order from least to greatest.

59, 61, 62, 63, 67, 67, 72

The median playing time is 63 minutes.

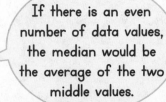

If there is an even number of data values, the median would be the average of the two middle values.

C Find the **mode.**

The mode, which is also a measure of center, is the value that occurs most often.

59, 61, 62, 63, 67, 67, 72

The value 67 occurs twice in the data set. Each of the other values occurs only once.

The mode, or most frequent playing time, is 67 minutes.

D Find the **range.**

The range is the difference of the greatest value and least value. It is a measure of variability.

Identify the least and greatest values from the ordered list.

59, 61, 62, 63, 67, 67, 72

Subtract.

$72 - 59 = 13$

The range of playing times is 13 minutes.

Convince Me! © **MP.1 Make Sense and Persevere** Trey made a mistake when recording the minutes for movie soundtracks and gospel music. His corrected data shows 60 minutes for movie soundtracks and 62 minutes for gospel music. What are the median and the mode of the corrected data set?

Name _____

☆ Guided Practice *

Do You Understand?

1. Why is it important to order the data when finding the median?

2. What does a large range tell you about the values in a data set? What does a small range tell you?

3. Why do you average the two middle numbers to find the median of a set of data with an even number of items?

Do You Know How?

In **4–7**, use the data table.

Test Scores
76, 92, 88, 76, 88, 75, 93, 92, 68, 88, 77, 84

4. Order the scores from least to greatest.

5. Circle the two middle numbers of the data. What is the median of the data?

6. Underline the numbers that appear most often. What is the mode of the data?

7. What is the range of the data?

☆ Independent Practice ☆

In **8–11**, use the data table.

States Traveled To or Lived In
1, 3, 5, 2, 5, 2, 10, 7, 1, 2, 4, 1, 2, 7, 12

8. Order the data from least to greatest.

9. What are the median, mode, and range of the data?

> Be precise when ordering numbers, so you do not drop or add values in the data set.

10. The student who traveled to 3 states visited three new states during a vacation. Does increasing the 3 to 6 change the median? If so, how?

11. Does increasing the 3 to 6 change the mode? If so, how?

*For another example, see Set C on page 776.

Math Practices and Problem Solving

In **12–14**, use the data table.

12. What are the median, mode, and range of this data?

13. What is the mean number of moons for the 8 planets, rounded to the nearest whole number?

14. **Math and Science** The dwarf planet Pluto was once considered a planet. If you include Pluto's moons in the data, the median is 5. How many moons does Pluto have? Explain your reasoning.

Known Number of Moons of the Planets	
Mercury	0
Venus	0
Earth	1
Mars	2
Jupiter	50
Saturn	53
Uranus	27
Neptune	13

DATA

15. © MP.6 Be Precise How can you tell the difference between the net of a triangular prism and the net of a triangular pyramid?

16. **Higher Order Thinking** Is the median always, sometimes, or never one of the data values? Explain.

17. A-Z **Vocabulary** What term is used to describe the difference between the greatest and least values of a data set?

18. © MP.3 Critique Reasoning Lewis thinks that since the data 5, 0, 4, 0, 0 has a mode of 0, the data has no mode. Critique Lewis's reasoning.

© Common Core Assessment

19. In a–d, use the data table to find the statistical measures.

    a. mean   **b.** median

    c. mode   **d.** range

Cost of Snowboards ($) at Ski Shop
265, 237, 325, 281, 265, 252, 494, 273

DATA

Name _____

Another Look!

Carlos surveyed 10 friends about how much television they watched. The table shows his data. Carlos wants to summarize his data using the median, mode, and range.

Number of Hours of TV Watched in a Week	
Juan	7
Tyrone	10
Abigail	16
Lateisha	9
Helen	12
Albert	21
Tim	14
Josh	8
Anita	13
Henry	15

DATA

To find each measure, he first orders the data values from least to greatest.

7, 8, 9, 10, 12, 13, 14, 15, 16, 21

Find the median: Since there are an even number of data values, find the average of the two middle values, 12 and 13.

$$\frac{12 + 13}{2} = \frac{25}{2} = 12.5$$

Find the mode: Every number appears just once. The data have no mode.

You can use these statistics to describe a set of data.

Find the range: Subtract to find the difference between the least and greatest data values.

$$21 - 7 = 14$$

The median of the data is 12.5, there is no mode, and the range is 14.

In **1–5**, use the data table.

1. Order the data from least to greatest.

2. What are the median and mode of the data?

3. How do you find the range of the data? What is the range of this data set?

4. A newspaper wanted to summarize the data without including Alaska and Hawaii. How does this affect the median?

5. How does deleting the data for Alaska and Hawaii affect the mode and range?

National Parks in Western States	
Alaska	23
Arizona	22
California	26
Colorado	13
Hawaii	7
Idaho	6
Montana	8
Nevada	3
New Mexico	13
Oregon	6
Utah	13
Washington	13
Wyoming	7

DATA

In **6–9**, use the data table.

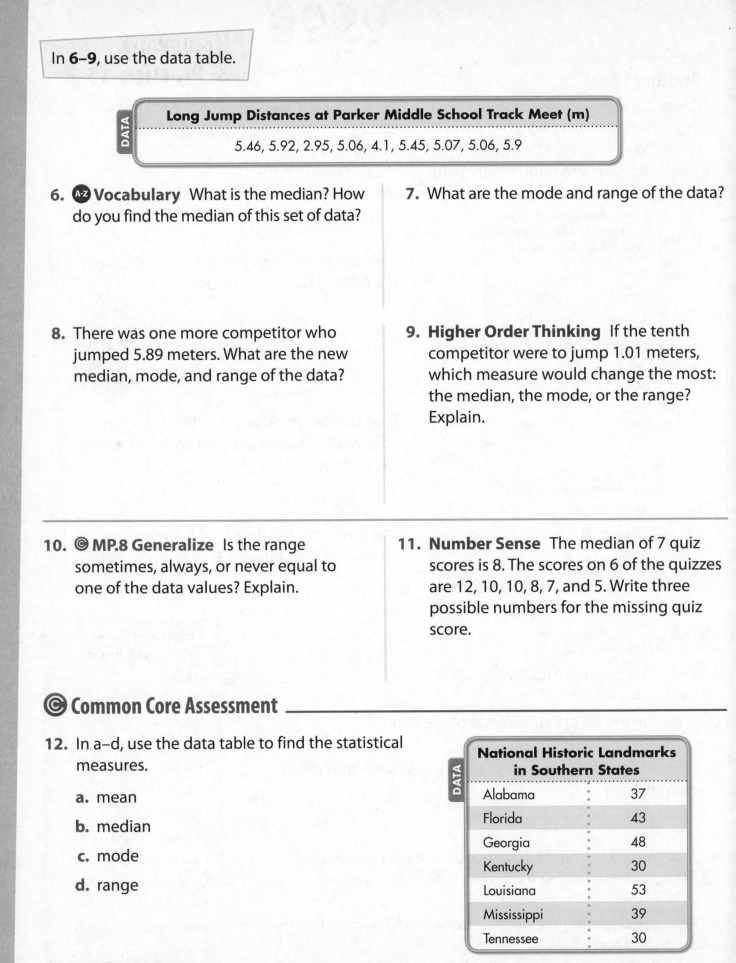

Long Jump Distances at Parker Middle School Track Meet (m)
5.46, 5.92, 2.95, 5.06, 4.1, 5.45, 5.07, 5.06, 5.9

6. **A-Z Vocabulary** What is the median? How do you find the median of this set of data?

7. What are the mode and range of the data?

8. There was one more competitor who jumped 5.89 meters. What are the new median, mode, and range of the data?

9. **Higher Order Thinking** If the tenth competitor were to jump 1.01 meters, which measure would change the most: the median, the mode, or the range? Explain.

10. **© MP.8 Generalize** Is the range sometimes, always, or never equal to one of the data values? Explain.

11. **Number Sense** The median of 7 quiz scores is 8. The scores on 6 of the quizzes are 12, 10, 10, 8, 7, and 5. Write three possible numbers for the missing quiz score.

© Common Core Assessment

12. In a–d, use the data table to find the statistical measures.

    a. mean

    b. median

    c. mode

    d. range

National Historic Landmarks in Southern States	
Alabama	37
Florida	43
Georgia	48
Kentucky	30
Louisiana	53
Mississippi	39
Tennessee	30

Name _____

Solve & Share

There are 5 children in the Brown family. Their median height is $58\frac{1}{2}$ inches. The range of their heights is 14 inches. How tall could each child be?

I can ...
make sense of problems and keep working if I get stuck.

Ⓒ **Mathematical Practices** MP.1, MP.2, MP.6, MP.7
Content Standards 6.SP.A.3, 6.SP.A.2

Thinking Habits
Be a good thinker! These questions can help you.

- What do I need to find?
- What do I know?
- What is my plan for solving the problem?
- What else can I try if I get stuck?
- How can I check that my solution makes sense?

Look Back! Ⓒ **MP.1 Make Sense and Persevere** How does knowing the median and the range help you solve the problem? Explain your reasoning.

Essential Question

How Can You Make Sense of Problems and Persevere in Solving Them?

A

A store sells 5 different kinds of milk in gallon jugs. No two prices are the same. List possible prices for the 5 kinds of milk.

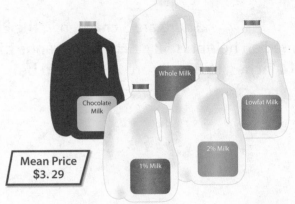

What do I need to do?

I need to make sense of the problem before deciding on a strategy. If I get stuck, I need to persevere until I find possible prices for 5 kinds of milk.

Mean Price
$3. 29

Here's my thinking...

B ## How can I make sense of and solve this problem?

I can

- identify what I know and what I need to find.

- identify how the quantities are related.

- choose and implement an appropriate strategy.

- check that my work and answer make sense.

C

The mean is the average price of the 5 different kinds of milk. So, the total for all 5 kinds of milk has to be 5 times the average: 5 × $3.29 = $16.45

I can try 5 different prices that add up to $16.45. Make the middle number the same as the average price of $3.29.

Try these possible prices: $3.10, $3.20, $3.29, $3.36, $3.50

Check to see if the total is $16.45. If it does not equal the goal price, use the difference to adjust one price.

The total checks.

These are possible prices for the 5 gallons of milk: $3.10, $3.20, $3.29, $3.36, $3.50

Convince Me! © MP.1 Make Sense and Persevere Use a different solution strategy to find another possible answer for this problem.

Name _____

☆ Guided Practice *

© **MP.1 Make Sense and Persevere**

There are 7 sunflowers in Tess's garden. Tess says that the mode of the sunflower heights is 70 inches, the median height is 68 inches, and the range is 10 inches. What are some possible heights of the 7 sunflowers?

> Make sense of a problem by asking how the quantities in the problem are related.

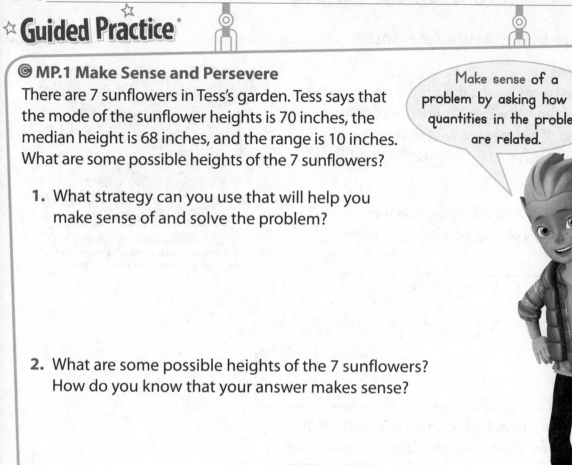

1. What strategy can you use that will help you make sense of and solve the problem?

2. What are some possible heights of the 7 sunflowers? How do you know that your answer makes sense?

☆ Independent Practice ☆

© **MP.1 Make Sense and Persevere**

The mean number of passengers on a daily flight from Tampa to Miami is 82. The plane holds a maximum of 102 passengers. What are some possible numbers of passengers on the flight over the past 5 days?

3. How can you use the information in the problem to help you solve the problem?

4. List possible numbers of passengers on the Tampa to Miami flight over the past 5 days. Show your work.

5. Explain how you know that your answer makes sense.

*For another example, see Set D on page 776.   **Topic 15** | Lesson 15-4   **769**

Math Practices and Problem Solving

Common Core Performance Assessment

Carnival Rides

Statistical measures about the time 8 people wait in line to ride the "Whirl and Twirl" are shown at the right. Two of the people wait in line the same amount of time. Make a list of possible wait times for the ride.

Median Wait Time: 38 minutes
Range of Wait Times: 32 minutes

6. **MP.1 Make Sense and Persevere** What do you know and what do you need to find to solve the problem?

7. **MP.2 Reasoning** How can you use the relationship between the quantities in the problem to make a list?

You can use reasoning to determine how the known and unknown quantities in the problem are related.

8. **MP.6 Be Precise** Make a list of possible wait times. Then explain why your list makes sense.

Another Look!

Six prairie dogs have a mean length of 30 centimeters. The shortest and longest prairie dogs differ in length by 5 centimeters. What are 6 possible lengths for the prairie dogs?

Make sense of the problem and then carry out a plan to solve it.

If one strategy does not work, try another.

How can I make sense of and solve the problem?

- I know there are 6 prairie dogs.
  Mean length = 30 cm
  Range of lengths = 5 cm

- I can make and implement a plan to solve the problem. I can use the values for the mean and range to determine 3 of the 6 lengths. Then I can try three more values as the possible lengths of the other prairie dogs.

- I can check that my work and answer make sense.

Here is my plan for solving the problem:

Multiply 30 cm by 6 to find the combined lengths of the prairie dogs.

6×30 cm $= 180$ cm

Make the mean, 30 cm, one of the lengths.

Choose two values on either side of the mean with a difference of 5: $28 + 5 = 33$, so I'll use 28 cm and 33 cm as the least and greatest lengths.

Find three more numbers that result in a sum of 180 when added to 28, 30, and 33.

Possible lengths in centimeters:

$28 + 28 + 30 + 30 + 31 + 33 = 180$

The mean length is 30 cm, and the range is 5 cm, so my answer checks.

© MP.1 Make Sense and Persevere

Mr. Austin toured his state. During the 9-day tour, the mean number of miles he drove each day was 96. On each of three days he drove 82 miles. This is the mode. What are some possible distances Mr. Austin could have driven each of the 9 days?

If your list does not match the requirements in the problem, you can persevere by adjusting one or more of the numbers.

1. How can you use the mean number of miles and the mode to help make sense of the problem and plan a strategy?

2. Use your strategy to solve the problem. Explain why your answer makes sense. Show your work.

Yard Sale

Joely is selling 7 of her old toys at her parents' yard sale. The median and mean prices are shown at the right. None of the toys are the same price. Make a list of possible toy prices.

3. **MP.1 Make Sense and Persevere** How can you use the given information to develop a strategy?

Mean Sale Price: $0.25
Median Sale Price: $0.30

When you use structure to solve a problem, you look for and use relationships between quantities. Listing them or putting them into a table can help.

4. **MP.7 Use Structure** Apply your strategy to find possible prices of the toys. Explain your reasoning.

5. **MP.2 Reasoning** Without calculating, is it possible that the mean and median of your list of toy prices could both remain the same if Joely were to remove one of the toys from the yard sale before it is sold? Explain.

Name _____

Fluency Practice Activity

Find a Match

Work with a partner. Point to a clue.
Read the clue.

Look below the clues to find a match. Write
the clue letter or symbol in the box next to
the match.

Find a match for every clue.

I can ...
add, subtract, multiply, and
divide decimals.

© **Content Standard** 6.NS.B.3

Clues

A Rounded to the nearest whole
number, the answer is 292.

M The answer is between 293 and
293.5.

U The answer is the greatest of
them all.

N The answer has a 1 in the
thousandths place.

= The answer is a multiple of 20.

H The answer is an odd whole
number.

F The ones and hundredths digits
are the same in the answer.

T The answer is between 300 and
305.

☐	☐	☐	☐
15.239 + 278.26	300 − 8.362	15.7 × 19.4	128.34 ÷ 0.46

☐	☐	☐	☐
348 ÷ 1.45	148.26 + 148.3	2.63 × 125.6	504.06 − 220.079

Glossary

Word List

- data
- mean
- median
- mode
- range
- statistical question

Understand Vocabulary

Choose the best term from the Word List. Write it on the blank.

1. The _____ is the value that occurs most often in a data set.

2. A _____ anticipates a variety of different answers.

3. The sum of all the values in a data set divided by the total number of values in the set is the _____.

4. To find the _____ of a data set, you need to know the least and greatest values.

5. The middle value in an ordered data set is the _____.

Circle the *median* of each data set.

6. 10, 15, 20, 25, 28, 30, 30, 40, 50   **7.** 8, 12, 12, 15, 16, 18, 22, 24, 32

The data set shows the ages of volunteers at a wildlife center.
Write T for *true* or F for *false*.

47, 12, 16, 12, 52, 30, 13

8. _____ The *range* of ages is 40 years.

9. _____ The *median* age is 12.

10. _____ The *mode* age is 12.

11. _____ The *mean* age is 26.

Use Vocabulary in Writing

12. Alicia earned the following amounts pet sitting: $28, $36, $15, $43, $28. Explain how you would describe the data. Use at least 4 words from the Word List in your explanation.

Name _____

Set A pages 749–754

Ramon asked this question to his classmates: "How much time, to the nearest hour, do you spend online each week?"

His question anticipated a variety of answers from his classmates, so it can be used to answer the statistical question "How many hours do my classmates spend online each week?"

Ramon made this dot plot to display the numerical data he had gathered.

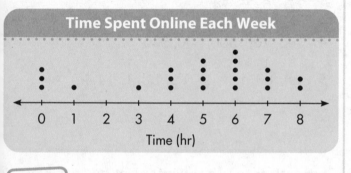

Remember that statistical questions anticipate that there will be different answers in the data.

In **1–3**, tell whether or not each question is statistical.

1. How many stations are there in a subway system?

2. How would passengers of a subway system rate the quality of service on a scale of 1 to 10?

3. How many passengers travel on each of the Green, Blue, Red, and Orange Lines of the subway system each day?

Set B pages 755–760

Find the mean of the data set.

Number of Kites Sold				
12	10	15	18	15

The mean is the sum of all the data in a set divided by the total number of data values in the set.

$(12 + 10 + 15 + 18 + 15) \div 5$
$= 70 \div 5 = 14$

The mean is 14.

Remember to divide by the number of values in the data set, even if one or more of the values is zero.

In **1–8**, find the mean of each data set.

1. 3, 6, 9

2. 5, 12, 0, 7

3. 9, 11, 22, 25, 38

4. 95, 87, 63, 0, 88, 87

5. 500, 0, 350, 750, 0

6. 28, 27, 26, 28, 23, 21, 22, 28, 22

7. 46, 52, 49, 55, 48, 57, 47, 54

8. 1.25, 2.5, 3.75, 1.75, 2

Find the median, mode, and range of the following set of data.

DATA	Total Game Points				
	129	124	128	120	124

The median is the middle number in a data set that is arranged in numerical order.

120, 124, 124, 128, 129

The mode is the number that occurs most often. The mode is 124.

120, 124, 124, 128, 129

The range is the difference between the greatest number and least number in a data set.

129 − 120 = 9

Remember to order the data values from least to greatest before you begin. The median is a measure of center. The mode is the data value that occurs most frequently. The range describes the spread of a data set and is a measure of variability.

In **1–5**, find the median, mode, and range of each data set.

1. 2, 5, 5

2. 11, 13, 13, 11, 13

3. 27, 26, 25, 24

4. 100, 200, 500, 300, 500

5. 1.4, 1.3, 1.1, 1.4, 1.9, 1.8, 1.7, 1.4

Think about these questions to help you **make sense and persevere** when you solve problems.

Thinking Habits

- What do I need to find?

- What do I know?

- What is my plan for solving the problem?

- What else can I try if I get stuck?

- How can I check that my solution makes sense?

Remember to use the information to solve the problem.

Jennifer harvested 5 pumpkins. She recorded this statistical information.
- Mean weight = 25 pounds
- Lightest pumpkin = 7 pounds
- Range in weights = 30 pounds

List possible weights for the pumpkins.

1. What do you need to find?

2. What is the weight of the heaviest pumpkin?

3. List the weight of 5 pumpkins that fit the given information.

4. How can you check your answer?

Name _____

1. In 1a–1d, choose True or False for each statement.

Number of Days Students Do Homework Each Week									
2	5	6	1	4	3	6	5	3	5

1a. The mean number of days students do homework is 4.

○ True   ○ False

1b. If the student who did 1 day of homework had done 5 days, the mean would be 4.5.

○ True   ○ False

1c. If another student who did homework 4 days per week were included in the data, the mean would stay the same.

○ True   ○ False

1d. If all students did one more day of homework, the mean would increase to 5.5.

○ True   ○ False

2. How do you know this dot plot displays the answers to a statistical question?

Number of Siblings Students Have

Number of Siblings

Ⓐ Various data are shown.

Ⓑ All data values are the same.

Ⓒ The data are numerical.

Ⓓ Students were all asked the same question.

3. The ages of ten boys are listed below. In 3a–3d, select Yes or No for each statement.

7, 6, 8, 6, 8, 7, 8, 7, 8, 6

3a. The range is 3.
  ○ Yes   ○ No

3b. The median and mode are 7.
  ○ Yes   ○ No

3c. The median is 7 and the mode is 8.
  ○ Yes   ○ No

3d. The median is 8 and the mode is 7.
  ○ Yes   ○ No

4. Five textbooks have a mean price of $82, and the range of prices is $16. What are possible prices for the textbooks? Select all that apply.

☐ $82, $82, $82, $82, $98

☐ $90, $90, $74, $74, $74

☐ $83, $83, $72, $84, $88

☐ $82, $82, $88, $76, $82

☐ $82, $84, $90, $80, $74

5. Chad earned the following test scores:

70, 85, 100, 87, 80, 70, 95, 91

Write the correct term in each box to make the inequalities true.

mean	median	mode	range

mean < ☐   mode > ☐

6. A coach asked each member of the cross-country team these two questions:

How far did Tony run during practice?
How many miles did you run on Sunday?

Part A

Which question provides data that can be used to answer a statistical question? Explain.

Part B

The results of the statistical question are shown below, in miles ran.

3 7 4 0 2 3 4 3 2 5 3 1 4 2 5 4 1 3

Make a dot plot to display the data. Describe one thing the data show.

7. Is the question *How many cats did the pet store sell last Saturday?* a good example of a statistical question? Explain your reasoning.

8. The number of students in different yoga classes are listed below.

8 10 7 9 5 8 10 12 10

Compare the median, mode, and range of the data set. Which value is the greatest? Show your work.

9. Suzanne recorded the distance she rode her bicycle each week for 5 weeks. The median distance was 32 kilometers. The range in distances was 18 kilometers. Suzanne rode a different number of kilometers each week. What could be the distances that Suzanne rode her bicycle each week? Explain your strategy for finding the possible distances.

Name _____

The students at Fairview School support many local community services. As part of their fund-raising project, the Marching Band is selling DVDs of the school's championship football season.

1. Before making the DVD, the band wanted to see if it would sell. They took surveys during two lunch periods. The results are shown in the tables.

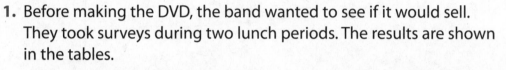

First Survey	
DVDs Wanted	Students
0	8
1	24
2	18

Total Students Surveyed: 50

Second Survey	
DVDs Wanted	Students
0	14
1	54
2	32

Total Students Surveyed: 100

What statistical question might have been asked? What makes the question a good statistical question?

2. The following list shows the number of DVDs sold each day during the first ten days of sales: 30, 21, 28, 23, 25, 23, 26, 23, 20, 21.

Part A

Make a dot plot of the data.

Part B

Describe what the data show.

3. Find the mean, median, mode, and range of the data for the first ten days of sales. Explain how the dot plot makes it easier to find some of these measures.

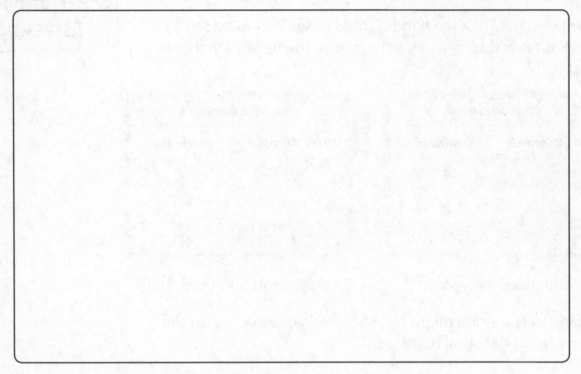

4. DVDs will be sold for 3 more days. Mr. Collins, the bandleader, set a goal of 26 for the mean number of daily sales.

Assess whether you think Mr. Collins' goal is reasonable, or whether it should be modified. If it should be modified, offer your own goal. Justify your answer.

Display and Summarize Data

Essential Question: How can graphs be used to represent data and answer questions?

Digital Resources

Solve · Learn · Glossary · Practice Buddy

Tools · Assessment · Help · Games

Check it out! My rayon shirt is made from wood pulp.

If rayon is made from wood pulp, then what makes it synthetic?

Let's find out. Here's a project about rayon and data displays.

Math and Science Project: Look for the Label

Do Research Use the Internet or other sources to learn more about rayon. When and why was it first invented? How do we use rayon today? Gather data to compare the costs of shirts made from rayon and shirts made from silk. Find the costs of at least 20 shirts made from each fabric.

Journal: Write a Report Include what you found. Also in your report:

- Represent your data using two box plots, one for the costs of rayon shirts and one for the costs of silk shirts. Draw the box plots on the same number line.

- Find the mean, median, and interquartile range (IQR) for each data set. Use these values to summarize rayon's impact on society.

Review What You Know

A-Z Vocabulary

Choose the best term from the box.
Write it on the blank.

• mean	• outlier
• median	• range
• mode	

1. Find the _____ of a data set by subtracting the least value from the greatest value.

2. An extreme value with few data points located near it is a(n) _____.

3. The average of the values in a data set is the _____.

4. The middle value in a data set is the _____.

Median, Mean, Mode, and Range

Use the data about the number of times students rode a bicycle last month.

Number of Times Students Rode a Bicycle
2, 4, 5, 11, 16, 12, 25, 16, 15, 26, 10, 16, 2, 15

5. What are the median, mean, mode, and range of the data?

6. The student who rode a bicycle 5 times recounted and said it should be 6. Does increasing the 5 to 6 change the median? Why or why not?

Analyze Data

7. The chart shows the minutes students spend doing chores each day. Which has the greatest value?

Minutes Doing Chores Each day
20, 25, 45, 20, 30, 40, 30, 25, 20, 15, 35, 40

Ⓐ Mean　　　Ⓑ Median　　　Ⓒ Mode　　　Ⓓ Range

My Word Cards Use the examples for each word on the front of the card to help complete the definitions on the back.

A-Z
Glossary

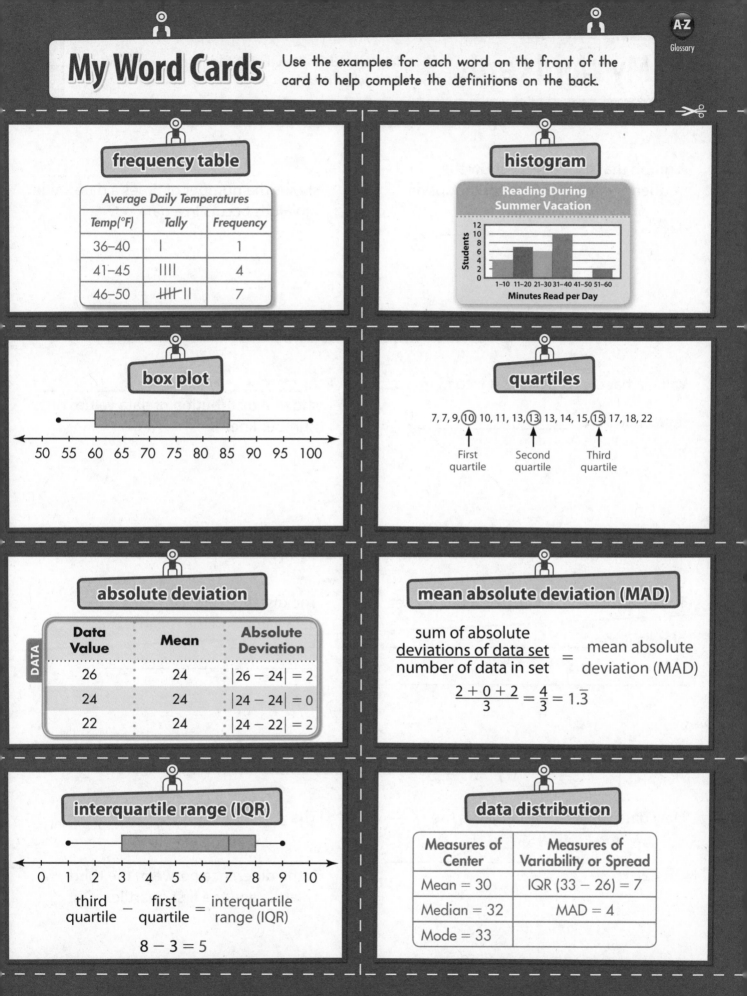

frequency table

Average Daily Temperatures

Temp(°F)	Tally	Frequency
36–40	I	1
41–45	IIII	4
46–50	HHT II	7

histogram

Reading During Summer Vacation

box plot

50 55 60 65 70 75 80 85 90 95 100

quartiles

7, 7, 9, ⑩ 10, 11, 13, ⑬ 13, 14, 15, ⑮ 17, 18, 22

First quartile   Second quartile   Third quartile

absolute deviation

Data Value	Mean	Absolute Deviation
26	24	$|26 - 24| = 2$
24	24	$|24 - 24| = 0$
22	24	$|24 - 22| = 2$

DATA

mean absolute deviation (MAD)

$$\frac{\text{sum of absolute deviations of data set}}{\text{number of data in set}} = \text{mean absolute deviation (MAD)}$$

$$\frac{2 + 0 + 2}{3} = \frac{4}{3} = 1.\overline{3}$$

interquartile range (IQR)

0 1 2 3 4 5 6 7 8 9 10

$$\frac{\text{third}}{\text{quartile}} - \frac{\text{first}}{\text{quartile}} = \frac{\text{interquartile}}{\text{range (IQR)}}$$

$$8 - 3 = 5$$

data distribution

Measures of Center	Measures of Variability or Spread
Mean = 30	IQR (33 − 26) = 7
Median = 32	MAD = 4
Mode = 33	

My Word Cards

Complete each definition. Extend learning by writing your own definitions.

A graph that uses bars to show the frequency of equal ranges or groups of data is a _____.

A _____ shows the number of times a data value or values occurs in a data set.

Values that divide a data set into four equal parts are _____.

A _____ shows a distribution of data values on a number line.

The mean of the absolute deviations of a set of data is the _____ _____.

The distance between each data value and the mean is the _____.

How data values are arranged is the _____.

The _____ _____ is the difference between the third quartile and the first quartile.

Name _____

☆ ☆ ☆
Solve & Share

A sixth-grade class recorded the number of letters in their first and last names combined. What was the most common length? Least common length? *Make a table to solve this problem.*

I can ...
make and analyze frequency tables and histograms.

© Content Standards 6.SP.B.4, 6.SP.B.5a
Mathematical Practices MP.1, MP.2, MP.4, MP.6, MP.7

Number of Letters in Sixth-Grade Students'
First and Last Names

15, 11, 14, 8, 10, 15, 17, 16, 19, 12, 13, 12, 14,
15, 11, 16, 9, 12, 13, 10

Remember to attend to precision and use equal intervals when you set up your table.

Look Back! © **MP.7 Look for Relationships** How does organizing the data help you see the numbers of letters that occur most often? Explain.

How Can You Make and Use a Frequency Table and a Histogram?

A

Mr. Maxwell timed the cross-country team in a 2-mile run. He wants to organize the data in a frequency table. A frequency table shows the number of times a data value or values occurs in the data set. How can Mr. Maxwell make a frequency table?

How can the data displays help you make sense of the data?

DATA

Times					
16:45	14:25	18:40	16:03	15:12	19:15
17:14	14:02	16:52	15:18	17:49	17:55

B Organize the data in a frequency table.

Running Times	Tally	Frequency
14:00–15:59	IIII	4
16:00–17:59	HHT I	6
18:00–19:59	II	2

C Use the frequency table to make a histogram.

A histogram is a graph that uses bars to show the frequency of equal ranges or groups of data.

Step 1 Title the graph.

Step 2 Choose the scale for the vertical axis.

Step 3 List the time intervals along the horizontal axis.

Step 4 Graph the data by drawing a bar for each interval.

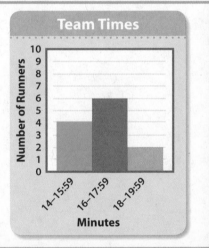

Convince Me! © MP.2 Reasoning How are frequency tables and histograms alike and how are they different?

© Pearson Education, Inc. 6

☆ Guided Practice *

Do You Understand?

1. Look at the histogram on the previous page. What does the tallest bar tell you?

2. How many runners had times of 18 minutes or more?

Do You Know How?

3. How would an interval of 3 minutes change the appearance of the histogram? Explain.

Independent Practice ☆

In **4–9**, use the data in the chart.

How many songs do you have on your MP3 player?
125, 289, 115, 203, 192, 178, 256, 248, 165, 233, 147, 209, 225, 184, 156, 201, 143, 125, 263, 210

4. Complete the frequency table below for the number of songs on MP3 players.

Song Range	Tallies	Frequency
100–149		
150–199		
200–		
–		

5. Use your frequency table to complete the histogram.

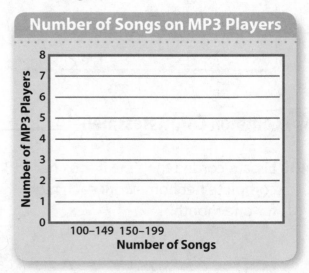

Number of Songs on MP3 Players

6. How many people have between 150 and 199 songs on their MP3 players?

7. Do more than half of the MP3 players have less than 149 songs on them?

8. Is the greatest number of songs on MP3 players between 200 and 249 songs?

9. Are there more MP3 players that have between 200 and 249 songs on them than between 150 and 199 songs?

Math Practices and Problem Solving

In **10–12**, use the data in the chart.

Bicycle Stopping Times (in seconds)
15, 25, 11, 8, 10, 21, 18, 23, 19, 9, 14, 16, 24, 18, 10, 16, 24, 18, 9, 14

10. **MP.2 Reasoning** Todd wants to know how many people took 20 seconds or more to stop a bike safely. Would a frequency table or a histogram be the better way to show this? Explain.

11. **Higher Order Thinking** When organizing the data, what interval should Todd use? Explain how you made your decision.

12. **MP.4 Model with Math** Make a frequency table and histogram for the data.

Time (in seconds)	Tallies	Frequency

Time It Takes to Stop a Bike

Common Core Assessment

13. Lissa recorded the time it took her to complete her homework each night for one month.

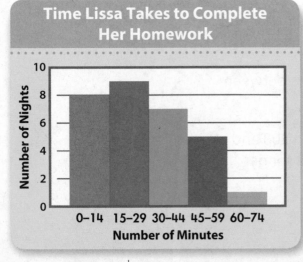

Time Lissa Takes to Complete Her Homework

Using the histogram, select all of the true statements that describe Lissa's data.

☐ Lissa worked on her homework for over an hour one time.

☐ More than half the month Lissa spent less than 30 minutes on her homework each night.

☐ The most time spent on homework each night was between 15 and 29 minutes.

☐ It took between 15 and 29 minutes more often than it took between 30 and 59 minutes.

Name _____

Help Practice Tools Games
        Buddy

Homework
& Practice 16-1
Frequency Tables
and Histograms

Another Look!

Maya recorded the number of bags of popcorn she sold each day at a carnival.

Making a frequency table will help you organize the data. You can use the frequency table to make a histogram.

Bags of Popcorn
62, 65, 58, 31, 64, 58, 66, 68, 56, 67, 68, 51

Represent the data in a frequency table and a histogram.

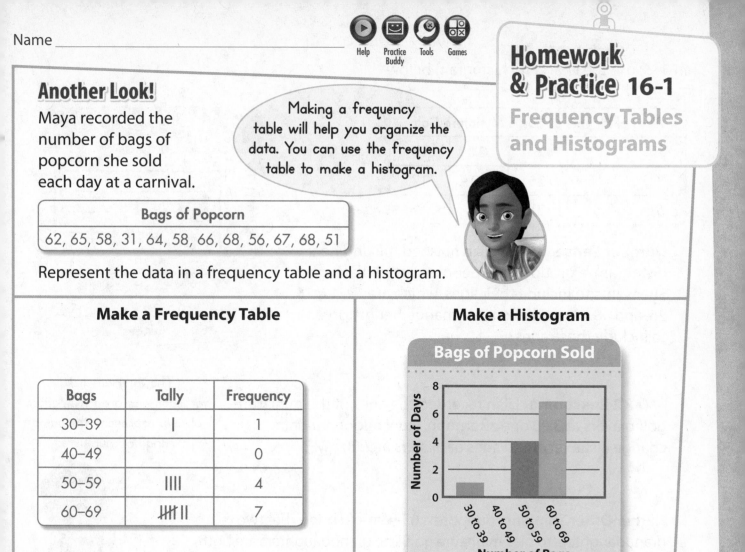

Make a Frequency Table

Bags	Tally	Frequency
30–39	I	1
40–49		0
50–59	IIII	4
60–69	HHT II	7

Make a Histogram

Bags of Popcorn Sold

In **1** and **2**, use the data in the chart.

Annual Ticket Sales for Charity Ice-Skating Event							
72	81	88	51	90	89	85	74
87	100	80	99	87	96	99	84
84	86	94	88	91	85	78	90

1. Complete the frequency table below for the number of tickets sold each year to the charity event.

Tickets Sold	Tallies	Frequency
45–54		
55–64		
65–74		
75–84		
85–94		
95–104		

2. Use your frequency table to complete the histogram.

Digital Resources at PearsonRealize.com   **Topic 16** | Lesson 16-1   **789**

In **3–5**, use the chart and histogram below.

Ages of Players at Castle Miniature Golf				
14	7	6	24	15
9	19	25	10	17
51	8	21	48	12

3. **Number Sense** Just as Lilah finished making her histogram, a group of five people started playing. She wants to include their ages, which are 12, 12, 16, 26, and 48. How should Lilah change her histogram to include these ages?

4. © **MP.2 Reasoning** Lilah recorded the ages of the miniature golf players at 3:00 one afternoon. How might her data change if she recorded ages of players at 7:00 P.M.?

The intervals used for each bar on a histogram always represent the same range of numbers.

5. **Higher Order Thinking** Suppose a 65-year-old brings her two granddaughters to play miniature golf. The granddaughters are both 5 years old. How can Lilah adjust the intervals to include these ages?

© **Common Core Assessment** _____

6. Each day for a month, Bo timed himself to see how many free throws he could make in 60 seconds.

Using the histogram, select all of the true statements that describe Bo's data.

- ☐ He made 15–19 free throws 6 times.
- ☐ More than half the month Bo made more than 10 shots.
- ☐ The greatest number of shots made in 60 seconds was between 10 and 14.
- ☐ Bo made fewer than 10 shots more often than he made more than 14 shots.

Name _____

Solve & Share

A quality control inspector at a food processing plant collected data for the number of raisins in small boxes. Find the minimum, maximum, and median of the data. Then find the median of the first and second half of the data. **Solve this problem any way you choose.**

I can ...
make and analyze box plots.

© Content Standard 6.SP.B.4
Mathematical Practices MP.1, MP.2, MP.3, MP.4, MP.5

Count of Raisins in Small Boxes:

27, 29, 27, 25, 25, 27, 32, 30, 28, 32, 26, 31

You can make sense of the data by ordering the numbers of raisins in small boxes from least to greatest.

Look Back! © **MP.3 Construct Arguments** What do you think the median of the data and the median of the first and second halves of the data show? Explain.

Essential Question How Can You Draw a Box Plot?

A

Helen wants to display the lengths of 15 fish she caught. How can she use the data to make a box plot?

A box plot shows a distribution of data values on a number line.

Length of Fish (in.)		
7	9	10
7	13	13
10	15	15
18	11	13
22	14	17

B Find the median, minimum, and maximum values of the data.

⑦ 7, 9, 10, 10, 11, 13, ⑬ 13, 14, 15, 15, 17, 18, ㉒

↑ minimum   ↑ median   ↑ maximum

Find the median for each half.

7, 7, 9, ⑩ 10, 11, 13, ⑬ 13, 14, 15, ⑮ 17, 18, 22

↑ First quartile   ↑ Second quartile   ↑ Third quartile

Quartiles are values that divide a data set into four equal parts.

C Draw the box plot.

Show a number line with an appropriate scale, a box between the first and third quartiles, and a vertical segment that shows the median.

Draw segments that extend from the box to the minimum and to the maximum values.

6 7 8 9 10 11 12 13 14 15 16 17 18 19 20 21 22 23

↑ minimum   ↑ median   ↑ maximum
↑ First quartile   ↑ Third quartile

Convince Me! © **MP.2 Reasoning** Write two conclusions about the data shown in the box plot above.

☆ Guided Practice ☆

Do You Understand?

Sarah's scores on tests were 79, 75, 82, 90, 73, 82, 78, 85, and 78. In **1–5**, use the data.

1. What would be a good scale to use for a number line that will include Sarah's scores?

2. What values are included inside the box of a box plot?

Do You Know How?

3. Find the median.

4. Find the first and the third quartiles.

5. Draw a box plot that shows the distribution of Sarah's test scores.

☆ Independent Practice ☆

In **6**, use the data given to answer each question.

6. The box plot displays data of home runs a major league player hit in 9 seasons.

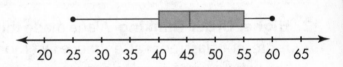

20 25 30 35 40 45 50 55 60 65

a. What is the maximum number of home runs the player hit for the seasons shown?

b. What is the minimum number of home runs the player hit?

c. What is the first quartile?

d. What is the third quartile?

In **7** and **8**, draw box plots using the data provided.

7. The sprint times in seconds of students who tried out for the track team:

44, 40, 40, 42, 49, 43, 41, 47, 54, 48, 42, 52, 48

8. Test scores earned on science tests:

73, 78, 66, 61, 85, 90, 99, 76, 64, 70, 72, 72, 93, 81

*For another example, see Set B on page 823.

Math Practices and Problem Solving

9. **© MP.2 Reasoning** The price per share of Electric Company's stock over 9 days, rounded to the nearest dollar, was as follows: $16, $17, $16, $16, $18, $18, $21, $22, $19.

Use a box plot to determine how many dollars greater per share the third quartile price was than the first quartile price.

10. **Math and Science** The temperature forecast for Topeka, Kansas, for the next 8 days showed the following daily highs in degrees Fahrenheit: 29, 31, 24, 26, 29, 35, 27, 32.

If the forecast is accurate, what would be the average high temperature rounded to the nearest degree?

---

11. **© MP.4 Model with Math** Coach Henderson clocked the speeds in miles per hour of pitches thrown during the first inning of a middle school baseball game as follows.

Draw a box plot to display the data and write two conclusions about the data shown in the box plot.

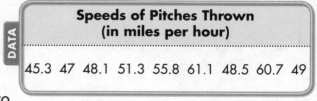

DATA

Speeds of Pitches Thrown (in miles per hour)

45.3 47 48.1 51.3 55.8 61.1 48.5 60.7 49

---

12. **Higher Order Thinking** Alana made this box plot to represent classroom attendance last month. Without seeing the values, what conclusions can you make about whether attendance was mostly high or low last month? Explain.

A box plot shows how data is distributed, or spread, around the median.

© Common Core Assessment

13. Use the data given to complete the box plot.

The ages in years of the students in Caryn's gymnastics class are as follows.

DATA

Age In Years of the Students

12 11 9 18 10 11 7 16 14 11 6

Choose numbers from the box to complete the box plot.

6   8   9   11   12   14   16   18

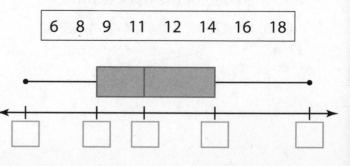

Help   Practice   Tools   Games
Buddy

Another Look!

Fabian created a box plot to record the number of points scored in the first half of 11 basketball games.

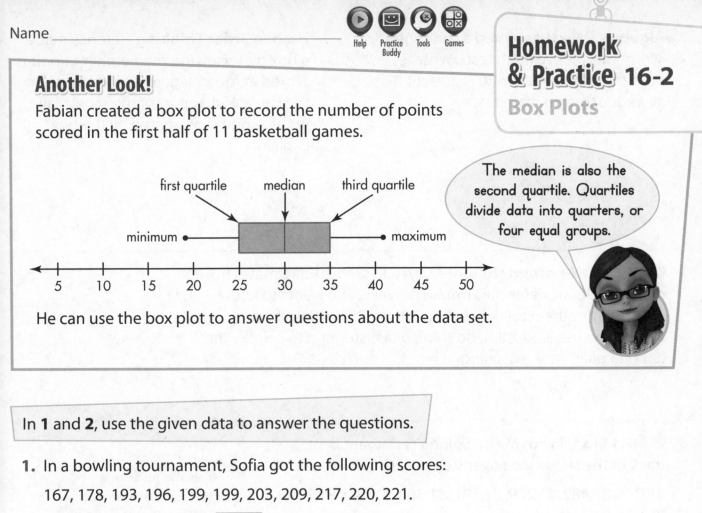

The median is also the second quartile. Quartiles divide data into quarters, or four equal groups.

He can use the box plot to answer questions about the data set.

In **1** and **2**, use the given data to answer the questions.

1. In a bowling tournament, Sofia got the following scores:

   167, 178, 193, 196, 199, 199, 203, 209, 217, 220, 221.

   a. What is the median? ☐

   b. What is the first quartile? ☐

   c. What is the third quartile? ☐

   d. Draw a box plot of the data.

   e. Write two conclusions about the data shown in the box plot.

2. Sabrina raised flowers. In a competition with other flower growers, she earned the following scores: 7, 10, 10, 6, 7, 8, 8, 7, 9.

   a. What is the median? ☐

   b. What is the first quartile? ☐

   c. What is the third quartile? ☐

   d. Draw a box plot of the data.

   e. Write two conclusions about the data shown in the box plot.

3. **Algebra** David has scored a combined 411 points on five math tests. Write a multiplication equation to represent his average score on math tests.

4. **Higher Order Thinking** Terence made a box plot showing the number of points scored at football games. Without seeing the values, what part of the scores fall in the range represented by the box? Explain.

5. ©**MP.5 Use Appropriate Tools** Crystal asked 20 classmates how many bottles of water they drink in a week. She wants to know how many of them drink between 20 and 25 bottles of water. Should she use a box plot, dot plot, or a histogram to display the data? Explain your reasoning.

6. ©**MP.4 Model with Math** Solon's restaurant kept track of the sales made over 9 days as shown below.

   $1,074, $1,482, $1,209, $1,391, $1,360, $1,442, $1,569, $1,601, $1,315

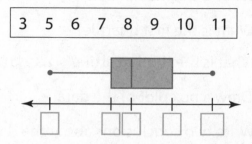

When the median or quartile falls between two values, find the mean of the two values.

   a. Draw a box plot of the sales figures.

   b. Between what two figures do the middle half of the sales for Solon's restaurant fall?

© **Common Core Assessment** _____

7. Use the given data to complete the box plot.

   Shantay tossed a pair of number cubes numbered 1–6 a total of 10 times. Below are the sums of the numbers on her cubes for each of her tosses.

   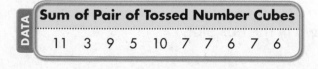

   Sum of Pair of Tossed Number Cubes
   DATA: 11 3 9 5 10 7 7 6 7 6

   Choose numbers from the box to complete the box plot.

   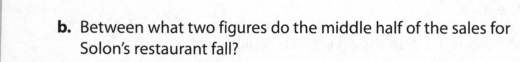

   3 5 6 7 8 9 10 11

© Pearson Education, Inc. 6

Name _____

Solve & Share

Suppose you collected data from 11 people about the number of letters in their first names. The median name length is 6 letters. Make two possible dot plots that could be used to display the data, one where the data varies a little and one where the data varies a lot. **Solve this problem any way you choose.**

Solve

I can ...
use measures of variability to describe a data set.

© Content Standards 6.SP.B.4, 6.SP.B.5c
Mathematical Practices MP.2, MP.3

You can use reasoning to find values that have the same median.

Look Back! © MP.3 Construct Arguments Describe the data distribution you generated and discuss the spread and clustering of the data.

Essential Question How Can Variability of Data Be Described with One Number?

The center of the data for Ann's math quiz scores can be described using a single number.

Median = 88   Mean = 86

How can a single number describe how much Ann's scores vary from the mean?

DATA

Ann's Math Quiz Scores (%)	
82	99
76	73
92	90
88	88

Variability describes the spread and clustering of data in a set.

Step 1

Find the absolute deviation, the distance between each data value and the mean. You can find the absolute deviation from the mean by computing the absolute value of the difference between these numbers.

DATA

Score	Absolute Deviation
73	$|86 - 73| = 13$
76	$|86 - 76| = 10$
82	$|86 - 82| = 4$
88	$|88 - 86| = 2$
88	$|88 - 86| = 2$
90	$|90 - 86| = 4$
92	$|92 - 86| = 6$
99	$|99 - 86| = 13$

Step 2

Find the mean absolute deviation (MAD), the mean of the absolute deviations of a set of data. Add the absolute deviations and divide by the number of data values in the set.

$$\frac{13 + 10 + 4 + 2 + 2 + 4 + 6 + 13}{8}$$

$$= \frac{54}{8} = 6.75$$ ← number of scores

Generally, Ann's quiz scores varied 6.75 points from the mean.

Convince Me! © MP.2 Reasoning Can the MAD ever have a negative value? Explain.

Another Example

How does the interquartile range describe Ann's Science Quiz Scores?

Another measure of variability is the interquartile range (IQR). This is the difference between the third quartile and the first quartile.

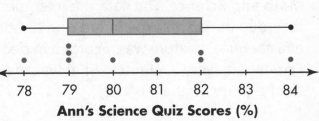

Ann's Science Quiz Scores (%)

Because at least half of the data values lie in this interval, it is easy to see the interquartile range using a box plot.

The dot plot shows Ann's quiz scores for science. The interquartile range is $82 - 79 = 3$.

So, at least half of Ann's science quiz scores were within an interval of 3 points.

☆ Guided Practice *

Do You Understand?

1. What does the MAD tell you about the variability of data in a data set?

2. What does the IQR tell you about the variability of data in a data set?

Do You Know How?

In **3** and **4**, use the data set 4, 5, 5, 6, 7, 8, 8, 10, 10.

3. Find the sum of the absolute deviations from the mean.

4. Find the MAD and the IQR.

☆ Independent Practice ☆

In **5** and **6**, use the data table showing the number of miles Jill biked in 9 days.

DATA	Miles Biked		
	5	9	11
	10	8	6
	7	12	4

5. Find the absolute deviation from the mean for these data values from the set: 5, 7, 12.

6. Find the MAD of this data set. What does this tell you about the number of miles Jill biked?

Math Practices and Problem Solving

In **7–10**, use the data set shown in the table.

7. **Math and Science** The data show temperatures recorded during an experiment. The temperature of a chemical mixture was recorded in degrees Fahrenheit every 5 minutes. What was the mean temperature for the mixture?

Temperatures (°F)			
11	17	20	16
19	16	15	22

8. © **MP.3 Critique Reasoning** Dina said that the greatest absolute deviation will be found from the greatest temperature, because it has to be the farthest from the mean. Is she correct? Explain.

9. **A-Z Vocabulary** What is the term used to describe the range of the middle half of the data set? Find that value for this data.

10. **Higher Order Thinking** What is the MAD for the data and what does it tell you about the temperature of the chemical mixture during the experiment?

© Common Core Assessment

11. Harlo recorded the tide, in feet, every hour during an 8-hour period as shown below.

Tide (in ft)
3, 7, 11, 15, 20, 31, 39, 42

Part A

What is the MAD for the data set?

Part B

Is the IQR greater than or less than the MAD? What does this tell you about the variability of the data?

Help Practice Buddy Tools Games

Another Look!

What is the mean absolute deviation (MAD) of this data set?

20, 40, 60, 80, 100

The mean absolute deviation (MAD) uses one number to tell how far the data is spread out from the mean.

Step 1

Find the mean of the data.

```
  20         60
  40      5)300
  60
  80
+ 100
  300
```

The mean is 60.

Step 2

Find the absolute deviation for each value in the data set.

Data Value	Absolute Deviation
20	$|60 - 20| = 40$
40	$|60 - 40| = 20$
60	$|60 - 60| = 0$
80	$|80 - 60| = 20$
100	$|100 - 60| = 40$

Step 3

Find the mean of the absolute deviations.

```
  40         24
  20      5)120
   0
  20
+ 40
 120
```

The mean absolute deviation (MAD) is 24.

In **1** and **2**, complete the tables to find the MAD of each data set.

1.

Data Value	Absolute Deviation
10	$|25 - 10| =$
15	
20	
30	
50	
MAD =	

2.

Data Value	Absolute Deviation
125	
138	
275	
178	
236	
90	
MAD =	

In **3–7**, use the data in the table.

3. At a carnival booth, people pay $1 to take 5 free-throw shots. They win a prize based on the number of baskets they make. Vera recorded the number of baskets 20 people made out of 5 shots in the table. Complete the frequency table.

Number of Baskets Made	Tallies	Frequency
0	III	
1	IIII	
2	IIII	
3	III	
4	III	
5	II	

4. **Higher Order Thinking** Without making the calculations, what do you expect the MAD to be? Explain your reasoning.

5. © **MP.2 Reasoning** Vera needs to find the mean number of baskets made. How can you find the mean of the tallied data?

6. What is the MAD of Vera's data? What is the IQR?

7. © **MP.3 Construct Arguments** Which measurement, the MAD or the IQR describes how close each person's number of baskets made was to any other person's number of baskets made? Construct an argument to support your answer.

When you find the mean and the mean absolute deviation (MAD), remember to include all of the numbers in the data set, even zeroes.

© **Common Core Assessment**

8. Jason recorded the number of hours of sunshine each day for 7 days as shown below.

Hours of Sunshine
12, 10, 3, 8, 13, 11, 5

Part A

What is the IQR of Jason's data?

Part B

Make one true statement about the IQR and how it relates to Jason's data.

Name _____

Solve & Share

The data set shows the price in dollars of athletic shoes in one store. Does the mean, median, or mode best describe what is a typical price for shoes at this store? **Solve this problem any way you choose.**

I can ...
select and use appropriate statistical measures.

© Content Standards 6.SP.B.5c, 6.SP.B.5d
Mathematical Practices MP.1, MP.2, MP.3, MP.4, MP.6, MP.7, MP.8

Athletic Shoe Prices

$60, $50, $90, $50, $50, $75, $80

You can look for relationships, such as the spread and clustering of data, to help you decide which statistical measures you should use.

Look Back! © **MP.3 Construct Arguments** Which measure would the store most likely use in its advertising? Explain.

Essential Question

Which Statistical Measure is Most Useful to Describe a Given Situation?

A

Gary says he usually scores 98 on his weekly quiz. Does his statement accurately describe his overall performance? Justify your answer using measures of center.

Variability describes the spread and clustering of data in a set.

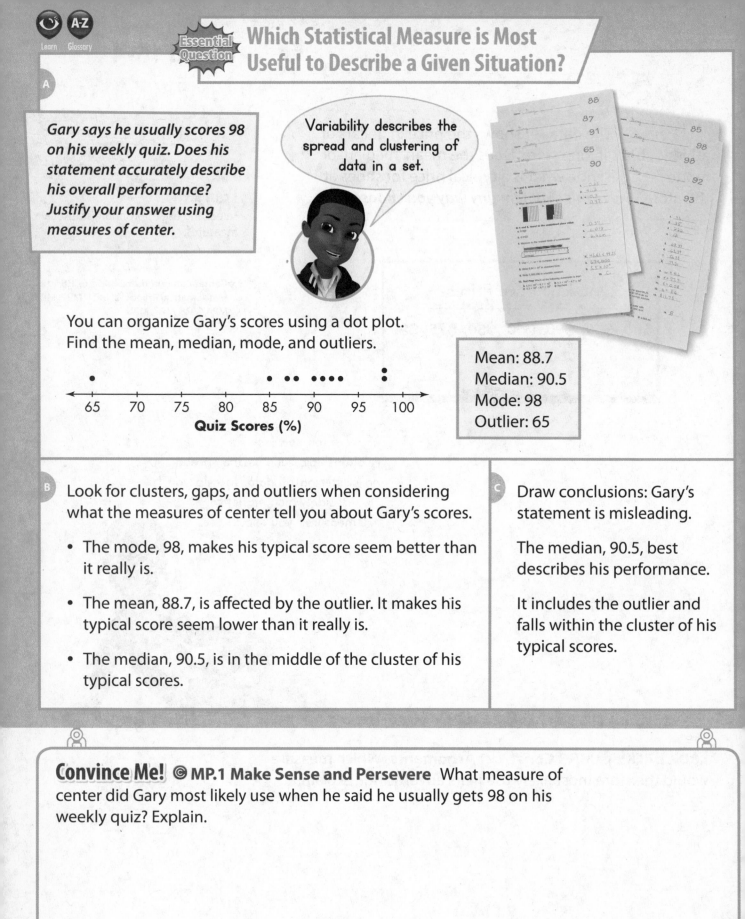

You can organize Gary's scores using a dot plot. Find the mean, median, mode, and outliers.

Quiz Scores (%)

Mean: 88.7
Median: 90.5
Mode: 98
Outlier: 65

B

Look for clusters, gaps, and outliers when considering what the measures of center tell you about Gary's scores.

• The mode, 98, makes his typical score seem better than it really is.

• The mean, 88.7, is affected by the outlier. It makes his typical score seem lower than it really is.

• The median, 90.5, is in the middle of the cluster of his typical scores.

C

Draw conclusions: Gary's statement is misleading.

The median, 90.5, best describes his performance.

It includes the outlier and falls within the cluster of his typical scores.

Convince Me! © **MP.1 Make Sense and Persevere** What measure of center did Gary most likely use when he said he usually gets 98 on his weekly quiz? Explain.

Another Example

When describing the variability of a given situation, it is helpful to know which measure of variability to use.

Quiz Scores	
Gary	**Yoshi**
65	80
85	80
87	82
88	82
90	84
91	84
92	86
93	86
98	88
98	88

DATA

Use the Interquartile Range (IQR)

Use the IQR when the *median* is the appropriate measure of center.

To find the IQR of Gary's quiz scores, find the difference between the third and first quartiles. $93 - 87 = 6$.

At least half of Gary's quiz scores are between 87 and 93. This accurately describes the cluster of his scores.

Use the Mean Absolute Deviation (MAD)

Use the MAD when the *mean* is the appropriate measure of center.

To find the MAD of Yoshi's quiz scores add the absolute deviations and divide by the number of values:

$24 \div 10 = 2.4$.

Yoshi's quiz score is typically within 2.4 points of her mean score of 84.

☆ Guided Practice *

Do You Understand?

1. A team's basketball scores for one season were 44, 43, 42, 40, 42, 45, 39, 38, 18. Is the median or the mean the best measure of center for these data? Explain.

Do You Know How?

2. Find the mean, median, and mode for the scores in Exercise 1.

3. Find the measure of variability that best describes the data set.

☆ Independent Practice ☆

In **4** and **5**, use the data to answer the questions.

Five different stores sell a quart of milk for one of the following prices: $1.50, $1.55, $1.80, $1.70, $1.50.

4. What are the mean, median, and mode of the data?

5. Which measure of center best describes these data? Which measure of variability?

Math Practices and Problem Solving

The table shows measures of center based on 5 data points. In **6–9**, use the table to answer the questions.

DATA	Mean	Median	Mode
	14,000	13,000	12,500

6. **A-Z** **Vocabulary** What is the term and the value of the middle number of the data set?

7. © **MP.1 Make Sense and Persevere** Which value in the data set occurs at least twice? Can it occur 3 times? Explain.

8. **Number Sense** Why must the other two numbers in the data set be greater than or equal to 13,000?

9. **Algebra** What must be the sum of the two remaining numbers, x and y? Write an equation to show how to find this sum.

In **10** and **11**, use the table.

Game Scores for the Bravo Bowling Team

Jessie	150	145	181	235	196	211	204	221	185
Sam	186	187	192	195	194	157	192	162	200

10. © **MP.6 Be Precise** The coach needs to choose the top bowler for the next meet. If the coach bases her decision on the player with the best average, whom should she choose? Justify your answer using measures of center.

11. **Higher Order Thinking** If the coach bases her decision on the player who is most consistent, whom should she choose? Justify your answer using measures of variability.

© Common Core Assessment

12. Choose True or False for each statement about the data shown in the table.

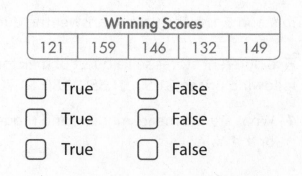

Winning Scores

121	159	146	132	149

There are no outliers. ☐ True ☐ False

The mean best describes the scores. ☐ True ☐ False

The measure of variability that best describes the data is the MAD: 11.92 points. ☐ True ☐ False

Name _____

Another Look!

Paige recorded the number of points scored this season by each member of her basketball team: 28, 30, 28, 30, 40, 30, 34, 32, 32. Find the measure of center and the measure of variability that best describe the typical number of points scored.

Make a dot plot to organize the data and identify any outliers.

The outlier, 40, distorts the mean. This makes the median, 30, a better measure of the data's center, and the interquartile range (IQR) is a better measure of variability.

The first quartile is 29. The third quartile is 33. The interquartile range (IQR) is $33 - 29 = 4$. At least half the team scored within 4 points of each other.

The mean is a better measure of center when all the data cluster together.

In **1–4**, use the data table.

Cost of Kick Scooters at Ted's Sports							
$125	$135	$130	$140	$135	$154	$135	$130

1. Make a dot plot of these data.

2. What are the mean, median, and mode of these prices? Which measure best describes the center of these data? Why?

3. Which measure would you use to describe the variability of these data? Explain your reasoning.

4. Describe the center and variability of these prices.

5.  **MP.4 Model with Math** Make a dot plot for the data.

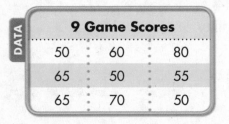

9 Game Scores		
50	60	80
65	50	55
65	70	50

6. What are the mean, median, and mode of the data, rounded to the nearest whole number? Are there any outliers?

7. **MP.8 Generalize** Use what you know about statistical measures to explain which measure of center best describes the data set.

In **8** and **9**, use the data table.

Cost of 6 Brands of Shampoo					
$1	$2	$4	$6	$7	$20

8. What is the outlier in this data?

9. **MP.2 Reasoning** Does an outlier affect the IQR? Does an outlier affect the MAD? Explain.

Common Core Assessment

10. Choose True or False for each statement about the home run data.

Home Runs Hit			
42	31	35	17
43	42	53	57

The median is the best measure of center to describe the data.　　☐ True　　☐ False

This data set has no outliers.　　☐ True　　☐ False

The measure of variability that best describes the data is the IQR of 15.　　☐ True　　☐ False

Name _____

☆ **Solve & Share** ☆

Toss two number cubes 20 times. Make a dot plot by plotting each sum you toss on the number line below. Summarize your data, paying attention to the shape of the data as well as measures of center and variability.

I can ...
summarize numerical data sets.

Ⓒ Content Standards 6.SP.A.2, 6.SP.B.4, 6.SP.B.5b, 6.SP.B.5c
Mathematical Practices MP.2, MP.4, MP.6, MP.7, MP.8

You can generalize by drawing conclusions about the data based on your observations.

2 3 4 5 6 7 8 9 10 11 12

Look Back! Ⓒ **MP.7 Use Structure** Based on the data you collected, which sums are you more likely to toss? Toss the number cubes 10 more times. Plot each sum and describe your results.

How Can a Data Distribution Be Summarized?

A

The fat content, in grams, was measured for one slice ($\frac{1}{6}$ pizza) of 24 different 12-inch pizzas.

The data are displayed in the dot plot. How can the data be used to describe the fat content of a slice of pizza?

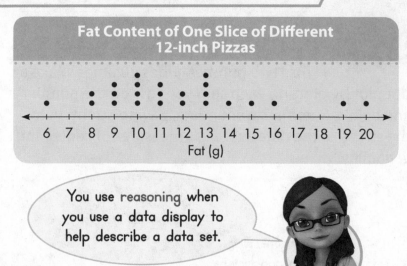

Fat Content of One Slice of Different 12-inch Pizzas

Fat (g)

You use reasoning when you use a data display to help describe a data set.

B To describe a data distribution, or how the data values are arranged, you evaluate its measures of center and variability, and its overall shape.

Measures of Center
Mean = 11.75 g
Median = 11 g

Measures of Variability, or Spread
IQR (13 − 9.5) = 3.5

The MAD is also a measure of spread, but because the mean isn't the best measure of center, use the IQR.

C **Overall shape**

- Most of the data points are grouped between 8 and 13.

- The data values are not symmetric. They are more spread out to the right.

- There are gaps in the data between 6 and 8, and 16 and 19.

The fat content of at least half of the slices falls between 9.5 g and 13 g, or an interval of 3.5 g. The typical slice of pizza has a fat content of 11 grams.

Convince Me! © **MP.2 Reasoning** What are some factors that might change the survey results?

Name _____

☆ Guided Practice *

Do You Understand?

1. Look back at the pizza data. How would the shape of the data distribution change if the outliers were removed? What effect would this have on the IQR?

2. How would the median and the mean be affected if the outliers were removed?

Do You Know How?

3. Five different students measured the length of a shadow in inches as follows: 38, $38\frac{1}{2}$, $37\frac{3}{4}$, 38, $38\frac{1}{4}$. Make a generalization about the data distribution of the shadow measurements.

4. What are the mean, the median, and the interquartile range of the data set in Exercise 3?

☆ Independent Practice ☆

In **5–7**, use the data table.

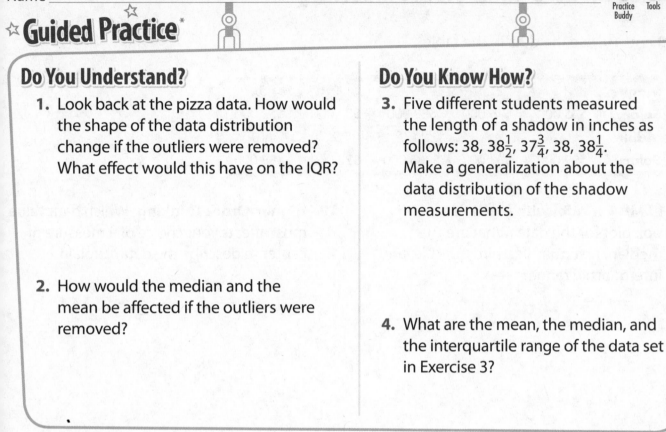

DATA	Number of Home Runs Hit by Players on My Team								
Player Number	1	2	3	4	5	6	7	8	9
Home Runs	21	9	12	20	7	11	9	10	9

5. What are the mean and the median?

6. Draw a box plot of the data.

7. Describe the overall shape of the data.

8. Make a generalization about the data distribution.

Math Practices and Problem Solving

In **9** and **10**, use the data in the table.

DATA	Adult	1	2	3	4	5
	Salary	$35,000	$46,000	$38,000	$34,000	$52,000
	Adult	6	7	8	9	10
	Salary	$99,000	$64,000	$435,000	$22,000	$88,000

9. © **MP.4 Model with Math** Make a box plot for the data. What are the median, first quartile, third quartile, and interquartile range?

10. **Higher-Order Thinking** Which data value most affects your choice of a measure of center to describe the data? Explain.

11. © **MP.2 Reasoning** How do you know that any value of x will be a solution to the inequality $x + 1.6 > x$?

© Common Core Assessment

12. Which statement about this data distribution is **NOT** true?

    Ⓐ The interquartile range is 4.

    Ⓑ The median is the preferable measure of center.

    Ⓒ The data cluster from 2 to 7.

    Ⓓ The distribution is symmetrical.

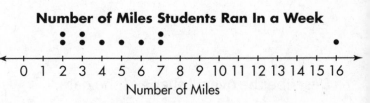

Number of Miles Students Ran In a Week

Number of Miles

Name _____

Help Practice Tools Games
      Buddy

Homework
& Practice 16-5
Summarize Data
Distributions

Another Look!

The box plot to the right displays data for the number of days the temperature was over 80°F for the month of July. The data were collected over a ten-year period.

You can summarize this data set by choosing some ways to describe it.

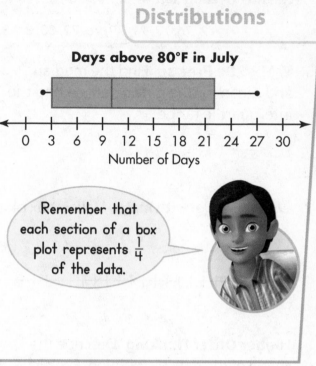

Days above 80°F in July

Number of Days

- The data are spread out to the right.

- The median is 10, and it describes the center of the data.

- The first quartile is 3 and the third quartile is 22. The box plot shows that half of the data fell between 3 days and 22 days. The interquartile range is 22 − 3, or 19 days.

- 25% of the time, the number of days with temperatures over 80° in July was only 3 days.

Remember that each section of a box plot represents $\frac{1}{4}$ of the data.

In **1–4**, use the data in the box plot.

1. Find the median for this data. What does it say about the data in this problem?

Students with Dogs in Each Classroom at Brookdale Elementary

Number of Students

2. What is the interquartile range?

3. Describe the shape of the data distribution.

4. If a dot plot were used to display the same data, what would it look like?

In **5–9**, use the data to answer the questions.

DATA

Lengths of Long Jumps in Mr. Hansen's Physical Education Class (in inches)

91, 72, 76, 77, 79, 79, 76, 72, 80, 83, 85, 89, 76, 80, 79, 82, 84, 80

5. © **MP.6 Be Precise** Find the median and mean for the data set. Then find the interquartile range.

6. What would be the preferable measure of center, the median or the mean? Explain your reasoning.

7. © **MP.4 Model with Math** Make a box plot and a dot plot for the data.

8. **Higher Order Thinking** Describe the shape of the data distribution. Explain how the dot plot and box plot are similar and different.

9. © **MP.7 Use Structure** Matt says that the mean would be more affected than the median if a long jump of 110 inches were added to the data. Do you agree? Explain how you know.

© **Common Core Assessment** _____

10. Which statement about the pet fish data is true?

Ⓐ The median and the mean are the same.

Ⓑ A good representation for the center of the data is 2.

Ⓒ The data are symmetrical.

Ⓓ The data show that most people have 3 or more fish.

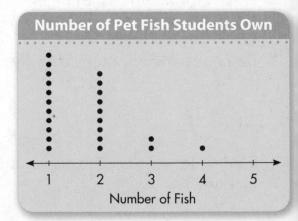

Number of Pet Fish Students Own

Number of Fish

Name _____

Solve & Share

Hal's class collected data to find out whether beef or chicken hot dogs have more sodium. Hal says, "Chicken hot dogs have more sodium since the median for the chicken hot dogs is higher than the median for the beef hot dogs." Does Hal's reasoning make sense?

I can ...
critique the reasoning of others using what I know about data distributions.

Mathematical Practice   MP.3, MP.1, MP.4, MP.6
Content Standards   6.SP.B.4, 6.SP.B.5c, 6.SP.B.5d

DATA	Milligrams of Sodium in One Hot Dog						
Beef	365	370	425	477	482	495	625
Chicken	358	426	513	522	545	581	588

Thinking Habits
Be a good thinker!
These questions can help you.

- What questions can I ask to understand other people's thinking?

- Are there mistakes in other people's thinking?

- Can I improve other people's thinking?

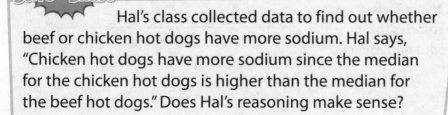

Look Back! ⓒ **MP.3 Critique Reasoning** What argument could you make to further support or improve Hal's reasoning?

Essential Question # How Can You Critique the Reasoning of Others?

A

Josie's mother thinks that cereals on the middle shelf at the grocery store have more calories than those on the top shelf. Josie collects data and makes dot plots to display her findings.

She tells her mother, "You are right. The cereals on the middle shelf do have more calories."

100, 100, 100, 110, 130, 140, 160

90 100 110 120 130 140 150 160
Calories in One Serving – Top Shelf

90, 90, 110, 120, 120, 120, 120

90 100 110 120 130 140 150 160
Calories in One Serving – Middle Shelf

What is Josie's reasoning to support her conclusion?

Josie found the median number of calories for each data set. The median for the top shelf is 110 calories. The median for the cereals on the middle shelf is 120.

Here's my thinking...

B How can I critique the reasoning of others?

I can

- ask questions for clarification.

- decide if the strategy used makes sense.

- look for flaws in estimates or calculations.

C Josie's reasoning is incomplete.

The data show that the cereals on the top shelf have some high calorie cereals that are not accounted for in the median.

The mean may be a better way to describe the number of calories in the cereals.

The mean number of calories of cereals on the top shelf is 120 calories. The mean number of calories of cereals on the middle shelf is 110 calories.

So, I can use the mean to argue that cereals on the top shelf typically have more calories than those on the middle shelf.

Convince Me! © MP.3 Critique Reasoning Josie collects more data. She adds two more data points for the middle shelf: 140 and 150 calories. She says that now the mean and the median for the middle shelf are higher than those for the top shelf. How can you decide if her reasoning makes sense?

© Pearson Education, Inc. 6

Name _____

Practice Buddy   Tools   Assessment

© **MP.3 Critique Reasoning**

Jack and Jennifer collected data about how many hours students in their class slept the night before. They made dot plots to compare the data for boys and girls. Jennifer said, "The boys slept more because most boys slept 8 hours." Jack said, "I agree because the median for the boys is greater than the median for the girls."

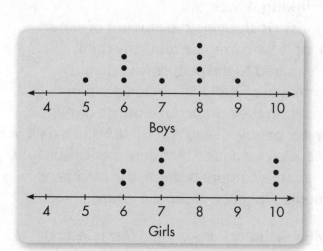

Boys

Girls

1. Does Jennifer's strategy for analyzing the data make sense? Explain.

2. Does Jack's reasoning support his conclusion? How might you critique his reasoning?

Independent Practice ☆

© **MP.3 Critique Reasoning**

The table shows the prices of some popular teen fiction in e-book and used print versions. Lynn compared the prices to find which version was less costly. She concluded that the prices for e-books and used print versions are equivalent because their median values are the same.

Prices for E-book and Used Print Fiction (dollars)									
E-book	10	6	9	11	10	9	10	9	5	8
Used Print	10	2	18	9	12	2	2	9	5	9

3. What strategy did Lynn use? What flaws in her thinking do you see?

4. How might you improve Lynn's reasoning? What would your conclusion be?

*For another example, see Set D on page 824.

Math Practices and Problem Solving

Drinking Water

Marissa is studying the amount of water people who exercise regularly drink compared to the people who do not exercise regularly. She made dot plots showing the number of 8-ounce drinks of water people in each group drink in a day. Marissa concluded that they drink about the same amount because the mean and median for each group are equal.

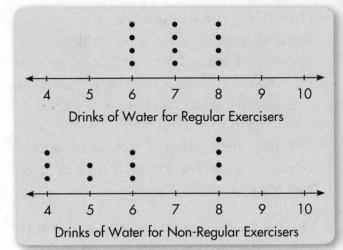

Drinks of Water for Regular Exercisers

Drinks of Water for Non-Regular Exercisers

5. **MP.3 Critique Reasoning** What question would you ask Marissa to clarify her reasoning? What flaw do you see in her reasoning?

6. **MP.6 Be Precise** How would you correct Marissa's statement?

To make sense and persevere with a problem, you can look for alternate strategies.

7. **MP.1 Make Sense and Persevere** In what other way can you describe the data? Explain what other measures you might use.

8. **MP.4 Model with Math** In what other way could Marissa display the data that would show something about the spread of the data?

Name _____

Another Look!

Bernie's Bike Shop has specialty wide-tire bicycles displayed in two rows. Victor used the price data to find the mean absolute deviation (MAD) of the prices of the bikes in each row. He concluded that the store places items with a wider range of prices in the front row.

Tell how you can critique Victor's reasoning.

- I can decide if the strategy makes sense.
- I can look for possible errors in his calculations.

Bicycle Prices (dollars)					
Front Row	200	290	160	350	150
Back Row	240	190	100	150	180

Critique Victor's reasoning.

The mean price of the bikes in the front row is $230. The mean price of the bikes in the back row is $172.

The MAD for the front row is $360 \div 5 = 72$. The MAD for the back row is $188 \div 5 = 37.6$.

$72 > 37.6$, so there is more variability in the prices of the bikes in the front row. Victor's conclusion is accurate.

When you critique reasoning, you explain why someone's thinking is correct or incorrect.

© MP.3 Critique Reasoning

The lengths, in miles, of the ten most popular paved bike trails and the ten most popular off-road bike trails in one state are listed in the table below. Louise found the mean length of each type of trail. She wants to publish a brochure saying that the typical lengths of paved and off-road trails in that state are similar. Critique Louise's reasoning.

Bicycle Trails Lengths (in miles)										
Paved Trails	5	5	10	15	5	25	25	5	5	25
Off-Road Trails	10	10	20	10	15	5	5	20	15	15

1. Is Louise's description of the state's bike trail lengths accurate? Did her strategy make sense?

2. How could Louise's statement about the state's bike trails be improved in the brochure?

Protein in Pizza

Dave is studying how many grams of protein there are in different kinds of pizza. He found this list of the number of protein grams in one slice of pizza in thick- and thin-crust varieties. Dave made box plots and concluded that, on average, thick-crust pizzas have more protein than thin-crust pizzas. They also vary more in the amount of protein in a slice.

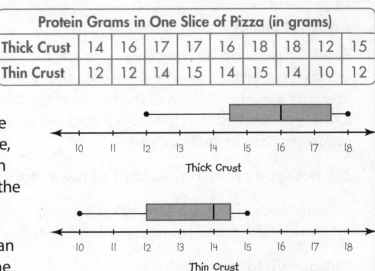

Protein Grams in One Slice of Pizza (in grams)									
Thick Crust	14	16	17	17	16	18	18	12	15
Thin Crust	12	12	14	15	14	15	14	10	12

3. **MP.4 Model with Math** Did Dave use an appropriate model or tool to analyze the data? Explain.

When you model with math, you display data in a clear way and use appropriate statistical measures.

4. **MP.6 Be Precise** Are Dave's calculations and box plots accurate? Explain how you know.

5. **MP.3 Critique Reasoning** Do Dave's statements about the protein in thick- and thin-crust pizzas show good reasoning? Explain.

6. **MP.1 Make Sense and Persevere** What other type of visual display would support Dave's statements?

Name _____

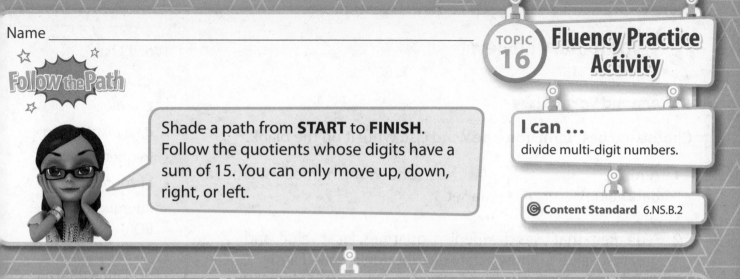

Follow the Path

Shade a path from **START** to **FINISH**. Follow the quotients whose digits have a sum of 15. You can only move up, down, right, or left.

I can ...
divide multi-digit numbers.

Content Standard 6.NS.B.2

Start				
41,964 ÷ 52	19,593 ÷ 21	8,322 ÷ 19	25,194 ÷ 38	9,216 ÷ 96
9,135 ÷ 87	6,952 ÷ 44	84,040 ÷ 88	19,712 ÷ 44	18,522 ÷ 63
41,310 ÷ 54	4,232 ÷ 23	25,425 ÷ 75	3,654 ÷ 42	43,068 ÷ 74
17,556 ÷ 84	42,032 ÷ 71	1,749 ÷ 11	21,941 ÷ 37	57,974 ÷ 82
7,372 ÷ 38	56,260 ÷ 58	1,170 ÷ 15	33,231 ÷ 53	6,693 ÷ 97

Finish

A-Z
Glossary

Word List

- absolute deviation
- box plot
- data distribution
- frequency table
- histogram
- interquartile range (IQR)
- mean absolute deviation (MAD)
- quartile

Understand Vocabulary

Choose the best term from the Word List. Write it on the blank.

1. A(n) _____ shows the number of times a data value occurs in a data set.

2. A diagram that uses the median, quartiles, least value, and greatest value to show a data distribution is called a(n) _____.

3. How data values are arranged is called the _____.

4. A graph that uses bars to show the frequency of equal groups of data is a(n) _____.

5. The _____ is the difference between the third and first quartiles.

Write *always*, *sometimes*, or *never* for each statement.

6. Intervals in a *frequency table* go beyond the values in a data set. _____

7. You can calculate the *IQR* from a *histogram*. _____

8. The third *quartile* in a *box plot* is an outlier. _____

9. The *MAD* is a negative value. _____

Use Vocabulary in Writing

10. Describe measures of variability and when you would use them to summarize a data set. Use at least 4 words from the Word List.

Name _____

Set A pages 785–790

The ages of the campers at a summer camp are listed below.

12, 14, 12, 14, 10, 11, 15, 13, 13, 11, 12, 12, 7, 14, 12

The data can be organized in a frequency table.

Divide the range of data into equal intervals and mark the frequency of the data using tally marks.

Ages of Campers	6–8	9–11	12–14	15–17
Tally	I	III	౼౼౼౼ ౼౼౼౼	I
Frequency	1	3	10	1

Reteaching

Remember that a histogram is a graph that uses bars to show the frequency of equal ranges or groups of data. It shows the shape of the data.

1. Represent the data in the frequency table on the left in a histogram.

Set B pages 791–796

At a paper airplane contest, seven airplanes flew distances, in feet, of: 60, 75, 45, 55, 70, 40, 65.

To find the first quartile, order the numbers from least to greatest, find the median value, and then find the median of the numbers to the left of the median. Do the same for the third quartile by finding the median of the second half of numbers.

40 (45) 55 (60) 65 (70) 75
1ˢᵗ quartile Median 3ʳᵈ quartile

Make a box plot. Show the minimum and maximum values, the median, and the first and third quartiles.

Paper Airplane Distances

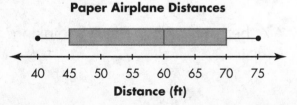

Distance (ft)

Remember that you need 5 values to create a box plot: the median, 1ˢᵗ quartile, 3ʳᵈ quartile, and the greatest and least values in the data set.

In **1** and **2**, use the data to create a box plot.

1. 27, 31, 30, 33, 29, 25, 28

2. 3, 1, 3, 7, 5, 2, 3, 6, 3

You can summarize data by finding the measures of center and measures of variability.

Games Sold Each Week						
81	90	85	86	82	53	90

Find the mean, median, and mode of the number of games sold each week.

Mean: 81, Median: 85, and Mode: 90

Since there is an outlier, the median is the best measure of center.

• The interquartile range (IQR) for this data set is 9.

• The mean absolute deviation (MAD) for this data set is 8.

The typical number of games sold each week is 85. This can vary by about 9 games.

Remember to use the IQR when the median is more appropriate and the MAD when the mean is more appropriate.

In **1–3**, use the data below.

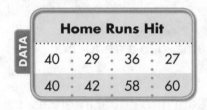

Home Runs Hit			
40	29	36	27
40	42	58	60

1. Find the mean, median, and mode of the number of home runs hit by 8 sluggers.

2. Which measure of center and measure of variability best describe the data set?

3. Summarize the data set.

Think about these questions to help you **critique the reasoning of others**.

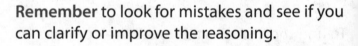

Thinking Habits

• What questions can I ask to understand other people's thinking?

• Are there mistakes in other people's thinking?

• Can I improve on other people's thinking?

Remember to look for mistakes and see if you can clarify or improve the reasoning.

Henry analyzed the March rainfall data in his town for the past 7 years: 3, 9, 14, 17, 19, 21, 24.

Henry concluded that March rainfall is usually less than or equal to 16 in. because the mean rainfall is about 15 in. and the IQR is 12 in.

Critique Henry's reasoning.

1. How did Henry support his conclusion?

2. Are there mistakes in Henry's thinking? Explain.

Name _____

1. The years of experience for a group of dentists are listed below. Which measure of center best describes the data set?

8, 6, 10, 7, 4, 4, 10, 35, 1, 5

Ⓐ Mode

Ⓑ Mean

Ⓒ Median

Ⓓ Outlier

2. The data show yearly rainfall for a 9-year period in inches:
29, 24, 19, 21, 23, 27, 26, 29, 18

What is the MAD for this set of data in inches?

3. The histogram shows students' scores on a math test.

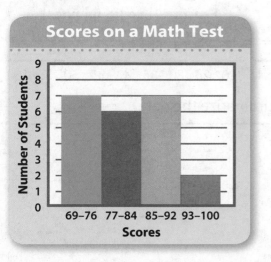

According to the histogram, how many students had scores between 85 and 100?

4. Sebby says that the mean is a better measure of center for the data below because the data is clustered together. Do you agree with Sebby's reasoning? Explain.

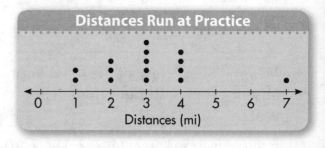

5. Choose the numbers from the box that make the statements correct.

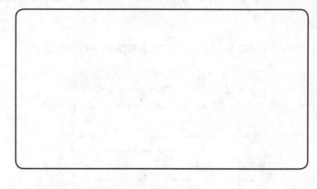

The third quartile is _____ and the first quartile is _____. The IQR is _____.

6. For each of 7 weeks babysitting, Kelly made the following dollar amounts: 16, 28, 28, 32, 21, 18, and 35. What is the first quartile of this data?

7. Eight homerooms in a middle school had the following distribution of students. What is the MAD of students?

29, 32, 33, 28, 30, 30, 29, 33

Ⓐ 1.25

Ⓑ 1.625

Ⓒ 2.25

Ⓓ 2.8

---

8. Ms. Smith kept track of the number of absences of her students for a school year.

5, 1, 6, 15, 2, 5, 3, 9, 2, 11, 7, 2, 1, 1, 7, 10, 1, 4

Make a histogram from the data.

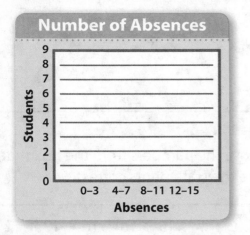

---

9. McKenna kept track of the number of miles she rode her horse each day for 2 weeks.

3, 2.5, 5, 2.5, 8, 10, 4, 0, 6, 6, 2, 2, 6, 9

Part A

Find the measures of center and variability that best summarize McKenna's data. Explain your reasoning.

Part B

McKenna says that she typically rides her horse for about 6 hours because the mode is 6. Is McKenna's conclusion appropriate? Explain your reasoning.

---

10. Twelve of Mr. Valerio's music students recorded the number of minutes they practiced each day. Mr. Valerio summarized the data using a box plot.

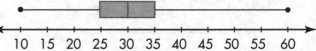

Summarize the data.

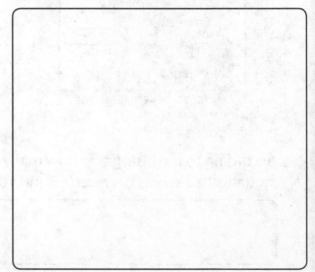

Name _____

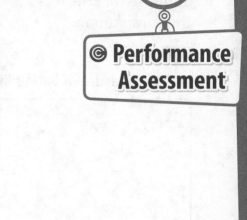

A Mazing Race!

Individual members of three teams raced through a maze.
Their times are shown in the table.

Performance Assessment

Maze Completion Times (in seconds)									
Blue Team	75	80	65	95	82	77	80	75	82
Red Team	80	86	83	83	84	78	87	88	87
Green Team	68	85	90	94	68	75	75	90	75

1. The team with the best mean time wins the competition.

Part A

Which team wins the A Mazing Race?

Part B

Why is the mean a better of measure of center to represent the overall
team score than the median?

2. Suppose that the team whose times have the least variability wins the competition.

Part A

Which measure of variability should be used? Explain.

Part B

Which team would win the competition? Explain your reasoning.

3. If you were a judge, what statistical measure would you recommend be used to determine the winning team? Explain.

Here's a preview of next year. These lessons help you step up to Grade 7.

Step Up to Grade 7

Lessons

Name _____

Solve & Share

Jessie and Kayla are scuba diving. They view a small school of fish at 4 feet below sea level. Then they descend 3 feet to view a sea anemone. At what depth, *d*, do they view the anemone? *Solve this problem any way you choose.*

I can ...
add integers.

© Content Standard 7.NS.A.1b
Mathematical Practices MP.2, MP.3, MP.4, MP.6, MP.8

How can you use a number line to model with math?

Sea Creatures Viewed	
Creature	Depth (feet)
fish	−4
anemone	*d*

Look Back! © **MP.4 Model with Math** How did the number line help you solve the problem?

Essential Question | **How Can You Add Integers?**

A

It was − 2°C when Jack left for school at 7:30 A.M. During the next three hours, the temperature decreased three degrees Celsius. What was the temperature at 10:30 A.M. that morning?

You can use reasoning to choose an operation. Add −2 + (−3) to find the temperature at 10:30 A.M.

B **One Way**

Think about walking a number line.

* Start at 0 on the number line, facing the positive integers.

* Walk backward 2 steps for −2 and stop.

* Walk backward 3 more steps to add −3.

Stop at −5. So, −2 + (−3) = −5.

C **Another Way**

Use these **rules for adding integers with the same signs.**

* Find the absolute values of the addends. $|-2| = 2$ and $|-3| = 3$

* Add the absolute values. $2 + 3 = 5$.

* Give the sum the same sign as the addends.

So, $-2 + (-3) = -5$.

Convince Me! © **MP.3 Critique Reasoning** Ava says that the sum of two negative integers is sometimes a positive integer. Do you agree? Explain your reasoning.

Another Example

Find $-2 + 3$.

Use these **rules for adding integers with different signs.**

- Find the absolute value of each addend. $|-2| = 2$ and $|3| = 3$
- Subtract the lesser absolute value from the greater. $3 - 2 = 1$
- Give the difference of the absolute values the same sign as the addend with the greater absolute value.

So $-2 + 3 = 1$.

> The addend 3 has a greater absolute value and is positive. So, the sum, 1, is also positive.

☆ Guided Practice

Do You Understand?

1. © **MP.8 Generalize** When is the sum of a positive integer and a negative integer positive?

2. Show how you could use the number line to find $-2 + 3$.

Do You Know How?

In **3–6**, find each sum. Use a number line or the rules for adding integers.

3. $-7 + 4$

4. $8 + (-3)$

5. $43 + (-19)$

6. $-16 + (-12)$

☆ Independent Practice ☆

Leveled Practice In **7–17**, find each sum.

> You can draw a number line or use rules to add.

7. $4 + (-3)$

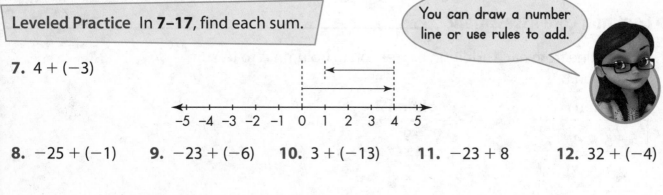

8. $-25 + (-1)$ 9. $-23 + (-6)$ 10. $3 + (-13)$ 11. $-23 + 8$ 12. $32 + (-4)$

13. $-7 + 15$ 14. $6 + (-19)$ 15. $-3 + (-7)$ 16. $-4 + (-8)$ 17. $-8 + 30$

Math Practices and Problem Solving

18. © MP.8 Generalize Use the rule to complete the table. Rule: Add −7.

In	3	−19	22	−43	−7
Out					

19. Math and Science In Antarctica, the temperature often drops below −40°F, and the wind speed can exceed 40 miles per hour (mph). A 40-mph wind makes −40°F feel 44°F colder. How cold does −40°F feel when the wind is blowing 40 mph?

20. Higher Order Thinking What is the sum of an integer and its opposite? Explain your reasoning.

21. © MP.6 Be Precise Write a number with the following characteristics.

- The digit in the hundreds place is 10 times the value of the digit in the tens place.
- The digit in the hundredths place is $\frac{1}{10}$ the value of the digit in the tenths place.

In **22** and **23**, use the table of scores.

22. Number Sense Who had the least score and the greatest score in each round?

Round	1	2	3
Hailee	−3	3	−6
Diego	4	−1	−5
Jon	−4	0	1

23. The person with the greatest total score wins. Who won the game?

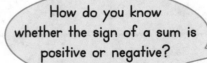

How do you know whether the sign of a sum is positive or negative?

© Common Core Assessment

24. Draw a line from each addition expression in Column A to its sum in Column B.

Column A	Column B
−2 + 11	−9
2 + (−7)	9
−4 + 9	−5
4 + (−13)	5

Name _____

Solve & Share

Sandi puts a container of juice in the freezer and records the temperature every hour. The temperature changes by −6° each hour. What is the total change after 3 hours? *Solve this problem any way you choose.*

Lesson 2
Multiply Integers

I can ...
multiply integers.

© **Content Standard** 7.NS.A.2a
Mathematical Practices MP.2, MP.3, MP.5, MP.7, MP.8

How can you use appropriate tools, like a number line, to help you solve this problem?

←|—|—|—|—|—|—|—|—|—|—|—|—|—|—→
−20 −18 −16 −14 −12 −10 −8 −6 −4 −2 0 2 4 6

Look Back! © **MP.7 Use Structure** How are addition and multiplication related? How can you use this relationship to find the total change?

Essential Question **How Can You Find the Product of Two Integers?**

A

When multiplying integers, the signs of the factors determine the sign of their product.

For example, 5 × 3 = 5 + 5 + 5 = 15

The product of two positive integers is positive.

Find −3 × 5 and 5 × (−3).

Then find −5 × (−3).

You can reason to identify patterns and apply properties when multiplying integers.

B Find −3 × 5.

$$-3 \times 5 = (-3) + (-3) + (-3) + (-3) + (-3)$$
$$= -15$$

Find 5 × (−3).

Use the Commutative Property of Multiplication.

$$5 \times (-3) = -3 \times 5$$

So, 5 × (−3) = −15.

The product of a positive integer and a negative integer is negative.

C Find −5 × (−3).

Continue the pattern in the table. The products increase by 5.

So, −5 × (−3) = 15.

The product of two negative integers is positive.

$$-5 \times 3 = -15$$
$$-5 \times 2 = -10$$
$$-5 \times 1 = -5$$
$$-5 \times 0 = 0$$
$$-5 \times -1 =$$
$$-5 \times -2 =$$
$$-5 \times -3 =$$

Convince Me! © **MP.3 Construct Arguments** Melanie says that when multiplying, if more than two factors are negative, the product is negative. Do you agree? Construct an argument with an example or counterexample.

☆ Guided Practice

Do You Understand?

1. Using the rules for multiplying integers, is the product of two positive integers and a negative integer positive, or negative?

2. Ⓒ **MP.8 Generalize** Explain why $(-4) \times (-3) = 4 \times 3$ without solving the equation.

Do You Know How?

In **3–5**, find each product.

3. $(3) \times (-8)$ 4. $(-9) \times (-6)$

5. $(4) \times (-2)$

In **6–8**, evaluate each expression for $n = -3$.

6. $5n$ 7. $n \times 0$

8. $n \times |-31|$

Remember, the product of any number and 0 is 0.

Independent Practice ☆

In **9–18**, find each product.

9. $3 \times (-7)$ 10. $(-8)(6)$ 11. -9×4 12. $15 \times (-8)$ 13. $(-14)^2$

14. $-1 \times (-27)$ 15. 4×24 16. $(7)(-18)$ 17. $-5 \times (11)$ 18. $17 \times (-3)$

In **19–28**, use order of operations to evaluate each expression for $a = -2$.

19. $3a$ 20. $-8a$ 21. $-2a + 4$ 22. $6a + 2$ 23. $-3a$

24. $-5a + (3)(-7)$ 25. $6 + 2a$ 26. $17a + 4$ 27. $4a + 6$ 28. $6a$

29. The product of 3 integers is -30. What could the 3 integers be? Write two possible sets of integers. Explain how you decided how many negative integers to include.

Math Practices and Problem Solving

In **30–32**, use the data in the table.

	Stock Name	Change in Value ($ per share)
DATA	Red Company	−2
	White Company	1
	Blue Company	−3

30. Haru has 30 shares of Red Company stock. How has the value of her stock changed? Find 30 × (−2).

31. © **MP.2 Reasoning** Kerry owns 15 shares of Red Company stock and 10 shares of Blue Company stock. Explain which of Kerry's stock values changed more.

32. © **MP.7 Use Structure** Sahil owns 6 shares of Blue Company stock. How many shares of White Company stock would Sahil have to own to make the total change in both sets of stock $0?

---

33. **Number Sense** Without calculating, determine which two integer factors will result in the greatest product. Explain how you made your choice.

−32   17   −16   18   20   −21   30

34. **Higher Order Thinking** Kari says that she knows that −83 × 109 has the same product as −109 × 83 without doing any calculations. Explain how Kari knows this is true.

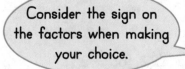

Consider the sign on the factors when making your choice.

© **Common Core Assessment**

35. Select the expressions that have a positive product.

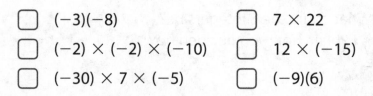

☐ (−3)(−8)   ☐ 7 × 22

☐ (−2) × (−2) × (−10)   ☐ 12 × (−15)

☐ (−30) × 7 × (−5)   ☐ (−9)(6)

Step Up | Lesson 2

© Pearson Education, Inc. 6

Name _____

☆ ★ ☆
Solve & Share

Aimee walked to her friend's house and back. Then she ran 3 miles on the treadmill. Her pedometer shows she traveled 5 miles in all. Aimee wrote the equation $2f + 3 = 5$, where f equals the distance to her friend's house, to represent the total miles she traveled. How far did Aimee walk to get to her friend's house? *Solve this problem any way you choose.*

Step Up to Grade 7

Lesson 3
Equations with More Than One Operation

I can ...
solve an equation that has more than one operation.

© **Content Standard** 7.EE.B.4a
Mathematical Practices MP.3, MP.4, MP.7

> You model with math when you write equations that represent situations.

Look Back! © **MP.3 Construct Arguments** Jon says that $f = 1$ because $2(1) + 3 = 5$, so Aimee walked $2f = 2(1) = 2$ miles to her friends house. Construct an argument to explain the flaw in Jon's reasoning.

Essential Question: What Steps Can You Use to Solve Some Equations?

A

The hiking club has hiked 5 miles of the trail shown. How many miles must they hike each hour to finish the trail in 4 hours? Let x equal the number of miles to hike each hour.

You can use an equation to model with math and represent this situation.

Hiking Trail
17 miles

miles left to hike + miles already hiked = total number of miles

4x + 5 = 17

B

Step 1

When an equation has more than one operation, first undo addition or subtraction.

$$4x + 5 = 17$$

$$4x + 5 - 5 = 17 - 5$$ Subtract 5 from both sides.

$$4x = 12$$

C

Step 2

Then undo multiplication or division.

$$4x = 12$$

$$\frac{4x}{4} = \frac{12}{4}$$ Divide both sides by 4.

$$x = 3$$

They must hike 3 miles each hour.

Convince Me! © **MP.7 Use Structure** How can you check that your answer is correct?

☆ Guided Practice

Do You Understand?

1. © MP.7 Use Structure In the example on the previous page, why do you subtract 5 from both sides of the equation?

2. Suppose the hiking club members in the example on the previous page had to complete their hike in 3 hours. How many miles would they have to hike each hour?

Do You Know How?

3. Complete the steps to find the solution of the equation.

$$\frac{x}{4} - 5 = 19$$

$$\frac{x}{4} - 5 + \square = 19 + \square$$

$$\frac{x}{4} = \square$$

$$\frac{x}{4} \times \square = 24 \times \square$$

$$x = \square$$

> When you solve an equation, you undo operations in the reverse order of the order of operations.

☆ Independent Practice ☆

In **4–11**, solve each equation and check your answer.

4. $\frac{x}{7} - 3 = 4$

5. $5b - 7 = 13$

6. $\frac{s}{4} + 3 = 9$

7. $24 + 12n = 60$

8. $25 = 11g + 3$

9. $18 = \frac{z}{3} + 3$

10. $2m + 5 = 6$

11. $n + 2.5 = 6.5$

Math Practices and Problem Solving

12. © **MP.3 Critique Reasoning** Marty recorded her work to solve the equation below. How do you know that Marty's answer is not correct? Explain Marty's mistake.

Marty's work: $\frac{x}{3} - 5 = 6$

$$3\left(\frac{x}{3}\right) - 5 = 3(6)$$
$$x - 5 = 18$$
$$x - 5 + 5 = 18 + 5$$
$$x = 23$$

13. © **MP.4 Model with Math** The month of April has 30 days. Corey's iguana eats $2\frac{1}{2}$ ounces of peas each day. How many ounces of peas will Corey's iguana eat during the month of April?

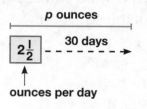

p ounces

$2\frac{1}{2}$ - - - 30 days - - - →

ounces per day

Is there another way you can model the amount of peas Corey's iguana eats?

14. Higher Order Thinking To solve the equation $x\left(\frac{12}{6}\right) - 100 = 0$, which operation would you use first? Explain.

15. Number Sense Without solving, how can you tell that $5(4 + 7) = 12 \times 6$ is not a valid equation?

© **Common Core Assessment**

16. Alejandro bought 4 T-shirts to give to his friends. After using a $10-off coupon, he paid $18 for the shirts. How much did each shirt cost? Use the equation $4s - 10 = 18$ to solve.

    Ⓐ $10   Ⓒ $7

    Ⓑ $8   Ⓓ $2

Name _____

Solve & Share

A walking path will be made around the lake shown. Find the length of the path in kilometers. *Solve this problem any way you choose.*

I can ...
find the circumference of a circle.

© Content Standard 7.G.B.4
Mathematical Practices MP.2, MP.5, MP.6

How can you use appropriate tools, like a measuring tape or a string and a ruler, to find the length of the path?

10 km

Look Back! © **MP.5 Use Appropriate Tools** What tools did you consider using to measure the distance around the lake? Why did you choose the tool you used?

Essential Question **How Can You Find the Circumference of a Circle?**

A

Anna is going to glue some lace around the top edge of a lampshade with a circular opening. How much lace does she need?

The circumference (C) is the distance around a circle.

Diameter is 5 in.

circumference

What do you know about the relationship between the circumference and diameter of a circle?

B One Way

Use the formula $C = \pi d$ to find the circumference, C, of the lampshade with diameter d.

$C = \pi d$

$C = (3.14)(5)$

In this book, equal signs are used for calculations involving π.

$C = 15.70$

Anna needs about 16 inches of lace.

π is approximately 3.14, or $\frac{22}{7}$. All calculations involving π are approximations.

C Another Way

Use the formula $C = 2\pi r$ to find the circumference, C, of the lampshade with radius r.

The diameter of a circle is twice the radius.

$C = 2\pi r$

$C = 2(3.14)(2.5)$

$C = 15.70$

Anna needs about 16 inches of lace.

Convince Me! © **MP.6 Be Precise** Refer to the problem on the previous page. Use the formula for circumference to find the length of the path around the lake. How close were your measurements to the actual circumference? What are some reasons for the difference in the measurement?

Name _____

☆ Guided Practice

Do You Understand?

1. **Algebra** What variables are used in the formula $C = 2\pi r$? What does each variable represent?

2. Ⓒ **MP.2 Reasoning** How could you estimate the circumference of the lampshade?

Do You Know How?

In **3** and **4**, use the diameter or radius shown for each circle to find its circumference. Use 3.14 or $\frac{22}{7}$ for π.

3. 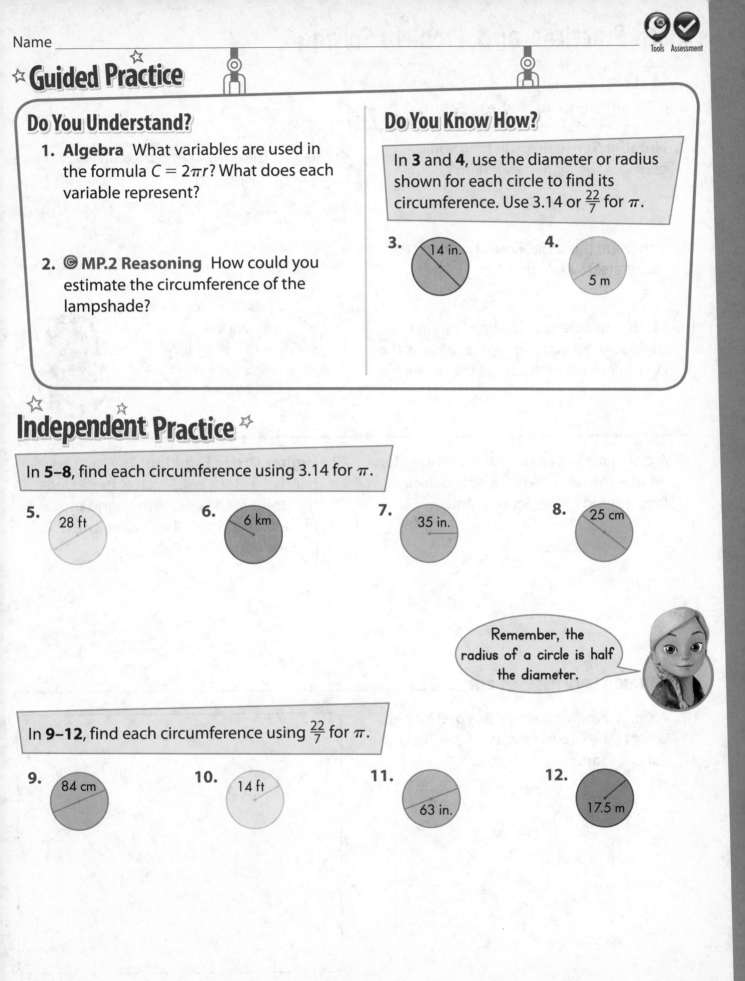 14 in.

4. 5 m

Independent Practice ☆

In **5–8**, find each circumference using 3.14 for π.

5. 28 ft

6. 6 km

7. 35 in.

8. 25 cm

Remember, the radius of a circle is half the diameter.

In **9–12**, find each circumference using $\frac{22}{7}$ for π.

9. 84 cm

10. 14 ft

11. 63 in.

12. 17.5 m

Math Practices and Problem Solving

In **13–15**, use the table showing the diameter and circumference for some of Saturn's rings.

13. Number Sense Explain how you can estimate the diameter of Ring G.

Ring	Diameter (km)	Circumference (km)
C	184,000	
B	235,000	737,900
A	273,600	859,104
G		1,091,464

DATA

14. Complete the table. Round answers to the nearest whole number.

15. Math and Science Saturn's D-Ring has a radius of 74,500 kilometers. What is the circumference of this ring? Use 3.14 for π.

If you know the diameter of a circle, how do you find the radius?

---

16. A clock face has a radius of 5.5 centimeters. What is the circumference of the clock face? Round to the nearest tenth.

17. Higher Order Thinking The minute hand of a clock is 4.2 inches long. Does the point at the end of the hand move more or less than 24 inches in one hour? Explain your reasoning.

© Common Core Assessment

18. A circular mirror has a radius of 9 inches. What is the circumference of the circle? Use 3.14 for π.

Name _____

Solve & Share

Nadia is remodeling her back yard. Landscaping plans include a swimming pool with a radius of 7 feet. Each square on the grid represents 64 ft². Find the approximate area of the yard covered by the pool. *Solve this problem any way you choose.*

I can ...
find the area of a circle.

Content Standard 7.G.B.4
Mathematical Practices MP.2, MP.7, MP.8

You can use relationships to generalize and solve problems.

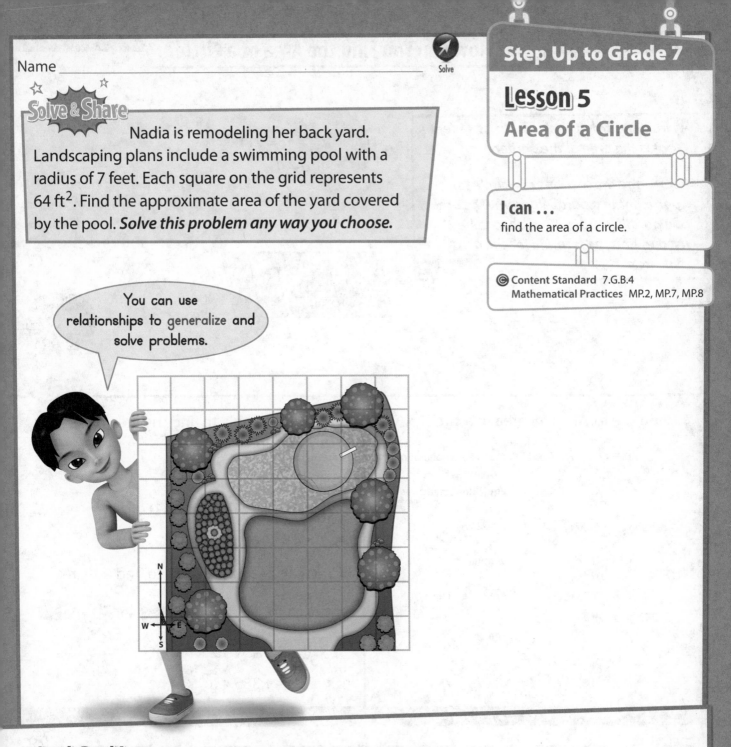

Look Back! © **MP.7 Look for Relationships** Divide the area of the pool by 3.14. How does the quotient relate to the radius of the pool?

How Can You Find the Area of a Circle?

A

A circular garden has a radius of 21 feet. What is the area of the garden?

Rearrange the sections of a circle to approximate a parallelogram. The area of a parallelogram, A = bh, can be used to find the formula for the area of a circle.

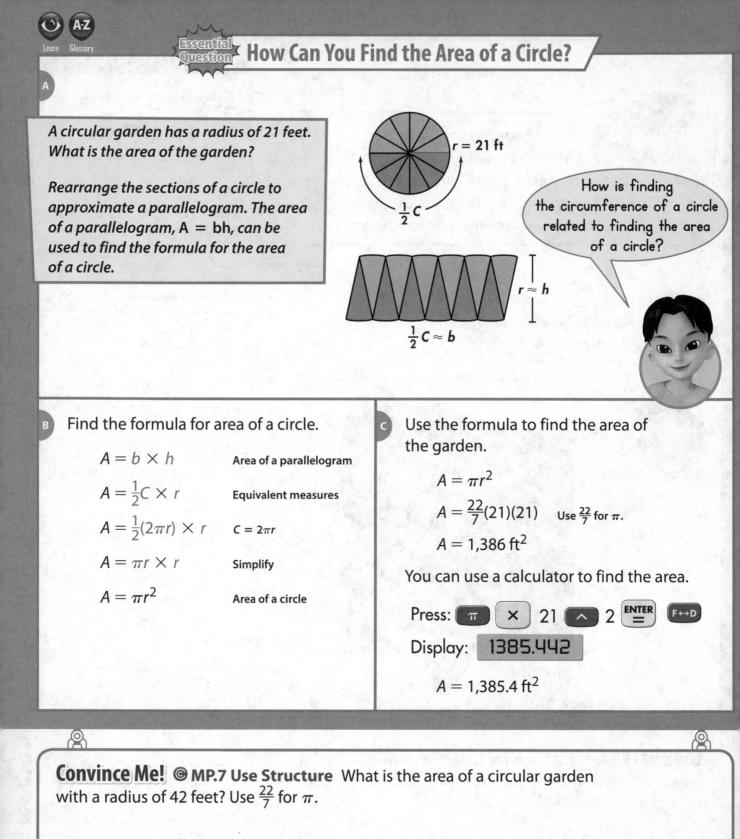

r = 21 ft

$\frac{1}{2}C$

$r \approx h$

$\frac{1}{2}C \approx b$

How is finding the circumference of a circle related to finding the area of a circle?

B   Find the formula for area of a circle.

$A = b \times h$ **Area of a parallelogram**

$A = \frac{1}{2}C \times r$ **Equivalent measures**

$A = \frac{1}{2}(2\pi r) \times r$ **C = 2πr**

$A = \pi r \times r$ **Simplify**

$A = \pi r^2$ **Area of a circle**

C   Use the formula to find the area of the garden.

$A = \pi r^2$

$A = \frac{22}{7}(21)(21)$ Use $\frac{22}{7}$ for π.

$A = 1,386 \text{ ft}^2$

You can use a calculator to find the area.

Press: π   ×   21   ^   2   ENTER =   F↔D

Display: **1385.442**

$A = 1,385.4 \text{ ft}^2$

Convince Me! © **MP.7 Use Structure** What is the area of a circular garden with a radius of 42 feet? Use $\frac{22}{7}$ for π.

Tools Assessment

☆ **Guided Practice**

Do You Understand?

1. ⓒ **MP.2 Reasoning** In the comparison on the previous page, how do the triangular shapes in the parallelogram relate to the circle?

2. **Algebra** How could you write the formula for the area of a circle in order to use the diameter instead of the radius?

Do You Know How?

In **3–6**, find the area of each circle to the nearest whole number. Use 3.14 or $\frac{22}{7}$ for π.

3.
10 yd

4.
35 m

5. $d = 54$ in.

6. $r = 10$ mi.

☆ **Independent Practice** ☆

In **7–10**, find the area of each circle to the nearest whole number. Use 3.14 or $\frac{22}{7}$ for π.

Remember, you use the radius of a circle when calculating the circle's area.

7.
16 cm

8.
12 km

9.
7 ft

10.
32 yd

In **11–13**, find the missing measurements for each figure. Round to the nearest whole number. Use 3.14 or $\frac{22}{7}$ for π.

11. $d = 8$ in.
$r = \square$
$C = \square$
$A = \square$

12. $d = \square$
$r = \square$
$C = 371$ mm
$A = \square$

13. $d = \square$
$r = \square$
$C = \square$
$A = 113$ sq in.

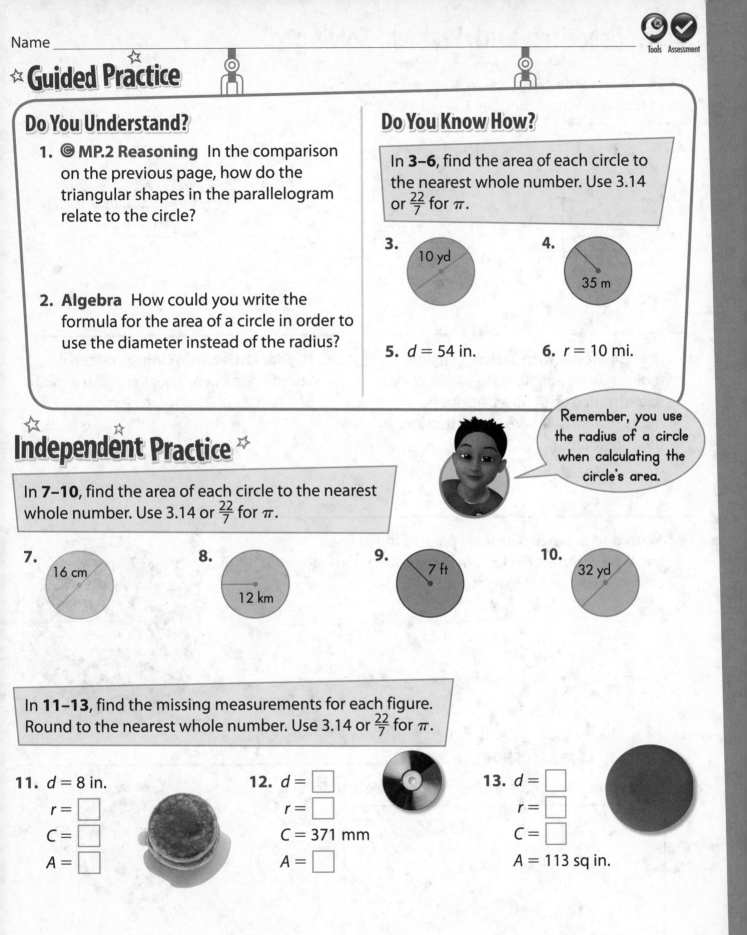

Math Practices and Problem Solving

In **14–16**, find the area and circumference of each coin to the nearest whole number. Use 3.14 or $\frac{22}{7}$ for π.

14.

24.26 mm

15.

17.91 mm

16.

21.21 mm

---

17. © **MP.4 Model with Math** A small radio station broadcasts in all directions to a distance of 40 miles. About how many square miles are in the station's broadcast area?

18. **Higher Order Thinking** How can you find the area of a semicircle with a radius of 5 feet. Explain your reasoning.

---

19. **Math and Science** Giant lily pads found in Brazil are almost perfect circles. What is the area of the top of the lily pad shown at the right?

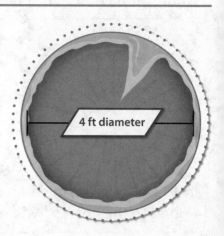

4 ft diameter

© **Common Core Assessment**

20. What is the area of the archery target? Use 3.14 for π.

122 cm

Glossary

A

absolute deviation The total distance between each data point and the mean.

absolute value The distance that an integer is from zero on the number line.

acute angle An angle with a measure greater than 0° but less than 90°.

acute triangle A triangle with three acute angles.

adjacent angles A pair of angles with a common vertex and a common side but no common interior points. *Example:* ∠*RSP* and ∠*PST*

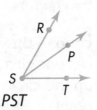

algebraic expression A mathematical phrase that has at least one variable and operation. *Example:* 10 × *n* or 10*n*

angle Two rays with the same endpoint.

arc A part of a circle connecting two points on a circle.

area The number of square units needed to cover a surface or figure.

associative properties Properties that state the way in which addends or factors are grouped does not affect the sum or product.

average The sum of the values in a data set divided by the number of data values in the set. Also called the *mean*.

axis (*pl.* axes) Either of the two perpendicular lines of a coordinate plane that intersect at the origin.

B

bar graph A graph that uses bars to show and compare data.

base (in geometry) A designated side of a polygon that is perpendicular to the height of the polygon; one of the two parallel faces on a prism; a particular flat surface of a solid, such as a cylinder or cone.

base (in numeration) A number multiplied by itself the number of times shown by an exponent. *Example:* $4 \times 4 \times 4 = 4^3$, where 4 is the base.

box plot A diagram that shows the distribution of data values using the median, quartiles, least value, and greatest value on a number line.

C

capacity The volume of a container measured in liquid units.

Celsius (°C) A scale for measuring temperature in the metric system.

center (in geometry) The interior point from which all points of a circle are equally distant.

center (in statistics) The part of a data set where the middle values are concentrated.

centi- Prefix meaning $\frac{1}{100}$.

central angle An angle with its vertex at the center of a circle.

chord A line segment with both endpoints on a circle.

circle A closed plane figure with all points the same distance from a given point called the center.

circle graph A graph that represents a total divided into parts.

circumference The distance around a circle.

cluster An interval with a greater frequency compared to the rest of the data set.

coefficient The number that is multiplied by a variable in an algebraic expression. *Example:* For $6x + 5$, the coefficient is 6.

common denominator A denominator that is the same in two or more fractions.

common factor A factor that is the same for two or more numbers.

common multiple A multiple that is the same for two or more numbers.

commutative properties The properties that state the order of addends or the order of factors does not affect the sum or product.

compatible numbers Numbers that are easy to compute mentally.

composite number A natural number greater than one that has more than two factors.

cone A three-dimensional figure that has one circular base. The points on this circle are joined to one point outside the base called the vertex.

conjecture A generalization that you think is true.

constant speed A rate of speed that stays the same over time.

conversion factor A rate that compares equivalent measures. *Examples:*

$\dfrac{4 \text{ cups}}{1 \text{ quart}}$ $\dfrac{12 \text{ inches}}{1 \text{ foot}}$ $\dfrac{1{,}000 \text{ meters}}{1 \text{ kilometer}}$

coordinate plane A two-dimensional system in which a location is described by its distances from two perpendicular number lines called the x-axis and the y-axis.

counterexample An example that shows that a statement is not true. *Example:* Statement: All odd numbers are prime numbers.
Counterexample: 9 is an odd number but is <u>not</u> a prime number.

cubic unit A unit measuring volume, consisting of a cube with edges one unit long.

cylinder A three-dimensional figure that has two circular bases which are parallel and identical.

D

data Information that is gathered.

data distribution How data values are arranged.

decagon A polygon with ten sides.

decimal A number with one or more digits to the right of the decimal point.

decimal point A dot used to separate dollars from cents in money or ones from tenths in a number.

degree (°) A unit for measuring angles or temperatures.

denominator The number below the fraction bar in a fraction; the total number of equal parts in all.

dependent variable A variable that changes in response to another variable.

diagonal A line segment that connects two vertices of a polygon and is not a side.

diameter A line segment that passes through the center of a circle and has both endpoints on the circle.

A   O   B

dimensional analysis A method that uses conversion factors to convert one unit of measure to another unit of measure. *Example:*
$$64 \cancel{\text{ ounces}} \times \frac{1 \text{ cup}}{8 \cancel{\text{ ounces}}} = \frac{64}{8} \text{ cups}$$
$$= 8 \text{ cups}$$

Distributive Property Multiplying a sum by a number produces the same result as multiplying each addend by the number and adding the products.
Example: $2 \times (3 + 4) = (2 \times 3) + (2 \times 4)$

dividend The number being divided by another number. *Example:* In $12 \div 3 = 4$, 12 is the dividend.

divisible A number is divisible by another number if its quotient is a whole number and the remainder is zero.

divisor The number used to divide another number. *Example:* In $12 \div 3 = 4$, 3 is the divisor.

dot plot A display of data values where each data value is shown as a dot above a number line. See also *line plot*.

E

edge The line segment where two faces of a polyhedron meet.

equation A mathematical sentence stating that two expressions are equal.

equilateral triangle A triangle with three sides of the same length.

equivalent expressions Expressions that have the same value regardless of which number is substituted for the same variable.

equivalent fractions Fractions that name the same amount.

estimate To find a number that is close to an exact answer.

evaluate To find the value of an algebraic expression by replacing each variable with a given value. *Example:* Evaluate $2n + 5$ when $n = 3$; $2(3) + 5 = 11$.

expanded form using exponents A number written in expanded form with the place values written in exponential form. *Example:* $3{,}246 = (3 \times 10^3) + (2 \times 10^2) + (4 \times 10^1) + (6 \times 10^0)$

exponent The number that tells how many times the base is being multiplied by itself. *Example:* $8^3 = 8 \times 8 \times 8$, where 3 is the exponent and 8 is the base.

exponential form A way of writing the repeated multiplication of a number using exponents. *Example:* 2^5

expression A mathematical phrase that can contain numbers, variables, and operations. *Example:* $12 - x$

F

face A flat surface of a polyhedron.

factor A number that is multiplied by another to get a product.

factor tree A diagram that shows the prime factorization of a number.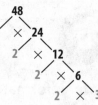

Fahrenheit (°F) A scale for measuring temperature in the customary system.

formula A rule that uses symbols to relate two or more quantities.

fraction A number that can be used to describe a part of a whole, a part of a set, a location on a number line, or a division of whole numbers.

frequency table A table that shows the number of times a data value or range of values occurs in a data set.

G

gap An interval with a lesser frequency compared to the rest of the data set.

gram (g) Metric unit of mass.

greatest common factor (GCF) The greatest number that is a factor of two or more numbers.

H

height The segment from a vertex perpendicular to the line containing the opposite side; the perpendicular distance between the bases of a solid.

heptagon A polygon with seven sides.

hexagon A polygon with six sides.

histogram A graph that uses bars to show the frequency of equal intervals.

I

identity properties The properties that state the sum of any number and zero is that number and the product of any number and one is that number.

independent variable The variable that causes the dependent variable to change.

inequality A statement that contains > (greater than), < (less than), ≥ (greater than or equal to), ≤ (less than or equal to), or ≠ (is not equal to) to compare two expressions.

input/output table A table of related values.

integers The counting numbers, their opposites, and zero.

interquartile range (IQR) A measure of variability that is the difference between the third quartile and the first quartile.

interval A range of numbers used to represent data.

inverse relationships Relationships between operations that "undo" each other, such as addition and subtraction, or multiplication and division (except multiplication or division by 0).

isosceles triangle A triangle with at least two identical sides.

K

kilo- Prefix meaning 1,000.

kite A quadrilateral with two pairs of adjacent sides that are equal in length.

L

least common denominator (LCD)
The least common multiple of the
denominators of two or more fractions.
Example: 12 is the LCD of $\frac{1}{4}$ and $\frac{1}{6}$.

least common multiple (LCM) The least
number, other than zero, that is a multiple
of two or more numbers.

like denominators Denominators in
two or more fractions that are the same.

like terms Terms that have the same
variable, such as y and $2y$.

line A straight path of points that goes
on forever in two directions.

line plot A display of data values where
each data value is shown as a mark above
a number line. See also *dot plot*.

line segment Part of a line that has two
endpoints.

linear equation An equation whose
graph is a straight line.

liter (L) Metric unit of capacity.

M

mass Measure of the amount of matter
of an object.

maximum The greatest data value in a
data set.

mean The sum of the values in a data set
divided by the number of values in the
set. Also called the *average*.

mean absolute deviation (MAD) The
mean of the absolute deviations of a set
of data.

measure of center A single number
that summarizes the center of a data set.
Example: mean or median

measure of variability A single number
that summarizes the variability of a data
set. *Example:* interquartile range

median The middle data value in a data set.

meter (m) Metric unit of length.

metric system (of measurement) A
system using decimals and powers of
10 to measure length, mass, and capacity.

midpoint The point that divides
a segment into two segments of
equal length.

milli- Prefix meaning $\frac{1}{1000}$.

minimum The least data value in a
data set.

mixed number A number that combines
a whole number and a fraction.

mode The data value that occurs most
often in a data set.

multiple The product of a given whole
number and any non-zero whole number.

net A plane figure pattern that, when folded, makes a solid.

nonagon A polygon with nine sides.

numerator The number above the fraction bar in a fraction; the number of objects or equal parts being considered.

numerical data Data where each value is a number.

numerical expression An expression that contains only numerical values and operations.

obtuse angle An angle with a measure greater than 90° but less than 180°.

obtuse triangle A triangle with an obtuse angle.

octagon A polygon with eight sides.

opposites Integers on opposite sides of zero and the same distance from zero on a number line. *Example:* 7 and −7 are opposites.

order of operations A set of rules mathematicians use to determine the order in which operations are performed.

ordered pair A pair of numbers (*x, y*) used to locate a point on a coordinate plane.

origin The point (0, 0), where the *x*- and *y*-axes of a coordinate plane intersect.

outlier An extreme value with few data points located near it.

parallel lines Lines in the same plane that do not intersect.

parallelogram A quadrilateral with both pairs of opposite sides parallel.

pentagon A polygon with five sides.

percent A rate in which the first term is compared to 100.

perimeter Distance around a figure.

perpendicular bisector A line, ray, or segment that intersects a segment at its midpoint and is perpendicular to it.

perpendicular lines Intersecting lines that form right angles.

plane A flat surface that extends forever in all directions.

point An exact location in space.

polygon A closed plane figure made up of three or more line segments.

polyhedron A three-dimensional figure made of flat surfaces that are polygons.

power The value of the base and exponent written as a numerical expression.

prime factorization The set of prime factors whose product is a given composite number. *Example:* $60 = 2^2 \times 3 \times 5$

prime number A whole number greater than 1 with exactly two factors, 1 and itself.

prism A polyhedron with two identical and parallel polygon-shaped faces.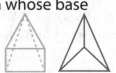

properties of equality Properties that state performing the same operation to both sides of an equation keeps the equation balanced.

proportion A statement that two ratios are equal.

pyramid A polyhedron whose base can be any polygon and whose faces are triangles.

quadrant One of the four regions into which the *x*- and *y*-axes divide the coordinate plane. The axes are not parts of the quadrant.

quadrilateral A polygon with four sides.

quartiles Values that divide a data set into four equal parts.

quotient The answer in a division problem. *Example:* In $45 \div 9 = 5$, 5 is the quotient.

radius Any line segment that connects the center of the circle to a point on the circle.

range The difference between the greatest and least values in a data set.

rate A ratio that compares two quantities with different units of measure.

ratio A relationship where for every *x* units of one quantity there are *y* units of another quantity.

rational number Any number that can be written as a quotient $\frac{a}{b}$, where *a* and *b* are integers and $b \neq 0$.

ray Part of a line with one endpoint, extending forever in only one direction.

reciprocals Two numbers whose product is one. *Example:* The reciprocal of $\frac{3}{4}$ is $\frac{4}{3}$ because $\frac{3}{4} \times \frac{4}{3} = 1$.

rectangle A parallelogram with four right angles.

reflection The change in the position of a figure or point that gives a mirror image over a line.

regular polygon A polygon that has sides of equal length and angles of equal measure.

repeating decimal A decimal in which a digit or digits repeat endlessly.

rhombus A parallelogram with four equal sides.

right angle An angle that measures 90°.

right triangle A triangle with one right angle.

scale The ratio of the measurements in a drawing to the actual measurements of the object.

scale drawing A drawing made so that distances in the drawing are proportional to actual distances.

scalene triangle A triangle with all sides of different lengths.

sector A region bounded by two radii and an arc.

side A segment used to form a polygon; a ray used to form an angle.

simplify To use operations to combine like terms in an expression.

solution (of an equation) A value that makes an equation true.

sphere A three-dimensional figure such that every point is the same distance from the center.

square A rectangle with four equal sides.

squared When a number has been multiplied by itself.
Example: 5 squared $= 5^2 = 5 \times 5 = 25$

statistical question A question which anticipates that there will be different answers in the data.

straight angle An angle that measures 180°.

substitution The replacement of the variable of an expression with a number.

surface area (SA) The sum of the area of each face of a polyhedron.

symmetric data Data distributed equally on both sides of the center.

terminating decimal A decimal with a finite number of digits.
Example: 0.375

terms The quantities x and y in a ratio. Also, each part of an expression that is separated by a plus or minus sign.

transformation A move such as a translation, reflection, or rotation that moves a figure to a new position.

trapezoid A quadrilateral with exactly one pair of opposite sides parallel.

triangle A polygon with three sides.

unit price A unit rate that gives the price of one item.

unit rate A rate in which the comparison is to one unit. *Example:* 25 feet per second

unlike denominators Denominators in two or more fractions that are different.

variability A measure of the spread of values in a data set.

variable A quantity that changes or varies, often represented with a letter.

vertex (in an angle) The common endpoint of two rays that form an angle.

vertex (in a polygon) (*pl.* vertices) The point of intersection of two sides of a polygon.

vertex (in a polyhedron) (*pl.* vertices) The point of intersection of the edges of a polyhedron.

volume The number of cubic units needed to fill a solid figure.

weight A measure of how heavy an object is.

x-axis The horizontal line on a coordinate plane.

x-coordinate The first number in an ordered pair that tells the position left or right of the *y*-axis.

y-axis The vertical line on a coordinate plane.

y-coordinate The second number in an ordered pair that tells the position above or below the *x*-axis.

Photographs

Photo locators denoted as follows: Top (T), Center (C), Bottom (B), Left (L), Right (R), Background (Bkgd)

001 Irin-k/Shutterstock; **013** Pearson Education; **079** Tlorna/Shutterstock; **139** Brykaylo Yuriy/Shutterstock; **146B** Sebastian French/Fotolia; **146CL** Corbis; **146CR** Corbis; **146T** Nicola_G/Fotolia; **223** Solarseven/Shutterstock; **228** Pearson Education; **256** Stockbyte/Getty Images; **271** Ginger Livingston Sanders/Shutterstock; **280** Pearson Education; **282** Steve Lovegrove/Fotolia; **317** Volodymyr Goinyk/Shutterstock; **332** Pearson Education; **344** Mikiekwoods/Shutterstock; **387** Chris Alcock/Shutterstock; **404** Pearson Education; **423** NatalieJean/Shutterstock; **428BC** Massimo Cattaneo/Shutterstock; **428BL** Pearson Education; **428BR** Ysbrand Cosijn/Shutterstock; **428TC** Capture Light/Shutterstock; **428TL** Rebeccaashworth/Shutterstock; **428TR** Marcel Jancovic/Shutterstock; **500** Sascha Hahn/Shutterstock; **504** Dmitry Nikolaev/Fotolia; **537** Wasu Watcharadachaphong/Shutterstock; **591** Sly/Fotolia; **602C** Jupiter Images; **602L** Jupiter Images; **602R** hotshotsworldwide/Fotolia; **604** Dmitri Gomon/Shutterstock; **655** TFoxFoto/Shutterstock; **664B** Carmen Steiner/Fotolia; **664T** johnnyraff/Shutterstock; **703** Ermess/Fotolia; **745** Razlomov/Shutterstock; **770** Nerthuz/Shutterstock; **781** Real Deal Photo/Shutterstock; **804T** Pearson Education; **804B** Pearson Education; **840** Inga Nielsen/Shutterstock; **849L** Image Source/Getty Images; **849R** Getty Images.